ESCAPE

ESCAPE

CHRIS DOBROWOLSKI

Supported by
ARTS COUNCIL
ENGLAND

British
Antarctic Survey
NATURAL ENVIRONMENT RESEARCH COUNCIL

firstsite Collectors' Group

University of Essex

ARTS
ADMIN.

ISBN 978-0-9565495-9-4
Jardine Press Ltd 2014
jardinepress.co.uk
cdobo.com

Preface

From the first time I saw Chris Dobrowolski's hand-made flame-throwing tank on TV I became fascinated with his work. Here was a tank camouflaged with reproductions of John Constable's Haywain and powered by four Suffolk Punch lawn-mowers. Clearly there was a lot going on with this artist, and I wanted to know more.

It was at one of his wonderful lectures that my curiosity was rewarded. Chris's performance was hilarious and self-deprecating, running from one unreliable salvaged slide and film projector to another. All this masks a courage and undaunted self-belief, that with the right found parts he can build and drive anything his heart desires, be it a boat, car, hovercraft or plane. His 'I can do' attitude had been kindled in childhood by the series of illustrated Ladybird Books which explain in an empowering way how things work and fire a child's imagination.

It was after one of these talks that I rather rashly offered to publish his story so far: the making of his vehicles of escape which culminates in his great escape to Antarctica to build a sledge from gilt picture frames.

This book only covers a small part of Chris Dobrowolski's prolific work. I hope it brings the art of this important conceptual artist to a wider audience, and that you find Chris Dobrowolski's life and work as powerful and poignant as I do.

I would like to thank Chris for his patience, Ladybird Books for permission to reproduce images of their publications, The British Antarctic Survey, Arts Council England, firstsite Collectors' Group and ArtExchange University of Essex, Catherine Dodds for doggedly and skillfully pulling together this publication, Paul Bourne and Elly Robinson for their editorial work, and Cheryl Pierce from Artsadmin for her help and encouragement.

James Dodds

Jardine Press Ltd

Contents

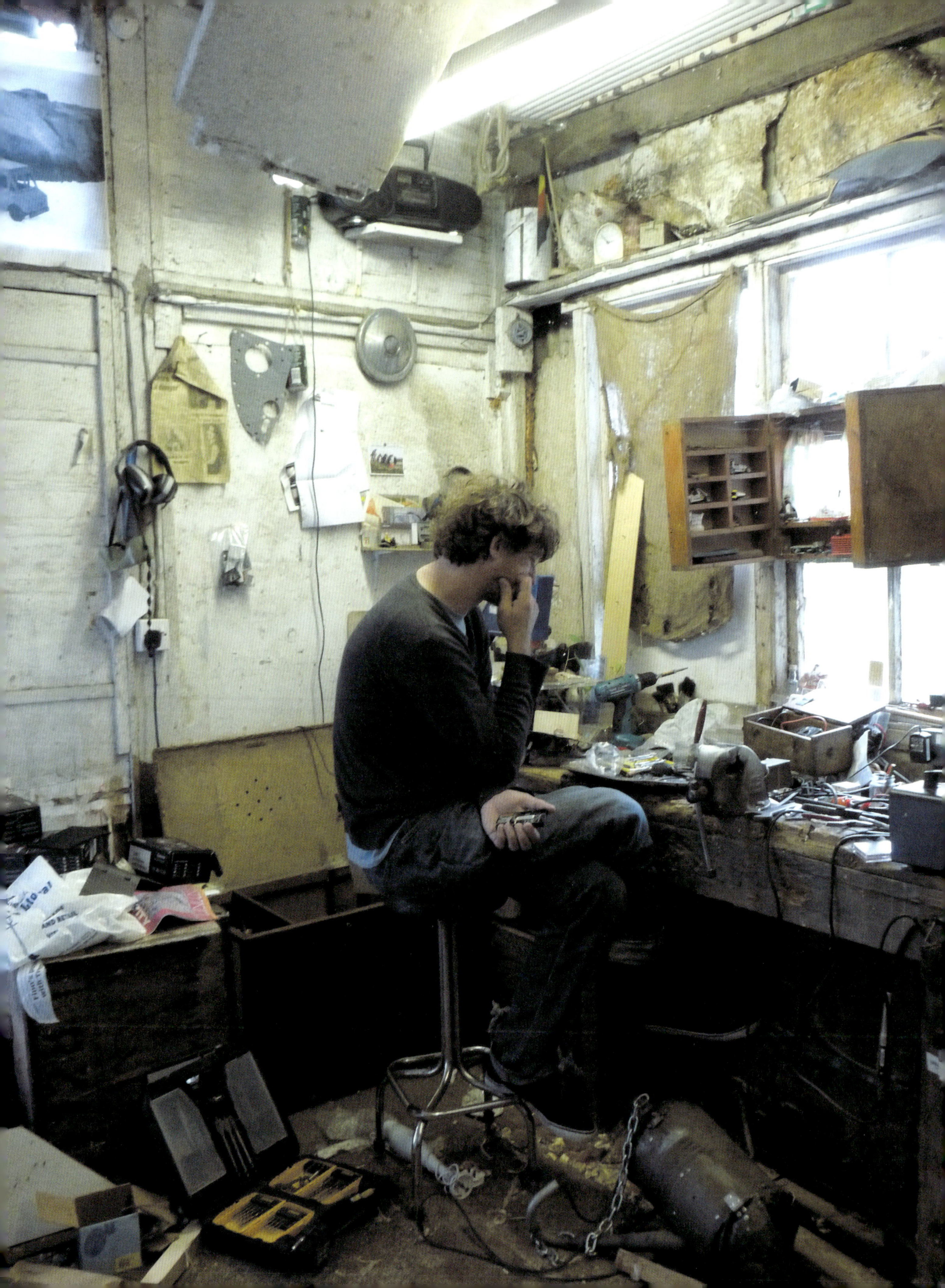

Prologue

If you do an internet search for my name followed by the word 'art' you will find the website The Art of Chris Dobrowolski. This is not me. This is the website of another artist, also called Chris Dobrowolski, who specialises in commercial paintings of marine mammals.

I'm not a commercial artist. I don't have a website to sell my art, I don't even have a digital camera, preferring 35mm slides to document work. I'm not a Luddite, I'm not trying to make a statement, it's just that a lot of my work was made before digital cameras became popular and I like the fact that the piece of film in a 35mm camera was physically present on the day the picture was taken. The image is part of the event and not just a representation of it.

Picasso said: 'Art is the lie that tells the truth.'

Images are representations of the real world; they are not the real thing. With a painting, for example, the artist might create an illusion of depth or distance but it's not really there, the painting is still a two-dimensional surface; a trick or a lie. Within this visual lie the artist creates a context, a platform or stage to represent the real world. From this fresh perspective, we can see something honest or truthful about the world that we couldn't see before.

In my work I find myself constantly occupying the territory between the lie and the truth, accentuating where the unreal becomes real.

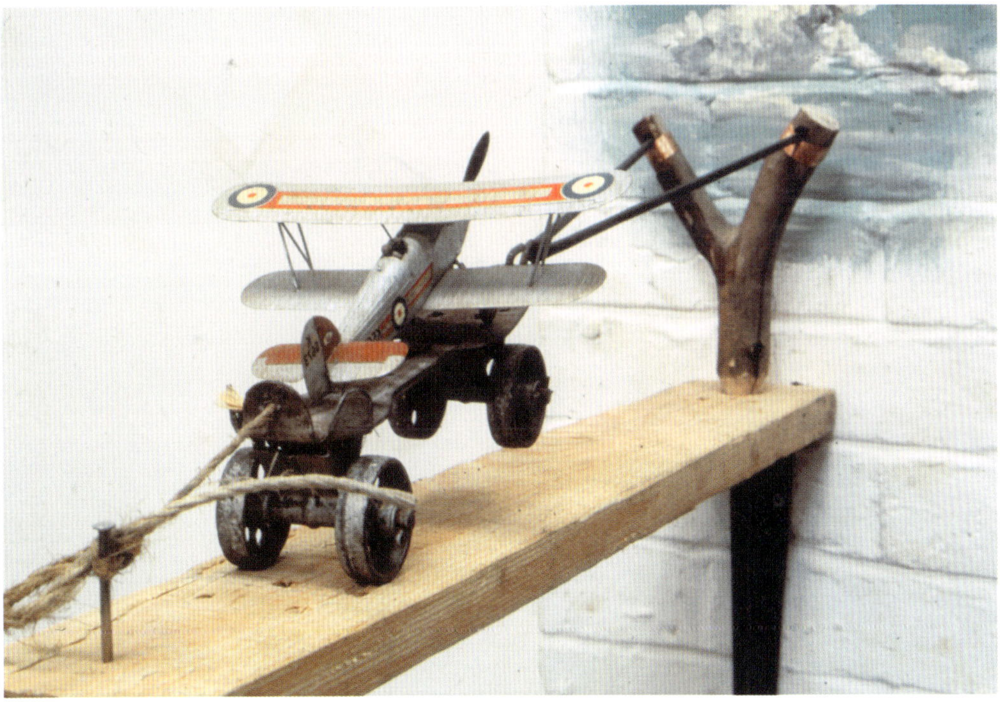

'Sketch for aeroplane No. 4'. Materials: string, nail, plank, bracket, roller-skate, Airfix model aeroplane, oil paint, brick wall.

left: The artist's studio. [Charlotte Bernays]

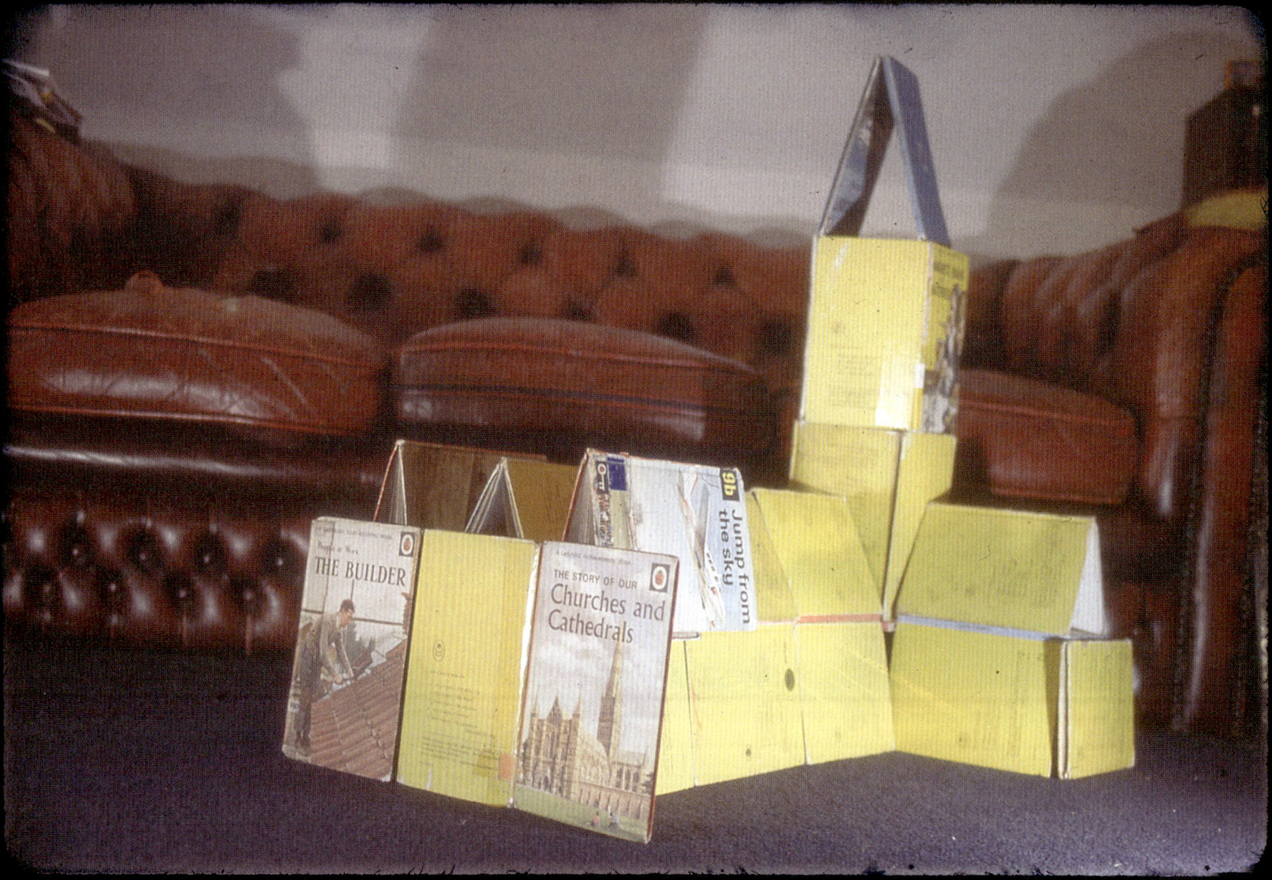
THE BUILDER
THE STORY OF OUR
Churches and Cathedrals
Jump from the sky

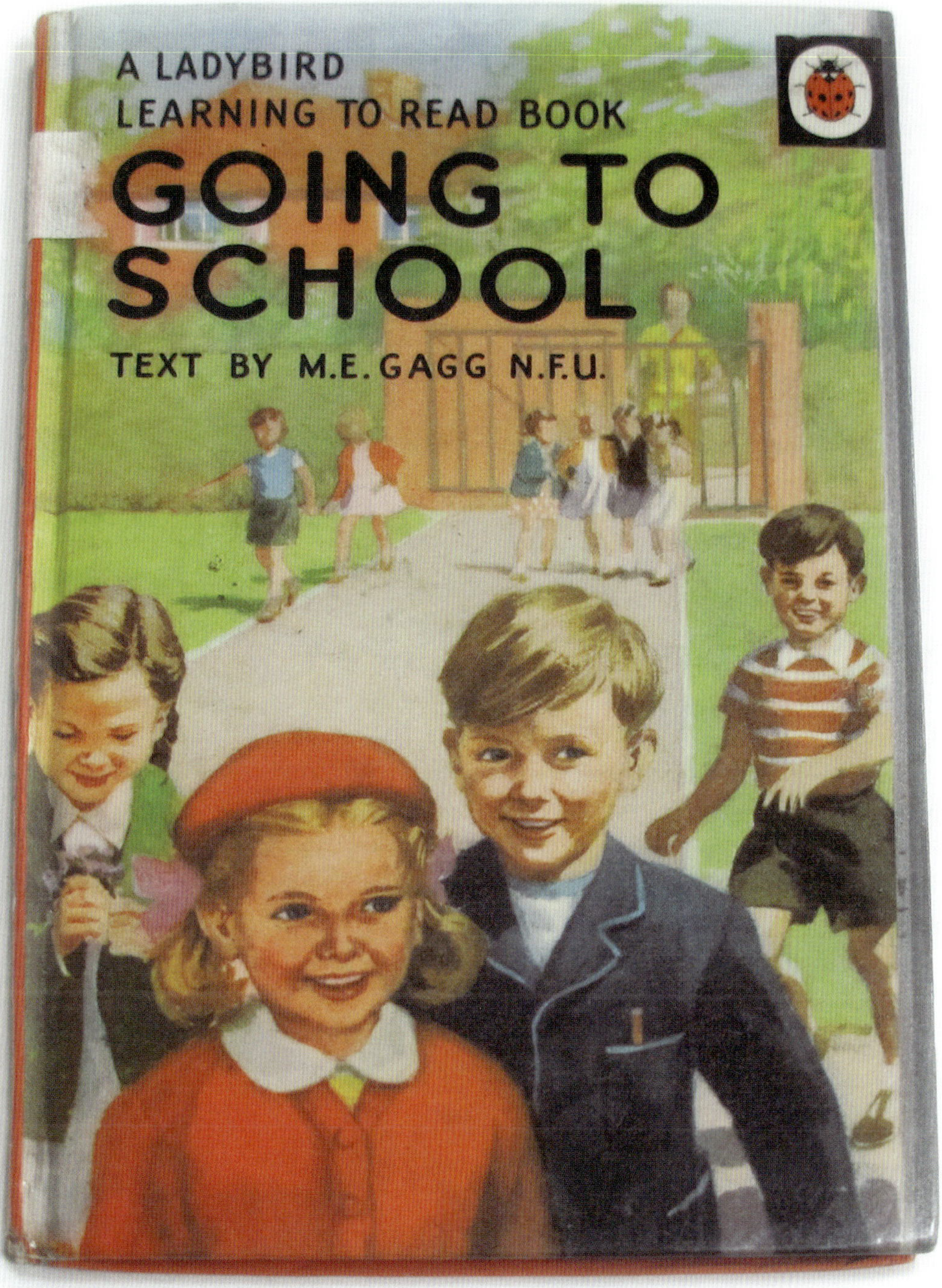

Some of my early work…

previous page:
Cathedral
made from
yellow backed
Ladybird books.

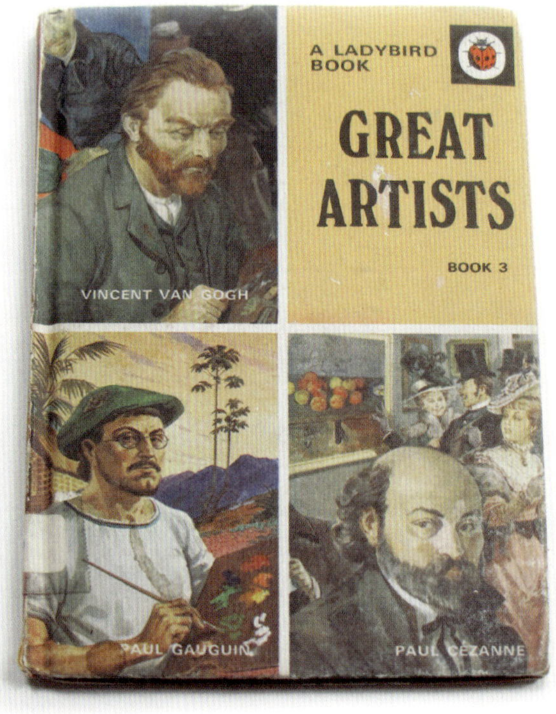

At art college we were all taught about the artist Marcel Duchamp. Although there has since been a lot of imitators, he was the first to display a toilet in an art gallery. From this we learnt that 'anything can be art.'

Another influence was Joseph Beuys. He emphasised the importance of process over product, a kind of anti-commodification of art. As well as valuing the process, it is easy to appreciate the egalitarianism of his approach. Every person's experience is as valid and important as everyone else's. The experience of going through a creative process is potentially far more valuable than looking at a painting by a great master. By this measure everyone can be an artist.

Seven years of art education taught me that everything can be art and everyone is an artist, which left me thinking… what's the fucking point of me? This is, admittedly, an abridged version of contemporary art history. In fact, it could be described as the Ladybird Book version. But with swearing.

The subjects covered by Ladybird Books were myriad and each would be condensed into simple text with illustrations. The books were designed for children but were also read by adults who wanted to understand the basics of a particular subject. They were, in a sense, the internet of their day. The back cover was always one of five pastel colours so that if they were turned face down they became anonymous flat units and I remember they worked quite well with my building blocks. If I got bored with reading them I could always make things from them.

The printing methods of the 1950s meant it was easier to reproduce colour paintings than photographs. Many of the Ladybird illustrations were, therefore, paintings of photographs. At first glance these looked like actual photographs but not quite as sharp. Today it is possible to buy mugs and fridge magnets with Ladybird Book illustrations on, exploiting their sentimental aesthetic nature. However I like to think that Ladybird Book illustrations sometimes also worked artistically on a far more conceptual level.

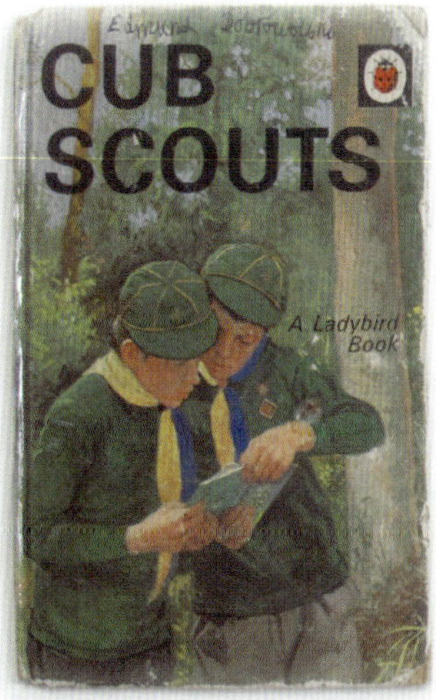

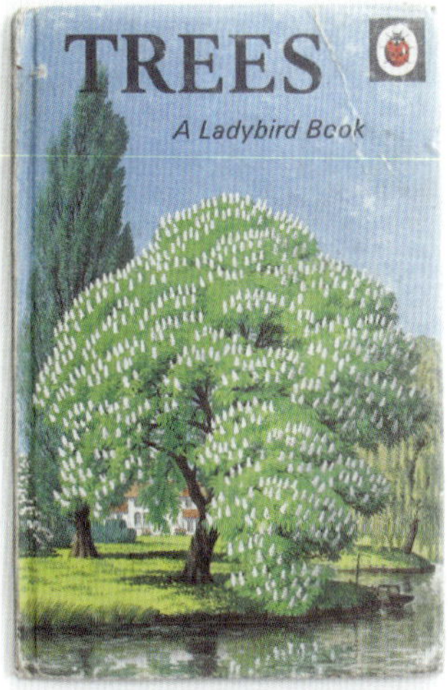

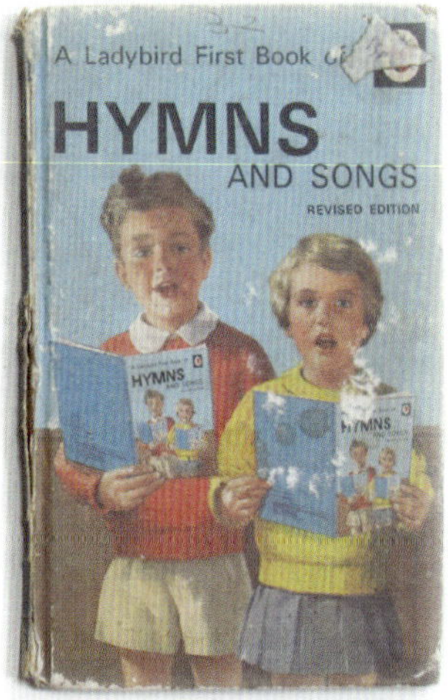

In the Ladybird Book of Cub Scouts, for example, we see two cubs earning a proficiency badge by tree spotting. To help them, they have a tree spotting book. If you look carefully, you can see that it is no ordinary tree spotting book, it is, in fact, the Ladybird Book of Trees. From a twenty-first century perspective we might call that product placement but I like to think it works on a level deeper than that. Similarly, on the cover of A Ladybird Book of Hymns and Songs, we see two children singing from a hymn book. In this example the book they are holding is actually the one that has their image on the front cover – A Ladybird Book of Hymns and Songs. Looking closer at the miniature book they are holding, they can be seen holding it again and again, so on and so on; into infinity, touching the sublime.

Another example is Printing Processes from the How it Works series which gives an illustrated, step-by-step guide to how a book is made; from blank paper to end product. This is not just any book, however, but the Ladybird Book of Printing Processes. The subject of the book is the story of its own creation. Logically, this can't happen but, in the parallel universe of the Ladybird Book, it can!

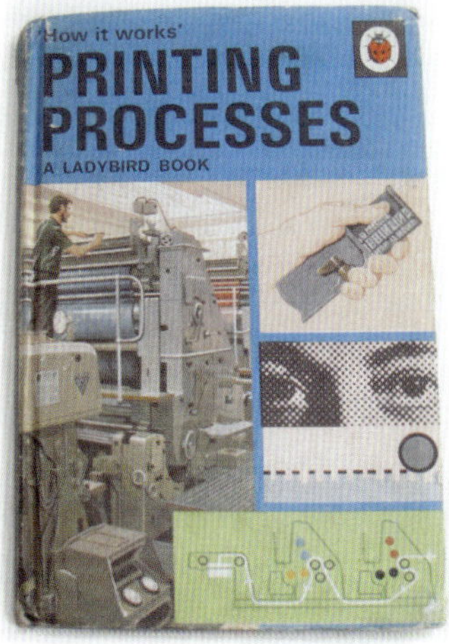

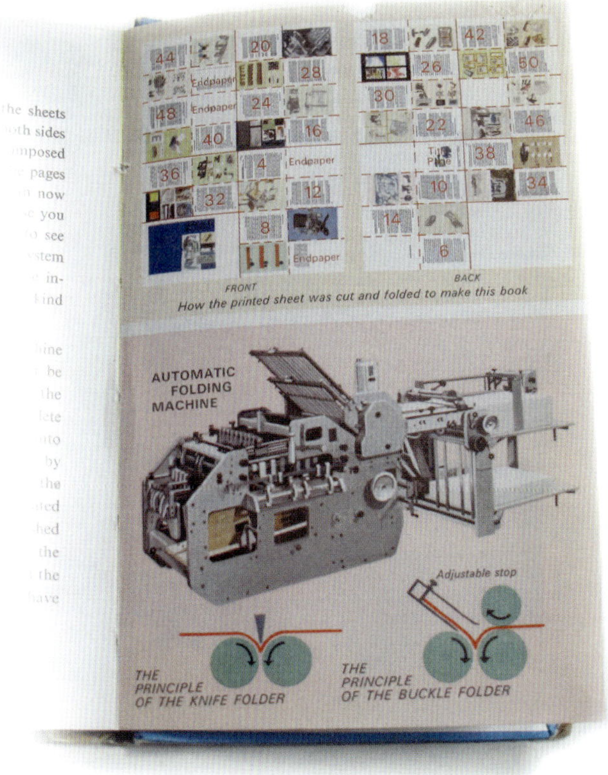

The Ladybird Book of Printing Processes

The page on the right is page 48. It shows an illustration of an automatic folding machine. In the illustration above it also shows all the pages of the book laid out on one sheet of paper (front and back) ready to be guillotined. One of the pages (in the top left hand corner) is page 48 showing the automatic folding machine and the paper waiting to be guillotined.

In Britain in the late 1980s, an art education usually entailed leaving school and applying to a Further Education College to do a Foundation Course in Art and Design. This course helped students put together a portfolio of work ready for an interview at an art college elsewhere in the country. The first term gave the student an experience of every application of the visual language. Students did week-long workshops in everything from Fashion and Textiles to Advertising Graphics, 3-D Design and Illustration. In amongst these subjects was a week-long introduction to Fine Art. At the time, we were all a bit vague about what Fine Art meant because the department seemed to cater for every kind of discipline. We had access to a workshop shared with 3-D Design and painting tutors who also taught Illustration. One of our tutors was a blunt speaking Yorkshireman known for his candour and no nonsense approach. To help delineate what the Fine art department was all about, he would defer to the painter Wassily Kandinsky.

As an abstract painter, Kandinsky's work could easily fall into the category of art that makes my mother say: 'Surely a five year old could have done that Christopher'. However, even she would agree the bright colours and patterns mean his work has an attractive quality. Regardless of its aesthetic virtues, Kandinsky's work itself was not the crux of our tutors pearl of wisdom. Instead he wanted to tell us about a comment he once made in an interview.

In an attempt to dismiss Kandinsky's work as 'only' decorative, a critic once asked him: 'What's the difference between your paintings and, say, for example, wallpaper?'

To this Kandinsky replies: 'An inner need.'

The tutor went on to explain that it was this 'inner need' that defined the activities in the Fine Art department as different to those of the rest of the art college. As students this definition suggested a level of involvement in the creative process that transcended the production of a mere commodity; the reward should be something more direct and personal.

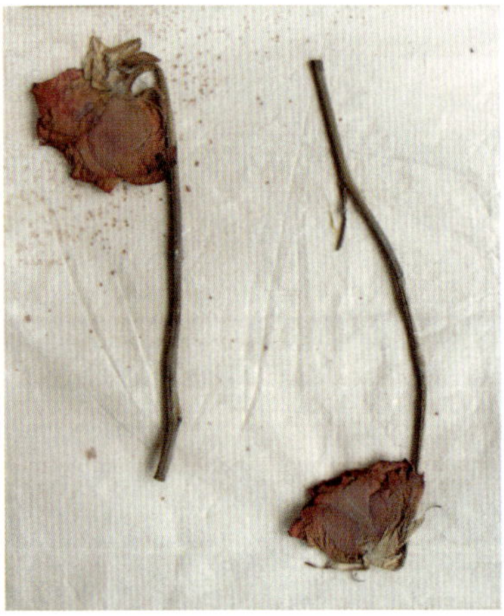

The original roses pressed flat, and copied in stamps.

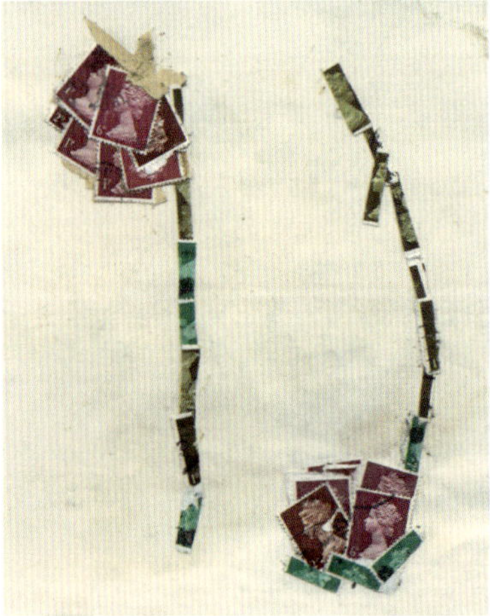

As part of the course experience, every year the students were sent on a research trip to Amsterdam. As well as being an opportunity to visit a few art galleries the trip was also a bonding exercise, a chance for that year's intake of students to get to know each other socially. On my trip to Amsterdam I met a girl.

Although she was an art Foundation student she wasn't actually from my college. By chance her college just had the same place in mind for their bonding exercise. It was fate. Luckily she didn't live that far away from me in Essex and gave me her phone number. When I got home I rang her to arrange a date. The first thing she said when she answered the phone was: 'Are you the bloke I met when I was drunk in that bar in Amsterdam?'

Not a great start and, when I steered the conversation around to meeting up, she quickly said: 'No, I don't think so, I'm washing my hair.'

I tried to forget about her then a few days later she posted a package to me: a cardboard box with two red roses inside. I took this as encouragement and rang her for a second time but, again, she was washing her hair. I was very confused and obsessed over my 'does she, doesn't she' situation until it became the focus of my art. In response to her offering, I found some old stamps and made two delicate sculptures of her roses from them; green stamps for the stems and red for the flowers. I put them in the same cardboard box and posted them to her.

It was a sincere poetic gesture but, importantly, before I posted them, I took a photograph.

I realise now that this was essentially self-preservation. I wasn't sure if she was playing hard to get or playing some kind of cruel trick. Taking the photograph gave me the comforting notion that I would have the last word or the last laugh. The photograph would go into my portfolio ready for my art college degree level interview. In this way I felt as if I had found my own interpretation of an 'inner need'.

The girl sent me another package and, again, I re-interpreted her gift in an artistically postal way, photographed it and sent it back. The same cardboard box went back and forth between us many times and I was beginning to think we may even meet. If we didn't: no matter. I was slowly amassing a pile of images that I could cow gum to a display board and take to my interview.

Being an important element in my work, naturally the girl would be mentioned in tutorials but one day my tutor actually met her face to face. He was a visiting lecturer and while the relationship was potentially blossoming he happened to be in 'her' art college one day. In a broad Yorkshire accent he introduced himself.

'Are you that bird that Chris is trying to get off with? Could you hurry up and send him some more stuff, luv? His interview date is coming up soon and he doesn't have enough photos for his portfolio.'

Needless to say our ongoing correspondence stopped very abruptly.

Many years later, I came across the box in the bottom of a cupboard at my parent's house. We had both used Sellotape to stick our address labels on with, one on top of the other. In the end there was a thick layer of them, alternately mine and hers. Now old and dry the yellowed Sellotape had long since lost its stickiness. When I picked up the box all the layers of labels separated, fell from the lid and fluttered to the floor like dry dead petals. On the back of one of the labels, about four addresses down, she had written a secret note:

'I don't know what you think about me Chris but I really do like you.'

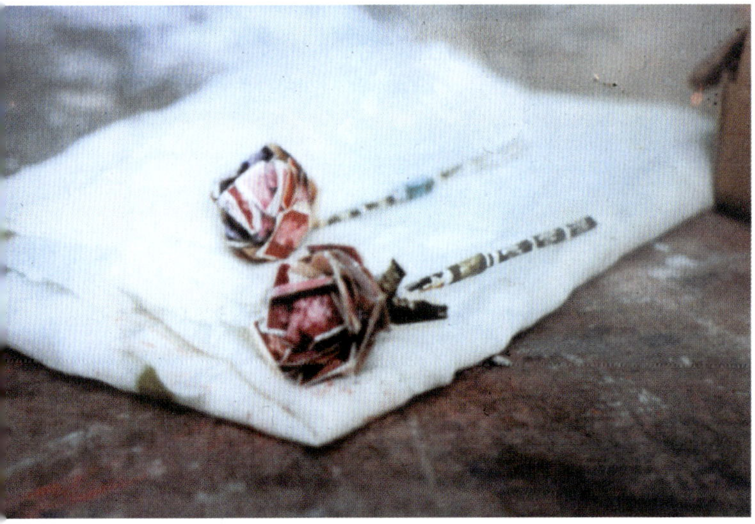

A terrible, out of focus photograph (I hadn't done the module in photgraphy yet) of the two roses made from red and green postage stamps.

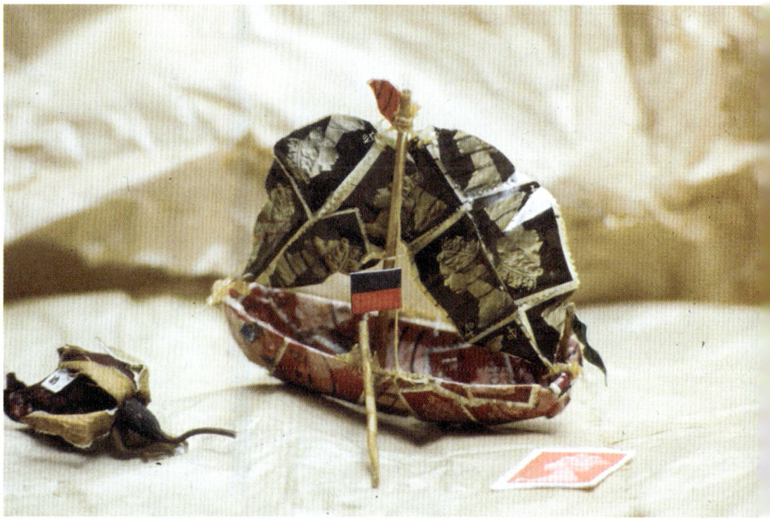

Another postal gift: toy boat made from stamps. [Mark Colyer]

The transition from Art Foundation to degree course meant applying to an art college and moving away from home. Which degree course depended on your skills and the recommendation of your tutors. There was a limited intake at degree level and foundation tutors were responsible for finding places for all their students. The most prestigious colleges were grouped around London or trendy places like Brighton and they could select the best students. If you failed to get into your first choice college, it became progressively harder to find a place so if a tutor had a student who was less talented or ambitious, they would diplomatically steer them towards a less prestigious college in a more provincial part of the country.

I was sent to Hull.

It was actually a great course, but Hull itself is a difficult place to sell. At the time, I don't think I had been further north than Suffolk, so Hull felt like alien territory. Going away to college was my first time away from home. Looking back on it now, I realise I was suffering from homesickness and this had an effect on the work I was making. It became quite sentimental and nostalgic.

When I was about six or seven years old my father bought my older brother and me two toy sailing boats for the boating lake. They were about eight inches long and made of wood with a steel plate that stuck out underneath for a keel. These mementos of home were the starting point of one the first art projects that I did as a student in Hull. I copied the simple design and made my own toy boats. Instead of painting them red like the originals, I made each from a different piece of wood that was made from several other smaller pieces glued together. After they were shaped into the form of a boat, sanded and varnished, the different patterns of the wood emerged and they became quite attractive, seductive objects. When I had finished I had made nine boats in total all the same shape but with a different pattern. I then glued address labels on them. Each address was of a friend or family member that I had left back home in Essex.

When you make something from a material such as wood or stone it is very easy to be seduced by the material yourself. A lot of the time at college, during tutorials, we were quite rightly challenged if we made an object that was purely aesthetic or was made well but had no intellectual enquiry. I think that I was trying to justify craft and making, something that I actually quite enjoyed. With this project the hope was that if a stranger came across one of the toy boats they might post it on to the address on the boat. For this to work the object had to be well made, intriguing and attractive otherwise this hypothetical stranger wouldn't be bothered to pick it up off of the beach in the first place.

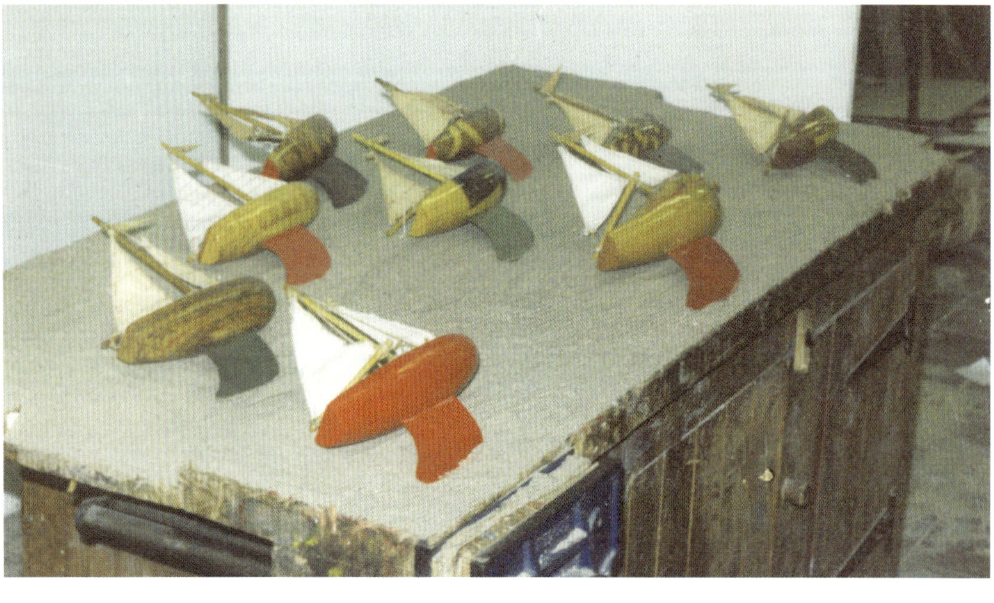

right: The nine toy boats.

far right: Launching the toy boats. Super 8 film. [Kerry Jones]

background: The last toy boat heads off down the Humber.

I launched my toy boats from the quayside and watched them go down the river Humber on the high tide. Each one represented quite a few hours worth of work. The wood was sanded to a perfect finish, I even made a corresponding pattern on each individual metal keel and stitched another corresponding pattern on the sails. They soon disappeared out of sight and I never saw them again.

For this cathartic experience I was given a grade. This was 1989 and English art colleges were under pressure to come into line with Margaret Thatcher's education reforms which were designed to make learning art more of a 'modular' system, similar to the model they have in the United States. So, after this term-long project, me and every other student were called into the office individually and given our grade. This meant that after a brief chat we were given a letter that was supposed to reflect our mark for that term. The letter represented how 'good' we were. I sat down in the office and the tutor told me how impressed he and all the other tutors were with the boats I had made and how they were equally impressed with what I had done with them and in recognition of this I was to be awarded a 'B'.

I was suitably grateful and thought I had done well until I heard that someone else had got an 'A'. My ego got the better of me and I started to wonder why I hadn't received an A? After all I put a lot of 'inner need' into my toy boats. Then the problem struck me, a problem that I have seen from both sides now, as I have worked in art education and had to grade students' work myself. The problem is that no matter how you look at it, you can't grade your 'inner need'.

I became totally disillusioned with the whole concept of art education and of course I was still homesick. In a sense I was doubly depressed.

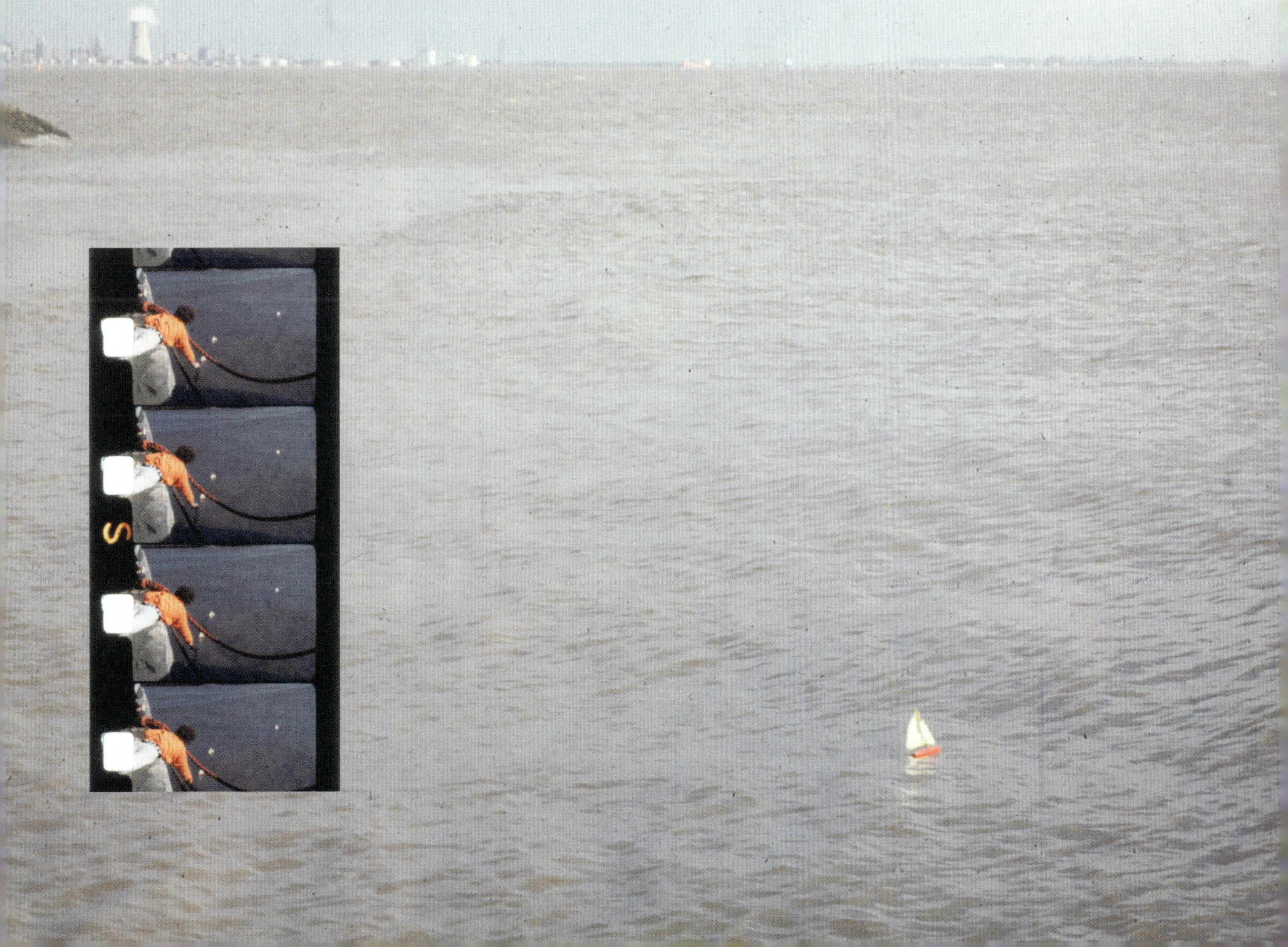

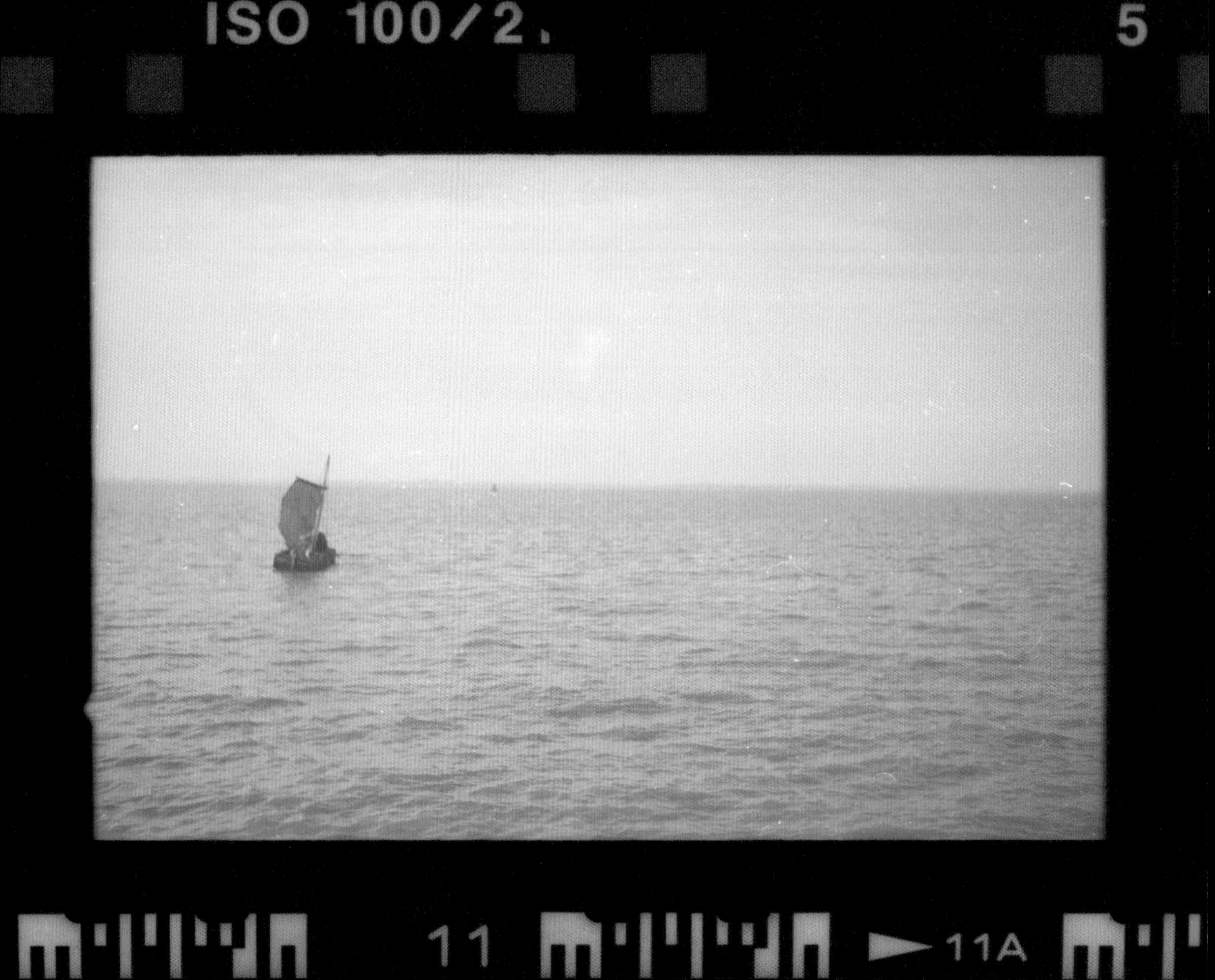
ISO 100/2.
5
11
11A

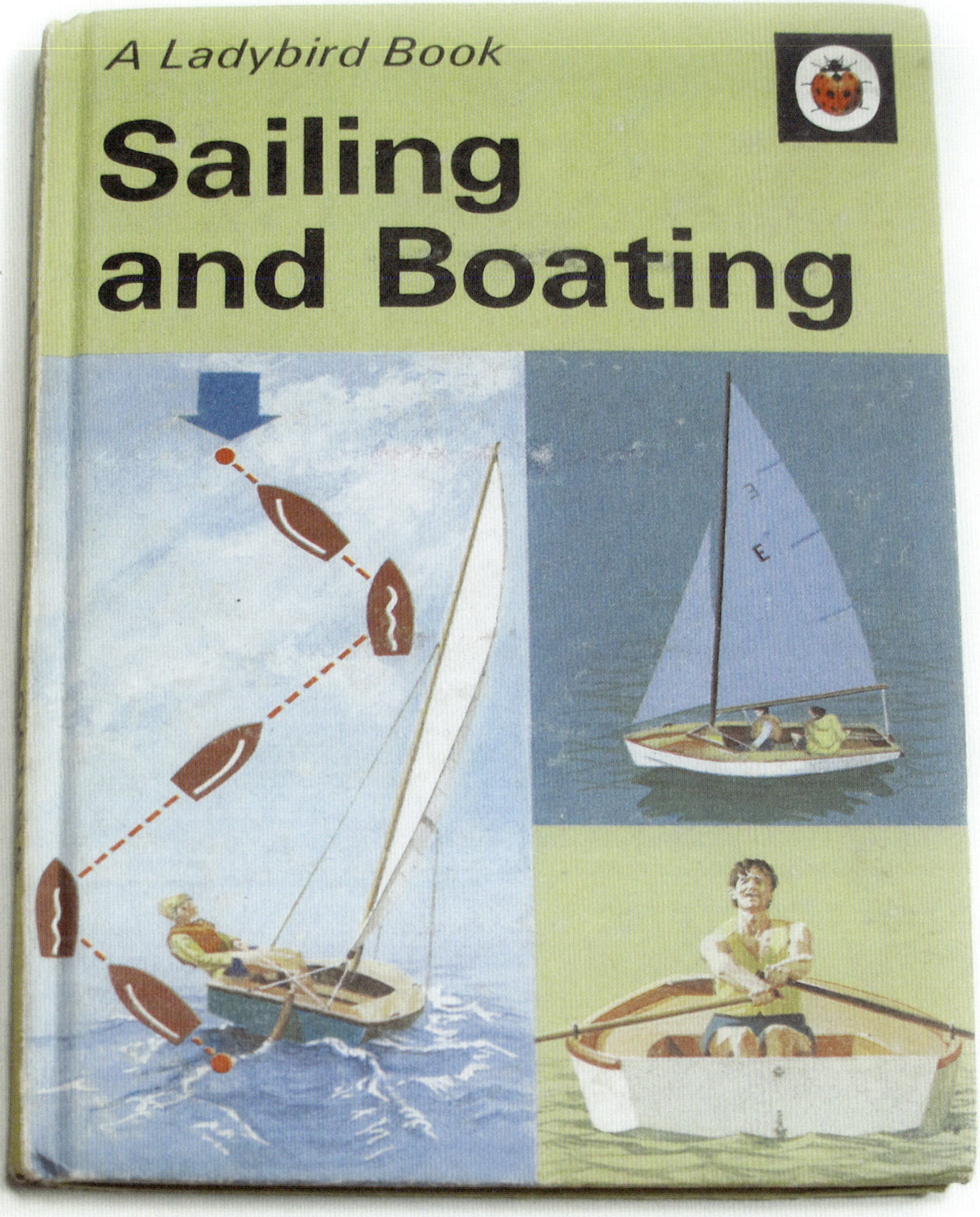

Seascape Escape

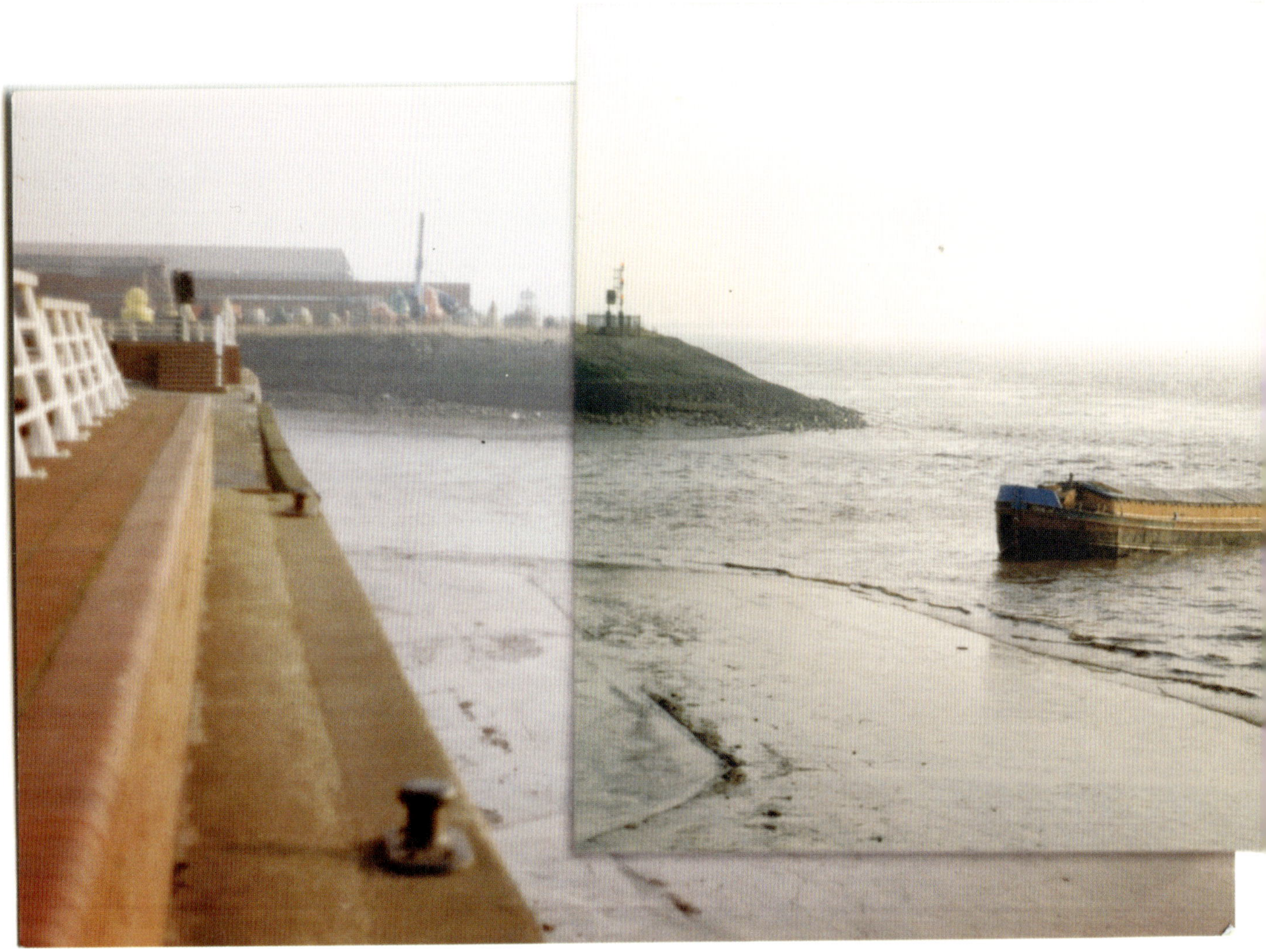

One afternoon during my first year, I found myself in the Ferens Art Gallery in Hull. The gallery has a large maritime collection and I was looking at a nineteenth century painting of a small rowing boat being tossed about on the sea. I wasn't really doing research I was just moping around feeling sorry for myself and contemplating what I should do next. I had probably had another tutorial earlier that day. Quite often when a tutor has no real input to give to a student, the last resort is to give a list of names of artists who do similar work. It's a well-meaning gesture but doesn't really help to find a fulfilling line of personal enquiry. I felt that everything I did had been done before.

We were often told at college that we were learning the visual language but, as students in our early twenties with limited life experience, we didn't have anything worth saying with it. The art college wasn't far from the River Humber and, if you went out of the back door and through the old town, you came to Drypool Bridge. This took you over the River Hull, down some steps to a path by the old flour mill. The path turned left to follow an inlet which was the entrance to the old Victoria Dock. Here it joined a road that followed a line of very old industrial buildings that fronted the River Hull and led to the Buoy Yard where there was a footbridge that crossed over a slipway onto an area called Sammy's Point. Here the River Hull entered the River Humber. The whole area was a bit run down. The grass was overgrown and the city felt a long way away. I went there because it was a great place to get away from things and find a bit of solitude.

The river Humber is over three miles wide at this point and, although sometimes this walk gave me time and space for contemplation, at other times it just accentuated my sense of isolation and

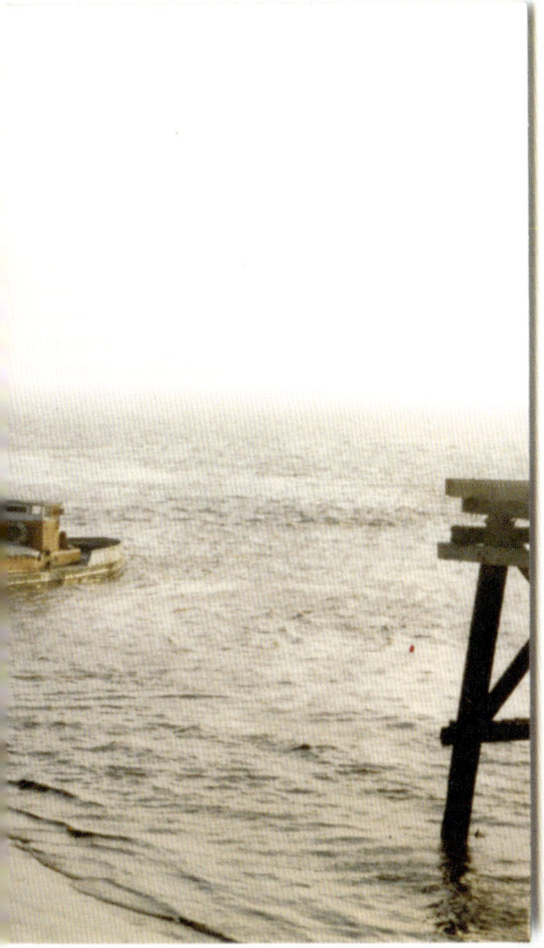

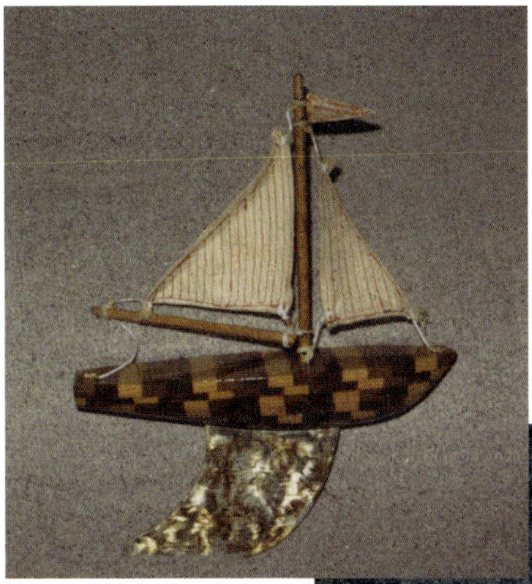

previous page: 'Friday' on the river Humber.

Two model boats –

left: addressed to myself.

below: addressed to an old friend called Paul Dorrington.

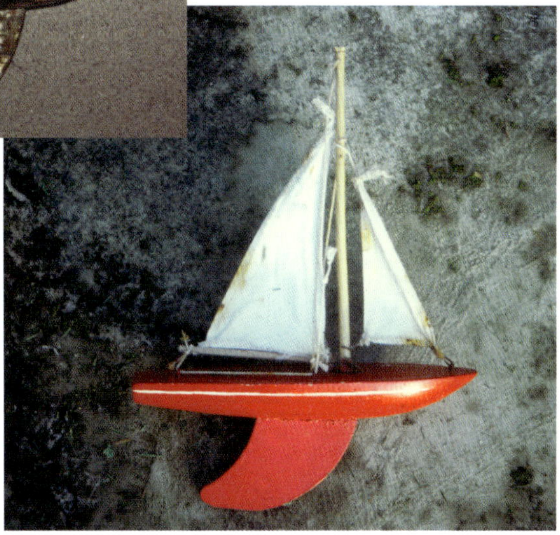

left: The river Hull as it enters the river Humber. The buoy yard on Sammy's point is visible on the other side of river.

depression. When I thought back to my time on the foundation course, I not only remembered the phrase 'inner need' but also 'doing it for real.' It was all about connecting with something on a more fundamental level and challenging our commitment to the subject. We had to 'do it for real' if we were to be taken seriously as artists and have any integrity. I found myself on the north bank of the River Humber in Hull thinking: 'What do I need to do next? What's my motivation?'

The answer, I concluded, was to get the fucking hell out of Hull!

I could have just left the course and gone home but that would have been giving up. Instead, on my next trip to Sammy's Point, I started to collect driftwood. I figured that, if I could get a lot, this time I could build one big boat and, if it was big enough, I could get in it and physically escape from art college.

I knew almost nothing about building a full-size boat so the toy boats I had made the term before became my model. I didn't always interpret them correctly. I thought the keel on the toy boats was designed to stop them from tipping over. It isn't. It's there to keep the boat going in a straight line so that it can sail at an angle to the wind but this basic ignorance didn't deter me at all. I just scaled up what I saw on my toy boats and found a big section of steel to act as my keel (although I thought I was making a counter balance). I knew I would have problems launching a boat with a piece of metal sticking out so I set about inventing a way to make it retractable. I didn't know about retractable keels used on small sailing dinghies that come up and into the boat via a slot, so I fixed the steel onto the bottom of the boat with chains that acted as a kind of hinge. The other end of the keel was connected at an angle of ninety degrees by ropes that ran from the tip of the keel to two old sash window pulleys connected to either side of the boat. With these ropes I could lower and then hold the keel rigid once the boat was in deep enough water.

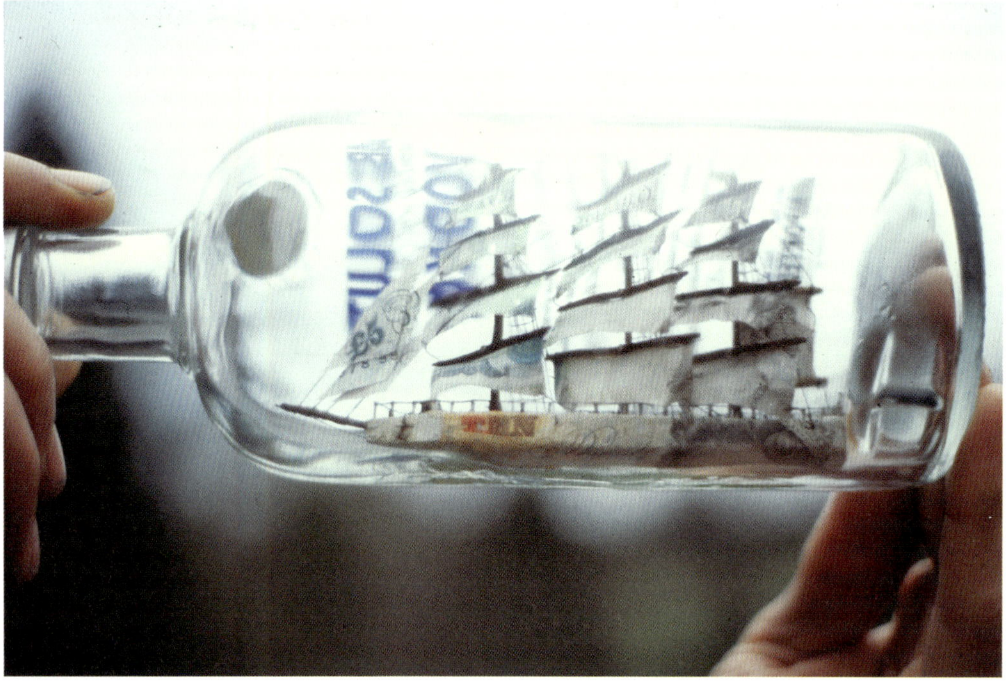

Ship in a bottle made from a ten and a five pound note. This was for an Absolut Vodka competition to use their bottle in an art piece using the word 'Absolut' in the title. The title was 'Absolut Ship'. I didn't win a prize.

My other boat-building experience came from making model ships in bottles. When I was a teenager, my aunt gave me a ship-in-a-bottle kit. It was pretty basic and consisted of a lump of wood that had to be whittled into a boat shape, some cotton (the rigging), a piece of muslin (the sails), glue, instructions and a bottle. Fortunately, my greatest asset, then as now, was my patience. The rigging on a ship in a bottle has to work pretty much like a real boat. When the model is put into the bottle, all the strings that elevate the masts and sails are extended so that they come all the way out through the neck of the bottle. The hull of the boat is just big enough to get through the neck of the bottle and, when all the sails are erected, it is this that gives the impression that the model couldn't possibly have got into the bottle. A good ship-in-a-bottle has a lot of detail; a tiny anchor, ladders and everything else that a real boat would need but in miniature. I just scaled things up.

A technique I learnt in the life-drawing room when 'scaling up', was to hold a pencil or thumb up to the subject from a distance and then bring it down onto the paper to create approximate proportions. I did this with my boat and its relationship to the River Humber. I would often walk down to the river and look out across the water holding up my finger and thumb, imagining the distance between the two was my boat about halfway across the river. On some days, with the tide on the turn, the water was surprisingly calm. On other occasions it could be quite windy with large waves breaking in mid-stream. It was on a day like this that I looked out across the river, panicked and thought, 'I need a bigger boat'.

Some tutors encouraged us to make sculpture in an 'intuitive' way and I like to think that my random scaling up of the boat against the River Humber was indeed intuitive but this all took much longer than I had anticipated. It was the last term of my first year and it was becoming apparent that I would not finish the boat before the end of term. This was vital because I needed to get the

right: The hull nearing completion.

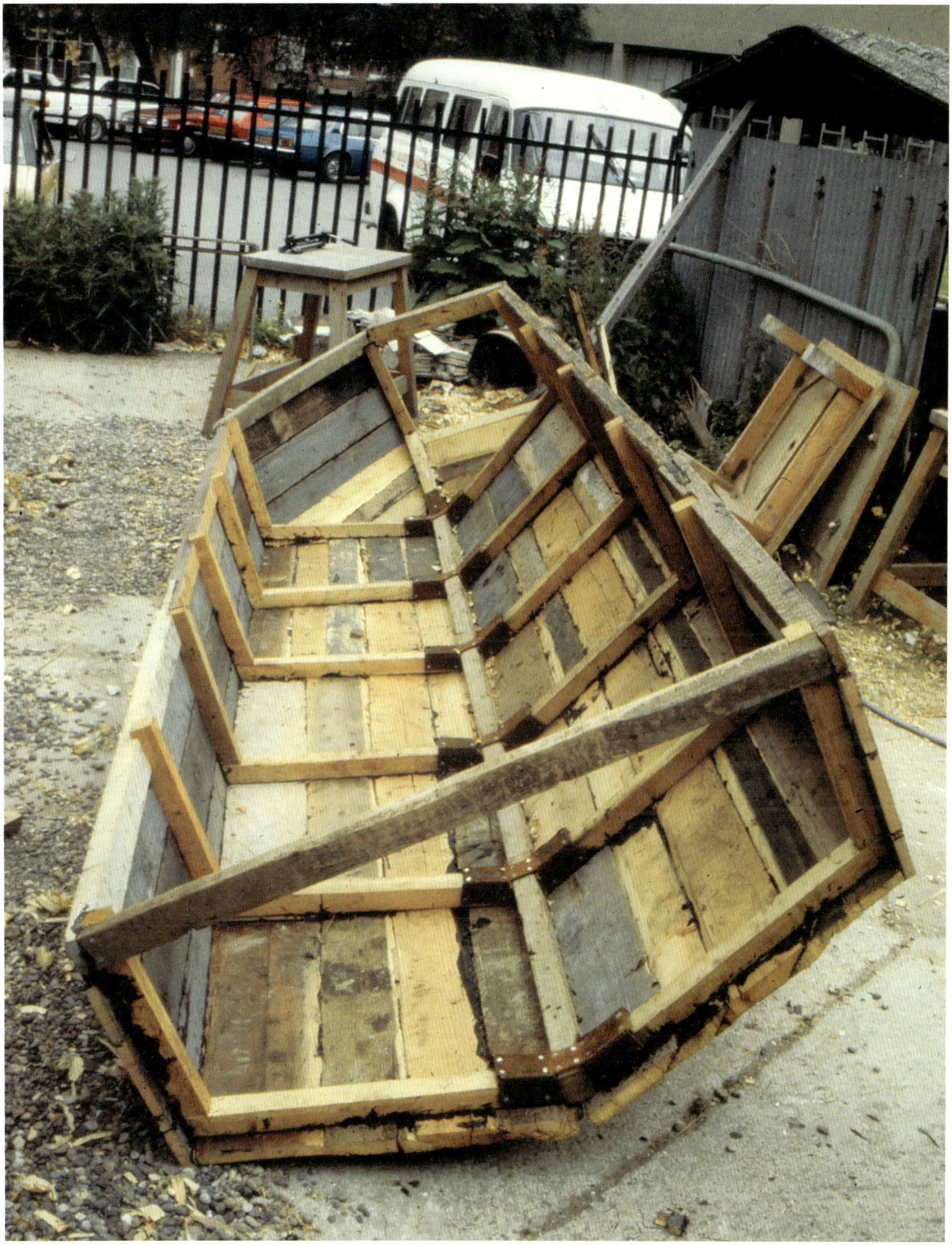

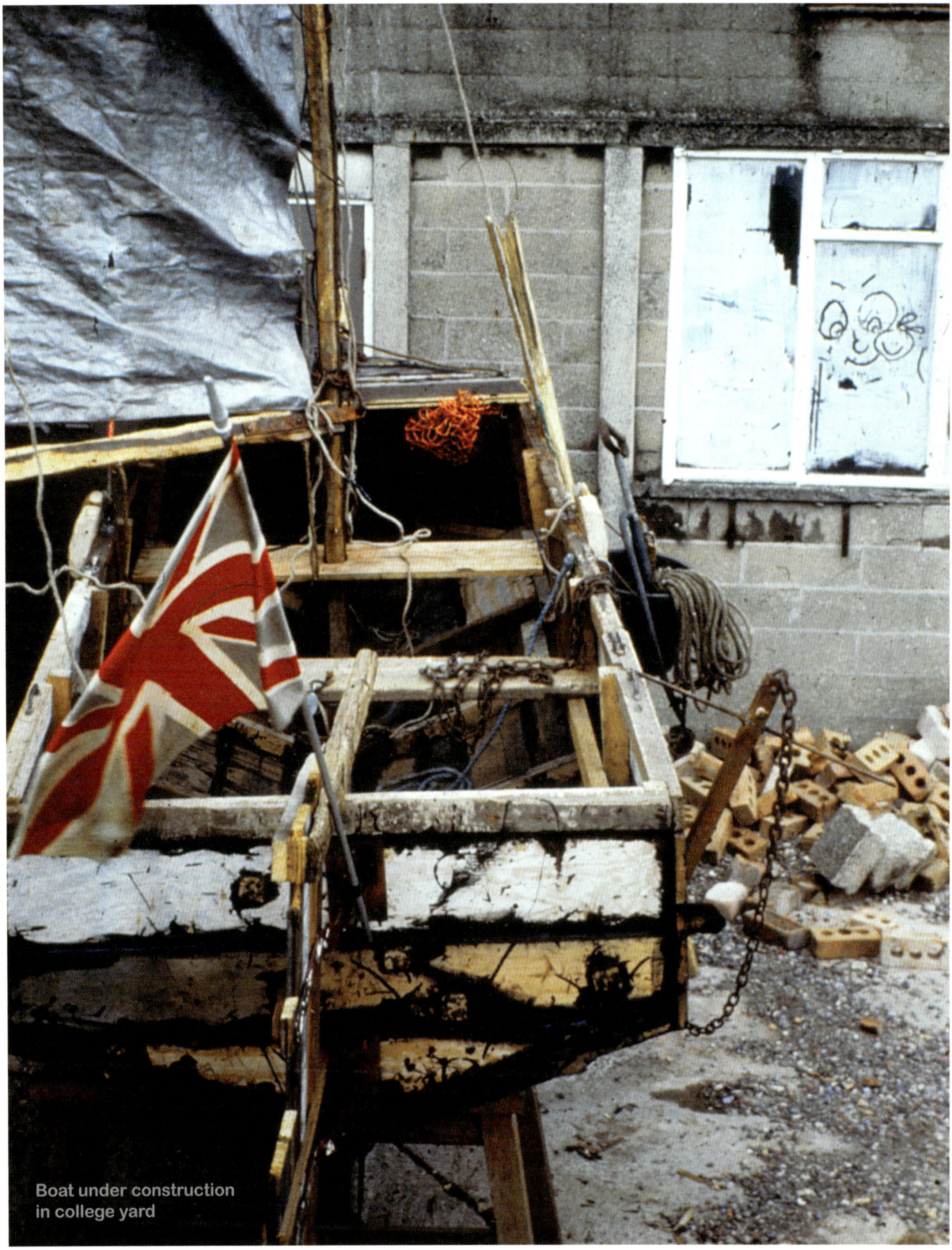

Boat under construction in college yard

boat launched before the weather changed. If I waited until September, just before the autumn Equinox, the water would be too rough for an escape attempt so I moved my part-built boat into the college yard. I devised ways to do most of the construction with hand tools so that I didn't rely on electricity and, when college shut for the summer, I still had access to my boat. Everyday I cycled to college, climbed over the fence and carried on building. I was lonelier than ever and, to cap it all, I was breaking into college to work on a boat whose function was to help me escape from art college.

One evening, I took a new route home through the municipal gardens in front of the college and stopped to read a small monument that had caught my eye. It was dedicated to Robinson Crusoe who had, apparently, set out on his travels from Hull. Here it was, immortalised in bronze, outside the Queen's Gardens Café. A monument to a fictitious character's imagined relationship to Hull. In recognition, I called my boat 'Friday'.

Eventually some of the technicians discovered me in the college yard, took pity and connected me to the power supply so I could speed things up with power tools. By late August, the boat was finished. The caretaker offered to move it with the college van and trailer and, with the help of the technicians and a small group of students, we took the boat to the river. The boat was lowered into the water and, to everyone's amazement, it floated.

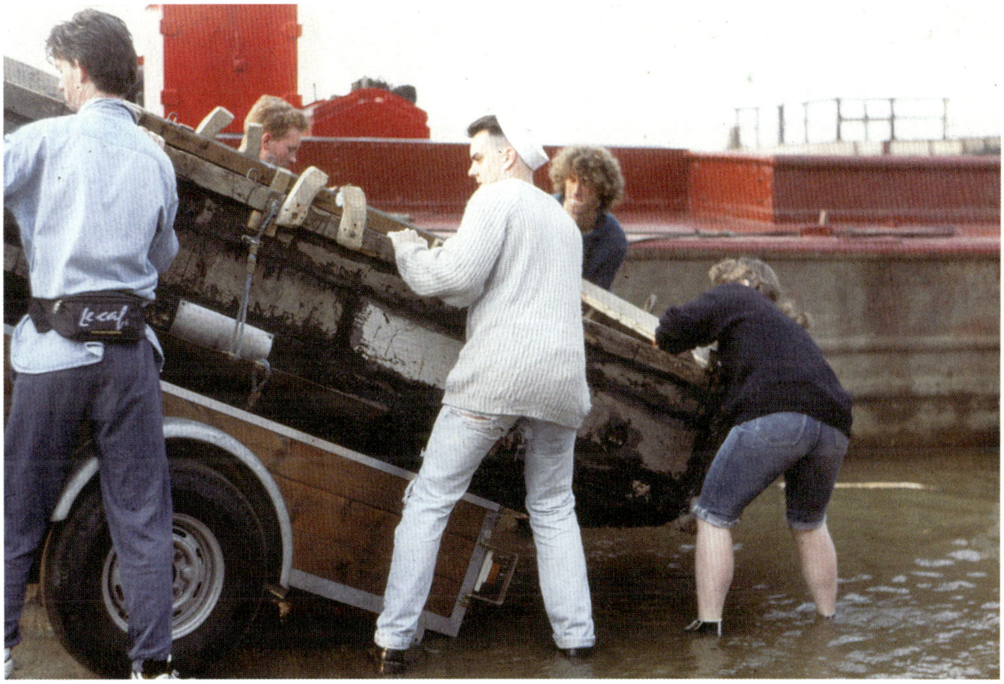

Launching the driftwood boat. [Clare Allen]

If I was going to escape from Hull in a boat, then the first obstacle was the river Humber. I knew very little about building a boat but I knew even less about sailing one. When you start doing a conspicuous project, however, it often attracts people who are keen to give advice and I picked up a few bits of knowledge along the way. One friend of a friend even lent me some life jackets.

Some of the other advice I received was less practical: 'If you are about to change direction in a sailing boat you have to say "lee-ho" to warn the crew that the boom will swing across the boat'.

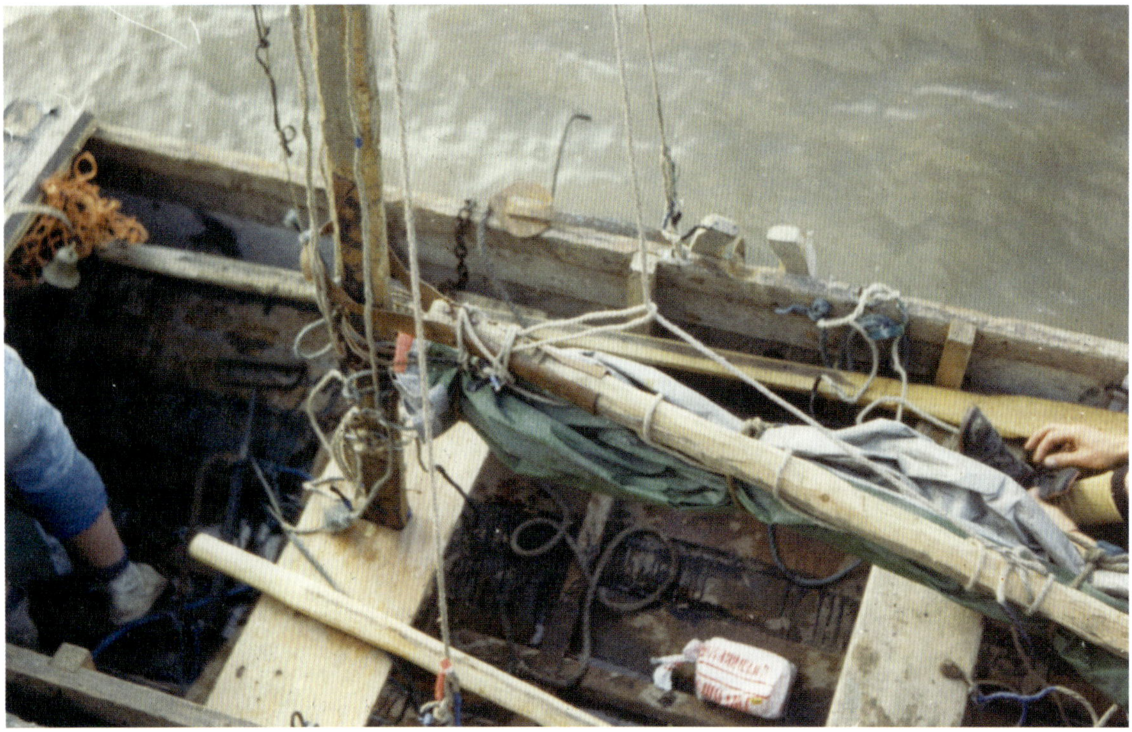

Interior of 'Friday'. In the top left-hand corner you can just about see Eddie's mum's front door bell. the red and white shape in the bottom of the boat is half a white sliced loaf of bread. [Clare Allen]

This was probably good advice for a racing dinghy but a bit pointless in a boat made from driftwood. All I really wanted to know was how to get it across the estuary in one piece and, eventually, with the help of a few handbooks, I pieced together all the information I needed. The plan was to get the boat into the water just as the tide was coming in and cross the river going upstream with the tide, aiming to get about halfway across before the tide changed and went out again. At this point, I planned to change direction and head for anywhere on the southern bank as I went downstream with the tide, crossing the river in a kind of 'V' pattern. The river was about three or four miles wide at this point and, with the right weather conditions, I thought I could make it.

I wasn't totally 'foolhardy', to quote the local newspaper. I had made an arrangement with the pilot launch at the end of the pier. The main function of the pilot launch was to transport navigational pilots onto the ships as they made their way up and down the river. Its other function was as a safety vessel in case of emergency. The crew had invited me and a couple of friends on board one afternoon for a cup of tea that had turned into a drinking session. We all got a little drunk and, at the end of the evening, the two-man crew said they would probably follow me all the way across the Humber when the day arrived. I was going to be perfectly safe.

The day arrived with a relatively calm wind blowing in the right direction so I rushed down to the river to get the boat ready to go. I didn't realise at the time, but I had picked possibly the worst conditions; a spring tide doing 5 knots. I had no idea what 5 knots was like, but I was about to find out. I had also underestimated how long it would take to get the boat ready to sail, we would have to work fast.

I had two other people in the boat with me; Paul Slater, a print student, and Eddie Weldon, a painting student. Eddie was my best friend at art college and had come back to Hull from his parent's farm for a few days to help me. Once we were in the water, the first task was for the 'crew' to help me lash all the rigging to the boat. I had made the mast removable so a lot of ropes needed tying. When we finished, I ran over to the pilot launch to let them know we were about to leave but they weren't the men we had got drunk with a few days before. I assumed they had been briefed, however, and quickly went back to the boat. By this time, the tide was going out instead of in. Oblivious to this, we launched and, as we drifted off downstream, I spotted the pilot launch going upstream in the opposite direction. We didn't see them again for the rest of the morning. By now, there was no wind and the sails just hung limply. We still had the oars I had made, however, and there was a point at which we could have turned around, rowed back and admitted defeat. We didn't. Very quickly, we drifted too far and had no choice but to carry on down river.

'Friday' floats for the first time. [Sue Hilder]

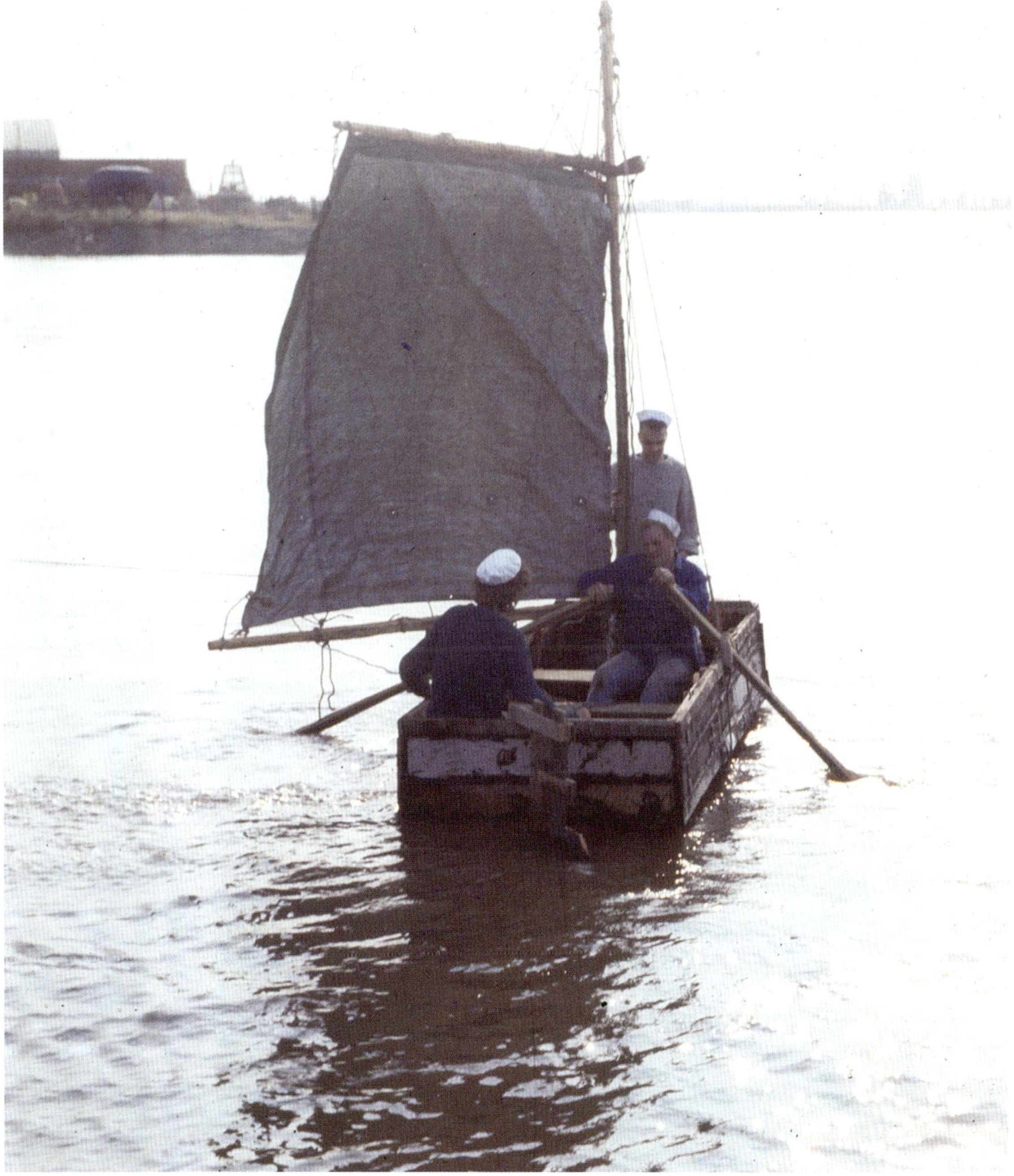

Documentation – SOUND

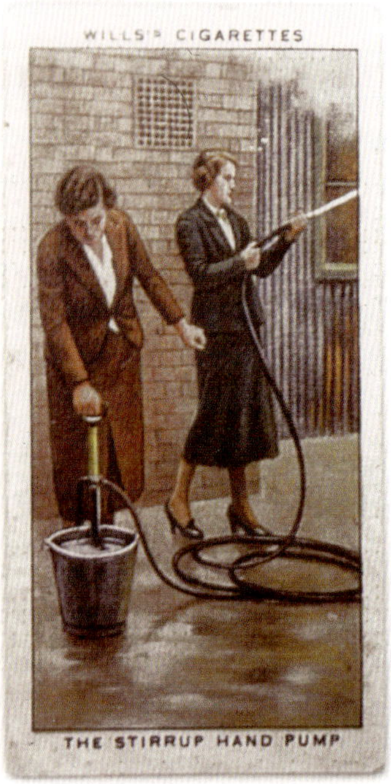

Cigarette card from 1939.

right: Collision with buoy.

I had an old cassette tape recorder in the boat with us. I thought it would give an interesting audio documentation of the event and capture the ambient sounds of our adventure. As it turned out, the cassette became a bit like the black box flight recorder that you get in an aeroplane. The sound quality wasn't brilliant, a lot of what could be heard was tape hiss interspersed with the sound of water sloshing around in the boat.

As well the water, the other background noise is something that sounds a bit like someone using a large bicycle pump. It is actually a stirrup pump, the kind that the air raid wardens use on 'Dad's Army'. They were standard issue in World War Two to put out fires during the Blitz. The 'stirrup' part is a kind of footplate that is kept on the floor by stepping on it. This enables the intake end to stand rigidly in a bucket of water while you pump the handle at the top up and down. There is a hose fixed to the other end and after a lot of vigorous pumping water (a dribble!) comes out of the end. I got mine from Eddie's granddad who used to be an air raid warden during the war. We hitch-hiked to Eddie's family farm one weekend and Eddie persuaded him to lend it us for our bilge pump (there were a few little leaks in the boat). While we were there I also quite liked the look of an old servant's bell that his mum had by the back door of the farmhouse. We borrowed it and on the cassette tape you can hear it 'ding dinging' as the boat rocks from side to side.

Over these background noises, the voices of me, Eddie and Paul can be heard.

The first thing of note is a conversation between the three of us that has a kind of self-congratulatory feel about it. A big wave had just swept up the river, I don't know where from, maybe a ship that had passed by a long way off. It felt quite big to us and we felt as if the boat had been picked up and dropped about three or four feet in the air. We were a little worried but then, as we had obviously ridden it successfully it felt like a little test that we had passed. I thought my large piece of steel underneath had obviously done its job and on the cassette tape you can hear Eddie say: 'We did it alright, if we can get through that we can get through anything'.

This was met by lots of positive noise from Paul and me.

At this point, while we are still congratulating ourselves, it is possible to hear Eddie say: 'We are going to hit this buoy'.

The the river was about three or four miles wide and we hadn't even made it half way across, we had however made it about maybe a quarter of the way. Unfortunately this brought us into the shipping lane. Consequently we were starting to come across the large navigation buoys that marked the channel. It was Eddie's job to man the rudder and steer us away from this sort of hazard but as there was no wind the rudder had nothing to steer against and it was next to useless. We were just floating with the strong tide. Although it was doing five knots, to us, floating as far out as we were, it didn't seem that fast. With no immediate point of reference there were moments when I wondered if we were moving at all. Occasionally we would look at the riverbank in the distance and see some familiar landmark go past and remind ourselves that we were in fact moving. Everything was a novelty to us, here we were the three of us, floating along in a thing that had only a short time ago been lots of separate lumps of wood, we had never seen a buoy in the river, up close before and it was becoming clear that they're really big. When we saw the buoy approaching Paul said:

'Quick, get the cine camera out'.

Documentation – FILM

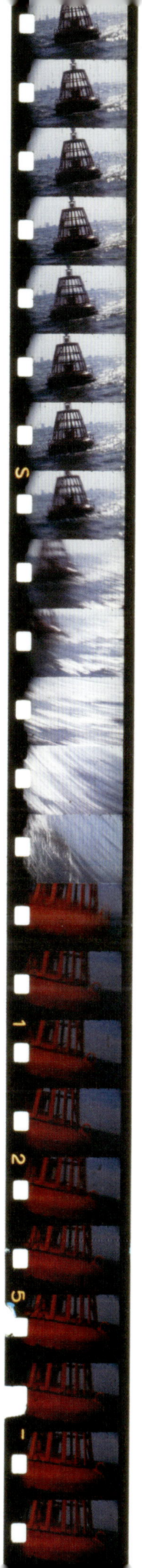

We had an old Super 8 cine camera on board. This was the late 1980s and, although video cameras existed, they were expensive and it wasn't easy to get hold of one. I'd have had to go to the AV Loans Department to book the college media equipment and, in the circumstances, I didn't think they would lend it to me. Super 8 cine cameras were, by comparison, very cheap and I managed to find one at a car boot sale for 50p. The camera cost less than the film inside and, in the event of an accident, I could afford to lose it.

Cine film was the camcorder of its day but with no sound. You can often see the same skills displayed nowadays in home movies; out of focus, shaky, zooming in and out for no apparent reason, wandering around with the camera and not keeping it still on any particular subject. The most famous Super 8 footage was taken in 1963 when a Mr Zapruda from Dallas accidentally filmed the Kennedy assassination. The footage is technically bad; out of focus, shaky and, at one point, the president's car disappears behind a signpost. Classic home movie stuff except someone gets shot at the end. The FBI immediately seized the film as evidence and it wasn't seen again until the 1970s when it was shown on national television. The film made such an impression that it spawned an entire film sub-genre called Zapruderesque. So, when people tell me 'Chris, your films are shit.'

I tell them: 'No, they are Zapruderesque.'

Our camera was so cheap and the viewfinder so tiny that we were finding it hard to fit anything in. It wasn't the ideal camera for a 12ft boat. The film begins with a shot of Eddie's ear, the back of Paul's head, a shot up a nose. The buoy presented a chance to film something far enough away to fit in the frame. I remember going to the front of the boat to begin filming the buoy and, suddenly, I had my first experience of what 5 knots was like. As I filmed the buoy through the tiny viewfinder, I noticed that it was getting bigger very quickly. The next words on the cassette tape are: 'Get the oar out.'

We still hadn't grasped how fast we were going so I was instructed to lean out with the oar to push us away. This was when I had my full-on encounter with the true meaning of '5 knots'. It's a bit like running as fast you can into a brick wall with a garden cane in your hands.

Retrospectively, I was very proud that when the boat smashed into the buoy, it stayed in one piece and I had 'done it for real'. As the bow slammed momentarily against the obstacle, the rear of the boat, still in the slipstream, kept going. It swung around and, slowly, started to point in the opposite direction. At this point on the recording you can hear someone say: 'Lee Ho.'

By this time, we had floated a few miles downstream and were drifting past George Dock, the main port of Hull. The captain of a tugboat, the Lady Joan, had just finished docking a ship and seen us floating past. We were flying the skull and cross bones and the captain said later that he had never seen pirates on the river Humber before and thought he should come and investigate. As he got closer, he realised we were in difficulty and offered to throw us a rope. I tied the rope to the front of Friday and we were pulled alongside the Lady Joan. Like most tug boats, the Lady Joan had enormous tractor tyres tied all along the side and we held onto these and clambered up onto the deck to safety.

It was all a bit of an anti-climax. The project, for me, had a romance about it. After I found out about Robinson Crusoe, I thought I was fulfilling my destiny. I was 21, the right age for an adventurous rite of passage. College tutors had told us that we didn't have anything worth saying and all I had done was float downstream a bit and get rescued. Apart from the collision with the buoy, there hadn't been the kind of intensity that made me feel truly alive.

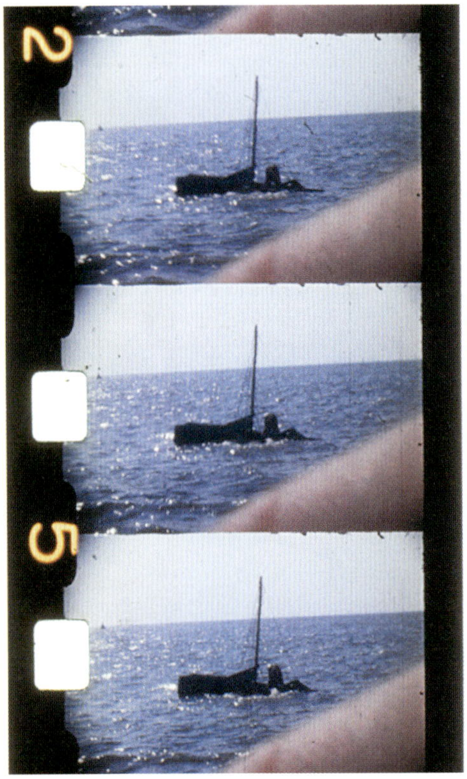

above: Background: Accidently cast adrift and taking in water, I'm keeping the boat afloat with a bucket. Foreground: Eddie's finger.

below: Salvaging the wreck of 'Friday' at Salt End jetty. [Sue Guthrie]

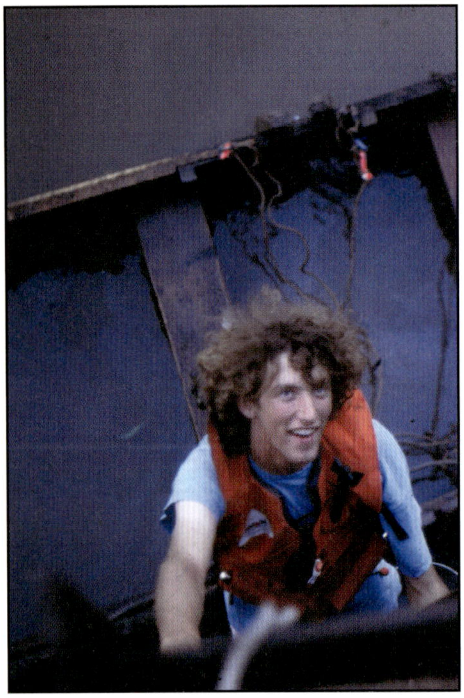

In the Disaster Movie genre, a much-used narrative technique is to send a character back into danger; back into the burning building or the sinking ship. My Super 8 home movie became a bit like that, but all horribly real. I looked down from the deck of the Lady Joan and noticed that the wake from the ship was creating big waves and the water was spilling over into my driftwood boat. In addition, my boat was tied beneath the outlet for the bilge pump so several gallons of water were being emptied straight into it. I could see the bell we had borrowed from Eddie's mum and the pump his grandad had lent us. I decided to climb back down into the boat to retrieve everything.

The water was just below my knees when I climbed in. The bell was screwed to the boat and, in my panic, I was all fingers and thumbs. I pulled at it a couple of times then gave up and turned my attention to the stirrup pump. It was connected to a long rubber hose that had tied itself in a knot around a piece of rigging. I couldn't contemplate untangling it but I managed to stretch out enough slack hose to lift the pump up to Paul on the tug. I told him to hold it firmly so that I could use both hands to yank off the hose.

What I didn't realise was that at the same time I handed the pump up to Paul, something else had happened. I don't know if it was my weight in the boat, the increasing level of water in it, or even the sudden motion of me yanking on the end of the hose and then the combined weight of me, the water and the boat snatching back onto it that caused it, but the rope tying me to the tug boat had snapped. When I yanked on the hose and pulled it off of the pump that Paul was holding, it was the only thing holding me to the tugboat. As I pulled, I noticed, slowly at first, that the tractor tyres on the side of the tug were going past me one by one. It took me a few moments to realise what was happening, by which time the last tractor tyre past by an inch out of reach. The tug steamed away from me up stream as I got taken in the opposite direction by the tide. The water in the boat by this point was above my knees as the front of the boat was below the water and each wave brought even more water into the boat. I was in serious trouble. Luckily, Eddie kept filming.

On the Super 8 film it's possible to see me in the distance finding a bucket and using it to frantically bail out water. I look quite comical but I kept the boat floating long enough for the Lady Joan to come back. The crew threw me a rope and I clung to it. A strong-armed deckhand reached down and lifted me up and I was unceremoniously landed on deck, like a big fish. There was more footage of this but when it came to using a camera Eddie could make a great composition but had a habit of putting his finger over the lens.

We didn't see the boat sink but we filmed it turning upside down just after I was lifted off. We could see it for a long time as it floated off downstream, became a tiny black dot and was lost in the diffuse light reflected off the water in the distance.

Aftermath

I thought that was the last I would see of the boat, it seemed pretty final, but, just in case, we drove along the river bank that afternoon to see if we could find it. A few miles downstream we found the rudder and I assumed the rest had sunk. The next day however, I indirectly found all of it. I was walking through Hull when I met the man in charge of all the pilot launches. His greeting was: 'You made a bloody balls up of that didn't you?'

He then went on to tell me that the rest of the boat had been found further downstream: 'They've found your boat. If you ring Captain Walker, Deputy Harbourmaster and… actually, now I think about it, don't. If I were you, I'd keep a low profile.'

I ignored his advice and rang Captain Walker. I had spoken to him at the beginning of the project and I thought he quite liked me. The Harbourmaster had a very official voice:

'WHO are you exactly?'

'I'm Chris, it's my boat'

'Then you're the one we're after.'

The semi-submerged boat had floated on until it had hit a petro-chemical jetty owned by British Petroleum. It was a restricted area and they weren't at all happy. The remains of my driftwood boat had got caught around one of the legs of their pier. Captain Walker wasn't very happy either. He told me I was a danger to shipping, disrespectful and foolish. I was summoned to meet him at the end of the pier. When I arrived, he was waiting imperiously, in uniform. I instinctively held out my hand as he walked towards me. He refused to shake it.

The boat was still upside down and tied to the bottom of a ladder. Captain Walker ordered me down to turn it over and bale it out with a bucket. The mast had broken off but, when I got all the water out, it still floated. His next order was to come back the next day to find a way of getting it to shore. A local boat owner kindly volunteered to tow the boat to the riverbank and, once on the beach, he left me alone to carry out Captain Walker's final orders. I took a can of petrol, set fire to the boat and destroyed it.

This left me with a bit of a problem when it came to my degree show.

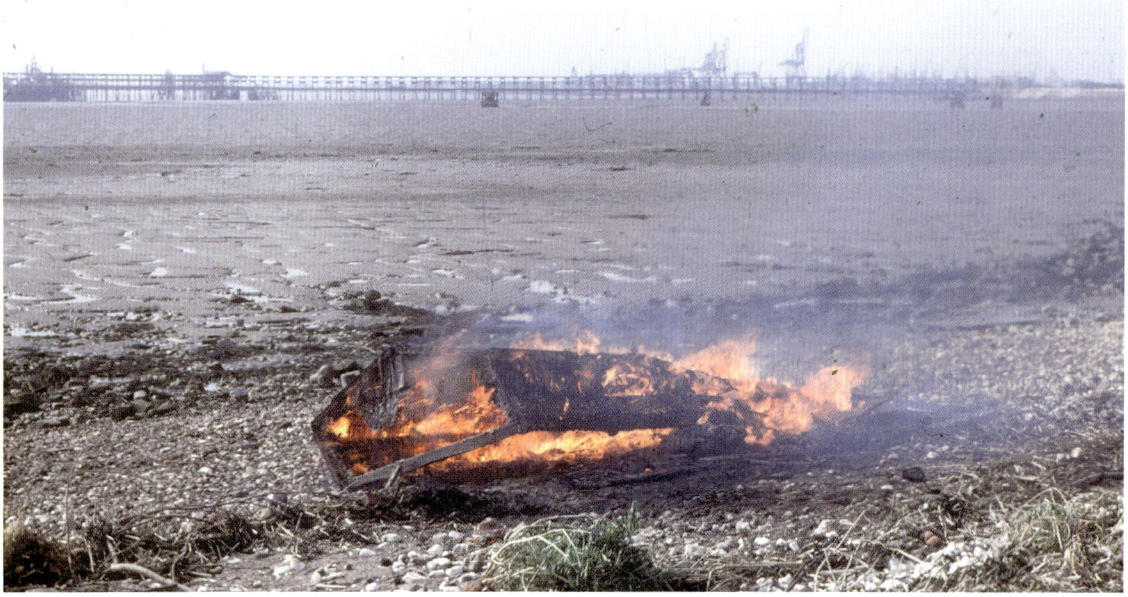

Destruction of the driftwood boat on Captain Walker's instructions.

The Hull degree show was quite typical of its time. The art college studios were cleared and partitioned with temporary white painted walls. Each student then had a space to show their work in. Since a big part of my course work had gone up in smoke, I needed something to represent my artistic output. Luckily, my art course was very conceptual and my tutors allowed me to go back to the beach, dig it up and show that instead. Somewhere in the sand my boat still existed, if only on a molecular level.

My space had a floor to ceiling window on one side and I laid out the beach so that it appeared to go through this and carry on outside. In actual fact I had carefully lined it up on the other side of the glass laying it on top of the grass the other side of the window. Outside it was in a strip dictated by the width of my designated space. The grass embankment sloped down and away from the window with the similar undulation of a real beach. Instead of ending at the water's edge however, mine terminated at the car park.

The art college degree show, or exam, is a very stressful time of year in the art student's calendar. Normal day-to-day things like washing, laundry, eating and sleeping all get disregarded as students stay up all night to finish their work. I have one good photograph of the beach and it has me sitting on it. I have torn jeans and shirt, scraggly hair and no shoes or socks. Although I look as though I'm trying to impersonate Robinson Crusoe, it was in fact just my normal student appearance at that busy point of my course.

Inside the gallery was a small detail of particular importance to me – a ship in a bottle. It was no ordinary ship in a bottle – it was a replica of my own ship, Friday, mounted on a sea green edition of Robinson Crusoe. It included a miniature Eddie, Paul and me and a model of the buoy we hit.

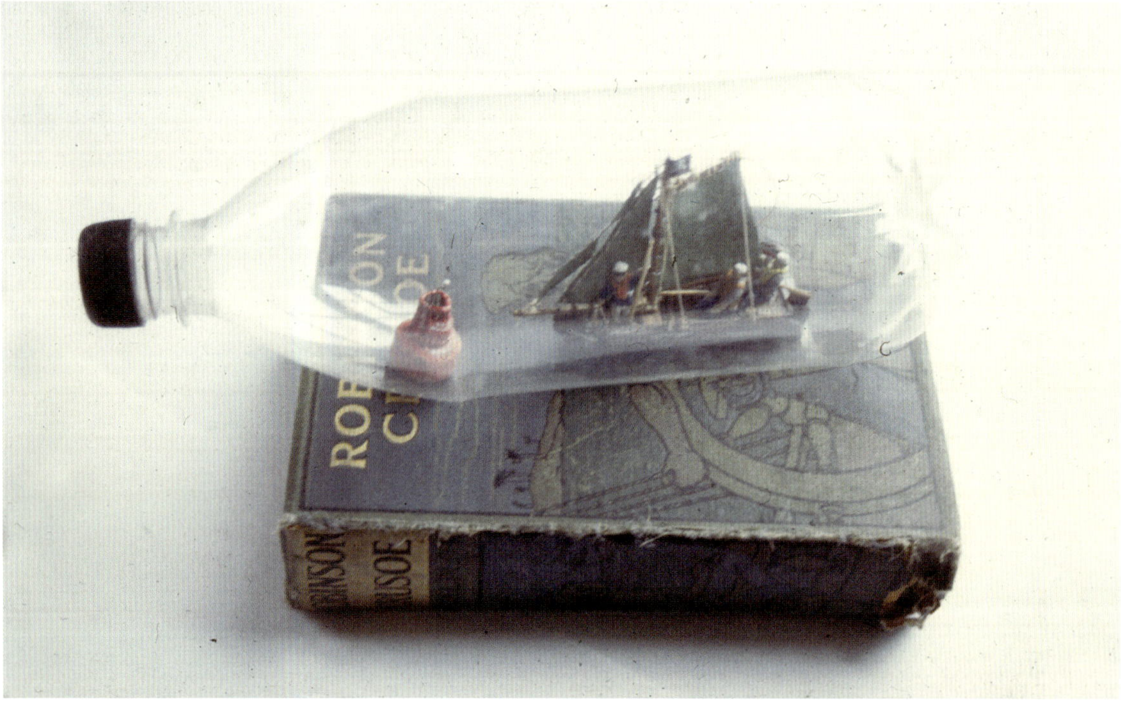

'Friday' as a ship in a bottle. [Sue Guthrie]

right: Me, the unwashed art student, looking uncannily like Robinson Crusoe on my artificial beach. [Anna Miszewska]

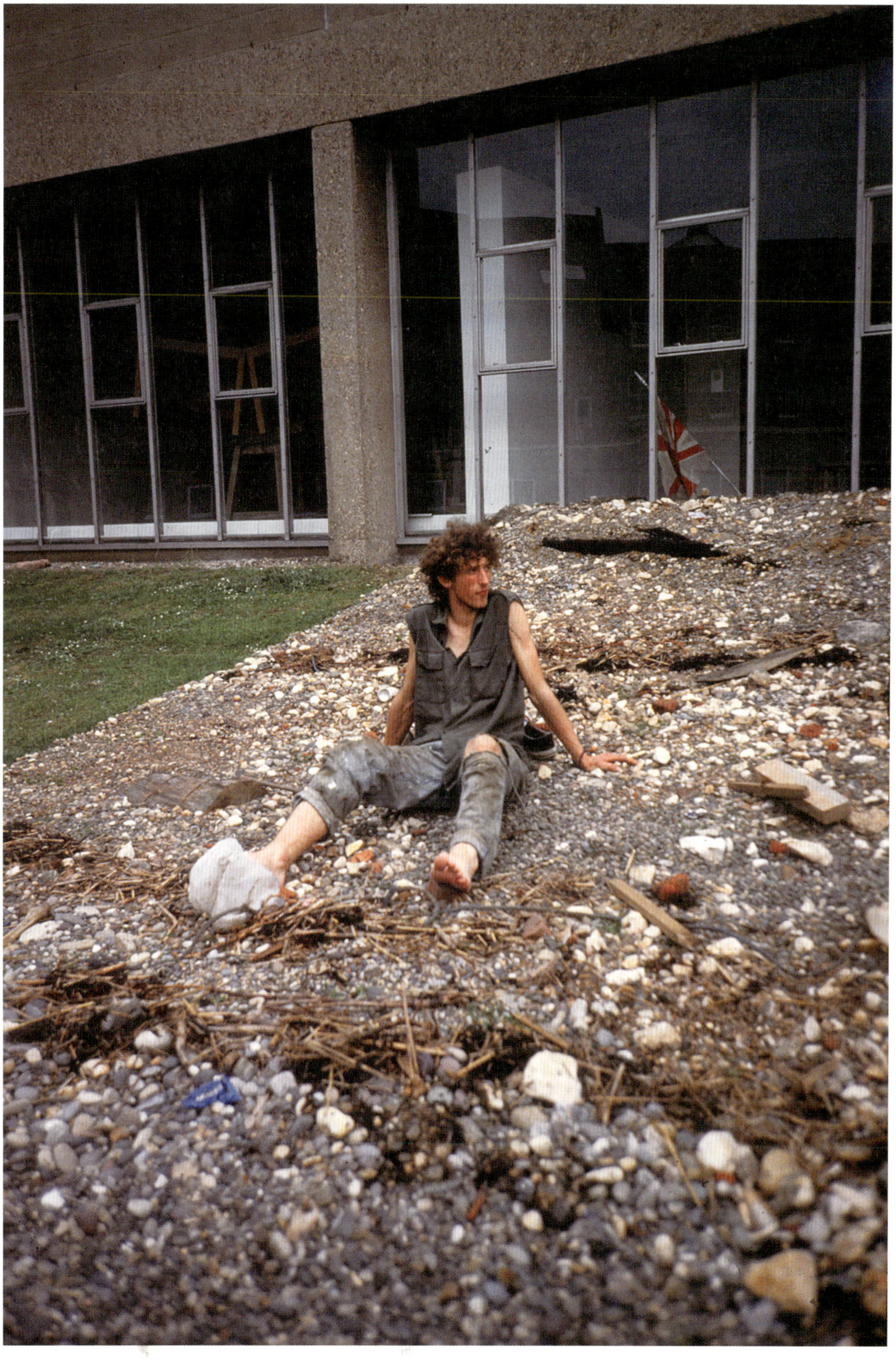

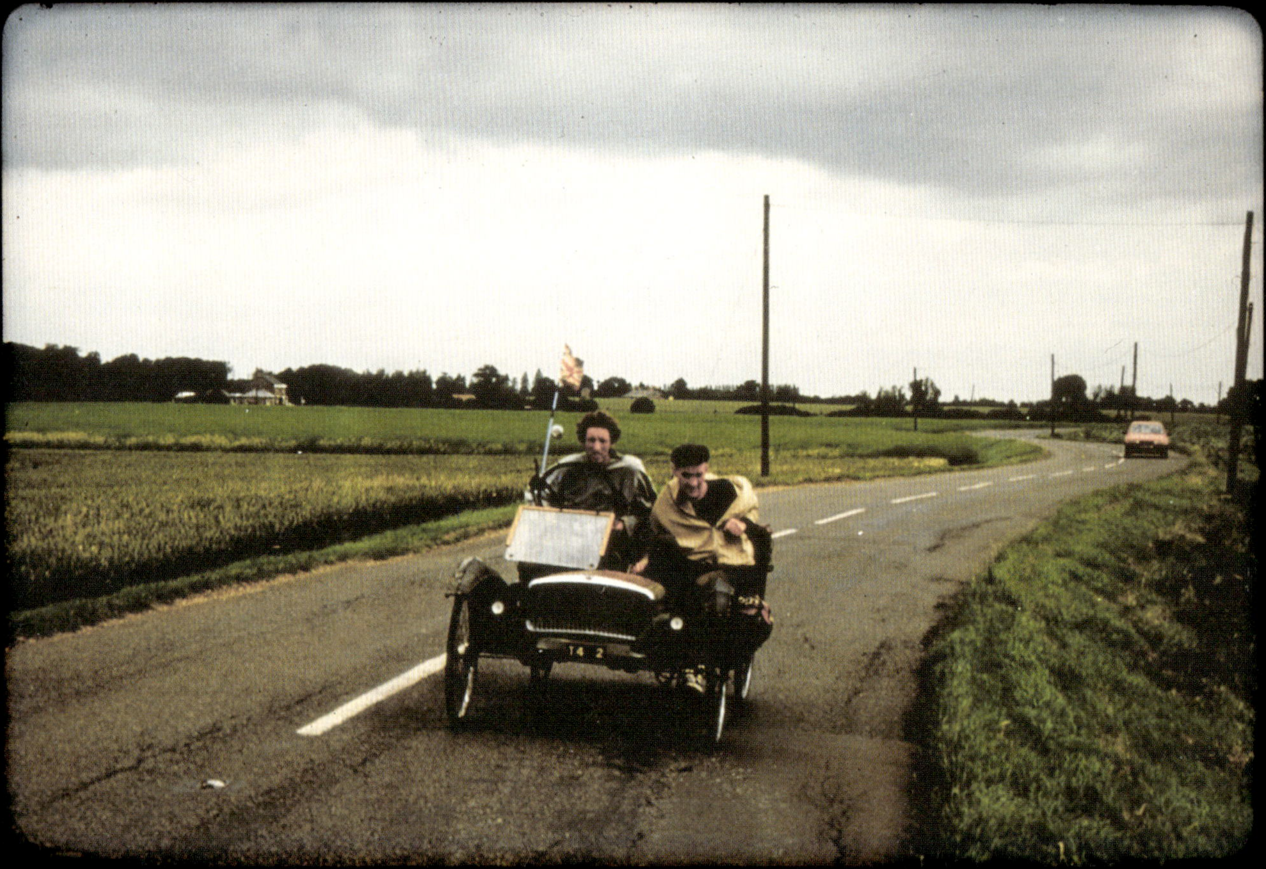

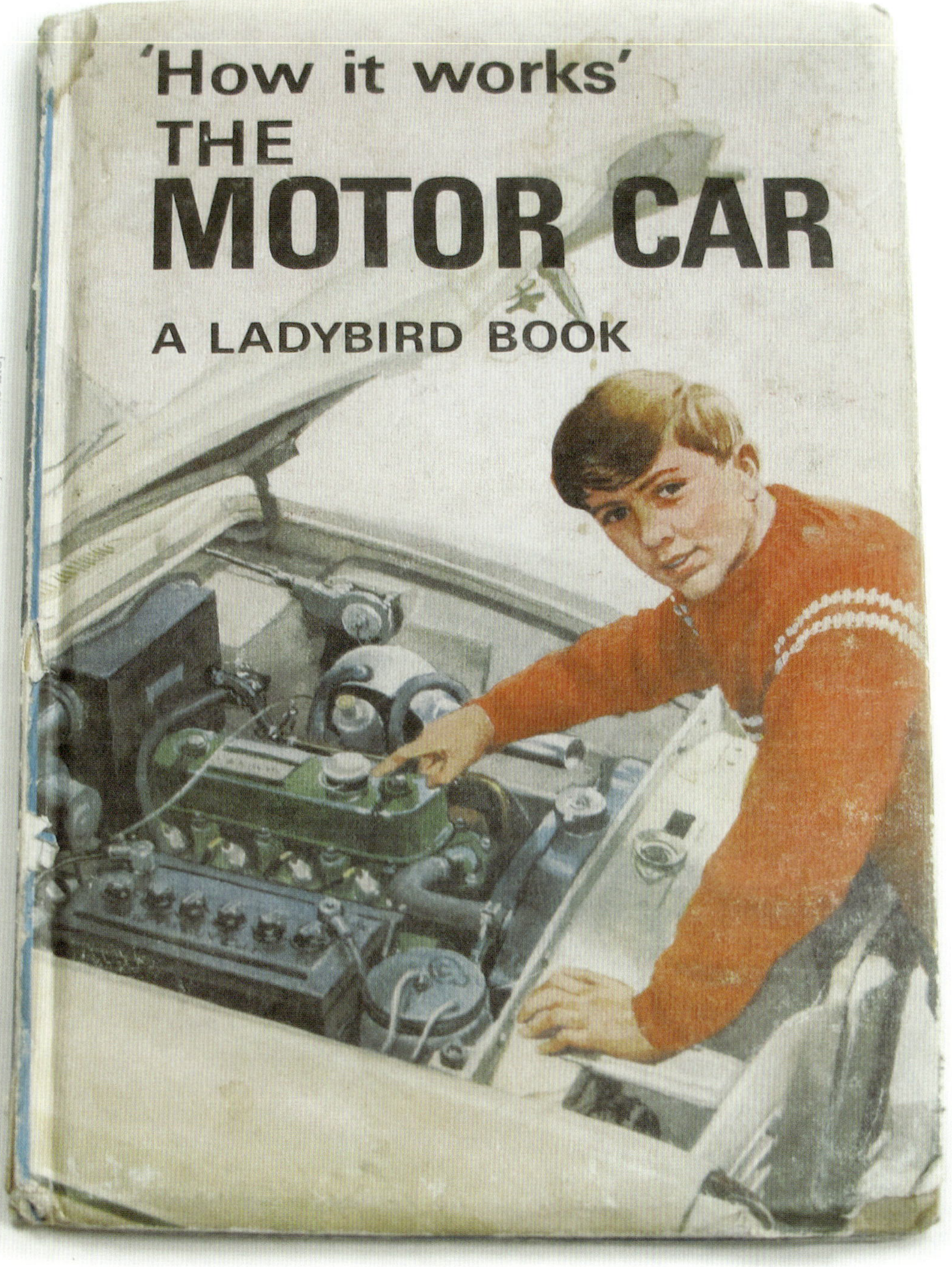

Landscape Escape

previous page: Pedal car at full speed.

When I was building my driftwood boat, I decided to fix all the wood together with screws rather than nails. Nails might have been strong enough but I felt the serious way it was built would show my integrity and commitment to the project. When we collided with the buoy, it may have been the choice of screws over nails that made all the difference because the boat stayed in one piece.

My history with screws goes back to when I was about eight or nine when I used to make pram-wheeled go-karts to roll down the road where I grew up. Nails were always a quick easy option when it came to making something – just keep whacking with a hammer until the nail disappears. This method was far better suited to the limited attention span of an eight year old than all the preparation or drilling needed for screws. Although my father was a carpenter, in the 1970s an electric drill was still a luxury. I only had access to an old fashioned hand driven drill at that time. I think that the personal screw-nail debate I had with myself led to a chain of thought that provoked memories of pram wheeled go karts and ultimately to my next attempt at escaping from art college… a great big go-kart.

When I built go-karts as a child, I wanted to build something that was like the family car. Not necessarily something fast but a mobile personal space that gave a sense of safety and reassurance, protected from the outside world. The family car was, somehow, a little bit of home that you took with you however far you travelled. I always wanted to make a go-kart that you climbed into, shut the door and felt safe.

The summer before I had to go back to college I had started to date an old friend from back home and I was very miserable with the fact that this new relationship was cut short by the beginning of the new term. I had to go back to Hull whilst she had to go back to her art college in Leicester. Behind my thinking was the secret plan to build a go-kart car and make Leicester my objective. I would be safe in the knowledge that if I could get there I would have no problems in justifying it in terms of fulfilling the requirements of my arts course because I had arrived there on my 'sculpture' as part of my project.

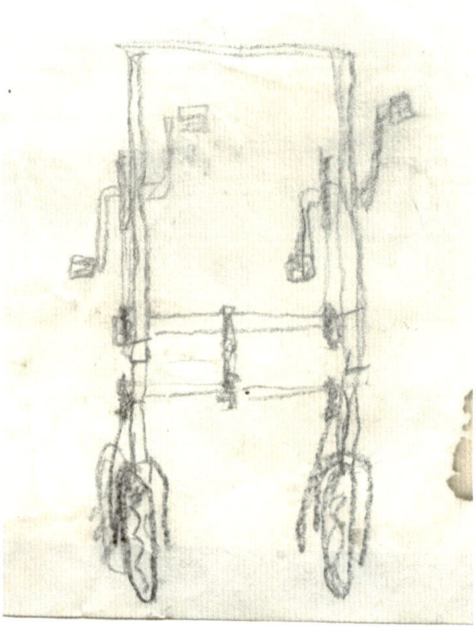

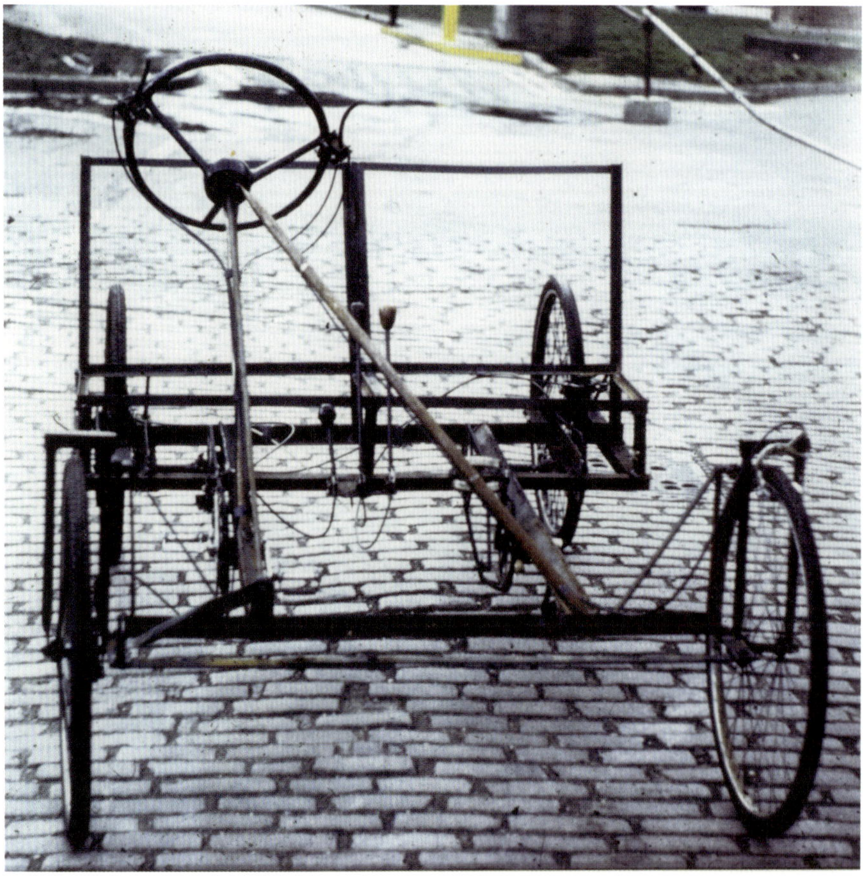

above: An early, rough sketch showing the pedals inline with the back wheel.

right: Pedal car under construction showing the chassis and the eventual staggered arrangement of the pedals and wheels.

Construction

The pedal car has two sets of pedals, each going to a separate back wheel. To offset the wheels, so that they weren't in line with the pedals and more like a real car, I had two sets of chains. The first set drove a shaft that had two cogs on it so that the drive chain had a kind of dog-leg in it to give a wider wheel base. The chassis was made of scrap metal with a mixture of bicycle and car parts fixed to it. I made two over sized bicycle type brake handles so there was extra leverage to pull two brakes up with each hand. These were bolted to an enormous car steering wheel that came from some old car from the sixties, but was also reminiscent of one I had bolted to the pram wheeled go-kart my father had built me as a child. The bonnet was made from an old tea chest and was double hinged and opened sideways in the same way that a veteran car bonnet opens. This and the trunk on the back (which I borrowed from Eddie) were used for the storage of the tent and camping stove etc. I used the normal Sturmey Archer 3-speed gears and kept the original changer leaver, which I welded a long gear stick to. Eventually I also made a windscreen from a gold picture frame.

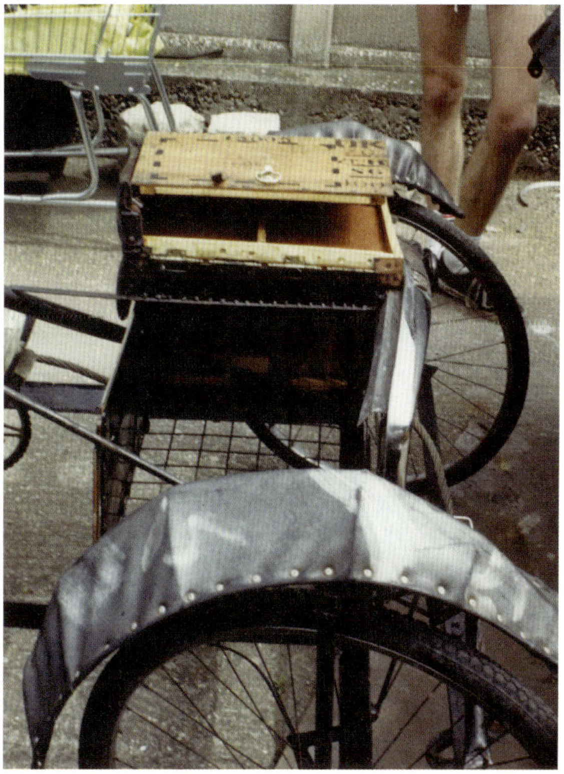

above right: bonnet opened. Interior luggage space.

right: Rear light made from a baked bean tin and a patch on one of the rear mud guards made from inner tubes.

below: Tea chest bonnet with the advertising slogan: 'It pays to buy good tea'.

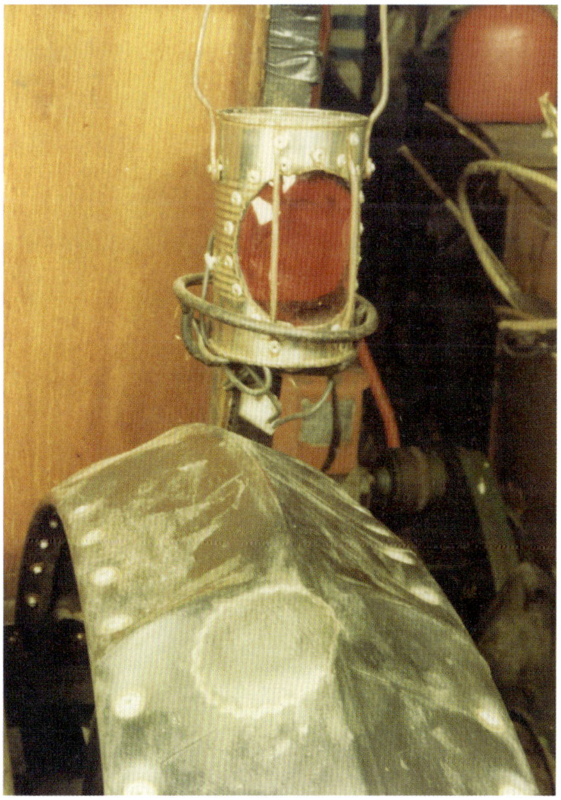

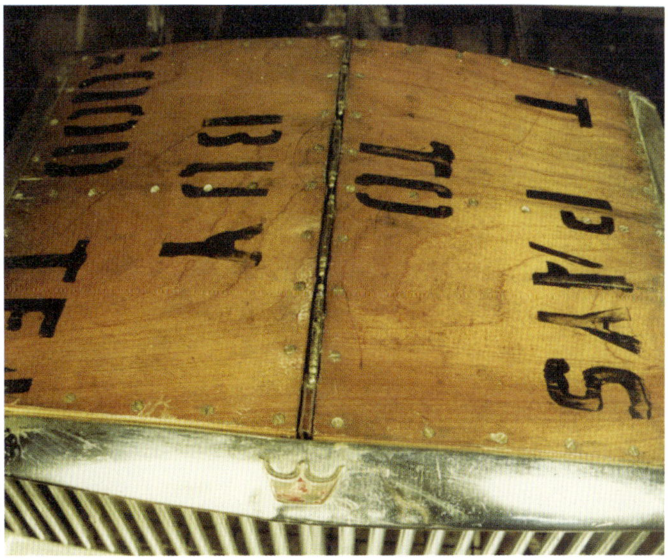

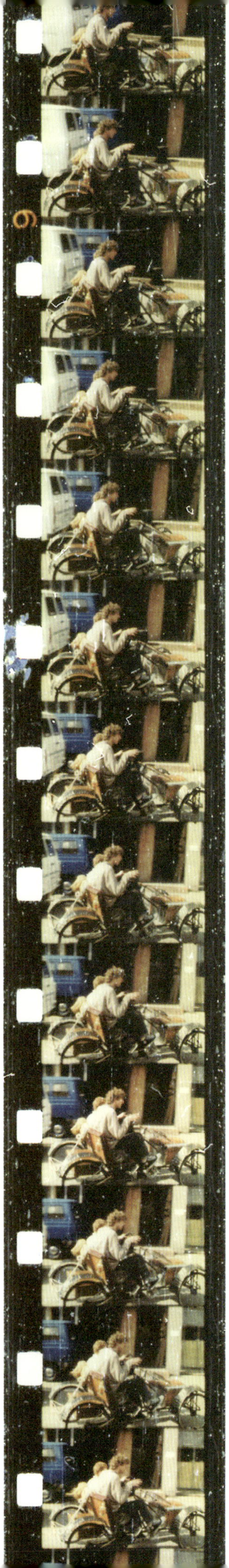

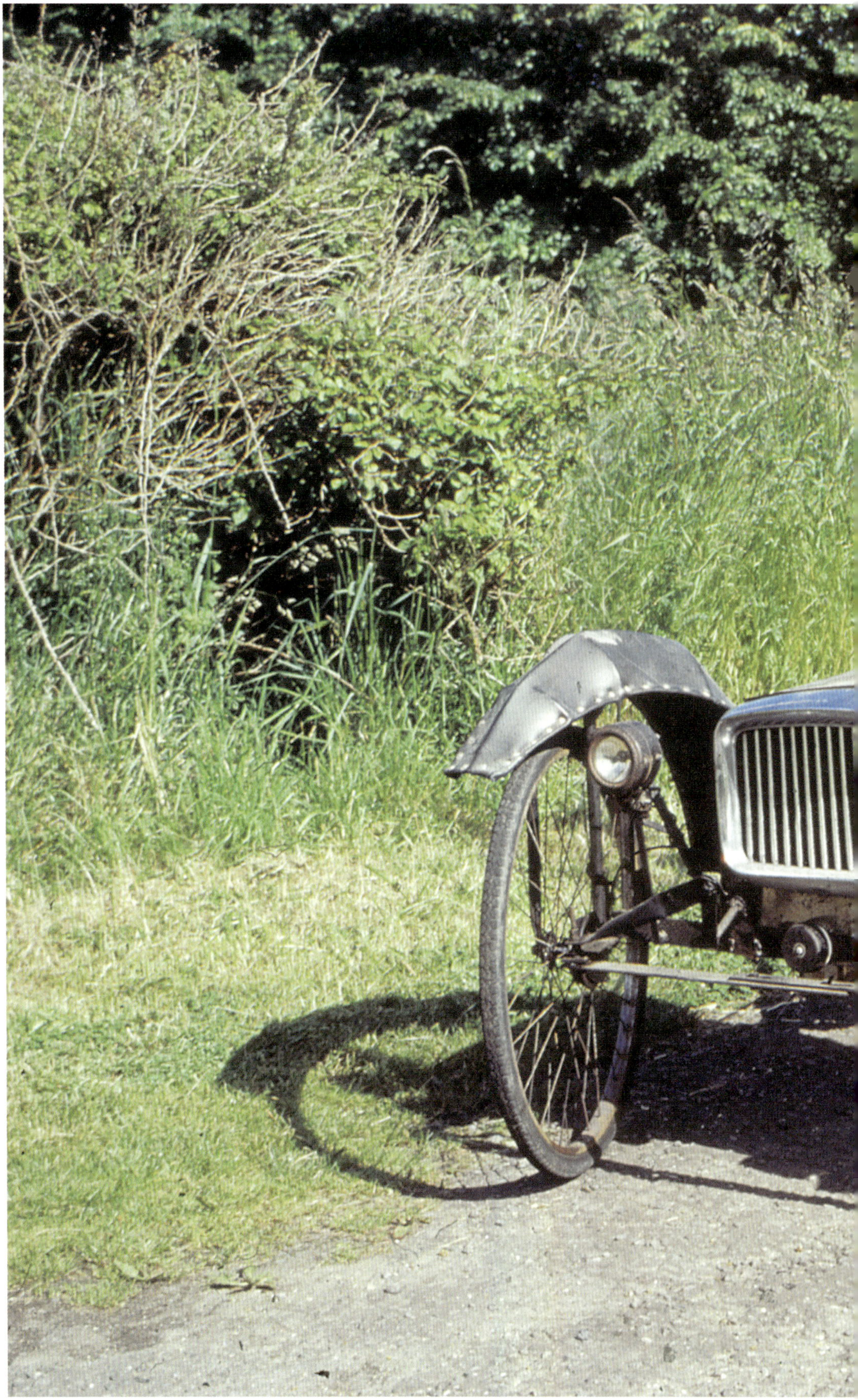

left: Pedal car on its first trip outside art college in Queen's Gardens Hull. [Clare Allen]

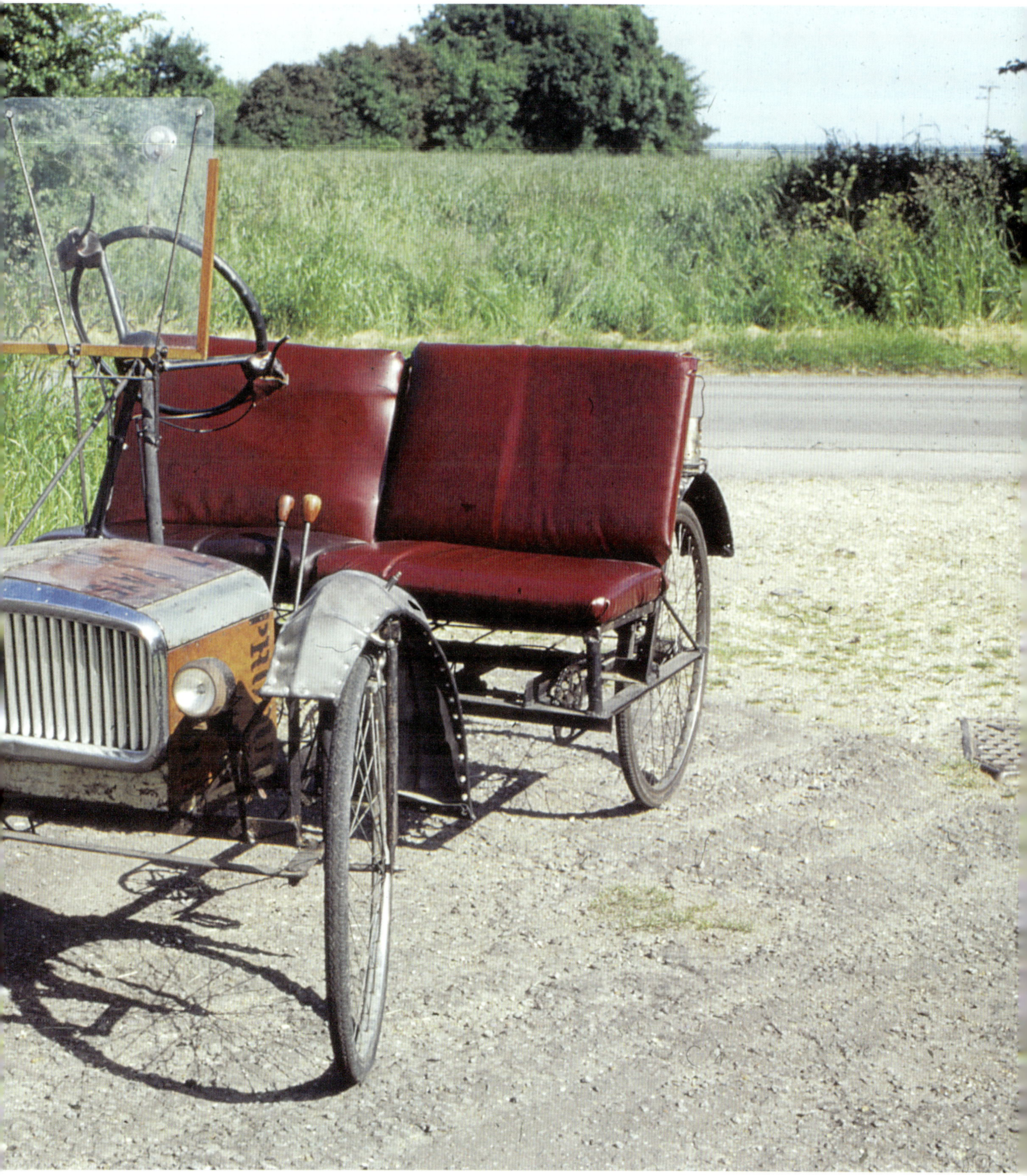

Pedal car before the gold picture frame windscreen was added. [Yusuke Toda]

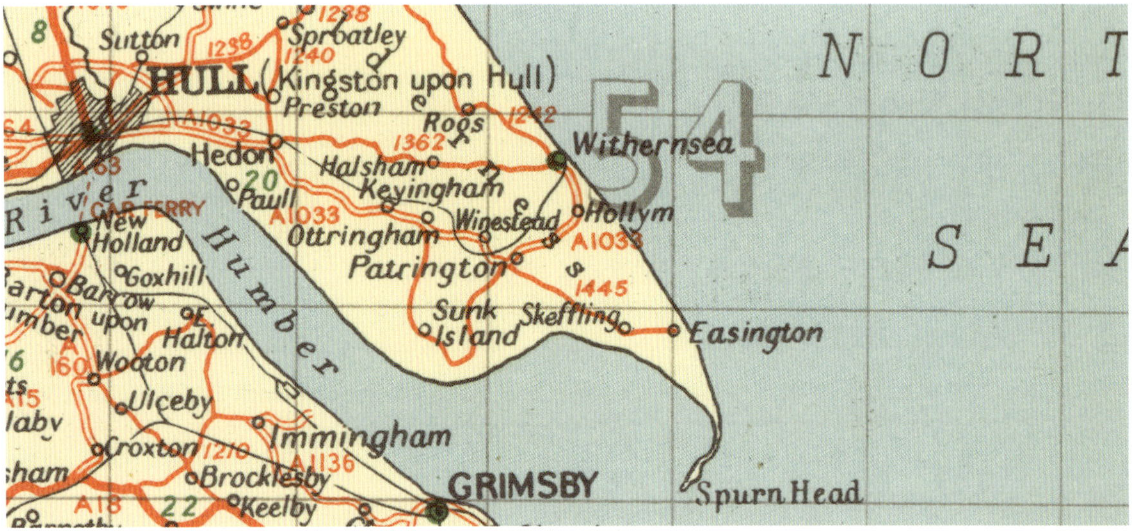

Map of Holderness.

The Journey

Looking at the map of Holderness, the land to the East of Hull becomes a thinner and thinner peninsular until it eventually becomes the single strip of land that makes up Spurn point. Looking for a clear objective that would test the capabilities of the pedal car I liked the visual poetry of Spurn point. It was the very end of the land so I made this objective my first journey. The distance was about thirty miles and I estimated it would take us about a day to get there and leave enough time to put up a tent and come back the next day.

Before I describe the pedal car journey, I need to elaborate more on the context it was built in, namely Art College. The art education I had was called a 'fine art' degree. In fairness, this definition doesn't really describe what happened in our department. Years later when I try to describe to the uninitiated an accurate picture of what we did I find the term 'visual philosophy' probably describes it best. We were encouraged to question the materials we used and to analyse the methods we used to manipulate them. We often found ourselves in an intellectual blind alley where we would revel in the grey area between definitions and quality. My favourite illustration of this is a hypothetical group tutorial I could have had whilst I was a student.

The format of the art college group tutorial usually consists of all the students from the tutorial group taking it in turns to stand around each other's work whilst trying to think of something clever or helpful to say. Imagine everyone is looking at a three dimensional object that is quite clearly sculptural but has paint applied to it that is quite clearly painterly. Someone in the group who likes the sound of their own voice that day says 'Sculptural yet painterly, is it a painting or is it a sculpture? It's a grey area. Very interesting.'

Imagine now that the sculpture-painting was photographed and the tutorial group is looking at the photograph. The image seems to be of more value than the subject. The leader of the tutorial group puts forward the case: 'The image seems to be of more artistic merit than the actual sculpture/painting. You should show the photograph instead of the object, it's much better. Is this image now more than just documentation,? And have we elevated it to the status of 'art' thus reducing the real thing to merely a prop for the photo..? Again, very interesting… it's a grey area.'

I have been a teacher so I have experienced this situation from both sides. Sometimes I have had to lead a tutorial and found myself looking at a construction that stands about four inches from the floor, made thoughtlessly from chicken wire and Sellotape. My job as the tutor is to find something positive to say, even if I suspect the student wasn't trying very hard. While I'm trying to find a diplomatic way of saying 'this is rubbish', I'm struck by the demeanour of the student and I'm tempted to say:

‘Yes, this is shit. But as I look at you, you are a kind of half-arsed slacker of a student and in some ways this ‘shit’ could actually be a true intellectual representation of your very soul and being. In those terms this ‘shit’ is actually quite good, hmmm… it’s a grey area.’

The antithesis of this culture is the mental approach needed by the police force. To make quick, important decisions there must be no ambiguity and no vagueness. No room for grey areas. It was on the A1033 driving the pedal car from Hull into Holderness that these two approaches met. As Eddie and I left Hull we saw a police car but, to our amazement, we shook it off. Later, however, as we pedalled through the countryside, we passed a police van in a layby. This is how I imagine the policeman’s thought process developed:

The car passes him and he can see that, although slightly odd, it does look like a car. Then he takes in our legs going up and down and recognises this as motion normally associated with riding a bicycle. This is how it computes:

‘Not a car – not a bicycle = grey area = must be illegal!’

This thought process obviously needs to happen quite quickly and he has already pulled us over before he has worked out why it is illegal. He is struggling to find a legal phrase to justify his action. When this phrase failed to materialise, he comes up with: ‘No, no, I’m sorry, but you are not… serious.’

Mindful of the fact that I had already spent two years having to justify my actions at art college as sincerely and philosophically as possible I instinctively set about stating how genuine I was, even to extent of explaining all about my ‘inner need’ and exactly ‘how’ serious I was. He wasn’t interested. I felt confident that I was OK legally as well because I’m pretty sure it doesn’t say in the Highway Code ‘you must be serious at all times on the highway’. It wasn’t long before another police car stopped, this time it was a plain-clothed policeman in an unmarked car. They conferred, then did ‘good cop bad cop’ on me. The first policeman (bad cop) was still trying to find words that best suited my traffic violation and came up with another nothing word that he picked out of the ether.

‘Reckless! That’s what you are, reckless!’

I couldn’t think of a less appropriate word. It was a giant, two-seater pedal car with a maximum speed of 10 miles per hour. Minutes earlier we had been overtaken by a milk float. Good cop then interjected with a suggestion that we took the next exit off the main road and picked our way through the narrow country lanes to Spurn Point. I agreed and we found ourselves in Sunk Island.

Sunk Island was reclaimed from the river estuary a few hundred years ago. It is virtually all arable land with only one or two houses. The roads skirt large, featureless fields without many signposts. We got lost. The Sunk Island diversion added another three hours to our journey and I ran out of film before we reached the end of the land.

I have subsequently done a few other journeys with the pedal car. Before the next trip I thought it was best to clear up the legal ambiguity of whether the car was legal or not. I decided to approach the police first and went to the main police station in Hull at Queen’s gardens and explained what I had built over the counter to the duty officer. He was surprised, went away, came back and told me to wait nearby for a visit from V.I.B. They turned up in a police van with V.I.B. written on the side and carrying clip boards. It turned out V.I.B. stood for ‘Vehicle Inspection Branch’. They looked at the car and said they would have to consult their legal books. I think it was probably a grey area and the final decision depended on their personal opinion. I thought it was best not to tell them I was going all the way to London.

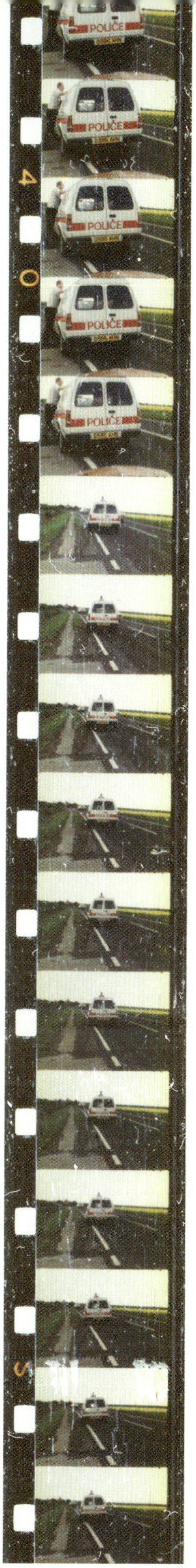

right: Meeting the police on the A1033 on the way to the ‘end of the land’.

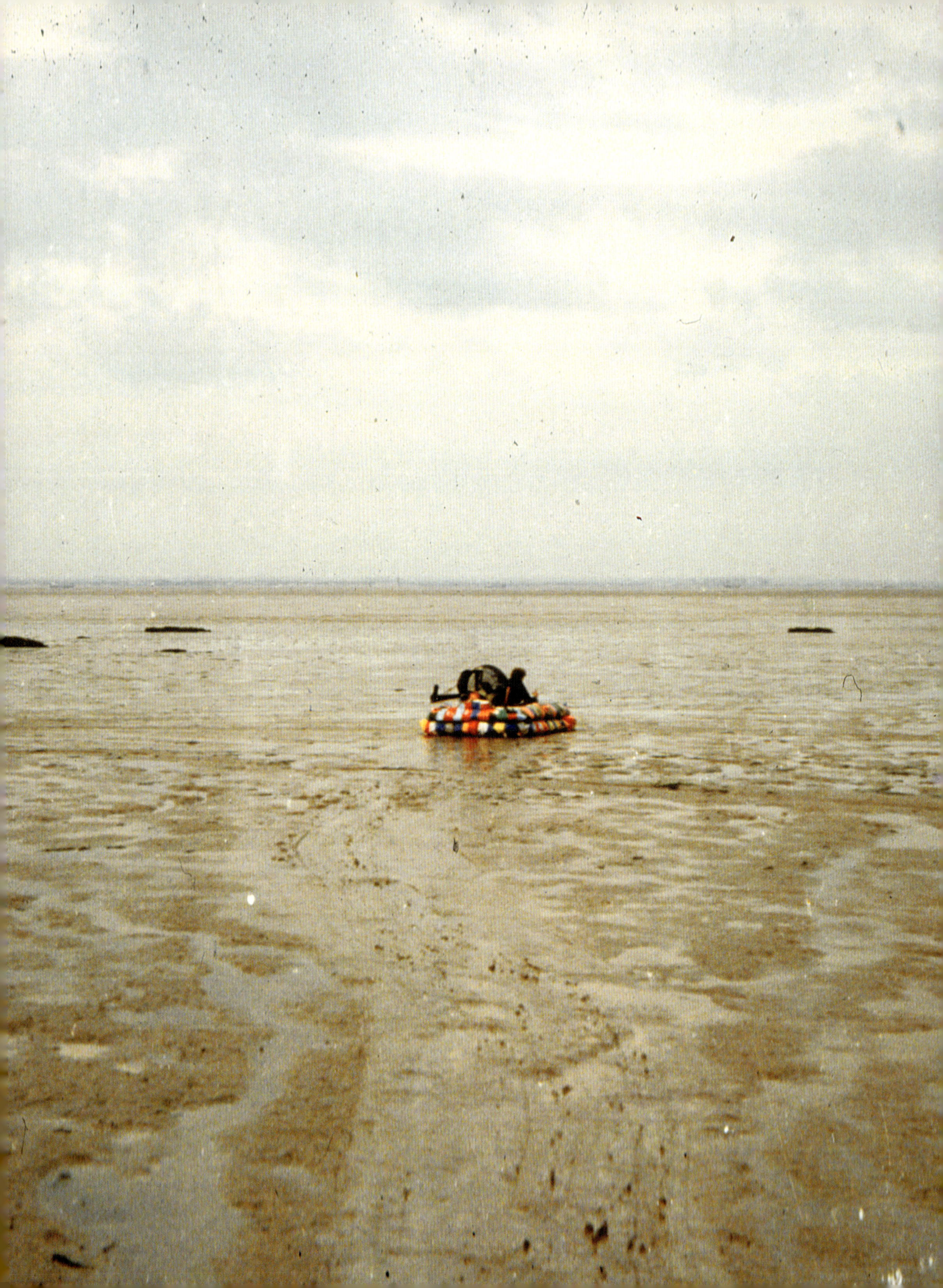

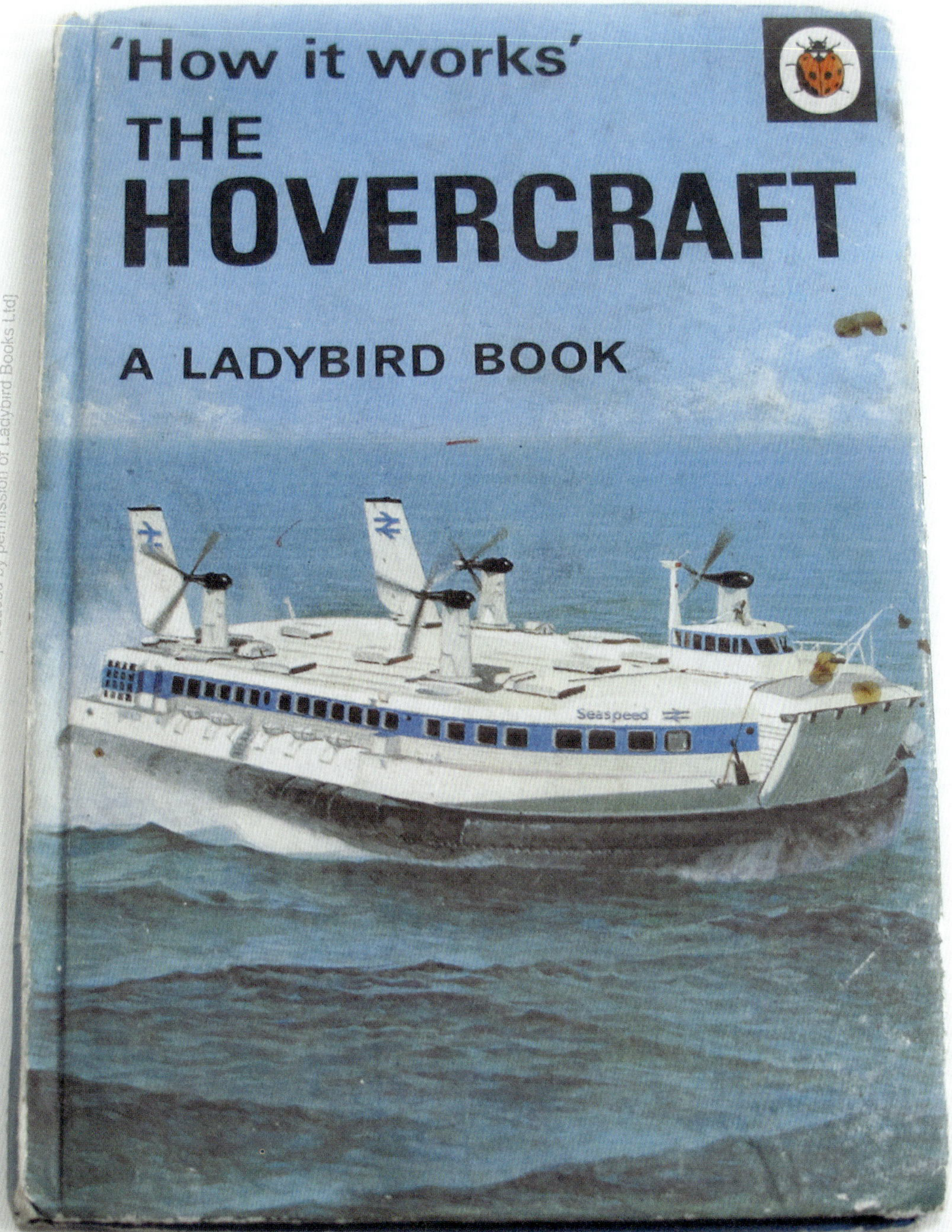

Seascape Escape No. 2

When I built the driftwood boat, I kept it on the Victoria Pier in Hull for a few weeks before the launch and it became quite an attraction. Mothers often left their children playing in it and we baby-sat the kids while the mums went to the nearby café. Other visitors included the large number of retired men who frequented the pier; ex-mariners who had stories to tell about the past. One guy was intrigued by the shape of the boat and told me that it reminded him of a small craft they used as a safety vessel when he worked on ship repair. According to him, they often had to work over the side of the ships while they were moored in the Humber. The safety vessel, he said, was woefully inadequate:

'It were useless. It was supposed to pick you out of the water if you fell off the side but if the current were strong, it could never catch you. We all had to wear life-jackets so when we fell in't water we would just float downstream. About four miles down, there's a bend in't river at Paull where things tend to wash up. The arrangement were, if you fell off before ten in't morning, you'd have to float to Paull, get out there and get on't bus to come back for afternoon shift.

'I never forget the day, five minutes to ten in't morning, I was working on the side of a coaster, I slipped and fell in't water. I bobbed to the surface and felt the current start to take me. I looked up as I floated past the bow of the ship. There, looking down, was the foreman. He tapped his watch and shouted: "back here for one o'clock".'

One day, a man came up to me on the pier, looked at the boat and said: 'Plastic bottles'. I asked him to elaborate and he told me that if I made a boat out of plastic bottles instead of driftwood it would never sink. I thought this was a terrific idea and I suggested to the man that he should go to art college.

Although I liked his thinking, the first obstacle was finding the amount of bottles needed to make something that big. Then, amazingly, when I took the pedal car on its journey to the 'end of land', I found them. Apparently, every time someone throws a plastic bottle into the Humber or any of its tributaries, they all end up on the same beach. When we got out of the pedal car and explored the beach on the estuary side of Spurn Point, I found hundreds of them. There were easily enough to do the job, but on this occasion I decided not to make a boat… I made a hovercraft.

I spent several days walking up and down the four mile stretch of beach collecting plastic bottles. Whilst beachcombing, I also came across other things that came in handy, including a life-jacket. In retrospect, it probably wasn't the best recommendation for a life-jacket; being found washed up on the beach, but I was pleased with it nonetheless. Another find, of far more importance, was the engine.

A small patch of land backed onto the beach where someone kept a caravan, a boat and a hovercraft made from a kit. I had no idea how I was going to power my hovercraft or where I was going to get the fan from and I could see this hovercraft was full of water and hadn't been used for a long time. The area was desolate but in the distance I could see a man in a woolly hat down on the beach. He gave me the name of the owner and I looked him up in the phone book. I rang him from a phone box and we agreed a price. I had to put £40 inside an envelope and drop it through the letterbox of an address in Hull. I had even found the engine on the beach!

On another occasion, I noticed a strangely familiar piece of wood. On closer inspection, it turned out to be the remnant of one of my own toy boats. Someone had obviously thought it was an interesting lump of wood and put it on the sea wall for safe keeping. I felt pleased that my craftsmanship had seduced a stranger into doing that much at least. The varnished paper address label had worn away and there was only a blank white square where the return address had been. As I scanned the horizon, I imagined the infinite number of places it could have washed up and here it was in front of me. I tried to read meaning into this chance encounter and considered repairing the damaged boat and putting it back in the water again. Luckily, before I did anything a tutor said: 'No, I think you were meant to keep that one.'

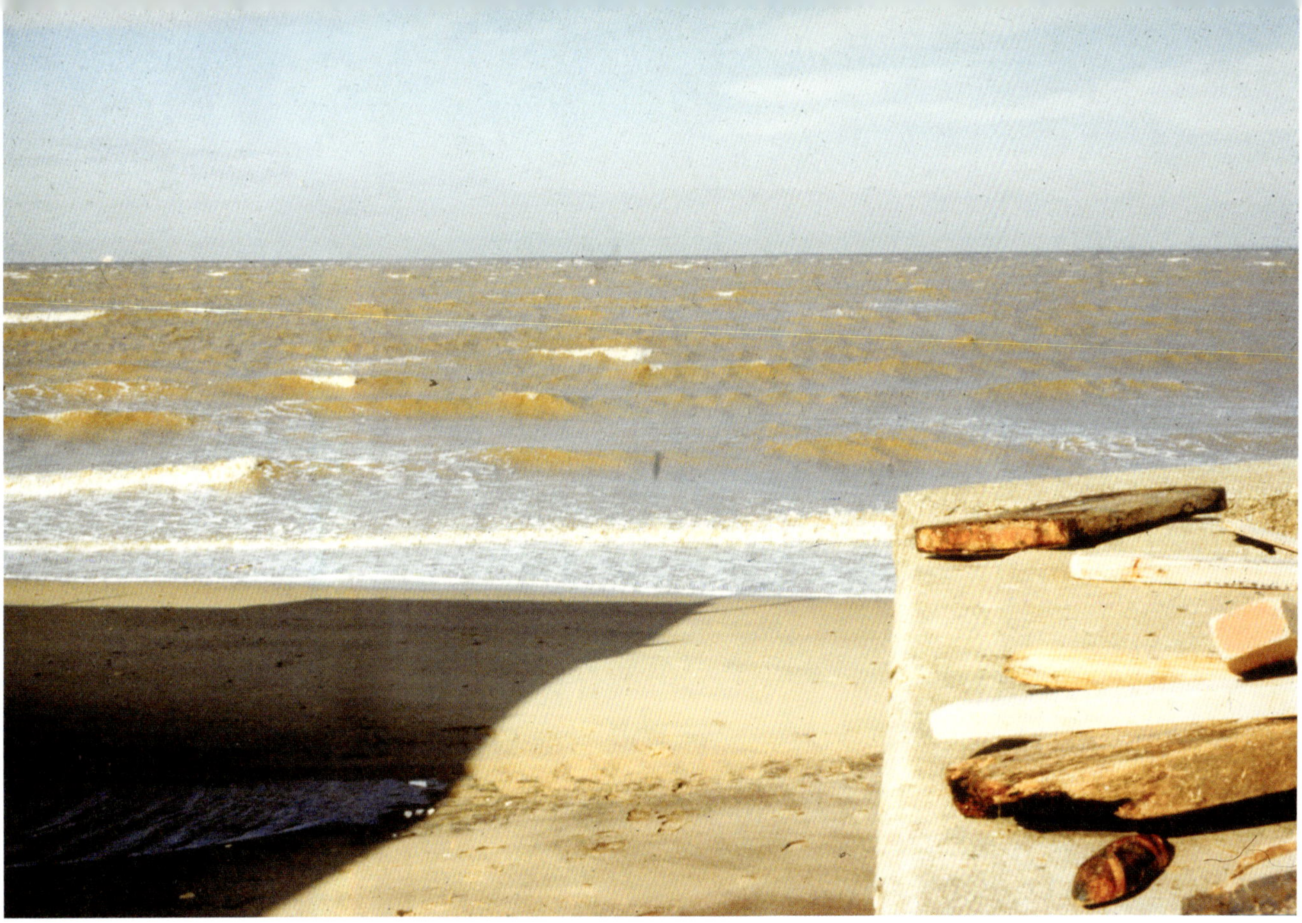

Finding the toy boat at Spurn Point (bottom right corner).

Construction

I got a rough idea of the dimensions of a hovercraft from a reference book I found in the library. I wasn't allowed to take the book out of the building or even to photocopy pages so I had to sit in the library and copy out the bits I thought were important in my notebook. Armed with the dimensions, I set about making the deck using two-litre plastic lemonade bottles. There were also a few green Lilt bottles (the only transparent green bottle in the UK at the time) and brown beer or cider bottles. The bottles had been in the river for a long time and looked like they had been sandblasted.

I lined them up end-to-end and cut off the top and bottom of each alternate bottle. This made them into hollow tubes or sleeves. I slotted this sleeve over the top of an intact bottle then slid the bottom of another bottle in from the other side. In this way, I had two plastic bottles held together with the middle section of a third. I then glued them in place and continued the process until I had a long tube of plastic bottles. I made several of these the required length of my hovercraft and finally fixed them together in rows inside a sort of wooden exoskeleton. I did this until I had a surface that was the correct size for the deck. The alternate Lilt and cider bottles made a nice green and brown stripe down the middle.

The next step was to make the air duct that went all the way round the outside of the hovercraft and transferred air from the fan to the skirt underneath. This big 14 inch diameter tube was made from the larger five-litre or gallon size bottles that I had found. These were the ones that oil sometimes comes in or industrial quantities of stuff like bleach. They always come with a handle moulded from the top and are often made from an opaque coloured plastic.

Hovercraft under construction in the sculpture studio, Queen's Gardens. The deck was made from wooden frames and 2-litre plastic bottles.

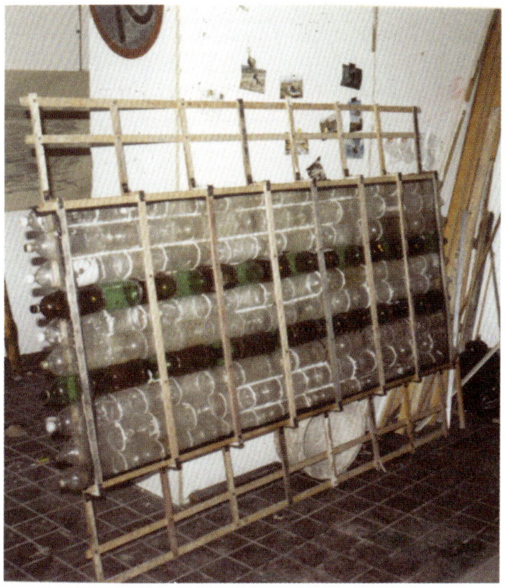

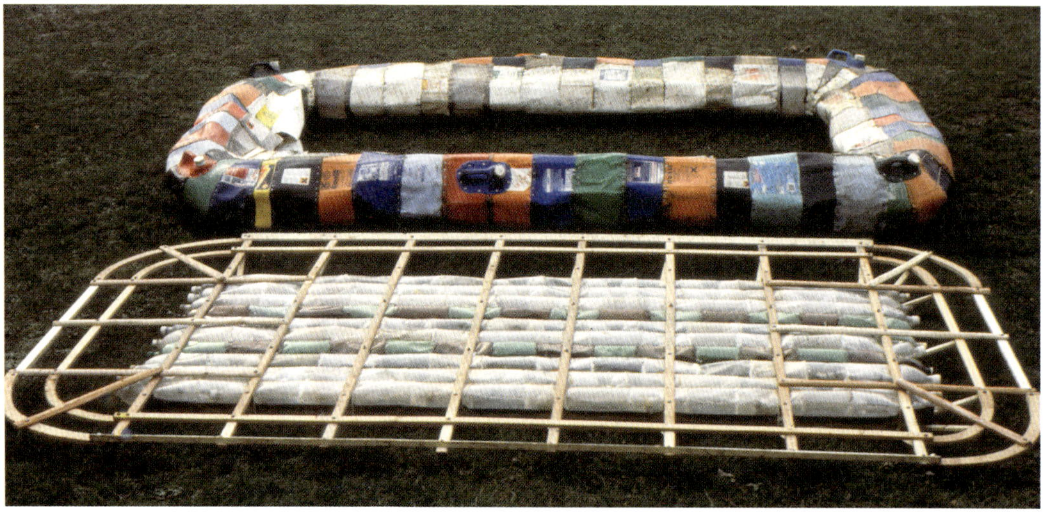

The deck and the main air duct before assembly.

The diameter of the bottle wasn't enough to allow a sufficient quantity of air to flow through so I had to double the size. The only way I could do this was to cut the top and bottom off, cut this tube open and rivet it to another section of plastic bottle that had also been opened out. The two sections together made a 14" diameter section of tube, but it was only 7" long. I had to repeat the process over sixty times, then join each little section together until I had enough tube to go around the circumference of the hovercraft. Each piece of bottle had to be pop riveted to the next one; it took thousands upon thousands of rivets and each one had to have a washer to stop the rivet pulling out after it had been fixed in place. Each join had weather-proof tape sandwiched in between to seal it. I had to reach inside and feel for the rivets to put the washers on. As a result my hands were constantly covered in the greasy goo that covered the tape. Sometimes the drill caught the tape and screwed it up into a tight ball around the drill bit and there was no other option but to drill all the rivets out and start the whole joint all over again. It was a truly horrible job.

After stopping to write my thesis, I made an air duct that went around the entire hovercraft. It had an opening at the back and this was pop riveted to a plastic dustbin with the bottom cut off to make an air intake which was mounted on the rear deck. Rotating inside the dustbin was a fan connected to the engine.

How it Worked

The dustbin was partitioned into two compartments which separated the air coming from the fan and diverted it in two directions. One part of this volume of airflow was diverted down and around into the air duct made from plastic bottles. It circulated all the way around the outside of the hovercraft and the tube inflated. Along its entire length, at intervals of about six inches, were holes about 10cm in diameter. These holes were on the underneath of the air duct, facing downwards. The air from each hole came out into a section made from a plastic sack which diverted the air in under the hull. These were mainly fertiliser bags which contoured themselves to the ground, trapping the air underneath. The trapped air lifted the hovercraft from the ground and made a cushion of air for it to sit on. Once it was off the ground, the lack of friction made it easy to move, so that the rest of the air from the fan in the dustbin – which pointed directly straight out from the back – could push it along.

On the nice, even, flat surface of the college car park it did this very well. There was a rudder on the back of the dustbin but most of the turning was done by leaning – like you would do on a motorcycle. The only difference was also applying friction to turn because weight caused the skirt (the fertilizer bags) to drag on one side and this assisted the turn. It also worked on water. As the man on the pier said, plastic bottles can't sink, so the sealed bottles made good buoyancy.

Because the bottles are transparent, they also let light through and, years later, when I worked out how to show the thing in an art gallery, I lit it from underneath and the bottles glowed like a stained glass window. In the gallery, I used several plastic bottles scattered around the gallery floor, each one with a light bulb inside and cut to suggest they were floating on an imaginary water surface. On each bottle I lit a transparent image of the different stages of the hovercraft's life, as if it were a light box. One of these images was of its inception; a photo transparency of me collecting plastic bottles on the beach at Spurn Point. I thought it would be appropriate to take the hovercraft back there to try it out.

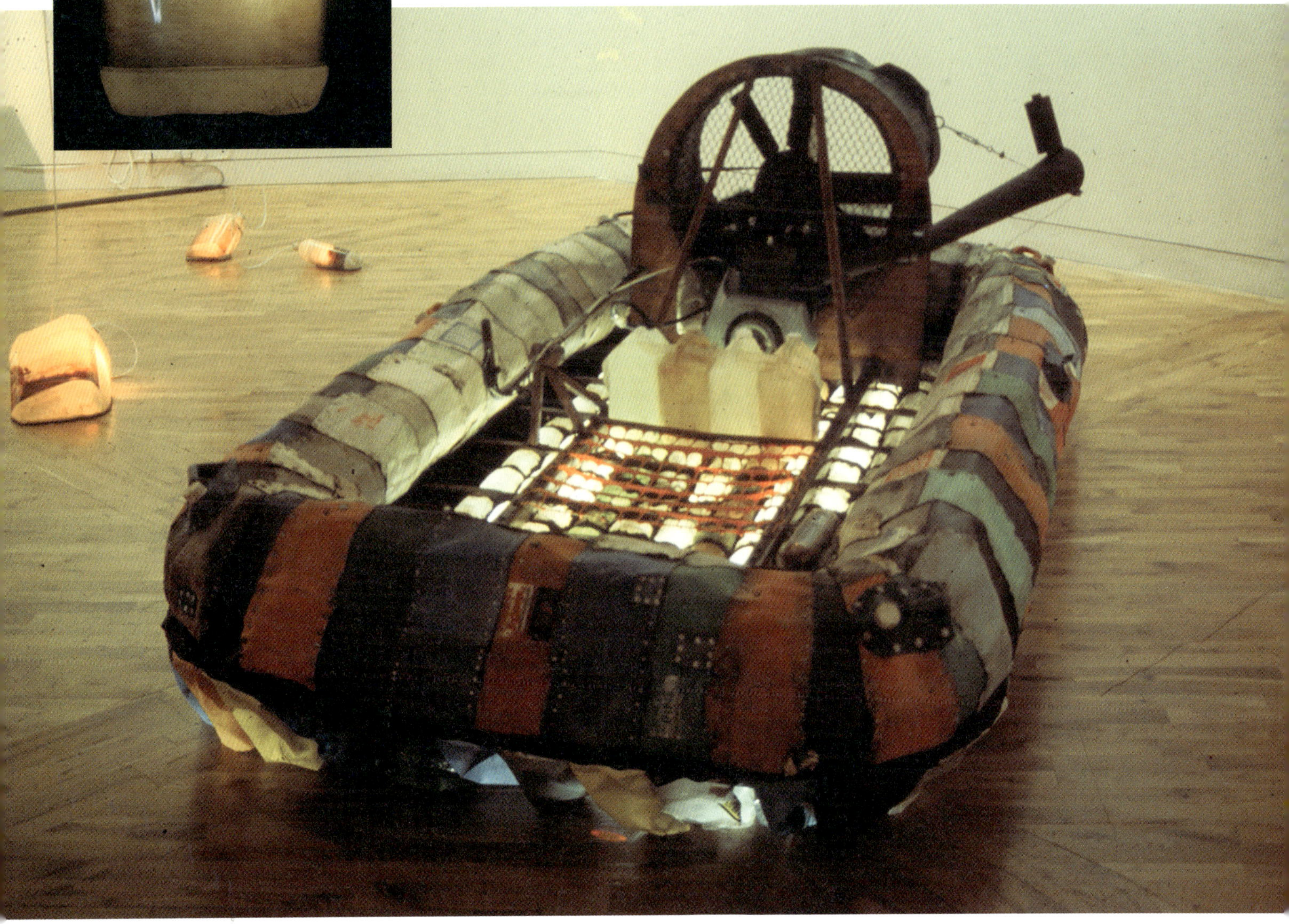

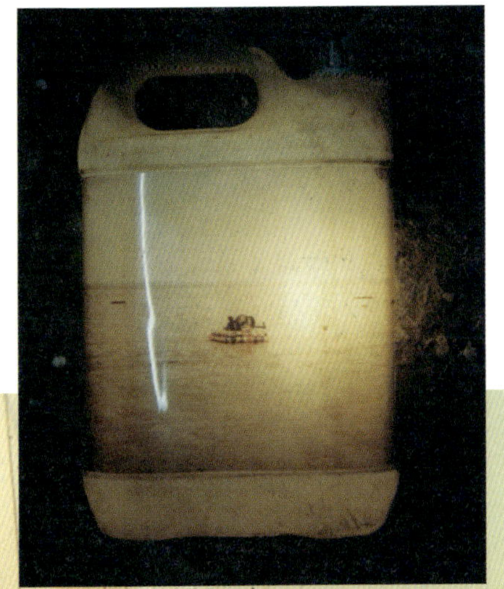

Hovercraft under-lit on display in the Ferens Gallery 2002. You can see three floating bottles in the background.

Inset: Detail of one of the floating bottles showing the hovercraft disappearing into the distance

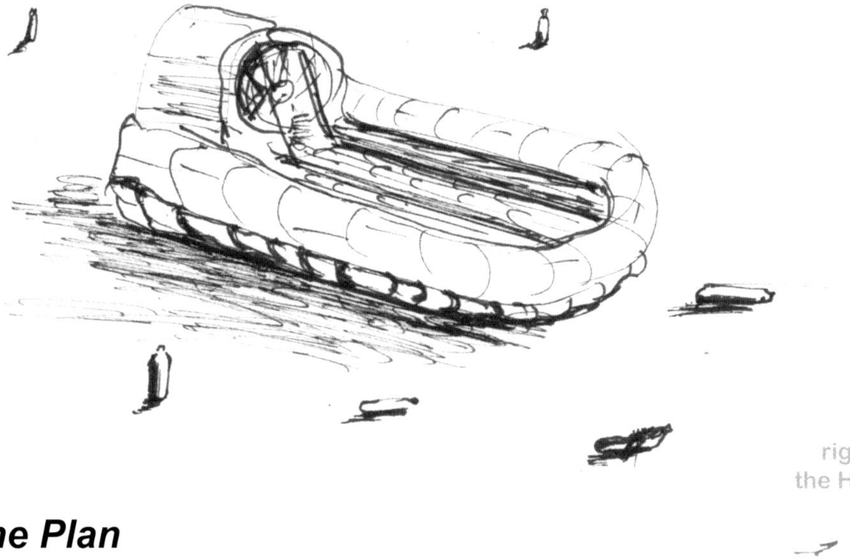

Sketch for
hovercraft in gallery.

right: Hovering out into
the Humber estuary mud.
[Tony Scott]

The Plan

The plan was to take the hovercraft to the beach where I found the bottles and come back upstream towards Hull. Although the hovercraft floated, I thought I should take advantage of its amphibious capabilities and go at low tide across the mud flats. When the tide goes out on the Humber, the water recedes a long way and leaves a muddy strip of exposed river bed hundreds of yards wide that stretches all the way to Hull. We took the hovercraft to the beach in the college trailer and borrowed a car from my sculpture tutor, Anna. The plan was for my friends to take the car back towards Hull whilst periodically finding ways to the river bank so they could see me going past and take the odd photo.

A hovercraft made from plastic bottles and old rubbish is never going to be the most efficient hovercraft in the world. There is a lot of rubbish in the Humber – lumps of concrete for example, the odd brick and bits of jagged scrap metal – and even the mud itself isn't perfectly flat. Although it worked beautifully in the college car park, it struggled to cope with the Humber mud. I eventually managed to negotiate the hazardous debris near the beach but realised if I was going to get any sort of speed up, I needed to get onto the smoother mud I could see glistening about 200 hundred yards away. I said goodbye to my friends and slowly made my way out. When I thought the surface had smoothed out, I turned right to follow the direction of the river. My friends disappeared in the car and I set off upstream alone.

Even on the smoother surface, the hovercraft struggled. The mud caused a lot of drag as it collected on the skirt. The slower it got, the more the mud stuck to it. The more mud that stuck to it, the heavier and lower it became; collecting more mud and getting slower still. Leaning to turn became impossible. If I leant, the thing just slowed and stopped. To keep the cushion of air under the hovercraft took every bit of power from the engine. Anything less than full power and it started to drag and stop. It was a two-stroke engine which revved very fast and at maximum power the sound was extremely loud. This was all very stressful and also disappointing, since the forward speed didn't reflect the amount of effort that was being put in. I often laugh at the photographs. I look very well protected in a full-face crash helmet but most of the time I was only travelling at walking pace so I'm somewhat overdressed.

The best thing to do was to get it pointed in the right direction and not stop but even this became a problem because, for some aerodynamic reason, it didn't want to go in a straight line. I think the dustbin on the back was mis-shapen in some way that the rudder couldn't compensate for. It only wanted to go corner first and so, at this skewed angle, I made my noisy way, eventually gathering momentum and picking up a little speed.

All my projects to date had been about escaping. Someone told me once that they were really just about getting some attention, like a child running away. Maybe I was just looking for attention or maybe I was searching for the sublime; a glimpse of something spiritually rewarding. I don't know the answer although it seems ridiculous to talk about spirituality in relation to a hovercraft made from plastic bottles. I did however have a moment when I felt as though I had found something.

I had travelled about a mile when I rounded a piece of headland. In the distance I could see Anna's car. It was probably the realisation that I was the focus of everyone's attention but it felt good. Then I looked in front of me and noticed a flock of birds feeding on the mud flats. I couldn't stop, turn or slow down so I had no alternative but to plough on towards them. They were slow to react despite the deafening noise and, as I reached them, they were still taking off so there was a moment when I was amongst them as they flew. I felt like I was one of the flock. I could still see my audience in the distance and I was struck by the glory of the moment. I shouted, 'Yes, this is it!'

At which point the engine blew up.

The engine barrel had snapped off all four lugs that held the bolts which fixed it to the crankcase. I was still two or three hundred yards out and stranded. I always imagine the conversation in the car as I came into view:

'There he is now, just coming round the corner. He's still going very slowly, isn't he? He's going to hit those birds, no, I think he's stopped actually, he's getting out, I reckon something's gone wrong. Oh no, he's coming over here, you know what he'll want don't you? He's going to expect us to help him bring it back!'

Anna's car was a very new Citroën. It had electric windows and central locking. It felt like a long fifteen minute walk towards them. As I got near the car, I made a pathetic gesture with my hand. All the electric windows glided up and shut firmly. This was followed by the familiar clunk of the central locking. I made the slow, muddy trek back out to the hovercraft. Eventually, as they watched from the car, each one in turn felt sorry for me, put on their wellies and came out to help. Apart from Mike who had big feet and couldn't find a pair of boots to fit. He remained on the beach.

They were right to be less than enthusiastic. Without the engine, the hovercraft had become a useless inanimate lump totally stuck in the mud. The mud was a particularly horrible clasping kind. It felt almost spiteful in the way it didn't want to let go of anything. For something that was supposed to float on air the hovercraft was surprisingly heavy. When we tried to lift it, we just pushed ourselves further down into the mud.

When I made the main air duct, I had cut the tops and bottoms off the 5-litre bottles and thrown them away. This was a shame because the handle is really the most distinguishing feature of a 5-litre plastic bottle. Without this visual reference, the air duct just looked like it was made from some multi-coloured plastic patches. The hovercraft reference book in the library suggested that grab handles should be fixed strategically all round the outside for safety so I retrieved some of the discarded bottle handles and pot riveted them onto the air duct. They looked very practical but also gave a visual clue to what all the segments of coloured plastic had once been. Now, stranded out on the mud, what had been an aesthetic decision became crucial to salvaging the hovercraft. They were the only thing to hold onto as we tried to pull the hovercraft to shore.

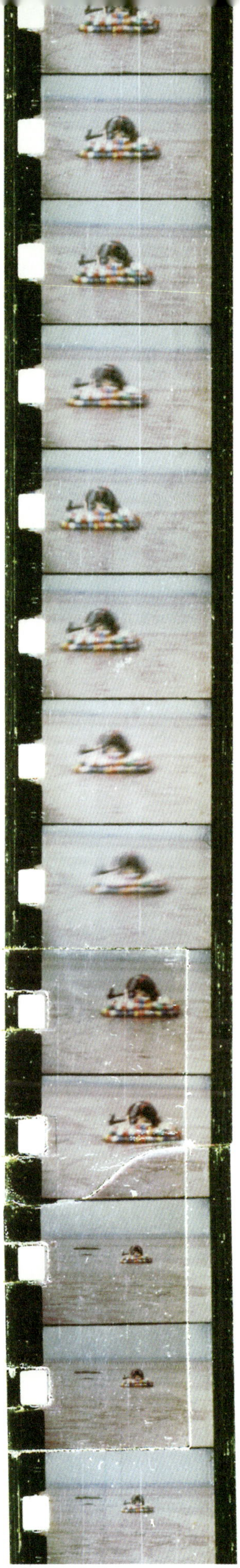

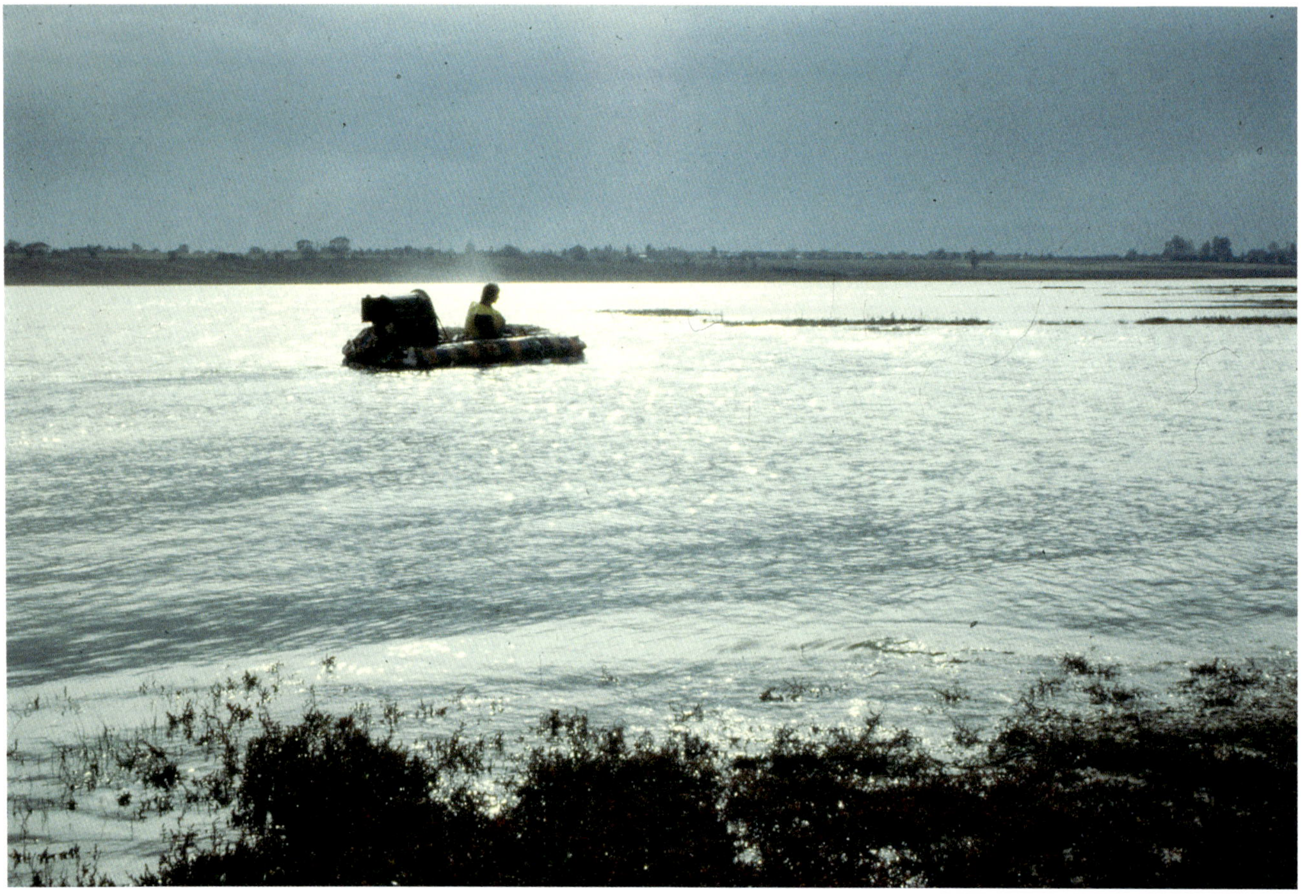

Hovercraft on water. [Sue Guthrie]

On the count of three, two people pushed on the dustbin at the back while the other two pulled on the plastic grab handles at the front. Once our combined force had unstuck the hovercraft from the mud it slowly slid across the surface but only for about a yard. We would then stop. The mud was so thick and viscous that nobody could push or pull whilst walking at the same time. At this point, we all had to use our hands to help free our boots from the mud which then allowed us to take another step or two, get in position and go again. As we were doing this, the hovercraft would be settling nicely back down in the mud so that, by the time we got to the count of three, it was stuck fast again. We repeated this process several hundred times and a few hours later we finally made it back to the beach. Mike greeted us on the edge of the beach and reached out to pull on the nearest handle to make up for his inability to help earlier:

'I don't know why you didn't wait for the tide to come in, surely it would have been easier to float it ashore wouldn't it?' he said.

Bastard.

When Mike put his full weight on the handle it came off in his hand and he fell flat on his back into a patch of mud. This raised our spirits momentarily but, once we had carried the hovercraft across the beach, there was still another obstacle; a tidal sea wall that ran along the estuary about 15 feet high. It could be climbed but not whilst carrying a hovercraft. There was a field on the other side which was sheltered from the wind and we lay there on the grass as we waited for the college trailer to come and pick us up. Cold, tired and covered in mud, we must have looked a bit strange. A woman came over to see us and then a farmer on a motorcycle.

'Have you been shipwrecked or are you just sunbathing?' The woman enquired.

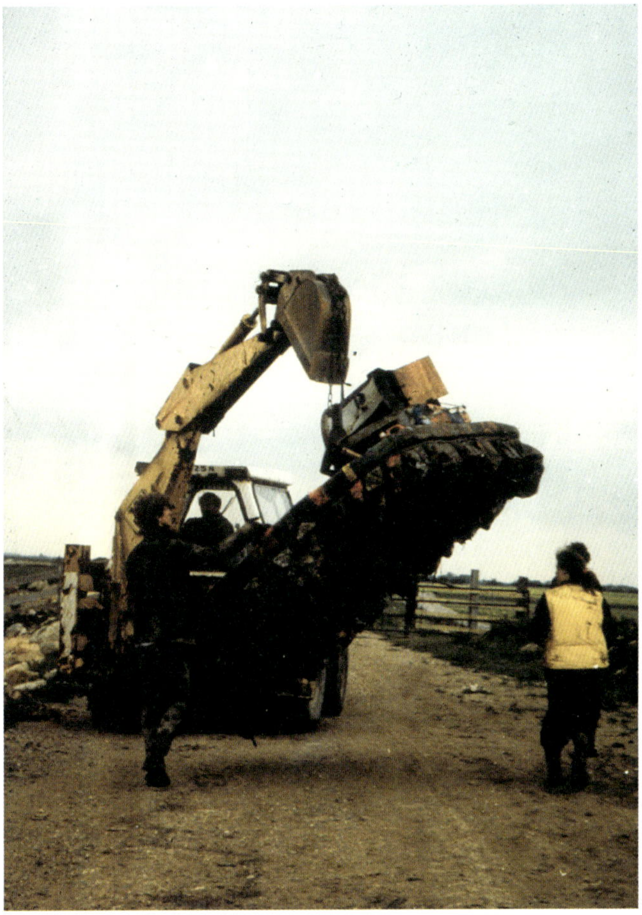

The helpful passing farmer
and his JCB.
[Chris Cannon]

'No, actually, I've just come up the river on a hovercraft made out of plastic bottles,' I replied.

The farmer got very excited: 'How are going to get it over the sea wall?' He asked.

'Don't know, don't care' I replied despondently.

'I've got a JCB.' he declared.

He quickly headed off on his motorcycle and came back with a digger. He tied the hovercraft to the hydraulic bucket and, using it like a crane, lifted it over the wall.

Back in Hull, a welding company offered to weld the broken engine so that I was able to hover around the college at my degree show. My girlfriend also came up from Essex. The relationship hadn't been going very well so I was keen to show her my hovercraft. I was having problems with the carburettor. I could hover for only a few yards before it stopped. Sometimes it was a fuel blockage, sometimes it just needed the adjustment of the mixture screws to get it running again. It didn't have a proper recoil starter rope so every time I made another attempt to start it, I had to laboriously wind the starting rope around the flange on the flywheel. Doing this repeatedly would make me increasingly frustrated and angry. I would pull on the rope and shout 'bastard!' when it didn't start. I would then carry on muttering to myself while I tried a few adjustments to the mixture screws, put the choke back on again, rewind the rope, pull it again 'you shit!' I would go through the process again and again getting more and more annoyed. Then pull it again 'Fucking, fucking fucker, I hate you.' I did this a lot, never gave up, just got more annoyed.

Eventually my bored girlfriend sat down in the hovercraft with me.

'Chris, it just isn't working,' she said.

I tried to explain my theory that the carburettor wasn't blocked and that it just needed to be adjusted correctly and the only way to do this was to persist with trial and error. To which she replied:

'No Chris… us.'

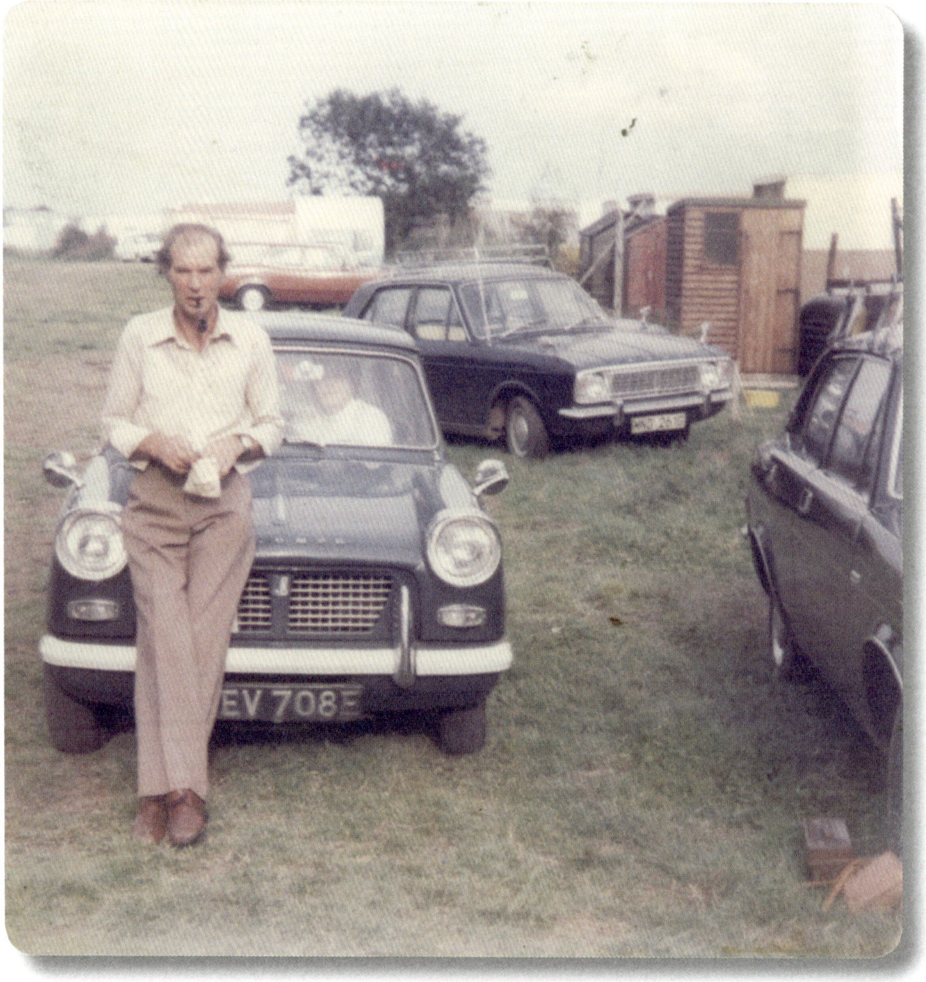
EV 708

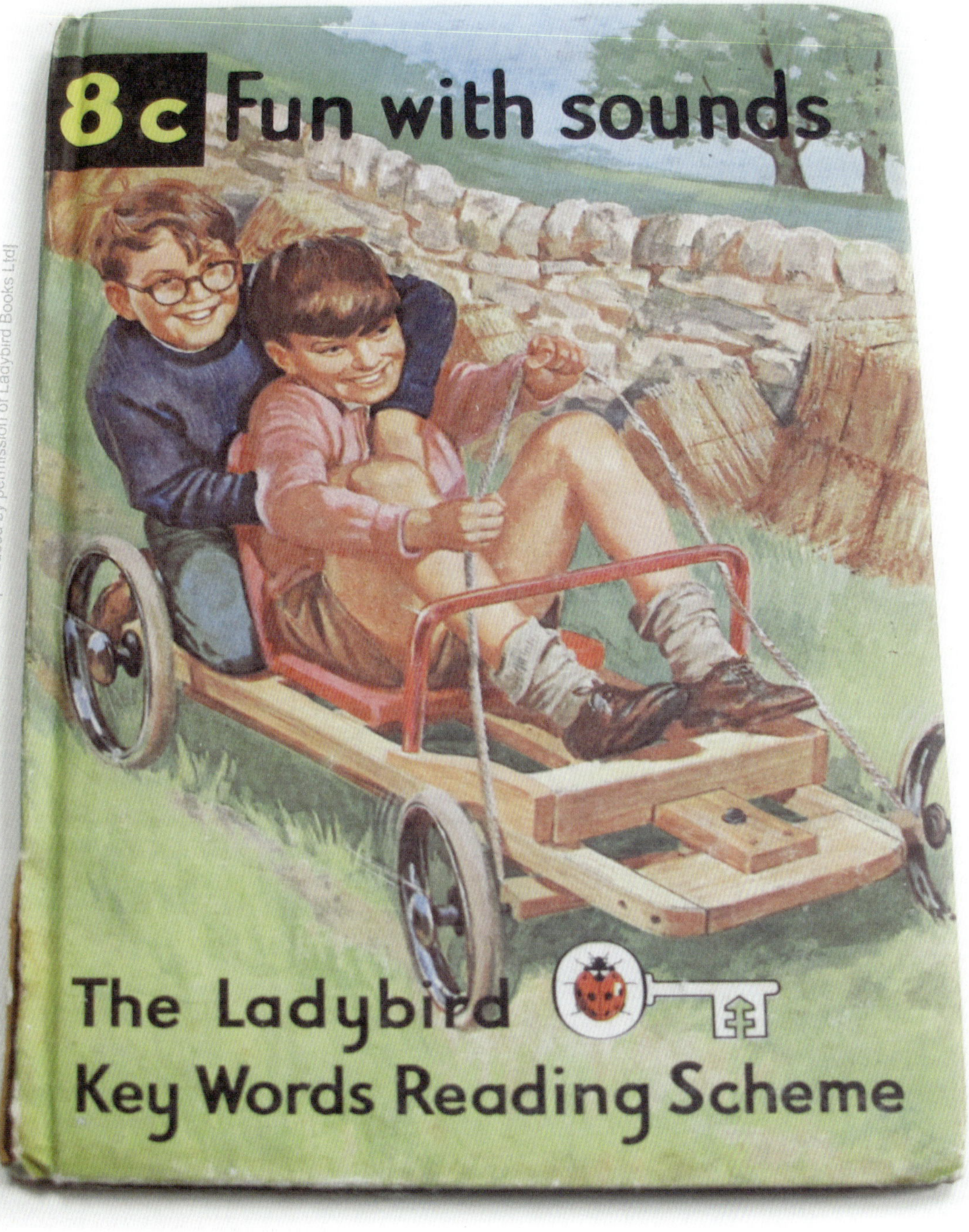

Timescape Escape

previous page: Mum and Dad and Triumph Herald, Mersea Island 1979.

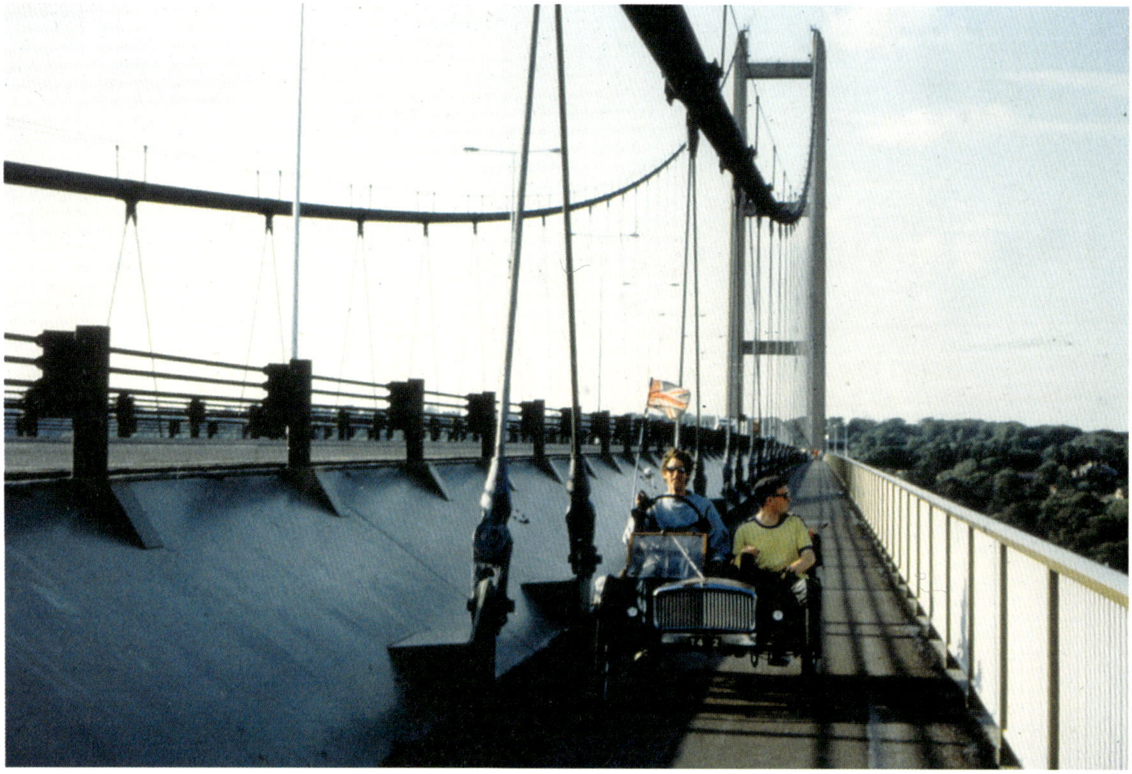

Crossing the Humber bridge. [Leo Hazelrigg]

When art college ended, we all had an opportunity to show our work at a graduate art fair in London. The college selected my pedal car to be part of the exhibition. I decided that the journey was an important element of the piece so it needed to arrive under its own steam. Eddie faithfully offered to help me pedal it from Hull to London. Another friend, Leo, offered to follow on a push-bike as our personal AA Man.

We set off from the art college and quickly arrived at the Humber Bridge. For me, crossing the river was a significant thing so we stopped to record the event by taking a photograph. There were no pedestrians there that day apart from one old man with a walking stick out for a stroll. He came over to us and wanted to know what we were doing. I told him we were off to London and he immediately sat back onto the fence, made himself comfortable, and launched into a story…

Apparently he had made the same journey himself when he was a young man back in 1930s during the depression. His tale painted quite an idyllic scene of sleeping in fields next to the road, and he proudly told us that the journey there had taken him only five days. It was an interesting to hear his story, but as we listened to him I have to admit I was getting a little impatient and anxious to take the photo and get going. Over the next few days I thought about the old man and realised that I was probably doing the same thing as him: going to London to seek my fortune.

The pedal car was quite heavy and pedalling was hard work. We had a few mechanical problems (most of them with the bicycle, not the car) but on the whole the journey was relatively uneventful. At the end of each day, we set up a tent by the side of the road or slept out in the open. Our route took us through a series of rural back roads so that we could avoid fast traffic. We crossed the Fens for a large proportion of the journey which meant we were on the flat. At one point I remember coming across an old millstone on the edge of a farmer's field. A plaque said that it marked the line of the Greenwich Meridian as it passed through Lincolnshire. We crossed the line and rode on.

A couple of days later we stayed in Cambridge with Leo's older brother who lived opposite the Scott Polar Research Museum. He let us sleep on his floor. The next day, just south of Cambridge, we had more problems with the push-bike and had to abandon Leo by the side of the road. Eddie and I went on ahead with the pedal car until we reached the next telephone box so that I could ring my father and ask him to come and rescue Leo and the bike. I suggested that we detour to stay at my parents' house in Essex, meet up with Leo and fix his bike. We left Leo sitting on the grass verge and gave him enough tobacco and cigarette papers to last until my father arrived.

We arrived at my parent's house just before Leo. My father thought it was hilarious that I had come home from college on a piece of art. We rested for a day, fixed the bike and then carried on to London. We camped the following night in Epping Forest and set off at sunrise to make our way into the city ahead of the rush hour. Our legs had grown strong on our trip down from Hull and after a day's rest we were a highly efficient machine and quickly found our way to the Business Design Centre in Islington. We were so quick, in fact, that it was only seven in the morning when we arrived and the only person there to greet us was a security guard. I said hello and proudly announced: 'We're here! We've made it!'

To which he replied, 'Who are you?'

He then went on to say that he knew nothing about a pedal car being delivered so he couldn't help us. I suggested we leave the car in the car park while we waited for a representative of the art fair to arrive. 'Only management are allowed to park in the car park,' he said with a half smile.

I asked if he would keep an eye on the car if we left it outside his window while we went for breakfast. His reply was less than supportive: 'I cannot be responsible for unauthorised vehicles in this vicinity.'

Eddie, Leo and I sat on the pavement next to the car and smoked hand-rolled cigarettes as we contemplated what to do next. As we did so a cleaner worked his way over to us with a broom and said: 'I wouldn't stay there lads.They're really strict about vagrants.'

I went back to the security guard's office. This time I was annoyed. I thought what I really needed to do was spell out exactly what it was we had done to get here.

'We have come all the way from Hull on this extremely heavy, home-made car. It's taken us a week to get here. It's 240 miles you know.'

'Hull? I know Hull! That is a long way, in fact I make it two hundred and forty 'two' miles – but you still can't leave it there!'

This was not exactly the Hero's Welcome I was expecting and, sadly, the security guard's welcome set the tone for the whole art fair experience. The organisers arrived at about nine o'clock and took the car off our hands and we went to find a place to get our films processed. After a fried breakfast, we went through the pictures we had taken over the last seven days. They were fairly unremarkable.

Art fairs are pretty tasteless, soulless, commercial events and what I had done could have been interpreted as a cynical publicity stunt. Apart from the fact that there was hardly any publicity. So, in fact, it looked like a failed publicity stunt. If an artist did something like this today then the project would take advantage of social media and have its own Facebook page. I didn't even have my Super 8 camera because I couldn't afford the amount of film we would need to document a week.

At the art fair, the pedal car looked like some irritatingly wacky thing that had very little to do with Fine Art. I hadn't conveyed anything about the relationship my work had to the landscape and, without this, there was no real intellectual or philosophical depth. The problem wasn't just that the work had failed to communicate with the audience; it was that I didn't even think I needed to engage the audience in the first place. I had made the car to escape from art college and I didn't give a stuff what anyone else thought. Consequently, nobody gave a stuff about me. Now that I wasn't an art student any more, the work didn't even have an education context. There was no reference to art at all that the viewer could see. There was nothing to denote the experience of crossing the countryside and it was this that gave the artistic content. The piece was totally lost on the viewer.

If I had added a label explaining the whole story then it would have become reliant on what was written, a departure from the visual to the written language. This approach, for me, always highlights the failing of the work to communicate on its own. At college I had spent all my time making vehicles to escape in and learnt technical things like how a hovercraft works, now all of a sudden I realised that while I was doing that, I didn't find time to learn how art 'works'. I was starting to learn but it was a number of years before I came up with a way to show the work effectively by referencing the landscape as part of the work and, indeed, inseparable from it. The art fair ended and I did what a lot of fine art graduates did at the time; signed on the dole and moved back in with my mum and dad.

I did not find my fortune.

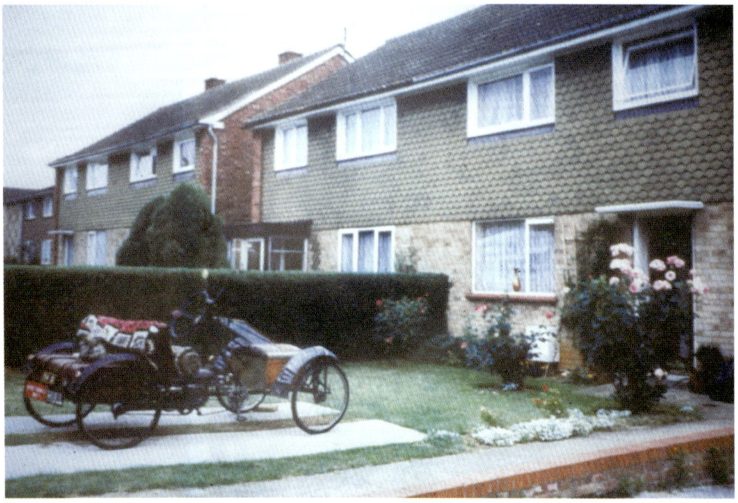

My parents semi-detatched house in Essex.

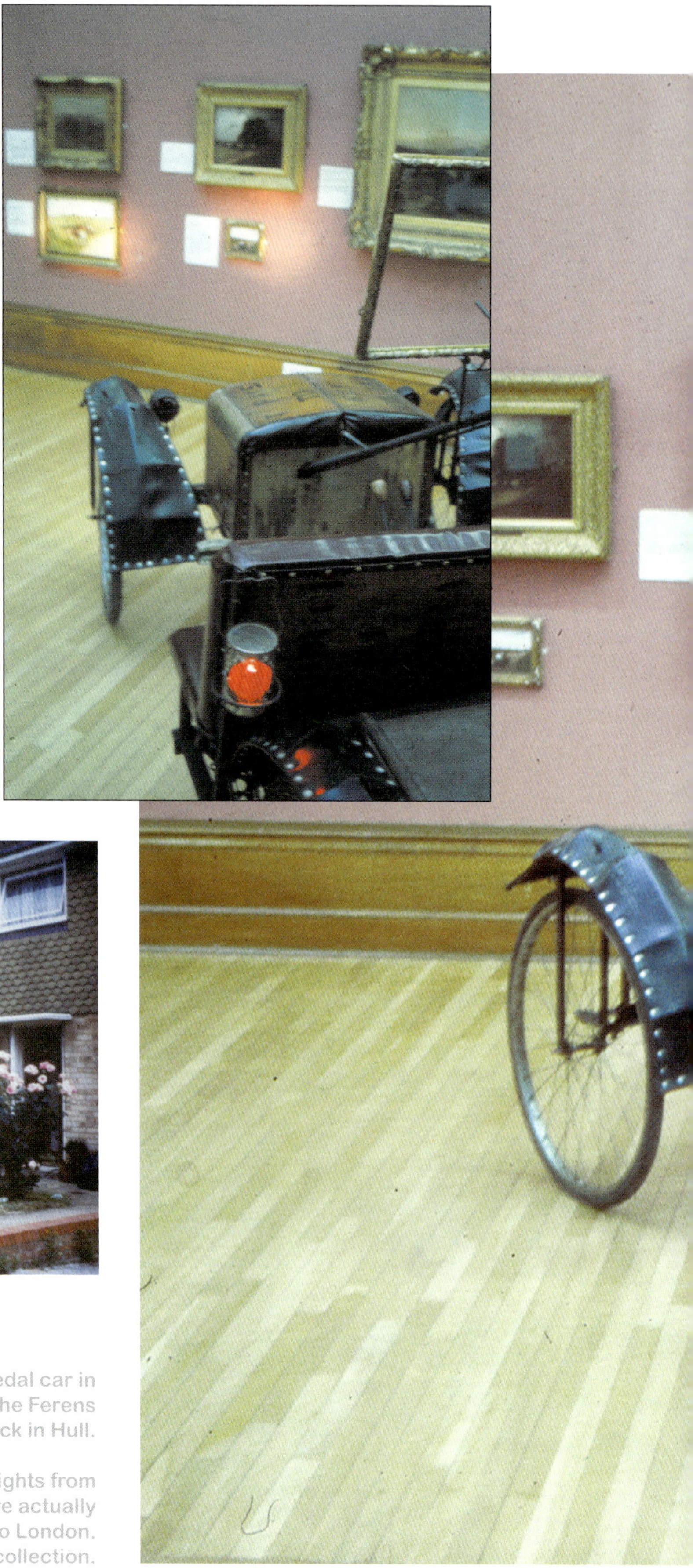

Many years later, I found a way of putting the pedal car in an art gallery that I was happy with. This was in the Ferens Art Gallery in 2002, ironically back in Hull.

Inset: Triggered by a movement sensor, the lights from the car spotlit two images on the wall that were actually photographs of the car on its journey from Hull to London. The other landscapes were part of the gallery's collection.

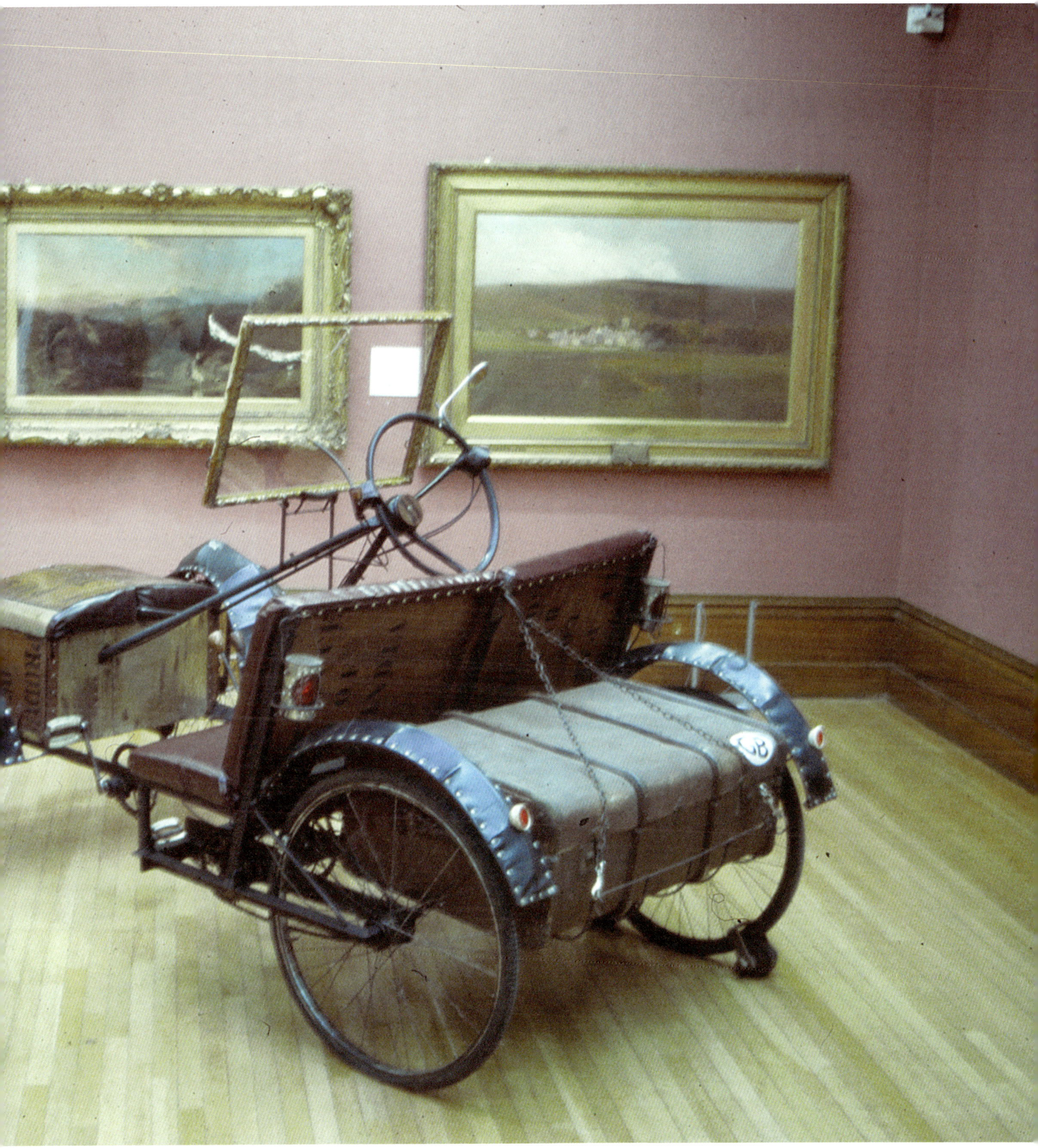

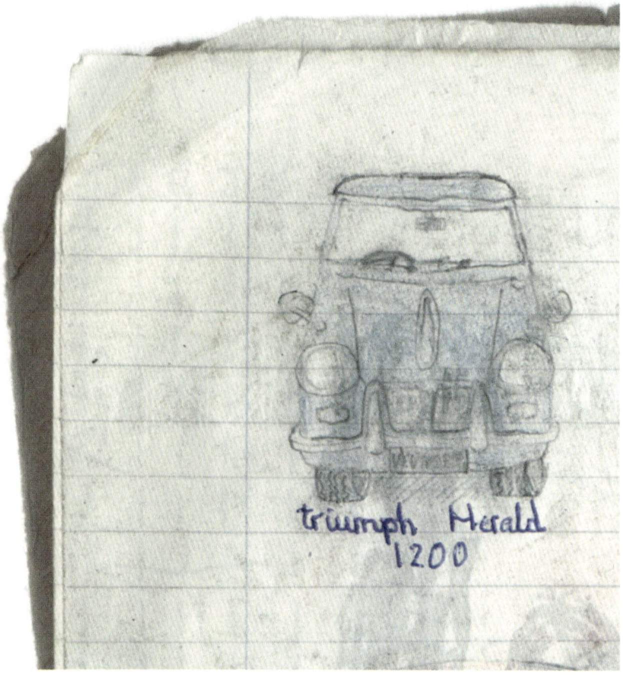

Drawing I did of our car when I was eleven years old.

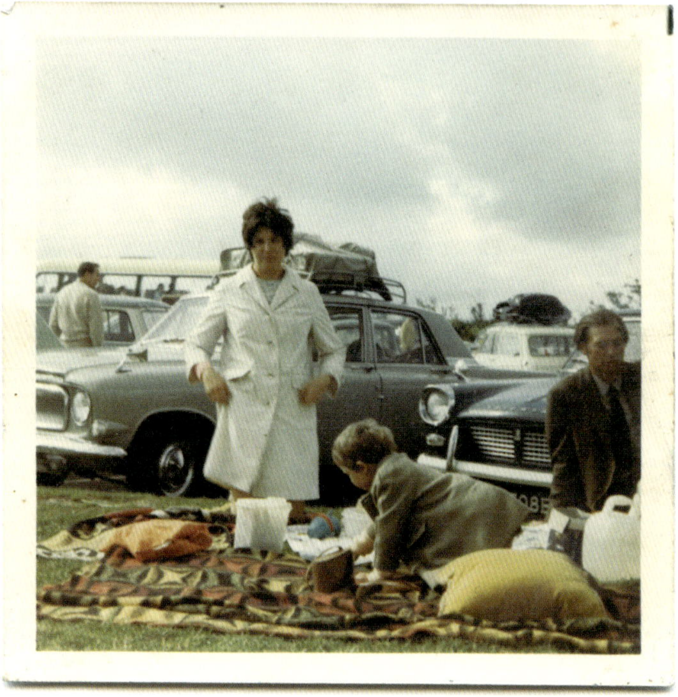

Me, Mum and Dad, picnicing in front of the car. Family holiday to Minehead 1971. [Edmund Dobrowolski]

In the three years since I had left home to go away to art college my father had retired. He was now at home all day and, sadly, so was I. My father didn't enjoy not being at work very much; it just gave him time to dwell on stuff and get annoyed. I, on the other hand, took the opportunity to tackle a long overdue project in the garage.

It was a 1967 Triumph Herald 1200 estate car I had left behind while I was away. Not in great shape when I initially parked it up, three years standing idle had caused further deterioration. It needed a lot of work to make it roadworthy. Through the 1970s and 80s, a serious amount of fibreglass filler had been used to disguise the various rust holes, much of this was now falling out. The main challenge, therefore, was the amount of welding it needed. The money it would cost to fix was far more than the car would ever be worth so there was nothing to justify the investment. Apart from one thing; I was emotionally attached to the car. This wasn't just a fondness for the shape or a nostalgic connection to 'my first car' it was something that went a little bit deeper.

This Triumph had originally been our family car and was the one and only, brand new straight from the dealership car my father ever bought. What was of more significance however was that he decided to buy it when mother became pregnant with their second child. That child was me.

When I passed my driving test he handed the car down to me and I meticulously cleaned and polished it, doing what I could to maintain it. The car had been in our family as long as I had and it still brings out a childlike sense of discovery in me. Sometimes it felt like a time-portal back to my childhood. Once when I was working underneath the car, I poked at an area of rust which quickly opened into a jagged hole. Putting my fingers inside to remove all the rust and other detritus I started to pull out stuff that had obviously been lost down the back of the seats over the years. I found pre-decimal coinage, a knife and a plastic model Russian soldier that had belonged to my older brother. It was like an archaeological dig but upside down.

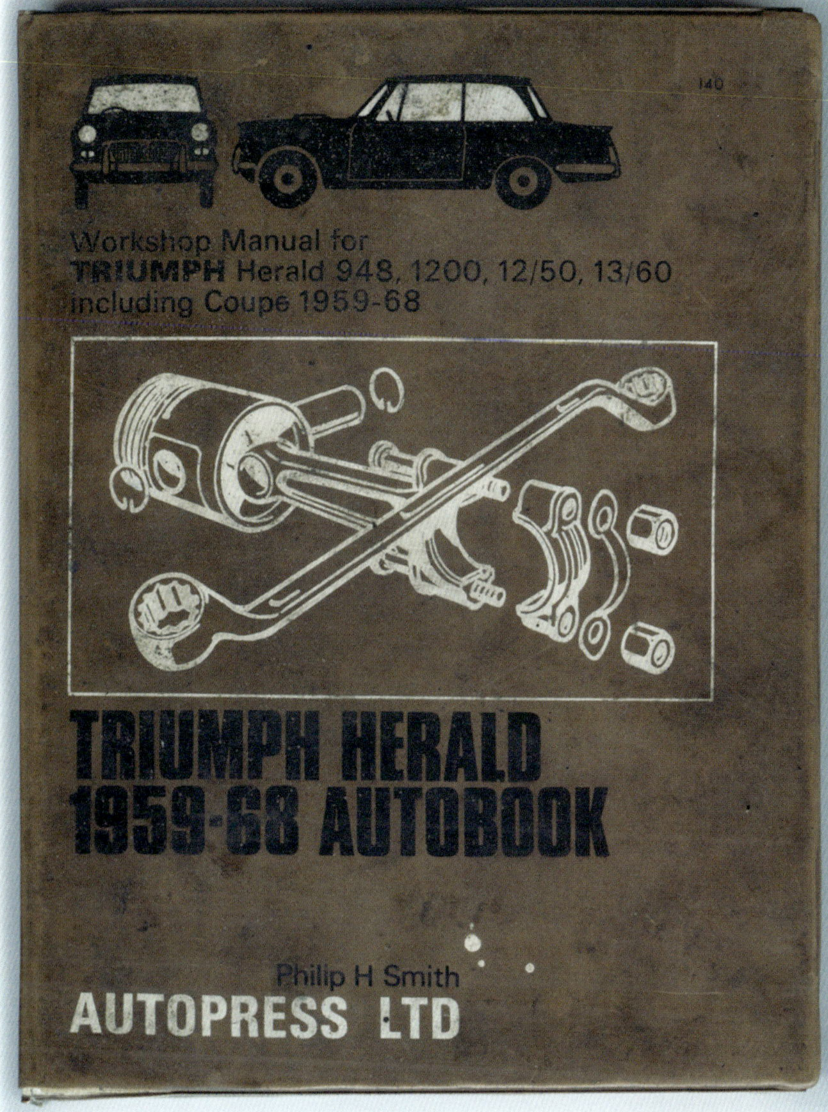

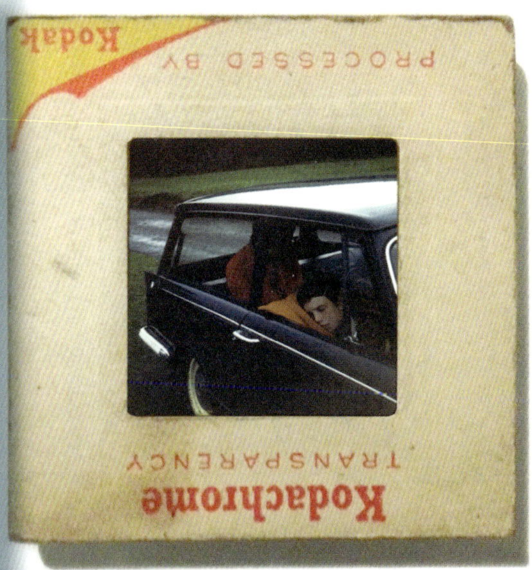

above: My older brother being travel sick on a family holiday to Wales in 1970. The longest journey we ever made in the car as a family. [Kazimierz Dobrowolski]

left: My well thumbed car repair manual.

below: Well worn set of keys

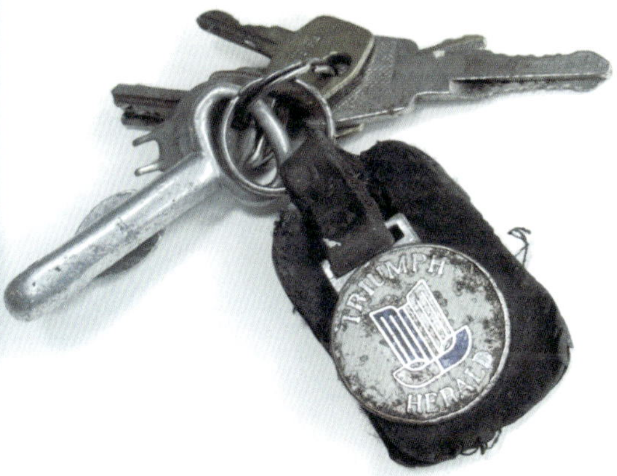

Although it would have been sensible to scrap the car, how could I? I had just come home from a place where I had spent my time making vehicles and pontificating about my 'inner need'. Surely a car that was synonymous with my own birth must hold some significant meaning that needed exploring? I committed myself to restoring it to its former glory. I had learnt a bit about welding in the sculpture department and I even managed to buy some cheap welding equipment. I realised I could save money by doing this work myself. The biggest bonus of all was my retired dad – a fantastic source of knowledge and experience.

The Triumph Herald was designed at a time when a lot of people fixed their own cars. The bonnet was enormous because it incorporated the front wings. When opened the improved access even made it possible to sit on the front wheel to change the spark plugs. My father was a very practical person and he always serviced and repaired the car himself. I assumed he had acquired his mechanical knowledge because he was a product of this more 'hands on' time. One day however, I found documentary evidence that shed fresh light on his relationship to car mechanics.

Service Schedule Maintenance Book showing all the intact tickets apart from 1000 mile, a 'Spring Seasonal', and the 6000 mile service.

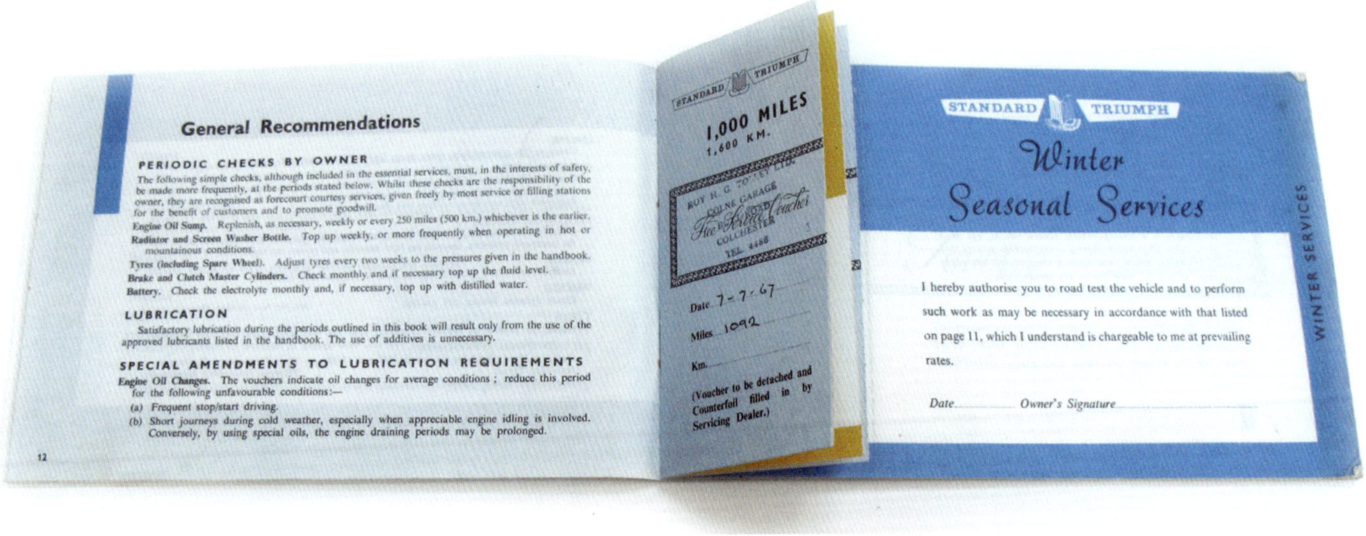

I was going through some old paperwork and came across a booklet with the Triumph logo on the cover. It was called the Service Schedule Maintenance Book. About 9 x 6 inches, The SSMB was designed like a big cheque book with numbered ticket stubs that went up in order of mileage; 500 miles, 6000 miles, 12,000 miles, 24,000 miles, and so on. Every time the car had been driven a certain amount of miles it was returned to the Triumph garage for maintenance. This was included in the price of the new car and the tickets were a coupon that the owner gave in exchange for the service. The reason this booklet struck me as interesting was that the car had obviously done more miles than were covered by the book. In my father's SSMB only a couple of tickets up to 6000 miles, had been torn out. Thereafter, he had not taken advantage of the free servicing schedule and I wanted to know why.

My father was Polish. He came to England after World War Two and was given work on building sites, which is where he picked up his carpentry skills. Unfortunately, this is also where he learnt a lot of his English and he picked up a fair amount of vernacular that permeated his day-to-day communication. I have heard it said that the Poles are a very passionate, hot-blooded people. Someone once described them to me as 'the Italians of the North'. To counter this, they often have a gloomy pessimism or a predilection towards the negative. A racial stereotype, perhaps, but one that my father lived up to very well. Armed with the SSMB, I approached my father, pointed out the discrepancy and pressed him for an explanation: 'Dad, why didn't you take the car back to the garage?'

He replied: 'I took the fucking car to the fucking garage once and they fucked it up! The Triumph Herald has very special independent suspension and you need a fucking special ramp to service it. You need a split ramp. You need to lift the fucking chassis with the first ramp then drop the fucking ramp under the fucking wheels so you can get at the fucking trunnions. Those STUPID fucking arseholes, caught the fucking brake hose on the second ramp – ripped the cunt out. Didn't tell me, didn't FUCKING tell me. I went to collect car... I could see this fucking piss on ground, it was fucking brake fluid. Got into car, drove off fucking forecourt, straight into side of Volkswagen fucking Beetle. Those bastards said I had driven it from the premises and they were not fucking liable. Never took it to fucking garage ever fucking again.'

He told me all this with a passion that suggested it had happened the day before when in fact it had happened nearly 25 years earlier. Ever since he had done all the repairs and servicing himself so he knew the car very well. He was going to be invaluable to me in the coming weeks of restoration.

I went down to the lock-up garage and began work. I thought that eventually my father would show an interest and would be glad to have something to do. Very soon I hit some minor difficulties. I wasn't sure how to repack the grease in the front wheel hubs. As this was supposed to be done every 12,000 miles, I knew my dad must have done it loads of times. I decided to ask him: 'Dad, when you pack the grease in the front wheel hubs are you supposed to fill the whole cavity with grease or just the roller bearing racer?'

After a short silence my dad replied: 'Christopher, don't fucking depress me with that fucking car! You are wasting your life! You fuck off to art college, waste three fucking years there, now you're wasting another six months fixing that piece of shit! Don't fucking depress me with that fucking car! If only I had pushed it in the fucking ditch when I had the fucking chance instead of giving it to you... you... fucking wanker!'

A few weeks later, I had moved onto the exhaust. It was pretty rusty and the best thing to do was buy another one but, unfortunately, the shop sold me the wrong one. I couldn't work out why it didn't fit. I know, I thought, I'll ask my dad. He's had a bit of time to calm down: 'Dad, I think they've given me the wrong exhaust pipe. I think this is the exhaust for the 12/50 Triumph Herald. Do you know if there's a difference between the exhaust manifold on the 1200 and the 12/50?'

To which my dad replied: 'Christopher, don't fucking depress me with that fucking car.' Then he changed tack slightly: 'Read the fucking manual. I had to read the fucking manual and I can't even speak fucking English properly.'

So I did.

Six months later I had the car MOT-ed, taxed, insured and on the road.

One Saturday evening my dad came to me wearing his going out clothes and said 'Christopher, give me lift to Club, I want all my friends to see what a beautiful car I have.'

And we bonded.

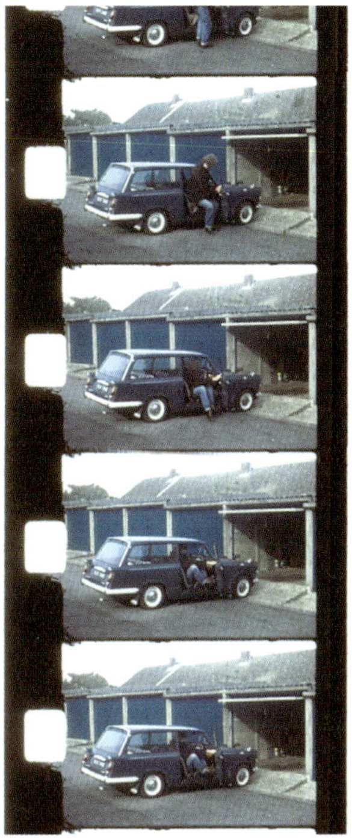

Putting the car into the lockup garage. [Kazimierz Dobrowolski]

Me and Dad in our road. Camera selotaped to the bonnet of the car.

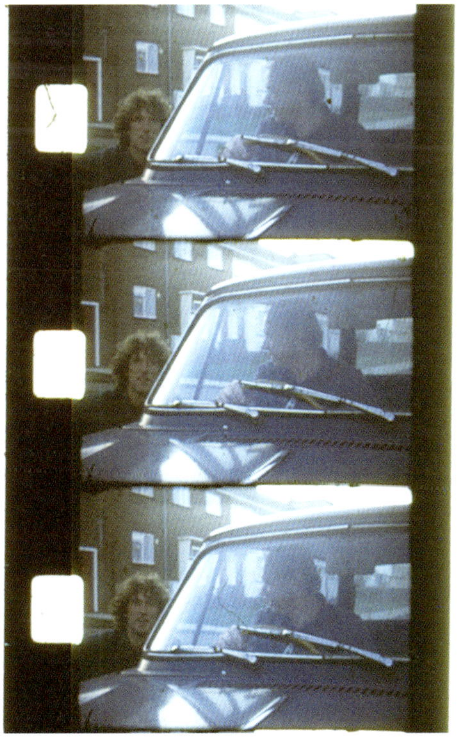

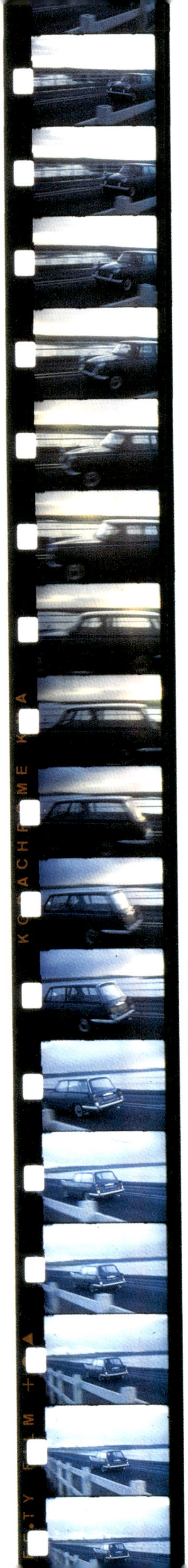

Years later, my Triumph made its way into an art gallery. I turned the whole thing into a display case by making different compartments that fitted each window exactly and painted them the same colour as the car. Inside there were all sorts of things related to it including the original bill of sale, my birth certificate and the Service Schedule Maintenance Book. There were also family photos, a drawing I had done when I was 11 and a model car that drove around a circuit in the back. In the middle of the track was a record player playing The Beatles' Abbey Road album. The sound came from a speaker in the radiator grill and the album cover was on display. It's the famous one with all four Beatles on a zebra crossing outside their studio in Abbey Road. In the image, behind George Harrison, there is a white Volkswagen Beatle and the number plate can be clearly seen. This car still exists because it's the one on the Abbey Road album cover and is consequently worth a lot of money. If you look a bit further down Abbey Road, above Paul McCartney's head, there is a blue Triumph Herald Estate exactly like mine. It's impossible to determine the number plate from such a distance so it could… possibly be mine.

I took great pains not to destroy my car making this piece of work. To assemble it, I simply had to remove the steering wheel then slot all the display cases together. I wasn't just being precious about my car, I wanted it to still be driveable.

To be invited to show your work, curators often want some kind of reassurance that the artist is worthy and, like anyone else, gallery curators are influenced by the opinion of others. The people who form these opinions often make their decisions based on the artist's CV and the other places the artist has shown their work can become as crucial as the work itself. In the art world, it's often not what you know, it's who you know and, if you don't have the connections, it's difficult to progress. It's a lot easier to get a show at a gallery if your CV shows that you have had exhibitions at places with the right kind of kudos. If you don't, you become stuck in a perpetual chicken and egg scenario. The car was supposed to be my kudos generator and, since I could still drive it, it could go anywhere.

One of the exhibits was all my old tax discs. I placed them in the windscreen display case and included the current disc so I could leave it anywhere I wanted. The plan was to find the most influential galleries, park outside, set up my art piece, take a photo and stick the name of the gallery on my CV.

Car crossing the causeway to Mersea Island, 1994. [Sue Guthrie]

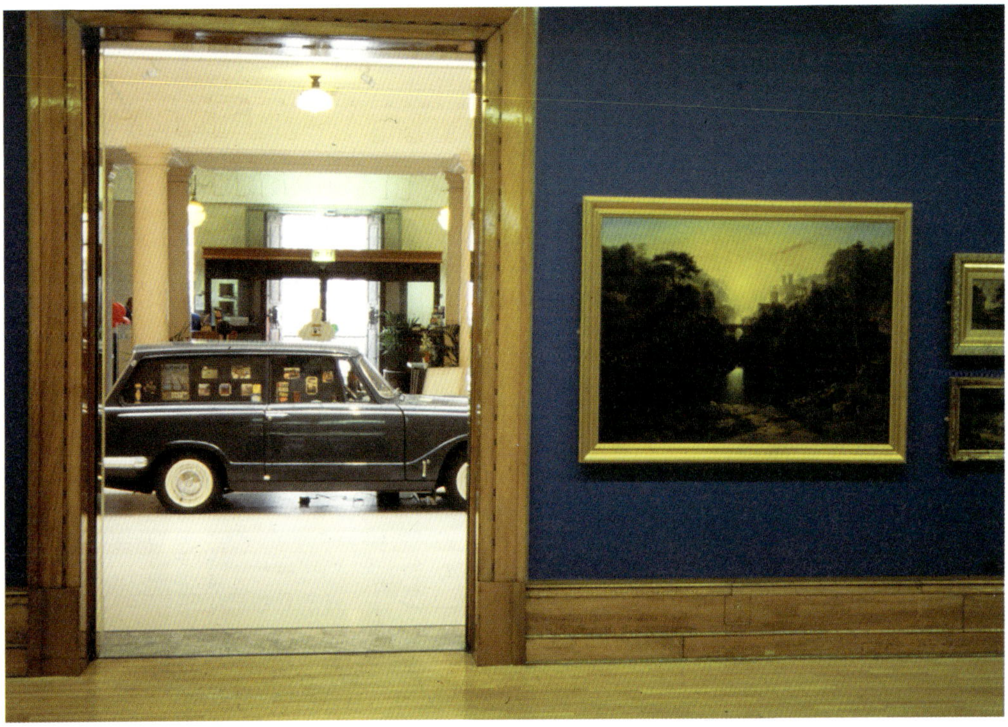

Ferens Art Gallery 2002.
The rear window displays the original order form for the car, and my birth certificate.

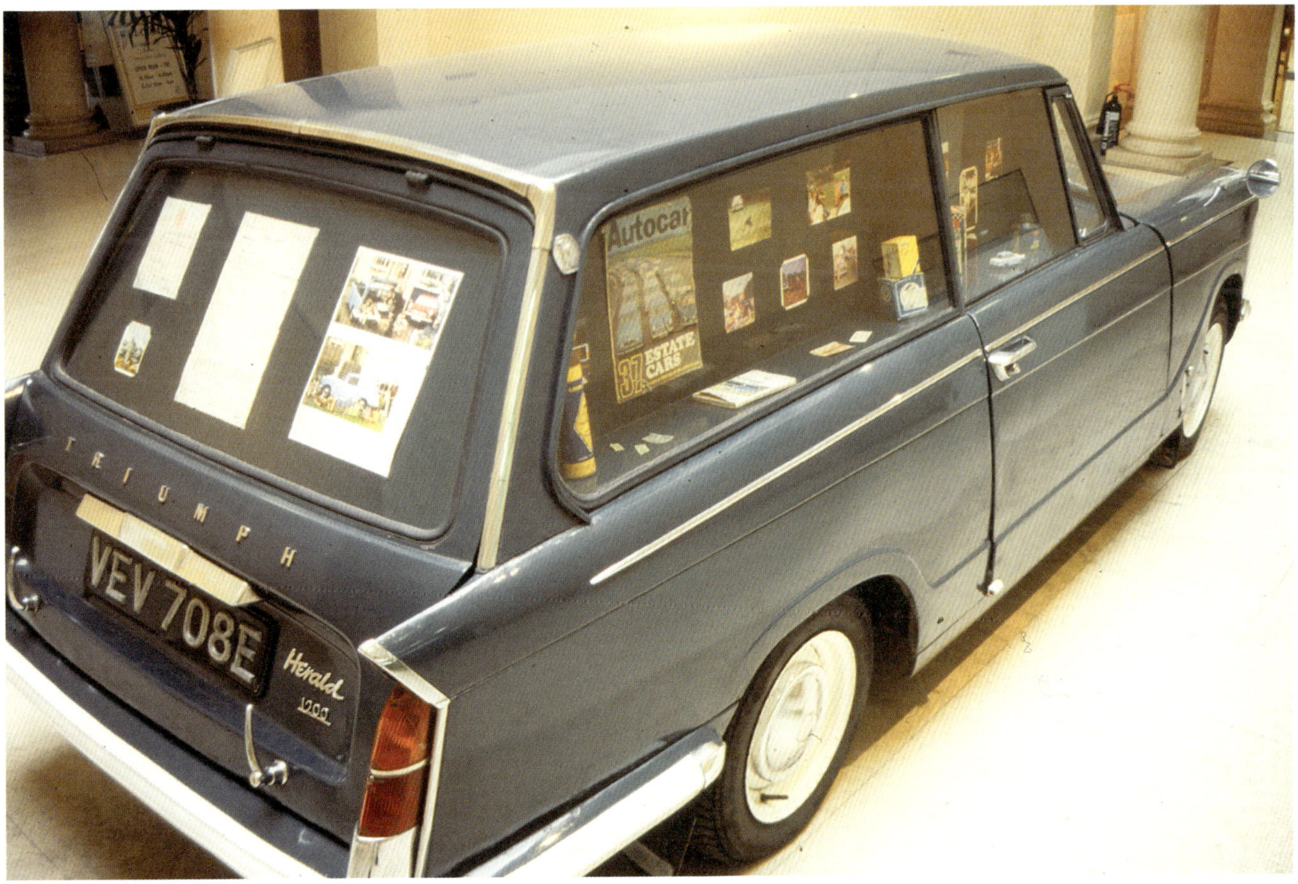

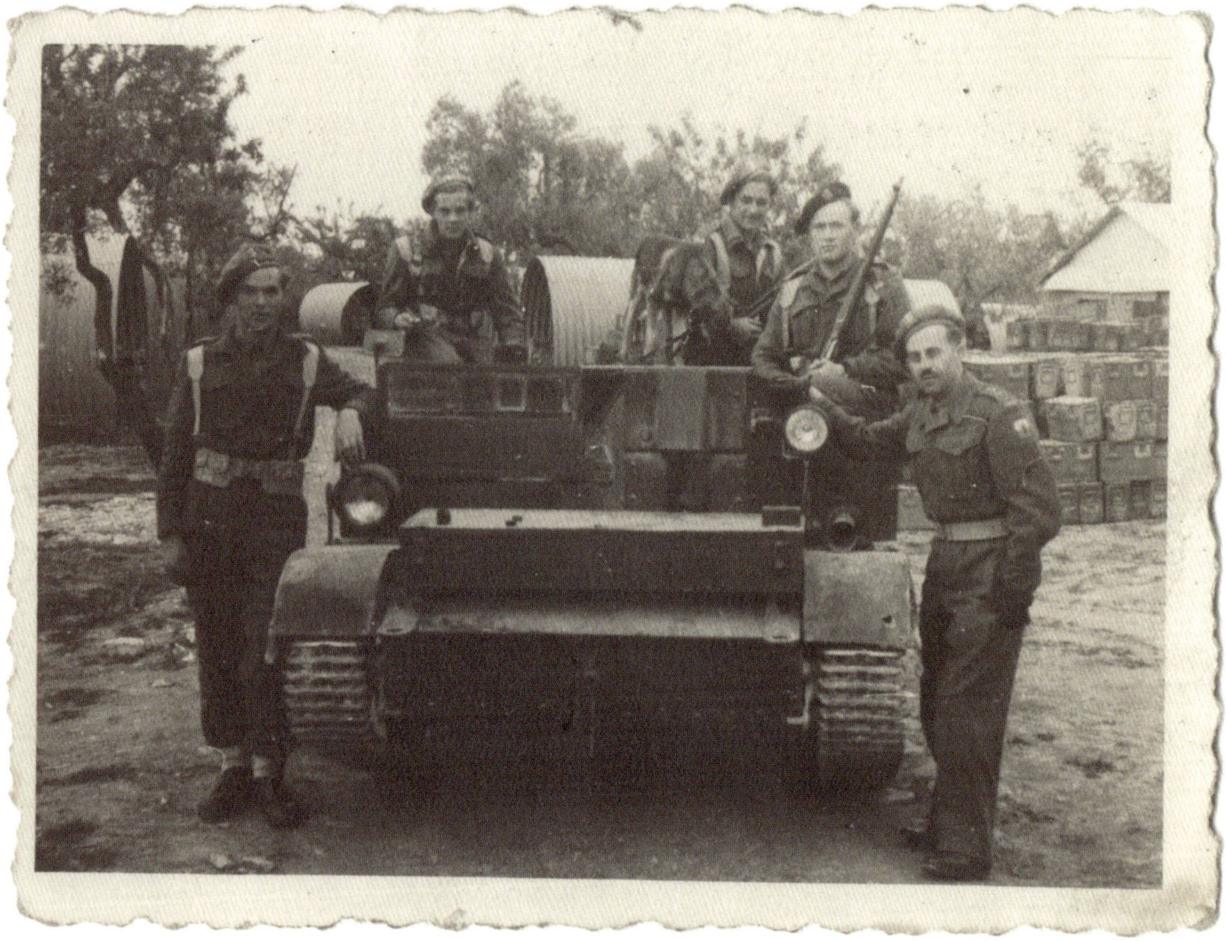

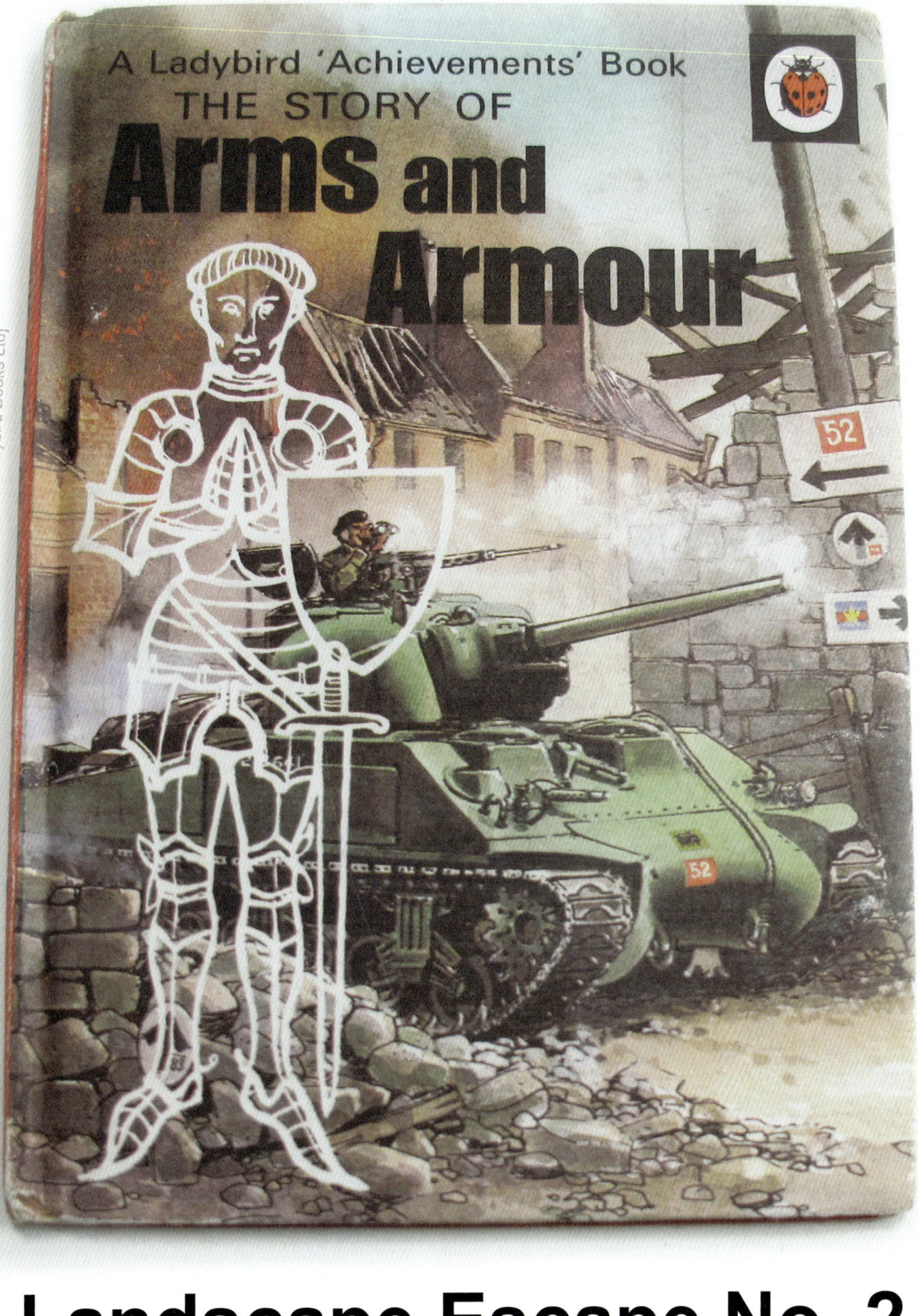

Landscape Escape No. 2

previous page:
Dad far left, 1945.

Here's a photo of my dad during World War Two. It was taken in Italy in1945 just as the war came to an end. My dad was about the same age in this photo as I was when I went to art college. He wasn't a tank driver, I think he was on guard at an ammo dump when the officer (the one on the far right) turned up in this Bren gun carrier instead of a jeep to do his inspection. The officer invited everyone to be in the photo.

My father's route to England was a long and convoluted one via Siberia.

World War two started in 1939 when Hitler invaded Poland. Whilst this was going on in Western Poland, Stalin's Soviet Union invaded Poland from the East. My dad came from Eastern Poland.

Stalin's people didn't like my Grandad very much – he had capitalist tendencies, he had an extra cow or something. For this misdemeanour my father said the Soviet forces rounded up the entire family, put them in cattle trucks and deported them to Siberia. It was technically Kazakhstan but to my father, and all those deported with him, Siberia was regarded as anything East of Moscow. I don't think he really knew where he was to be honest, just that he was somewhere in the middle of a vast inhospitable abyss.

In 1941 Hitler invaded the Soviet Union as well, so Stalin changed sides and looked for an alliance with Britain. Suddenly, the exiled Poles weren't the enemy anymore and Stalin allowed them to form a free Polish army and leave the Soviet Union. The army was equipped by the British and left Russia via Iran. From there, they became part of the British Eighth Army and saw action in the Middle East then North Africa and finished fighting the war in Italy.

After the war Stalin decided to keep Eastern Poland with the acquiescence of Britain and the USA. Since Stalin had a habit of secretly killing anyone associated with the free Polish army my dad couldn't go back and, out of embarrassment, Britain and the USA gave Polish soldiers the option to pick a country that had been on the allied side and start a new life.

My dad picked Canada.

Unfortunately he was on guard duty the night the truck left and he missed the boat. England was his second choice. He never really wanted to come here.

From Italy, his ship went to Liverpool where they were put on a train to East Anglia. At the time this part of the country had lots of redundant airfields with empty barrack huts. Their train took them straight across the country to Essex:

'We got out of the train in this funny little town we found out later was called Halstead and the whole battalion had to march to a transit camp, an old air force base at Gosfield. We turned right from the main road and quickly found ourselves in the countryside.

Everything was so incredibly green! Thick green hedges growing so high that they joined with thick green trees which joined in the middle. We were marching through a thick green tunnel. After a while we came across a gap in the hedge and had our first view over the countryside – a beautiful field of ripe golden corn... The sun was shining, the captain said we could all undo our top buttons and then we thought... What a beautiful country we have come to! And Christopher – you know?

It's fucking rained ever since!'

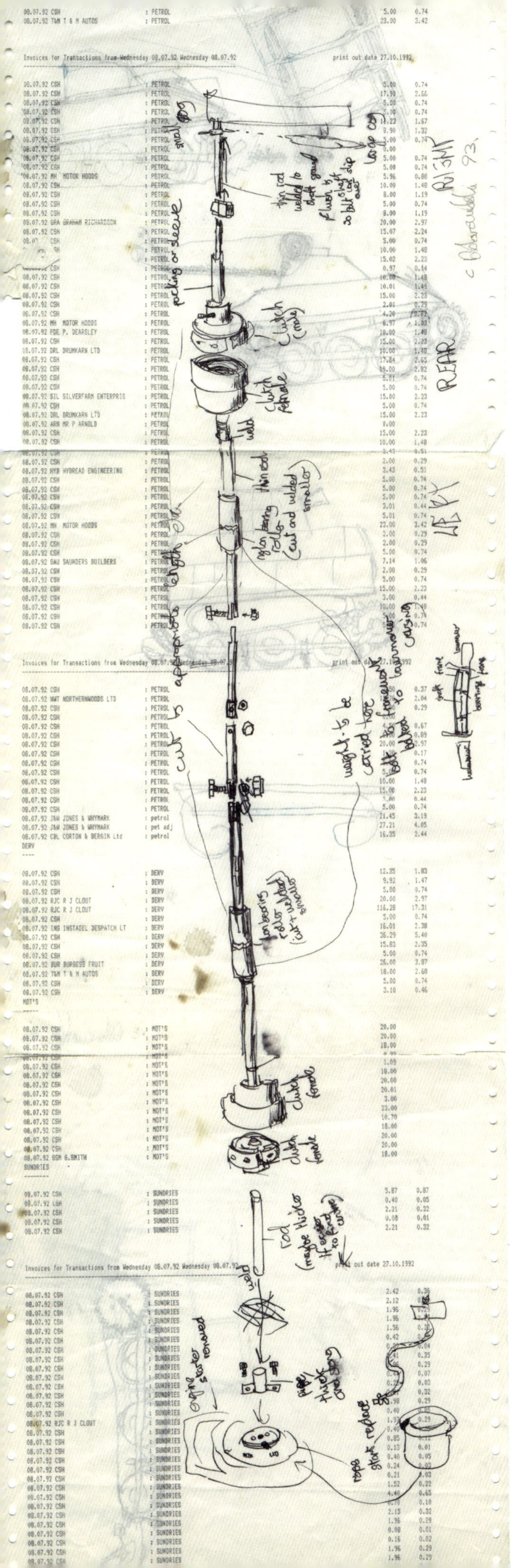

Construction

I always knew I wanted to make a tank because it's the land equivalent of a boat. Unlike a car, a tank can drive a direct line across the countryside like a boat plots a direct course across the open sea. The word 'tank' started out as a code word. When it was invented in World War One, its given name was Landship.

In making its own path, a tank creates a new relationship to the landscape. Although ultimately a destructive relationship, I still thought there was a beautiful simplicity in transcending physical constraints and going in a straight line over the horizon. In reality, unless you are crossing the Russian Steppe or a desert, that straight line freedom doesn't really work.

I was living with my parents in their ex-council house in Essex at the time and, like all the other houses in the road, it had a strip of back garden. Although I couldn't justify crashing through Mrs Smith's vegetable patch in an effort to carry out my artistic mission, the domestic garden environment was the source for most of the building materials for this project.

The chassis was made from the tubular metal frames of old wheelbarrows and lawnmower handles. I ran the tracks around ten wheelbarrow wheels (five each side) and the floor was made from sheets of metal from lawnmower grass boxes and the remaining bits of wheelbarrow. The driver's seat was a deckchair, the petrol tank was an old watering can and I used a spring-loaded garden broom triggered by one of the wheels to sweep the inside of the tracks. This stopped them from clogging up. The gun was a garden flame gun used to burn down weeds. It was, in effect, a large blow torch. Paraffin was piped around the flame several times so that it heated up and vaporised before it was ignited. It burnt with a short but intense flame, however, if you insulated the pipes as they ran around the flame, it could squirt as far as sixteen feet.

I used the engines from the lawnmowers for the power source. I eventually needed four – two for each side. I had a brake on each individual track and separate accelerators. By braking one side and accelerating on the other, it was possible to turn very sharply. The brand name for the lawnmowers was the 'Suffolk Punch'. It was a reference to a breed of

Rough sketch trying to work out how to get the separate lawnmower engines to work together.
They were joined via a complicated system of chains, shafts and centrifugal clutches.

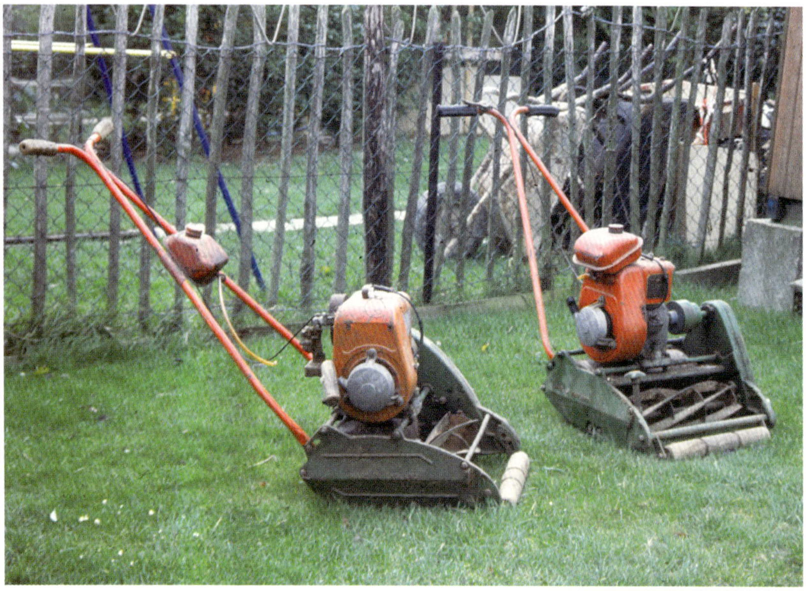

My Dad's two Suffolk Punch lawnmowers in his garden.

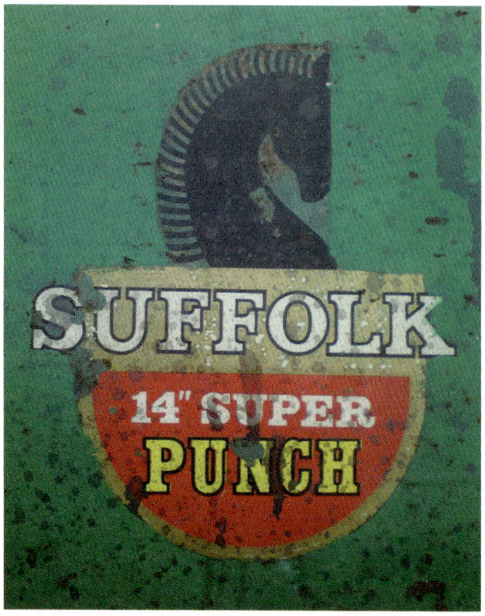

Detail of Suffolk Punch logo on the grass box.

work horse common in the nineteenth century but also alluded to the fact that the manufacturer was based in East Anglia. This was an important geographical reference for me but after my experience with the pedal car, I knew that I also needed some sort of reference to art; a visual cue that would link the tank to the landscape. For the bodywork therefore I reverted to something more traditional – painting.

Initially, I thought of making the bodywork by stretching canvas over a wooden frame. I would then paint landscapes on this tank shaped painting stretcher. I scrapped this idea because I felt that my painting technique would detract from the overall composition of the piece. I do not claim to be a virtuoso painter and in the wrong context my skills can send a counter-productive message. For example this was a girlfriend's critique of some of my early work:

'I really like your painting Chris, just looking at the way the paint is applied you really get a sense of how they were made. When you look at one of your paintings you can tell that the artist has tried really hard.'

As well as putting me off of painting for several years, this comment helped me realise that I didn't want this sort of message complicating the way someone relates to this artwork. The quality of a painting is always open to opinion. What I needed was painting that was already established as 'proper art'. The important thing was the visual connection between the thing I made and the landscape it travelled through.

Each weekend I went to car boot sales and bought all the John Constable reproductions I could find. The Essex/Suffolk border is commonly known as Constable Country and Flatford Mill, subject of The Haywain, is still preserved as close as possible to how it was in Constable's day. I had moved to Colchester where I'd found an incredibly cheap studio in an old barn and found myself, in effect, working in Constable Country. Even my Suffolk Punch lawnmowers were from Constable country. Usefully, both the lawnmowers and the Constable reproductions were green and, therefore, already camouflaged.

At the time, it was unfashionable to have Constable reproductions on the wall and most of them had quite garish gold frames around them. They had all been mass produced and the images were not framed behind glass but glued directly onto hardboard so that the hardboard was part of the picture and inseparable from it. I had to buy each one individually and each was unique – either faded or damaged in some way that showed that it had spent most of it's life in someone's house.

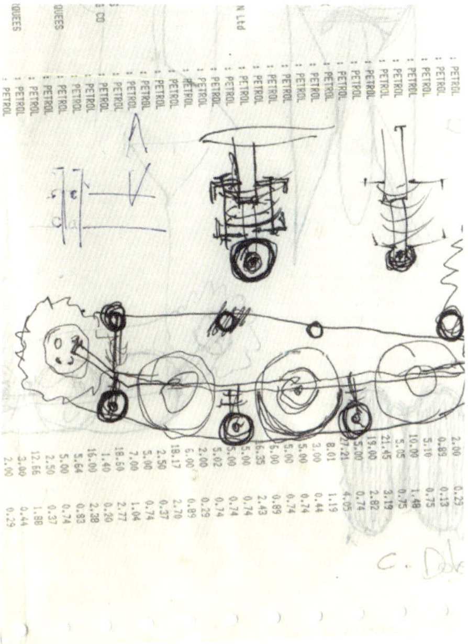

left: Side view of the wheel arrangement showing the tracks passing around 5 wheels. The front one, held off the ground, was actually 2 wheels side by side with toothed panels cut from lawnmower grass boxes and wheelbarows bolted to the side. The smaller wheels were designed to keep the tracks on and were sprung by bed springs.

right: Detail of the tracks. Wheelbarrow wheel with a Constable hubcap, one of the bedsprings, and a garden broom used to clean mud off the inside of the tracks. With each revolution of the wheel the red lever knocks the mud off the broom into the chute.

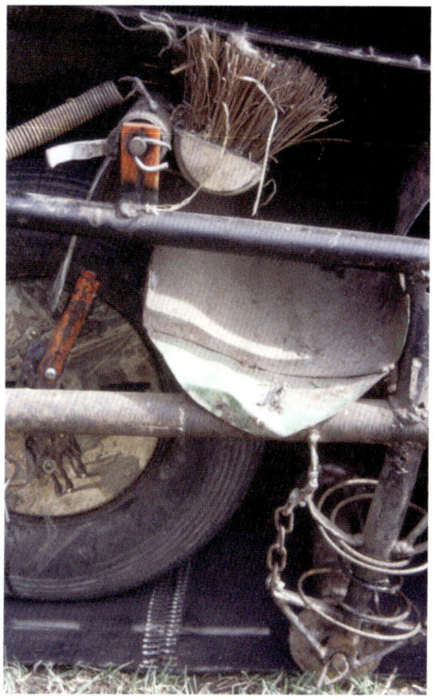

The hardboard gave me a section of bodywork for the tank and I used the frames to join these sections together but on the back instead of the front. The inside was an ornate gold-lined compartment and the only gold on the outside were the vision slots that I looked through when driving.

It is an important sculptural distinction to note that the tank was not a tank with Constable pictures stuck on afterwards. It was made from the pictures and this forged a new relationship to the landscape. When I look at a framed picture of a landscape, it invites me to look in on an imaginary world. With the tank this was reversed. I physically climbed into the picture and looked out of the frame onto the real world. It was a painting turned inside out.

I needed about sixty Constable pictures to make the tank and they took a few months to collect. I would go to four or five different car boot sales in a twenty mile radius every weekend and they usually cost about £1. One weekend, after I had been collecting for a while, I found quite an ordinary Constable picture. I already had about forty so I knew how much it was likely to cost. I was surprised, therefore, when the stallholder told me how much he wanted.

'Five pounds!'

When I showed my surprise, he assured me it was the going rate: 'People collect these you know.'

I didn't want to buy it at that price – I knew another one would eventually turn up. I also knew that nobody else was likely to buy it but, as I walked away, it suddenly dawned on me that it wasn't 'people' collecting them, it was me! I had bought so many Constables in the area that I had single-handedly inflated the price.

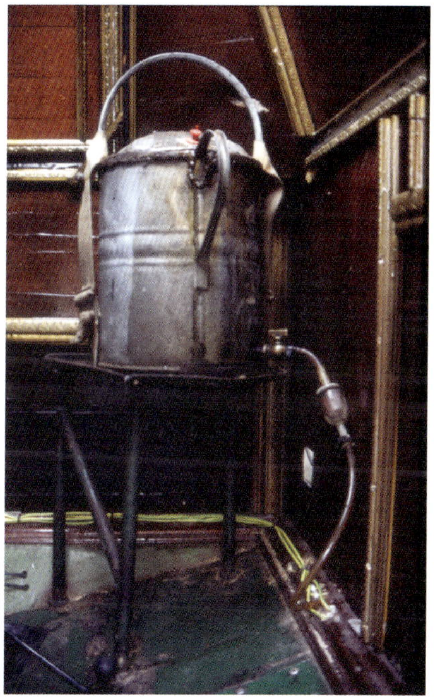

Interior shot showing the gold frames holding the pictures together from inside. Also the petrol tank made from a watering can.

The Journey

The finished tank was quite temperamental but I eventually got it working reliably enough to drive out of the barn and across the road to the farmer's field. The crop had just been cut so I thought it was an ideal time to film it with my Super 8 camera before the farmer ploughed it up again. I made it to the other side of the field and Eddie drove it back the other way so that I could film it. As I filmed, I just caught the farmer's tractor starting to plough in the distance.

Colchester is a garrison town and the location for the army prison. Sometimes they send soldiers on punishment marches around the countryside near the studio. On the film I was also lucky enough to capture a column of soldiers as they marched past in the background.

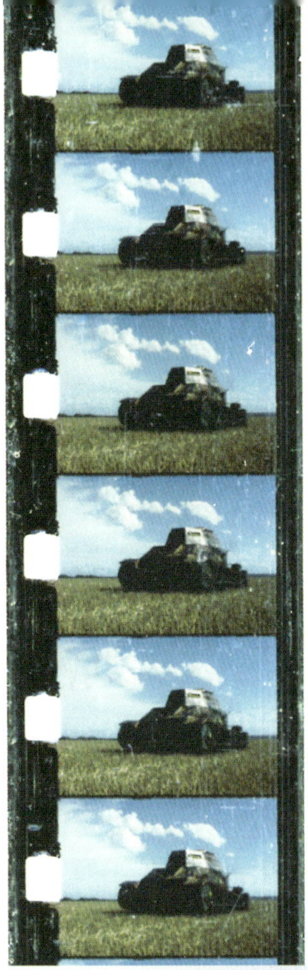

right: Tank crossing the farmer's field.

below: Tank at my old studio in Essex.

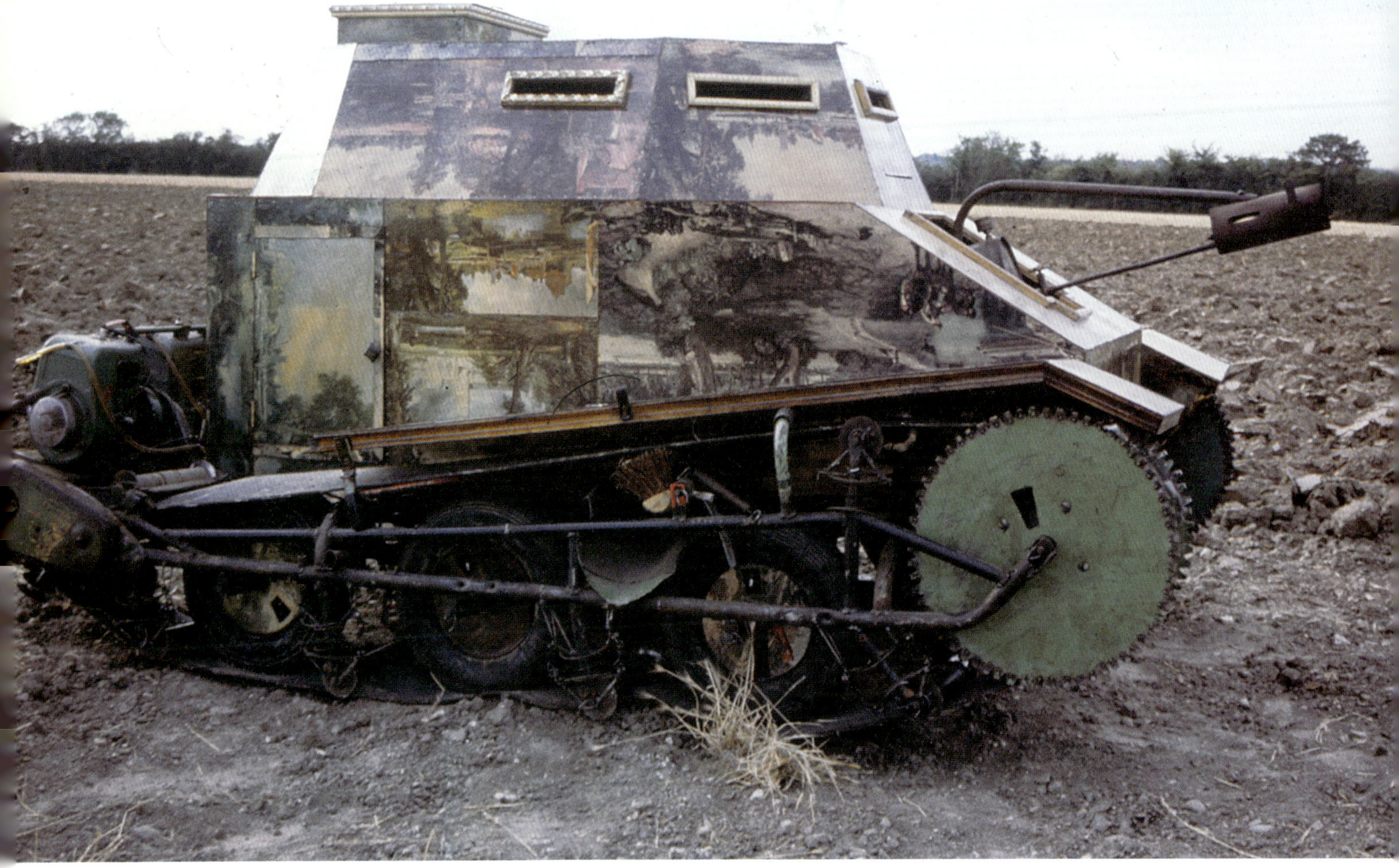

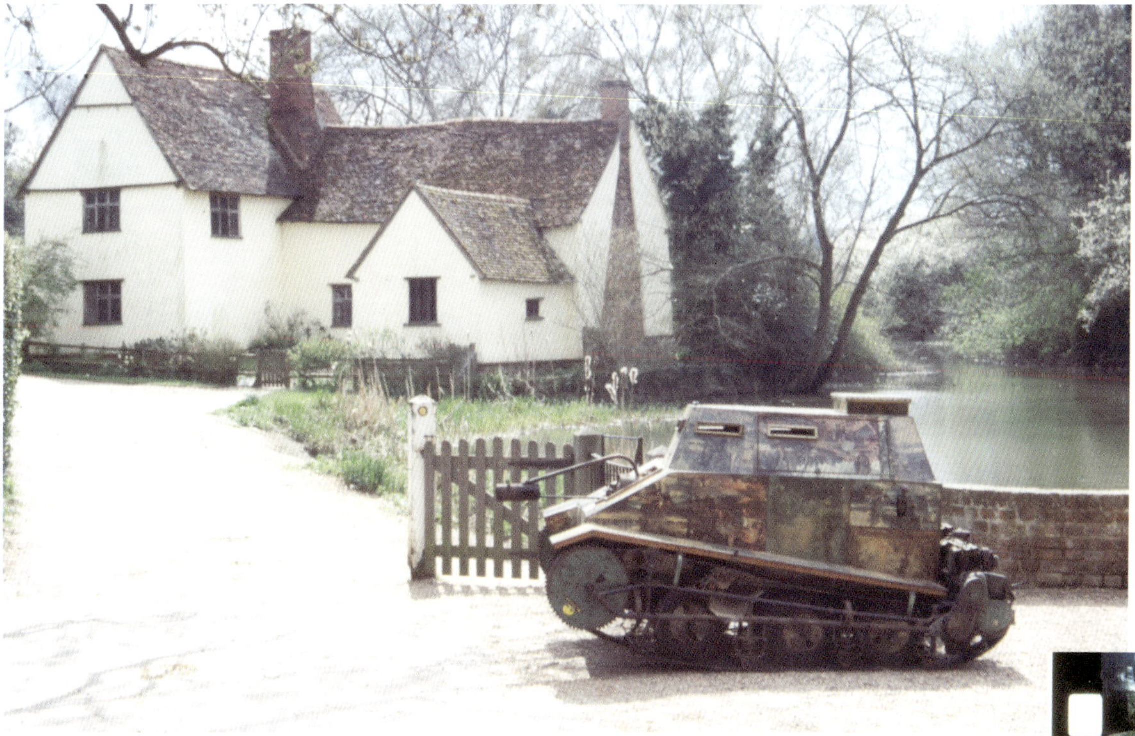

Tank at Flatford Mill, the scene of 'The Haywain'. 2001.

right: Flame-thrower in action.

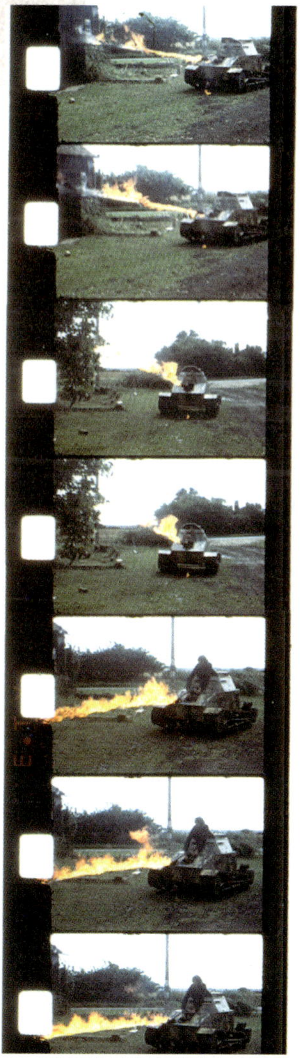

Detail of tank bodywork behind one of the lawnmower engines.

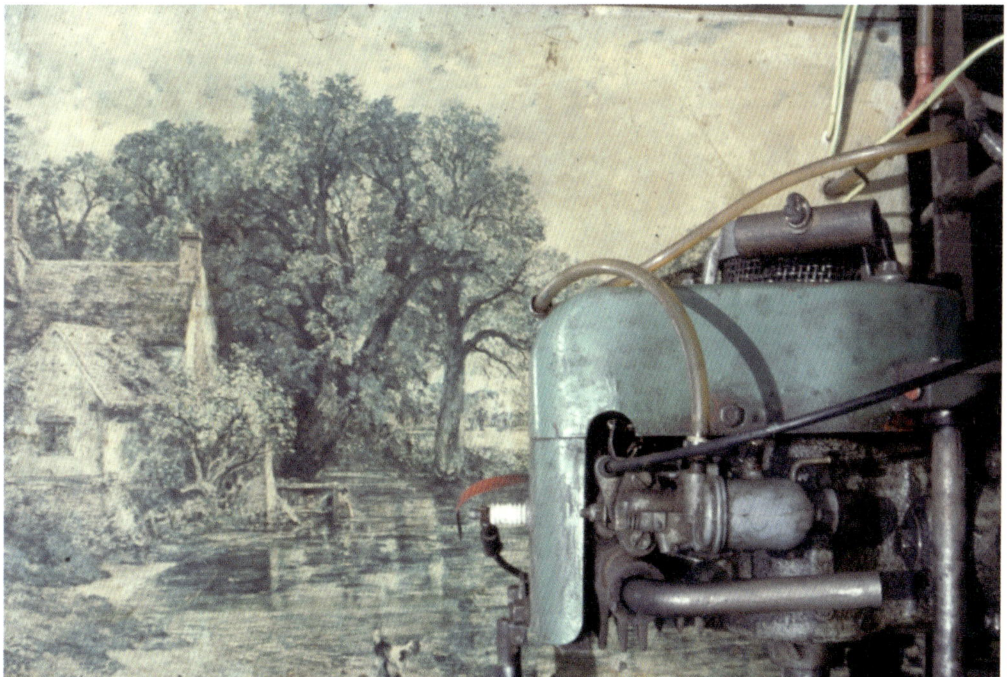

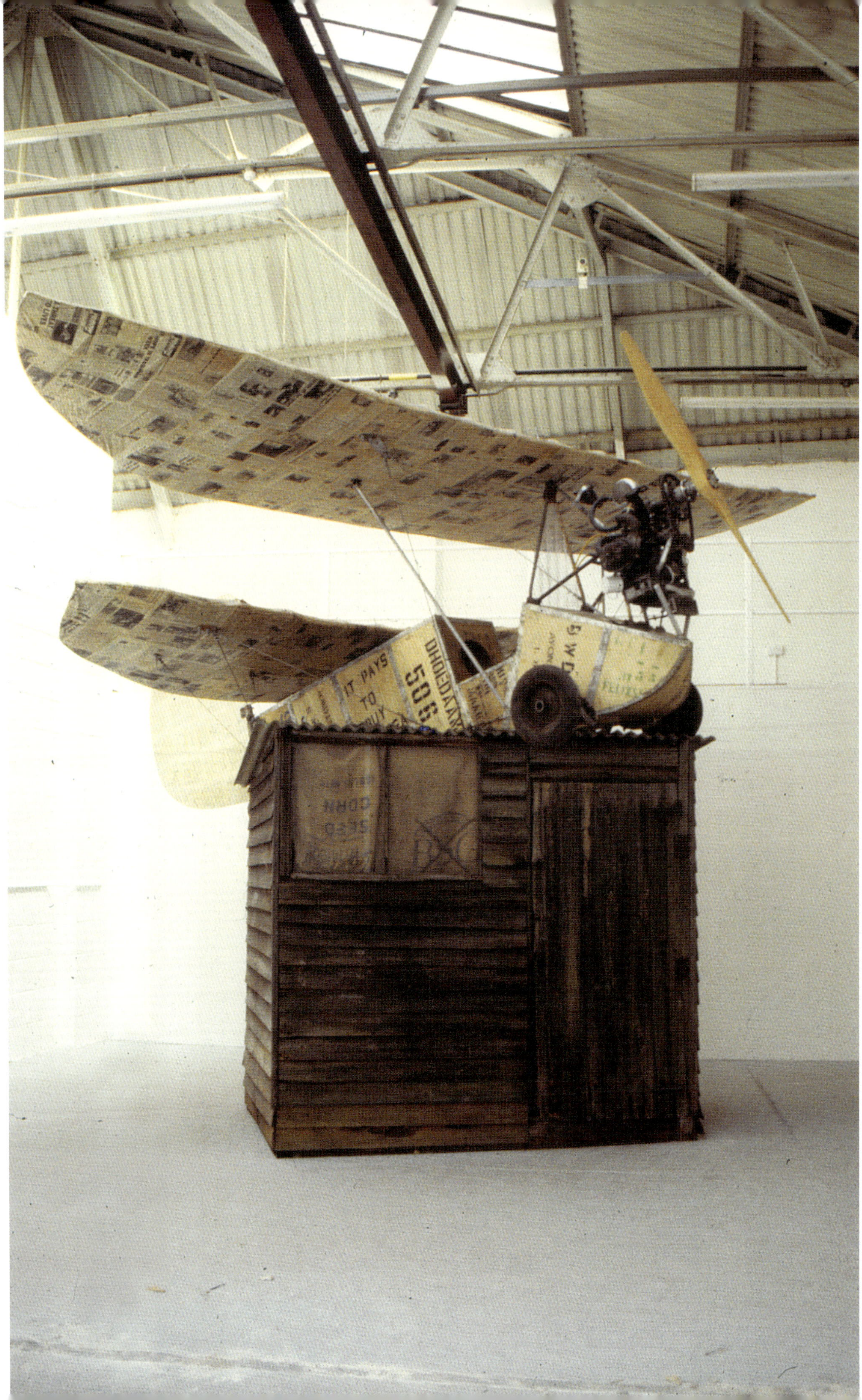
IT PAYS TO BUY

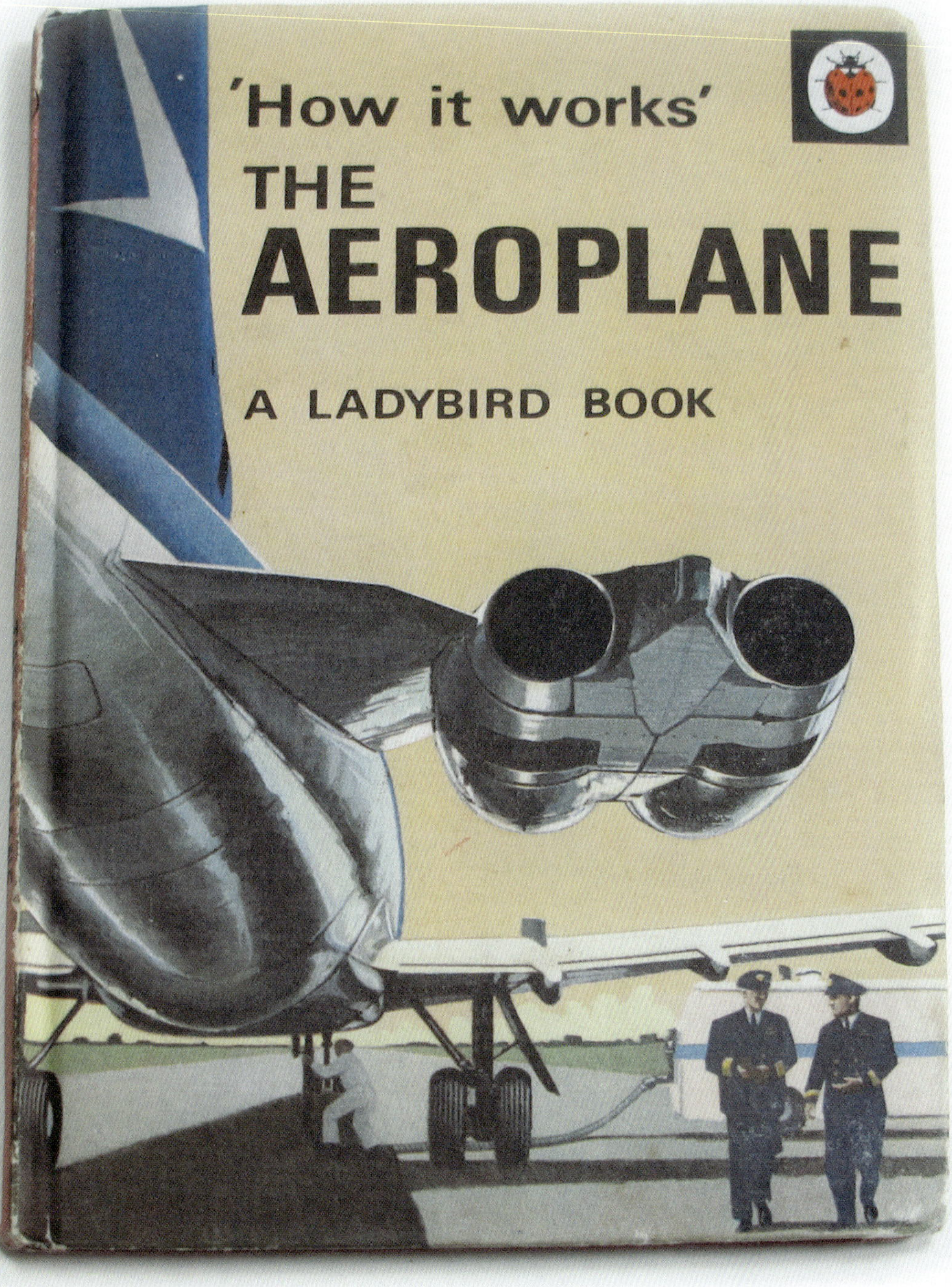

Skyscape Escape

previous page: 'Skyscape Escape'. My MA show, Royal College of Art, 1996.

Can I make an aeroplane?

There was a certain sense of inevitability to my next project. After making a boat, car, hovercraft and a tank, I lost count of how many times I heard: 'When are you going to make an aeroplane, Chris?'

Though I considered it, I didn't think it was possible to tackle a plane given my previous track record. My methodology involves too much trial and error and everything I make has a knocked up in the garden shed aesthetic not suitable for making something as exacting as an aeroplane. But then, one day in the library, I stumbled upon a reference to a rather intriguing book called The Flying Flea – How to Build and Fly it. I went to a second-hand bookshop and ordered an English translation.

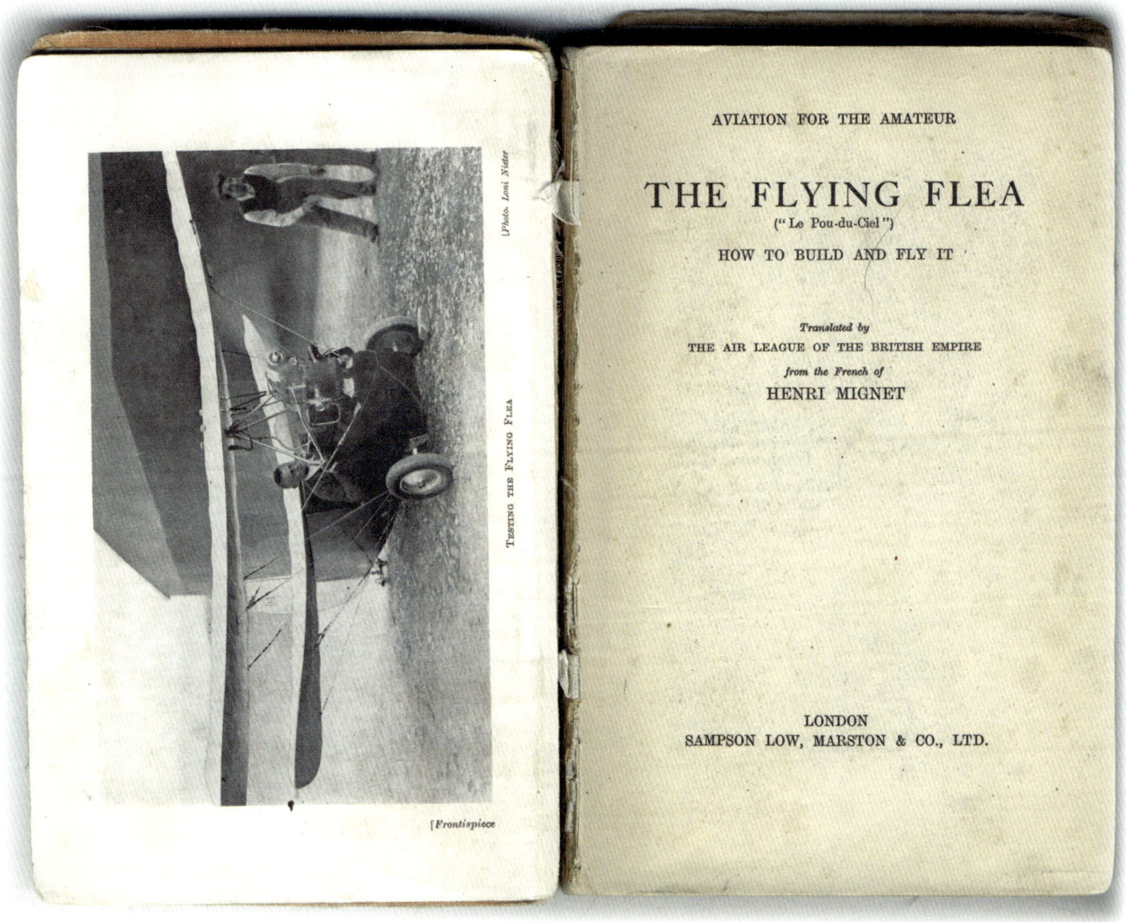

AVIATION FOR THE AMATEUR

THE FLYING FLEA
("Le Pou-du-Ciel")
HOW TO BUILD AND FLY IT

Translated by
THE AIR LEAGUE OF THE BRITISH EMPIRE
from the French of
HENRI MIGNET

LONDON
SAMPSON LOW, MARSTON & CO., LTD.

It was written in the 1930s by Henri Mignet, an idealistic French aircraft designer who wanted to encourage amateur engineers to make their own aeroplanes. The design incorporates short wings in order to make it easier to build in a garage, large shed or the spare bedroom. People who know about aircraft often talk about the subject in very technical terms. By contrast, Henri Mignet's Flying Flea is written in an accessible style that makes building an aeroplane seem really easy. Mignet's encouraging language is reminiscent of Harry Enfield's comedy sketch character, Mr Cholmondley-Warner, and its disarming innocence makes everything seem plausible. This is how the chapter on building the fuselage begins:

Chapter IX

TO WORK

The amateur is an enthusiast, an artist who obeys his impulses.
The amateur wishes to get on with his wings. He would glue the feathers to the egg before the chicken comes out in order to go faster. He would like to start by making the wings!
No, he must follow the logical order.
First: THE FUSELAGE.
Constructive Principles. The fuselage is constructed like a packing case...

Mignet estimates that the fuselage will take four days to construct – this is grossly inaccurate. It is true, however, that the fuselage is similar to a packing case and it is a lot less daunting to make one after this comparison has been made. As the components become more critical, Mignet's descriptions remain laid back and genial. The instructions for making the propeller are jolly and amiable:

Chapter XII

THE AIRSCREW

The airscrew... can one make it? Would it be better to buy it?
We shall cut our selves a helicoid of twisted wood. Five hours' work with a saw, chisel and a hammer, to file and sandpaper that is all. Calculation is easy, the drawing is easy, and construction easy.
Follow me and you will soon see... we shall cut our airscrew out of a slab of walnut or beech, bought in the city. Every carpenter or cart-maker of a village has in his stock good slabs of this kind, quite dry and probably covered with the dust of ten years. Wood sellers are everywhere.
A slab of wood about 0 metres 08 thick x 0 metres 18 wide x 2 metres long will cost about 25 francs.
Choose one with the grain more or less straight, without any big knots and with no splits. A good deal of wood can be cut away roughly, and this will take a carpenter about 5 minutes, and will cost you about 5 Francs. Do not forget to give a tip to the workman, and crack a few jokes with the master...

As the hypothetical aeroplane takes shape, the engine is started for the first time. The conventional way to do this is to swing the propeller by hand. I always imagined this to be quite hazardous but in the book it is approached in the same gung-ho fashion:

STARTING UP

Turning it in its direction of rotation; firmly grip the propeller blade with both hands 40 cms. from its access and swing it powerfully, stepping clear at the same time, and taking care not to slip or fall forward. You will practice this manoeuvre in fact many times with the contact switch off. It appears to be difficult. It would be if one did it timidly. It is not when one 'goes at it.'

I found it a bit worrying that apart from 'careful not to slip or fall forward' there didn't seem to be much in the way of health and safety. Surely it couldn't be that simple and, if it seemed unrealistic at the 'starting the engine' phase, how implausible would it be to get the thing off the ground? What I needed was someone to bridge the gap between the written word and reality.

In another library book, I found a picture of a man standing next to a finished Flying Flea. His aeroplane had the same engine and I noticed that he had a sofa cushion in the cockpit to sit on. To

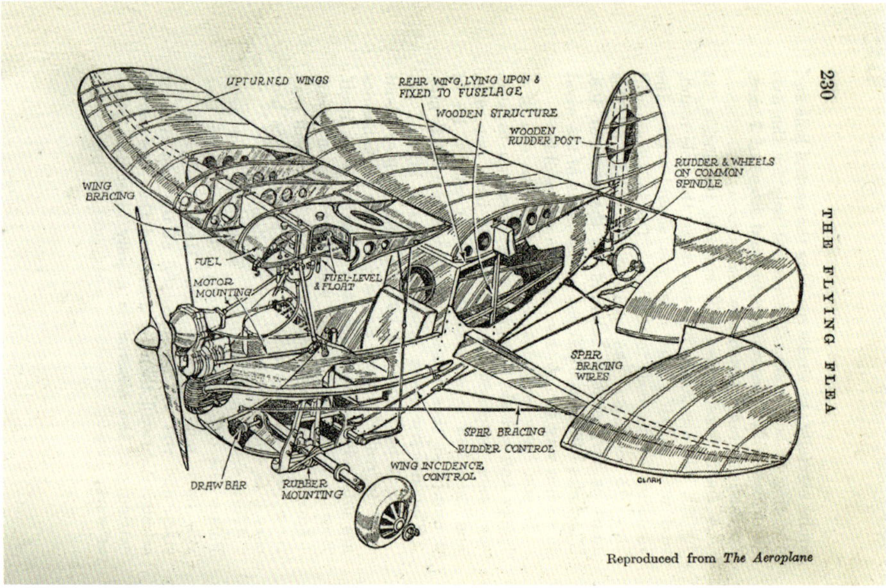

Cutaway technical drawing by Henri Mignet.

me, for some reason, this made him appear more approachable. In the text it also gave the name of the village he lived in so I could track him down via directory enquiries (these were the days before the internet). His name was Mick Ward and I went to North Scale in Lincolnshire to meet him. His wife answered the door and took me straight out to the garden shed where Mick was waiting for me surrounded by pictures and models of aeroplanes.

As well as details about how he mounted his engine, I was there to get his opinion on how likely he thought it that someone using Mignet's book could build the Flying Flea and get it off the ground. I didn't even know how successful Mick had been because the photograph I'd seen showed his Flea quite firmly on the ground.

When I asked Mick if he had 'hopped' his Flea he said 'No.'

I got a sense that he thought I was stupid for even asking. Mick had, however, made and flown other homebuilt aircraft so he had plenty of tips to impart. When I asked him if he thought it was feasible for me to build and fly a Flea he said:

'If you get to the point where you have finished building your own plane, the next thing you have to do is find somewhere to try it out. Ideally you want an airfield that will let you take it down the runway and get it up to take off speed. In the Flying Flea that could be anything between 40 and 50 miles per hour. It will seem a lot faster because the undercarriage means it's very close to ground. At that sort of speed there's a hell of a noise and lots of vibration; the engine is almost in your lap. Just before you pull back on the stick to lift off, a strange thing happens… you suddenly become acutely aware that all of these noisy vibrating components – the bolts, pieces of wood, screws, glue, nails, and fabric – were all put together by YOU! At that point you will have to make your own mind up about whether you pull back the stick and get the thing off the ground – I want nothing to do with it thanks very much.'

This was my one and only visit to Mick but as well as firsthand experience of flying he told me another thing that I found useful; his reason for building a Flying Flea in the first place. He was a small boy in the thirties when Henri Mignet came to England. Mignet had successfully crossed the Channel and landed in Kent with a motor-cycle inner tube over his shoulder in case he fell in the sea. He then did several short flights around the UK promoting the book. Mick saw the plane and met the man himself. Building the plane later in life was the fulfilment of a childhood ambition:

'I was only eleven years old at the time, I was so excited, I saved up all my pocket money and bought old tea chests from the local shop because I thought I could use the plywood to build it from.'

'What a silly idea,' he concluded.

'What a great idea,' I thought.

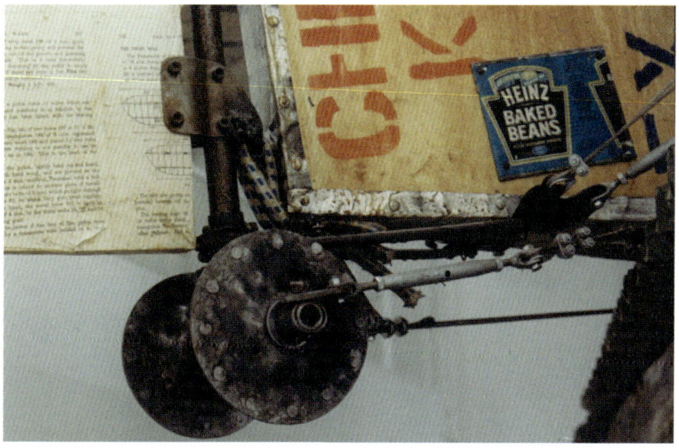

Flattened Heinz baked bean tin covers an access hole for the bolts that secure part of the rear undercarriage.

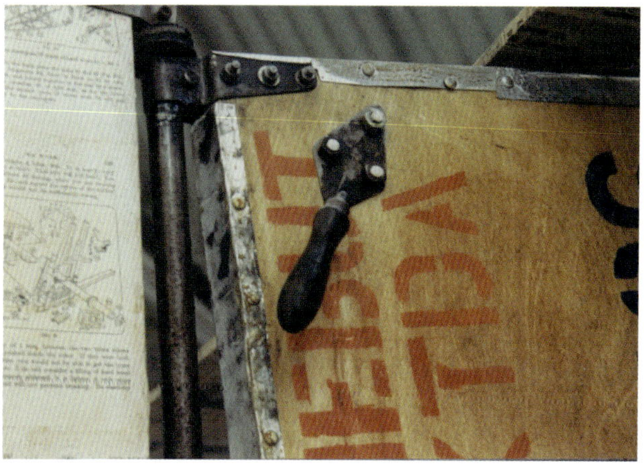

The trowel was actually used as a grab handle.

The Materials

If I was going to make an aeroplane from recycled materials following a 1930s design then tea chests were the perfect material. They were around in the 1930s and they are still in use today. This history-based thought process dictated what I made other parts from. I used wheelbarrow wheels for the undercarriage and small metal components were Heinz baked bean tins. In the centre of the propeller was a boss cut from a Lyons golden syrup tin bearing the company motto, 'Out of the strong came forth sweetness.'

Even the engine, from a Citroën 2CV, was influenced by the historical context. The French 2CV has a lightweight, air-cooled engine developed before the war, put into production in 1948 and still manufactured in the 1980s. I added one or two accessories. The oil filter was inside an enamel mug and the air filter was made from an aluminium teapot. The air came in through the top of the teapot and I covered the hole with some fine metal gauze. I attached the oil breather pipe to the spout. The book suggests an oil reservoir to supply a slow drip feed of gear oil onto the chain that connects the engine to the propeller. I made this reservoir out of a milk bottle. The drip of oil travelled down through two feet of copper tubing and emerged close to the chain. The accelerator control lever was made from a teaspoon and I bolted this to the side of the cockpit. I increased the engine revs by pushing the spoon forward with my thumb. More often than not, the propeller would then blow the oil from the chain straight into my face.

The wing covering needed to be in keeping with the rest of the plane so I used newspaper, but not just a random collection of old papers. Over the years, I have accumulated a variety of press clippings and I used these to construct the wings. From tip to tip the wings were covered in images of my own face. This was not just an excuse to revel in my own media coverage, I was trying to tackle an important issue.

We live in an age in which image often triumphs over content – in contemporary art as much as in politics and there's often a blurring of the boundaries between critical analysis and marketing. Making the plane took such a long time to do that technology had moved on before I finished it. The internet plays a much bigger part in self-promotion and will, hopefully, democratise the art world. At the time, however, the art press seemed to be the key to success. I even once met an artist who had come all the way from Japan to Britain to network and told me that he only wanted to talk to artists who had featured in Frieze magazine.

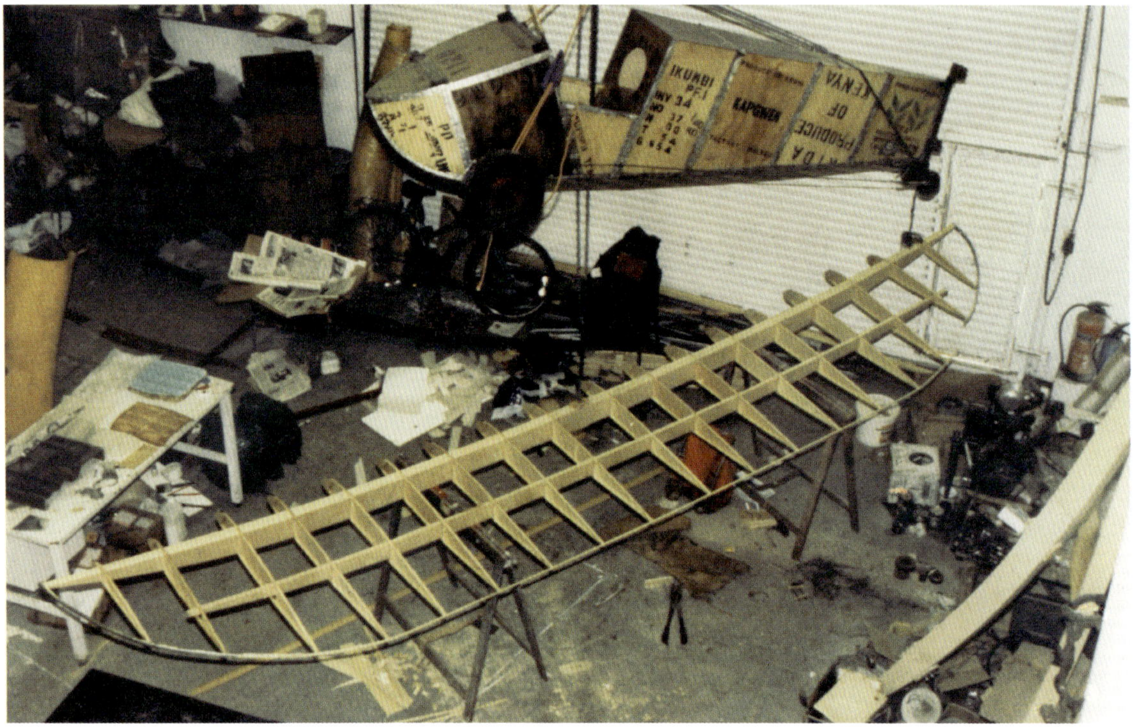

My studio at the RCA. Fusilage suspended in mid-air to save space.

Anything can be art and anyone can be an artist. There are more artists now than at any other time in history. Post Modernism means that nothing is new and everything can be appropriated. Marketing can be what makes the difference and it could be argued that it is often in this area that the real creativity happens. Therefore if I go into an art gallery it would make sense to admire the marketing, not just the art, as the marketing is arguably 'part' of the work. Instead, in the gallery, it is treated as a separate entity and I find this slightly duplicitous. I thought this issue was interesting enough to bring into the gallery by making it part of the work. Instead of denying a connection, I physically made the artwork from my publicity. The work and the media image were indivisible. A lot of my publicity, however, was from tabloid and local newspapers and a bit low brow. Though I like to think there is a lot of content in my work, I would be the first to admit that my image is terrible.

Whenever I met a journalist I tried to present the full story of what I was doing. On most occasions, despite my explanations, it became apparent that they had already made up their own mind. My favourite example is when a reporter came to college to do a piece on the hovercraft. The cameraman persuaded me to hover around outside the college. It was a nice flat piece of car park so I got some speed up and the picture did capture the movement. Then the reporter got out his note-book and began the interview: 'Why is this art?'

I started to tell him all about Duchamp and then launched into my explanation about how the vehicle related to the landscape. I told him how I found the bottles on the beach and about my epiphany with the birds out on the mud flats. I explained that I was essentially a landscape artist and, when I disappeared into the distance, I was working within a romantic tradition that included artists such as Caspar David Friedrich. The journalist sold the story to the Daily Star under the headline:

'HOVERCRAFTY!

Chris Dobrowolski's gotta lotta bottle… Lot less bother with a hover… Weirdo art student… Waste of tax payer's money!'

I had to deliver a lecture about my work once to art students and the issue of image versus content surfaced. I told anecdotes about the boat rescue, my encounter with police on the pedal car and the press coverage of the hovercraft in the Daily Star. The students found it all very amusing. When I came to talk about the aeroplane and the superficiality of image and marketing, I suddenly became aware that my delivery was yet another marketing tool so I tried to counter this by drawing attention to it so that I did not appear divisive. This led me into a strange area of paradox and double negative and, instead of coming across as candid, I looked more and more insincere:

'I know that I am making you laugh and the failure of a lot of my work does make it quite endearing. But I don't want you to think that this lecture is some kind of ploy to get you to like me. I'm not trying to "act" like some kind of loser to make myself appear less of a threat. I'm the real thing. I really AM a loser!'

After the talk, the host took me to the student union bar for a drink. Some of the students were in the bar and one of them made a point of coming over and talking to me:

'When you got into that self-evasive stuff about how you weren't an act but actually were a loser, I thought you were pulling a double bluff on us and that, in fact, you were some kind of a secret success. I had to come over and talk to you because I needed to meet you in a real context outside the lecture theatre to disprove my doubts. Now I'm talking to you, I can see you REALLY ARE a loser!'

I remember saying, 'Thanks very much for that', without any sense of irony.

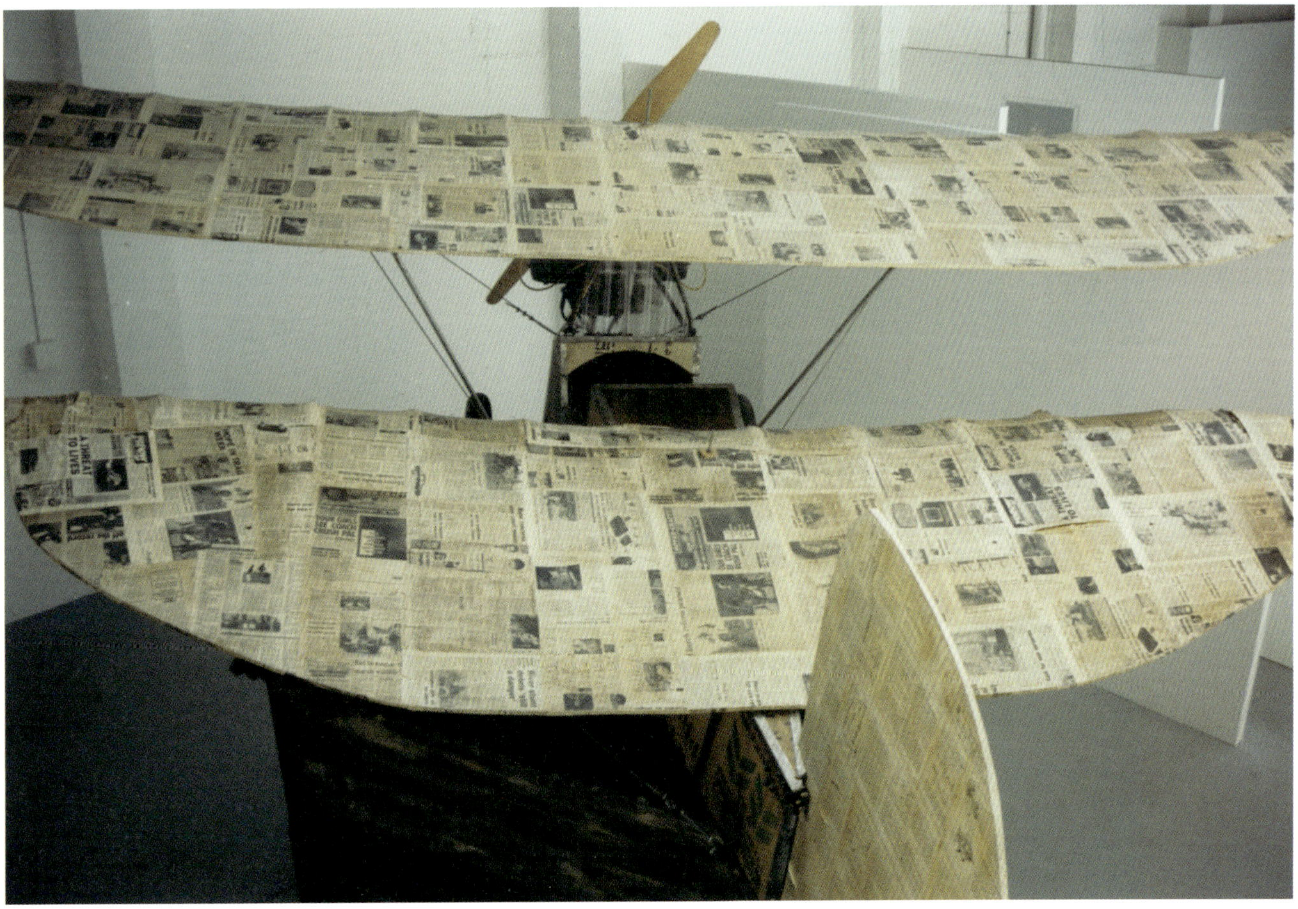

The newspaper wings.

An aerial sensation

I chose a slightly different material to cover the rudder frame. The 269 pages of Mignet's book gave me more than enough to cover the 3m square of rudder. The first 110 pages are all about how he arrived at his theory, the following 140 pages are instructions about how to make the aeroplane. The last 19 pages are entitled:

HOW TO FLY THE FLEA – Piloting

1. On the first outing one should merely taxi. A number of runs backwards and forwards... Very slowly first of all, at a jog-trot, so as to accustom oneself to moving the throttle and steering on the ground...
It is quite certain that at the end of this first trial you will accelerate too much, for a second just to see what happens. Careful!... Come on now! Steady. You are not yet ready.
2... To-day, speeding up your engine a little you are going to get a glimpse of an 'aerial' sensation... by pulling on the joystick, you hold it in the attitude of flight, that is with the engine on the horizon...
... There is no reason why you should not let it run along with the tail up, in flying position. Bumps will make you bounce up, you are lightened-you are almost in flight. Being impatient, you accelerate a little more... it is done! You are flying. Throttle down slightly. Without moving anything else, you come back to the ground...
That is enough for today. Do not hasten with the matter. Go home.
ONE'S TOUCH IN THIS SPORT IS PERFECTED LESS BY PRACTICE ON THE TRAINING GROUND THAN BY MATURE REFLECTION WHEN RESTING. YOUR TRIALS WILL BE SHORT, AT INTERVALS OF ONE OR TWO DAYS.
3. THIRD OUTING: Speed up your engine little more. Amuse yourself by flying the whole length of the ground.

Although I loved the idea of an 'aerial sensation', there seemed quite a big leap between outings two and three. As far as I was concerned no amount of 'mature reflection when resting' was ever going to bridge the gap between the initial 'aerial sensation' and amusing myself by flying the whole length of the airfield. I needed professional help and this time it came in the form of the Flying Flea Squadron.

In the early stages of the project, I bought a copy of Pilot Magazine. I knew very little about the world of aviation and I thought it might help. In the small ads I found a short advert entitled Homebuilt:

'A HOMEBUILT for less than £1000? Flying Flea/Pou du Ciel Squadron SAE INFO to... '

I wasn't quite sure what was on offer here and I had mixed emotions about meeting other Flying Flea enthusiasts. I had come across the aeroplane through my own research. In my own little way I felt that 'I' had 'rediscovered' the Flying Flea. Knowing that there was already an established organisation took that sense of ownership away. It was a silly but natural reaction. However, making contact would mean access to a support network and specialist knowledge so I sent my self addressed envelope. The reply came from a man called Graham Priest who sent me a hand-made, black and white magazine, Le Sport De l'Air. It looked like a fanzine. Inside was information about Flying Fleas in museums and others found falling apart in sheds. It also contained images of various half-built aeroplanes. On the front cover there was an image of a Flying Flea fuselage carefully wrapped in black polythene and tied to the roof of a car. In the top right hand corner of the page was the club's circular logo with the words 'Flying Flea Squadron' written around the outside. The magazine didn't really have the in-depth information I was looking for so I rung up the contact number and

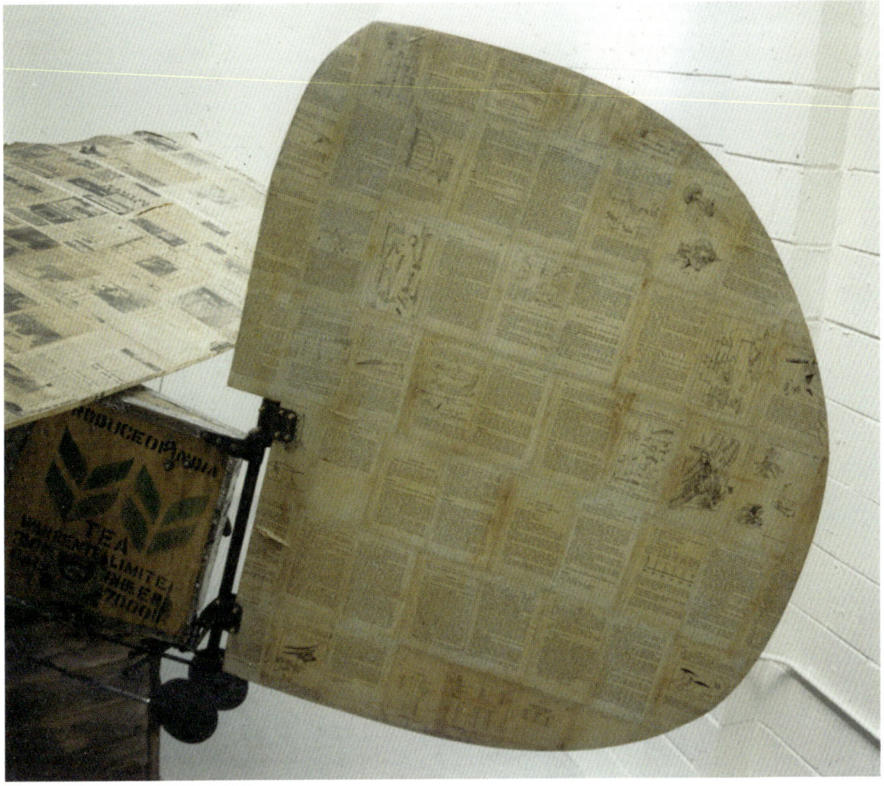

Rudder covered in pages from Mignet's original book.

spoke to the head of the organisation; Graham, or as I like to call him 'Squadron Leader'. He quickly wanted to know where I was based. When I told him I was from Essex but living in London (I was on a postgraduate course at the time at the RCA) he said: 'We're looking for a co-ordinator for London and the South East, maybe you should consider the post?'

He then went on to say, 'You do know about the ban don't you?'

The ban is a thorny issue that inevitably comes up when discussing the Flying Flea. The book came out in 1935 but the design was banned in 1936 because thirteen people had been killed in it.

I was aware of this because my introduction to the plane was via a book entitled Worlds Most Disastrous Aeroplanes.

The crashes were not only due to inexperienced people learning how to fly but also to an inherent design fault. What made the Flying Flea special was its simplicity and compactness, a simplicity that extended to the controls. There are no foot pedals and the whole plane is slung beneath the wings so that it banks automatically. The oversized rudder forces the plane to swing, pendulum fashion, into a skidded turn. The key to the design was the wing formation – the tandem wing. This gave a lot of lift with a short wing span and made the plane only about 4 metres in length. The largest wing was hinged so that the whole thing lifted or dropped at the back edge. It was controlled by pushing the joystick backwards or forwards. This pitched the aeroplane up or down determining lift and speed. A conventional aeroplane has a rigid wing but uses an elevator at the very back of the tail to tilt the aircraft up or down. Pulling on the joystick in the Flea is a different feeling and good for someone who knows nothing about flying. You can actually feel the weight and response of the aircraft in the same way you can feel a kite if you pull on its string.

As the wing hinges down, the trailing edge comes close to the rear wing positioned below and behind it. The gap between the two becomes narrower and the air is squeezed through the slot that is created between the two wings.

An aeroplane wing creates lift because the air is split into two paths – one above and one below the wing. The underneath of a wing is more or less flat whereas the top is curved. The air has to move faster over the top and this creates a loss of pressure which sucks the wing upwards. As the air is squeezed through the slot, it is also moving faster. This fast moving air travels over the rear wing and consequently creates more lift. If the plane goes into a slight dive angle of 15 degrees, the increased speed exaggerates the lift of the rear wing so that it actually starts to lift the plane higher at the back than the front putting it into a more pronounced dive. This dive becomes steeper and steeper the faster the plane heads towards the ground and is impossible to recover from. The fatalities often hit the ground nose first or even upside down – that's quite a serious design fault.

Graham had a solution – different wing profile and a longer fuselage so that the wings were further apart.

'I have the updated plans.' He said. 'Would you like me to post them to you?'

'YES' I replied.

He sent the updated wing profile measurements. They were photocopies of blueprints – white lines on a blue background. They reproduced as light grey lines on an ever so slightly less grey background. I could only read them if I held them up to the light at an angle and read the slight indentations on the paper. The dimensions were given to a tenth of a millimetre and they were in French. I followed the updated plans to the best of my ability and amalgamated them with the parts I had already made from the book.

The fuselage is probably the easiest bit of the plane to make because it takes shape quite quickly and you can see it evolve each day. The Flying Flea instructions had each component drawn with a little circled number exactly like Airfix model kits. The difference was that each component in the Airfix kit had the corresponding number moulded into the plastic part.

The wings for standard Airfix kits rarely comprise more than four separate pieces (top and bottom, left and right wing) and the fuselage is often made of two halves, left and right. Apart from sticking the transfers on, the most exciting part of making these plastic kits was putting the two halves together. Very quickly, it is possible to see the outline of the aeroplane illustrated dramatically on the packaging. I never once started an Airfix aeroplane kit without first holding the two halves of the fuselage together and trying to make the wings stay on just to get the instant thrill of seeing it come together. The fuselage of the Flying Flea comes together in almost the same way. Making the wings was a different story.

The process was laborious, repetitive work. The wing profile has to be copied over and over again to make the ribs. These are then connected in parallel to one another on the main wing spar. Until the day that all the ribs are finished and connected together it is just a boring production process. The end of each day's work just resulted in more of the same wooden shapes to add to the pile. Consequently, many Flying Fleas never get past the fuselage stage.

I stuck at my Flea on and off for several years. Early on, when I was still at college, my supervisor called me into the office for a meeting. I realised that, sensibly, the college didn't want to be responsible for me flying the plane. I told them I would sign a disclaimer and they said:

'We've already been to the college legal department and looked into that, actually.'

Eventually we agreed a compromise: 'The requirements of the course do not include flying the plane'. They needn't have worried, the plane was still a long way from completion.

After graduation, I moved back to Essex and was offered an artist's residency in a large house in the country. I was offered a flat to live in and a studio. Always one to look a gift horse in the mouth, I decided not to take the residency because the studio wasn't big enough to build my aeroplane wings.

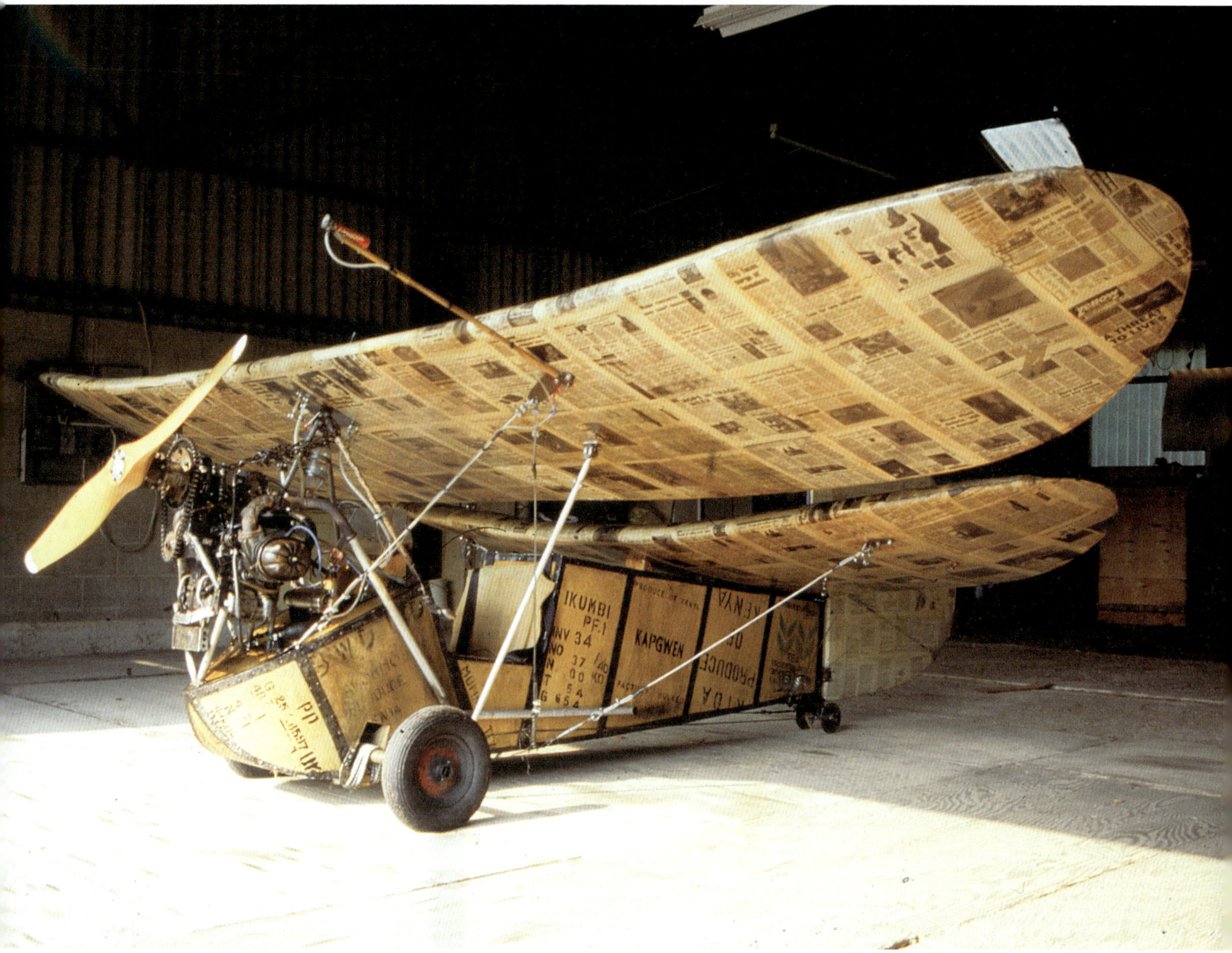

Flying Flea in the hangar at Bill's airfield, 2003.

To my amazement, the lady of the house said: 'Why don't you use the double garage? My husband can just as easily leave the Bentley on the drive.'

This idyllic environment was where I built the wings. The residency lasted a year and a half until the couple sold up and moved on. They gave me fair warning of their departure and tried to give me some hope by saying: 'You never know, the new people might keep you on.'

At the time I remember thinking…

'They may keep the maid and the gardener but I'm sure they won't keep the free loading artist.'

They didn't. I eventually put the finishing touches to the plane back at my old studio in the barn. After several years, I had what looked like a finished aeroplane in front of me. The only thing to do now was find somewhere to try it out. It was time to get back in touch with Squadron Leader Graham.

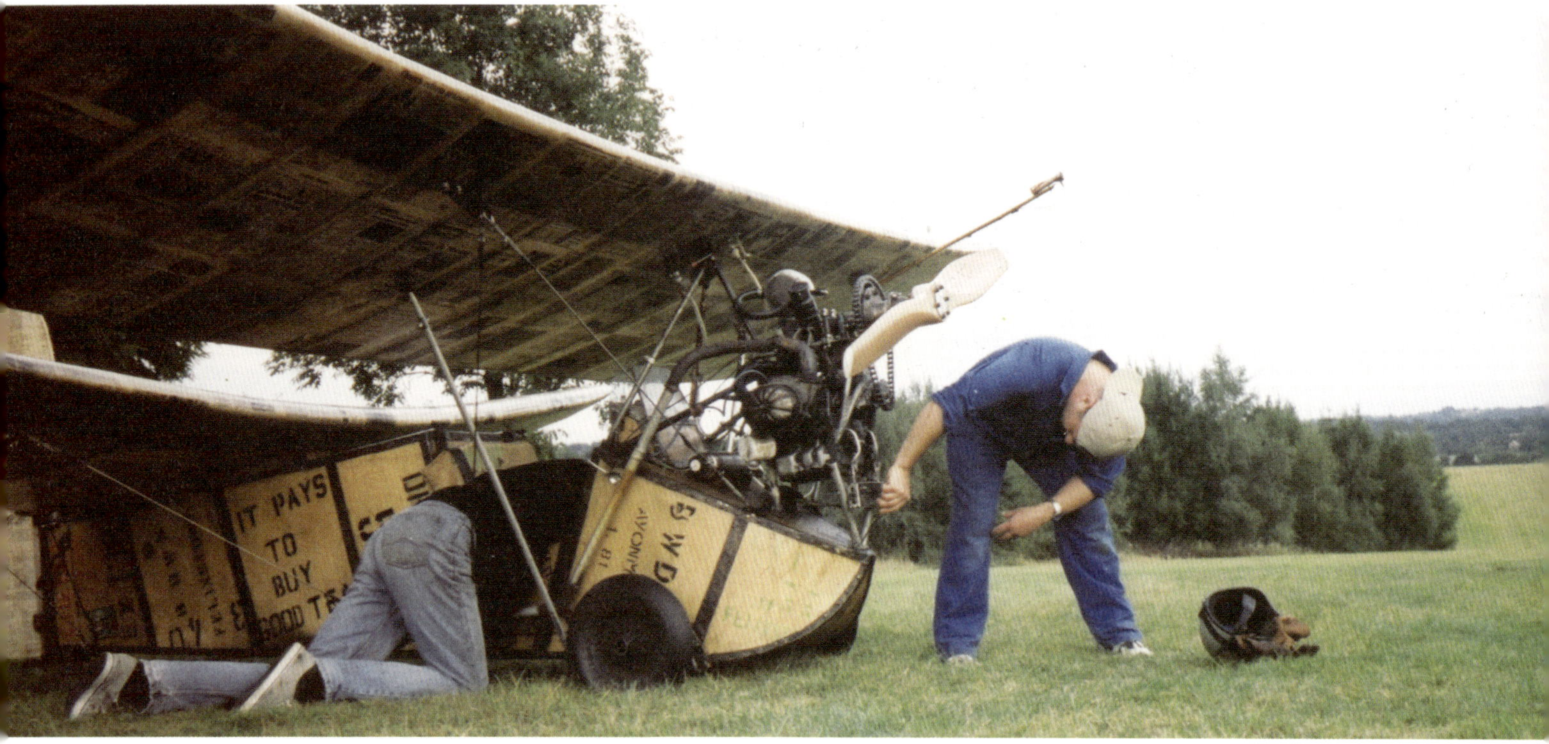

Me and Tony doing some last minute repairs at Bill's airfield. The taxiway can be seen disappearing over the hill on the right of the photo [Jo Newman]

The attempt at flight

On the phone to Graham, I could tell he was quite excited that I had finished my Flea. He said that it was perfect timing as he had organised a Flying Flea rally and was keen to have my plane there. In fact, he said, 'We NEED your plane there.'

I was very pleased with my invitation but I was rather puzzled by the word 'need'. I questioned Graham further. 'You NEED my plane? Why do you NEED my plane?'

'Because it's the only one.' He replied.

When I met the squadron at the airfield they were all very enthusiastic; mainly middle aged or retired men who all had a copy of the book, some of them even had red and white Flying Flea Squadron hats on. But none of them had a plane.

Bill was the most accomplished member of the Flying Flea Squadron. He had a pilot's licence, his own airstrip and hands-on experience of building a modern derivative of the Flying Flea for which he had obtained a licence, making it the only legal Flying Flea in Britain. He was the obvious choice as test pilot, but when I asked him, he ever so politely declined:

'The thing is, Chris, we're more of a historical organisation. It wouldn't be right if I flew it. I have a pilot's licence. The whole concept of the Flying Flea is that an ordinary person builds and flies it, someone who DOESN'T have flying experience. If I did it, it just wouldn't be historically accurate. It would be far better if an enthusiastic amateur taught themselves how to do it… We'll give you all the help you need… Stay here as long as you like…'

So here I was at Bill's airstrip, miles from home, with group of lovely old men who, in the nicest possible way, were trying to kill me!

Bill's airfield was set amongst rolling hills near Hastings. I travelled there in my friend Mark's van. The approach was down a narrow sunken lane and then a turn right up a short, steep driveway. At the top, the landscape suddenly opens out onto a view down a long grass hill that rises up again in the near distance like a miniature valley. This depression was the taxi way at the start of the runway. Officially, the runway began over the brow of the hill. I knew I wasn't going to fly off into the distance, taking off and landing was going to be a big enough achievement, and this area was just long enough to do that in. The squadron had decided that the steep hill on one side might give a useful bit of momentum while the other side might be useful for stopping as I tried to taxi faster and faster over the coming days.

The chapter in Mignet's book entitled How to Fly the Flea doesn't take into account the days spent in-between each 'outing' repairing the damage and replacing things that have vibrated loose or just fallen off. I did a lot of taxi-ing up and down the little valley but I remained firmly on the ground. I usually spent twenty minutes on the runway and about two weeks putting everything right again. The undercarriage was one of the early problems. The wheels kept seizing on the crude axle which would then start to rotate. It was held on by yards and yards of bungee cord wrapped around it on either side of the fuselage as the suspension. A long bolt stuck out of the axle as it came through the cockpit. This T-bar at right angles to the axle was designed to stop it rotating but, instead, it did one of three things; snapped off, bent and wound itself around the axle or just rotated with the axle smashing a hole in the cockpit floor.

On the first few days, the squadron was at the airfield in force and they turned themselves into an improvised ground crew. Graham delegated himself to start the plane by swinging the propeller. They were helped by Mark and another old college friend, Giles. Every time it broke down, my ground crew would all come running over and carry the stricken craft from the runway. If we could remedy the problem quickly, I had another go and they lined the side of the runway to watch me go down the hill again – apart from Giles who covered his eyes with his hands.

The technical problems continued. In an attempt to fix something else I had taken the teapot air filter from the top of the engine. For some reason small amounts of petrol kept coming out of the air intake. The propeller blew this immediately into my face. I was continually spitting it out of my mouth. Then, one early evening, just before sunset, it happened. I had an 'aerial sensation!' It was a bit rubbish and there was so much noise, vibration and spitting that I had no idea I had very briefly left the ground. The first I knew about it was when I returned to the top of the hill and saw everyone applauding and cheering with their hands in the air: 'For at least 3 yards you were possibly a full three or even four inches from the ground!'

I was told excitedly. Bill opened a bottle of champagne and Graham got drunk. Later that night, he said: 'I know it wasn't very high but it was only a few inches from the bottom of the ladder of the space rocket to the surface of the moon. It was one small step.'

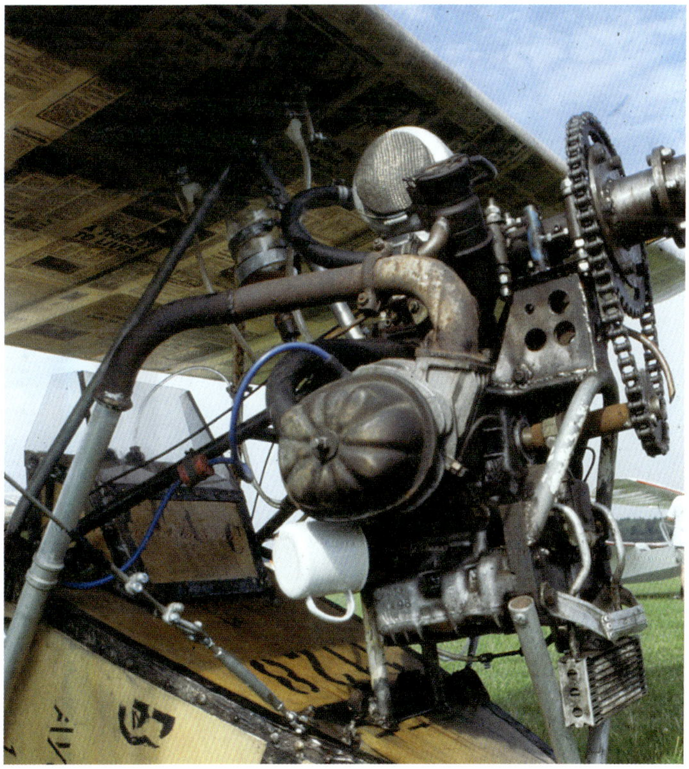

The Citroën 2CV engine

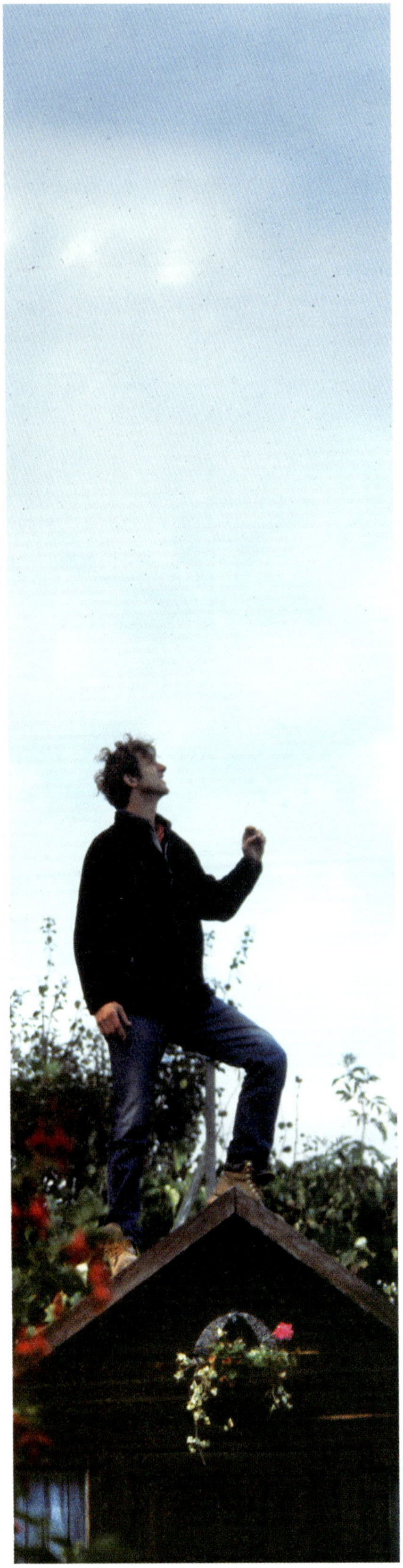
Me on the roof of my Dad's shed.

I could see his logic but four inches didn't really feel like a rite of passage. With a favourable wind, I managed to coax the plane a little higher but it was still plagued by teething problems. The frame I had designed to hold the reduction gear system fractured and took a long time to rebuild. I had to make a trip back to Essex and, while I was there, I met up with a colleague from the local art college. He wanted to know how things were going at the airfield and we started to have an impromptu tutorial about where I should draw the line on the project. If height was the key, I needed to decide how high that was. At some point something was going to break that I couldn't fix so I wanted to go back with a clear objective before that happened.

At first, the height of a person seemed appropriate but I wasn't quite sure why. I then started to think about my earliest memories of aeroplanes, height, discovery and adventure and this thought process took me to my childhood for inspiration.

The house where I grew up in Essex has a shed in the garden that I enjoyed climbing on. It was at the end of the garden and from its roof I had a completely new view of my world. Once when I climbed onto the shed roof, I remember an aircraft flew quite low over the neighbourhood – so low that I could see the people inside. This thing was literally out of my world. Then I thought I saw someone in the plane wave to me. I made a connection. The contact suddenly made this magical object part of my world. It was the lowest I had ever seen an aircraft over our garden and I knew there was a limit to how far down it could come. I also knew there was a limit to how high I could climb so there would always be a space between us: higher than I could reach on the shed roof and below the lowest aeroplane there was theoretically unexplored space. It wasn't on the moon, it was inches from my fingertips and I could see it every day when I looked up from my parent's garden. No matter how familiar it seemed, no-one had ever been there ever before.

This was the height I wanted to fly my aeroplane.

It doesn't sound that high but the thing to remember is that, in a plane crash, it isn't the sky that kills you, it's the ground. One of the thirteen people who had died in a Flying Flea had made a successful forced landing but carried on into a ditch and broken his neck. To save weight, there are no brakes on the Flying Flea but with a good pair of gloves it is possible to slow down a little by leaning out of the cockpit and grabbing the wheels.

I had access to a lot of information at the airstrip and the How to Fly chapter in Mignet's book but this information was useless until I had the experience to make it instinctive. For example, the book tells you to make a note of what the airspeed indicator reads. As I descended the hill at forty mph, everything happened very quickly and I never felt safe enough to take my eyes off the runway, let alone start looking at instruments. I even hesitated before doing basic things like move the joystick. In a way, I had too much information. Luckily, there was another member of the Flying Flea Squadron to simplify things for me.

Tony had a pilot's licence and kept his own plane at the airfield. He was from Dagenham. His plane was a shapely, bright red sports plane and it reminded me of a flying Ford Capri. We spoke the same language.

Tony took it upon himself to teach me how to fly. Before beginning, he established my existing knowledge of aeronautics by asking a few basic questions: 'What is meant by an aircraft's wing chord?' He quizzed.

'err…' I answered.

'Oh Shit! You're not joking are you? You REALLY know fuck all!'

He was very careful not to give me too much information so that I wouldn't get confused. At one point I sat on a chair by the side of the runway in an imaginary cockpit with a broomstick as joystick. Tony suggested a basic scenario:

'OK, you're going down the runway, you've pulled back on the stick, gone up, reached your desired height. You've kept it in a straight line and now you want to descend again. What do you do?'

I pondered. 'I know this one, Tony. I keep the stick in the same position but I slowly ease off on the spoon, not sharply, very slowly. I should make a more or less smooth landing.'

'Correct!'

'OK Chris, This time I'm going to give you a dilemma and you have to make a fast decision so you have to give me an answer as quickly as possible. You've gone down the runway and reached the required height but you've run out of runway to land safely. The hedge at the end of the runway is coming up fast. Do you:

'A. Pull back on the stick as hard as you can, apply more spoon, hop the hedge and take a chance on what's in the field on the other side?

'or B. Come down as quick as you can and take your chances in the hedge?'

I didn't think either option sounded appealing so I hesitated.

'Come on Chris, I need an answer NOW! This is a realistic scenario. What are you going to do?'

Under pressure I said, 'I'm going to hop the hedge Tony.'

'WRONG ANSWER!

'LET ME TELL YOU NOW CHRIS, AN AIR ACCIDENT AT FORTY MPH IS FAR MORE DANGEROUS THAN A GROUND ACCIDENT AT SIXTY. If that hedge is coming up, I want you to plough straight into it. I've got the fire axe, the first aid kit and the extinguisher in the back of my car and I can be at the end of the runway in under five minutes – I've been trained!'

At this point in time, my personal life had not been going well. I had been a student when I started the project, now, years later, I had a regular teaching post at the local art college which I loved. I was, in fact, employed by the tutor who had instilled in me the virtues of the 'inner need'. I had an opportunity to pass on everything I believed in but, unfortunately, my boss didn't agree so I was fired.

The aeroplane and all the other vehicles were stored in my studio in the country. It was idyllic; incredibly cheap with plenty of space. Then I got kicked out. Revelling in self pity, I had an argument with my girlfriend and we split up. I wouldn't go so far as to say that

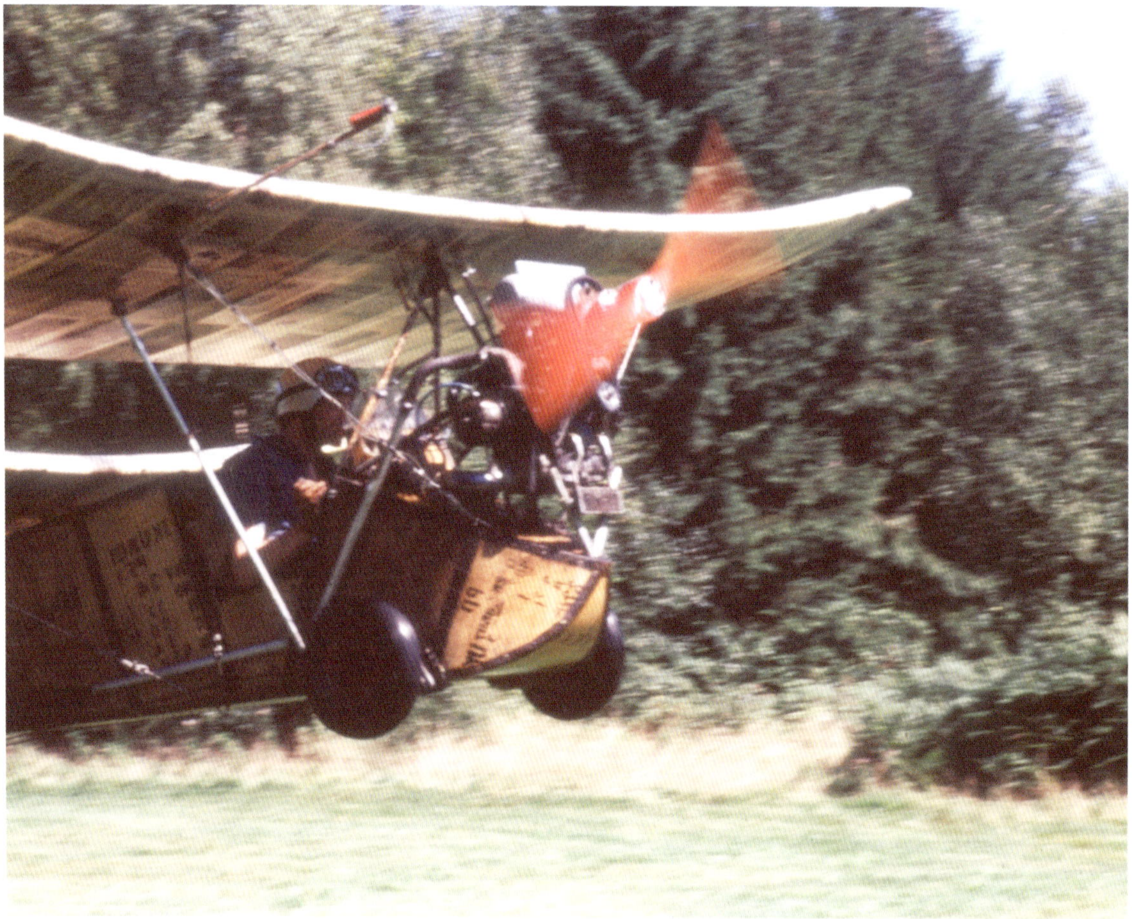

An aerial sensation… [Jo Newman]   right: Flying over the Super 8 camera. [Jo Newman]

my personal life had made me suicidal but it did give me the reckless edge I needed to get the plane off the ground! I confided my woes to the Flying Flea Squadron and, like Sirens singing, they said: 'Don't go back to Essex, stay here with us.'

Staying at Bill's was a blessed relief and I ended up staying the entire summer. Most of the squadron went back to their day jobs come Monday morning and I was alone for a lot of the time, fixing things. I lived in a Portakabin and on a couple of occasions I slept in the hangar with the plane. I read somewhere that the Wright brothers had camped under the wings of their plane when they carried out early trials and I realised it was exactly 100 years since the first flight.

Slowly the plane got better and the opportunities for flight, between repairs, became longer. I had adjusted the gearing by buying a smaller cog in a motorcycle shop to bolt onto the drive shaft. This seemed to give a little more power and I felt the plane lift off the ground more than three feet before I decelerated and landed again. I knew that I could get higher but evening was drawing in and I wanted to make sure there was enough light to film it with my super 8 camera before it broke again or was smashed up entirely. This was the first time I had put the plane back into the hangar unbroken so tomorrow looked like it was going to be the day.

It was a Sunday. The Flying Flea Squadron had all gone home ready for work the next day. Tony had hung on to see me three feet in the air and then he also had to leave. The only other person there was a 20 year old student, Joanne, who had come to help me out on her summer break. Even

Bill had to go off somewhere in the morning. As we pushed the plane off the field, I remembered all the different people who had helped me over the years. Apart from the Flying Flea Squadron, there were college technicians, friends, ex-girlfriends and my father who had died some years earlier. It was about ten years since I had bought Mignet's book and the only person present to witness the flight was someone who would have been only ten years old when I began. It was as if everyone had grown up and got a life while I stuck at it, trying to get my glorified go-kart to fly. The next day was going to be a Pyrrhic victory at best but it was no less exciting.

There was a slight breeze scheduled to get stronger towards lunchtime. We pushed the plane out of the hangar and discussed how Joanne would film it. As we stood next to the plane at the top the runway, Bill came by in his car. He was incredibly trusting and nonchalantly gave a few words of safety advice before he drove off and left the two of us alone on the airfield.

The undercarriage of my Flea was quite low so I was able to swing the propeller, climb in and reach out of the cockpit to throw out my own chocks. I looked down the hill and I could see Joanne positioned with the camera where we thought the plane might leave the ground. She gave me a wave to indicate that all was clear and the camera was working. I accelerated the engine to full throttle and slowly descended the hill. I quickly picked up speed and pulled back hard on the stick. I felt the plane lift but it wasn't very high and quickly the undercarriage touched the grassy slope of the other side. It couldn't climb faster than the gradient of the hill.

I carried on trundling along the ground, up and over the hill, and steered the plane into the edge of the runway where the longer grass slowed me down. I revved the engine to swing the plane around in an arc to face back up the runway. Joanne was out of view over the brow of the hill and I couldn't signal to her so I just had to assume she was ready. From this direction it was a bit tricky because there wasn't as much space to come to a stop. It was beginning to get a little breezy as I accelerated again and came over the hill, this time into the wind. I pulled back on the stick and felt the ground smooth out; the plane was leaving the ground! As I went past, I took a quick glance to my left to make sure that Joanne was filming – she was there but, to my surprise, I had to look down to see her. I was up!

I took another glance to my right and realised that I was at the same level as the tree branches. I don't know if I imagined it but I thought I was banking slightly to the right. I instinctively moved my stick a tiny amount and then it was time to come down before I ran out of runway. I decelerated slowly and landed quite heavily but without damage. When we processed the film, it confirmed that I had been higher than a garden shed!

We flew a couple more times so that Joanne could film it again and take some shots with her 35mm camera and then we buried the super 8 camera in the runway so that I could fly over it while Joanne used a remote control to film from underneath. Even with two remote leads joined together, I still felt quite close as I careered down the hill at her. We eventually stopped as we felt it get windier.

In the early evening Graham came back. The wind had died down and I was keen to show him how I had progressed. He waited with his video camera as I came over the hill. On maximum revs, as I pulled back the stick, there was a loud crunch and the engine revved very high – the propeller had come off. I had made a bad weld which snapped under the strain, shattering the blade into two pieces on the ground.

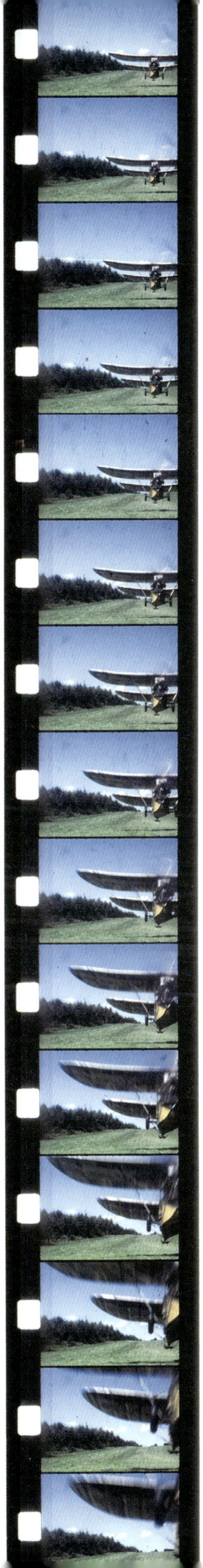

Secretly, I was a little relieved. The propeller had missed me when it came off but it takes a long time to make and I knew that I could not produce another one quickly. It was September, summer was over and the broken propeller was effectively my ticket out of there. It was addictive to keep trying to get higher and higher but I had achieved my goal and it was time to go home.

Because the squadron had had so much fun, the following year I was presented with a new propeller and the next summer I went back to the airfield. It was a short visit because the plane was scheduled to be in an art show a few days later. I arranged to meet Dan, a documentary film-maker, at the airfield so that he could film the plane flying. I was still going down the hill and taking off in the bottom of the dip. Dan said it would look better if he filmed from behind and caught me against the blue sky instead of the grass of the bank. To do this, I would need to keep the power on as I reached the top of the hill so that I was still flying. It was a manoeuvre I hadn't tried before because, by now, I was instinctively powering down as I reached the top; I climbed as the ground rose up with me. This time I reached the top of the hill and suddenly found myself climbing very steeply. I did what I had always done and decreased the power slowly – I fell like a brick from about four metres up. As I saw the ground coming up to meet me I instinctively held on to the sides of the cockpit to brace myself and felt the impact in my arm. It hurt for about an hour or so and then I was OK.

The aeroplane was relatively unharmed too. I thought I was going to smash the new propeller but the underneath of the fuselage hit the ground first. The suspension had bottomed out and the underneath of the cockpit had gouged a long hole in the grass. When it came to rest, I could see grass around my feet and assumed the floor had been ripped off with the impact. Afterwards, I discovered that it had only split but the forward momentum had pushed a long turf of grass through the split like a carpenter's plane takes a shaving of wood.

I was later told that what I had technically done was stall. I should have pushed the joystick forward to come down and left the spoon where it was. Tony's flying lessons did not cover going beyond the top of the hill. In effect, I had learnt how to take off but not how to land properly. I described my accident to a microlight pilot I met at the airfield one day who told me he had done a similar thing a few years ago. He had dropped from 5 metres and had been in hospital for several months.

The next summer, I repaired the cockpit floor and went back to the airfield. I was still having a problem with petrol coming from the air filter and realised that the valve timing was totally wrong. Combustion was happening at the wrong time in the engine and, instead of igniting all the petrol, some of it was being blown back. When I adjusted it, I realised as soon as I swung the propeller that it felt completely different since the compression was a lot higher. It had been giving a lot less than full power ever since the first time I used it. When I went down the hill the engine sounded different too and I could lift off the ground whichever way the wind was blowing. My flights were longer, more controlled but a lot closer to the ground. The incident the previous summer had cost me my nerve. I did a bit more filming from all angles before Mark came back with the trailer and we went home.

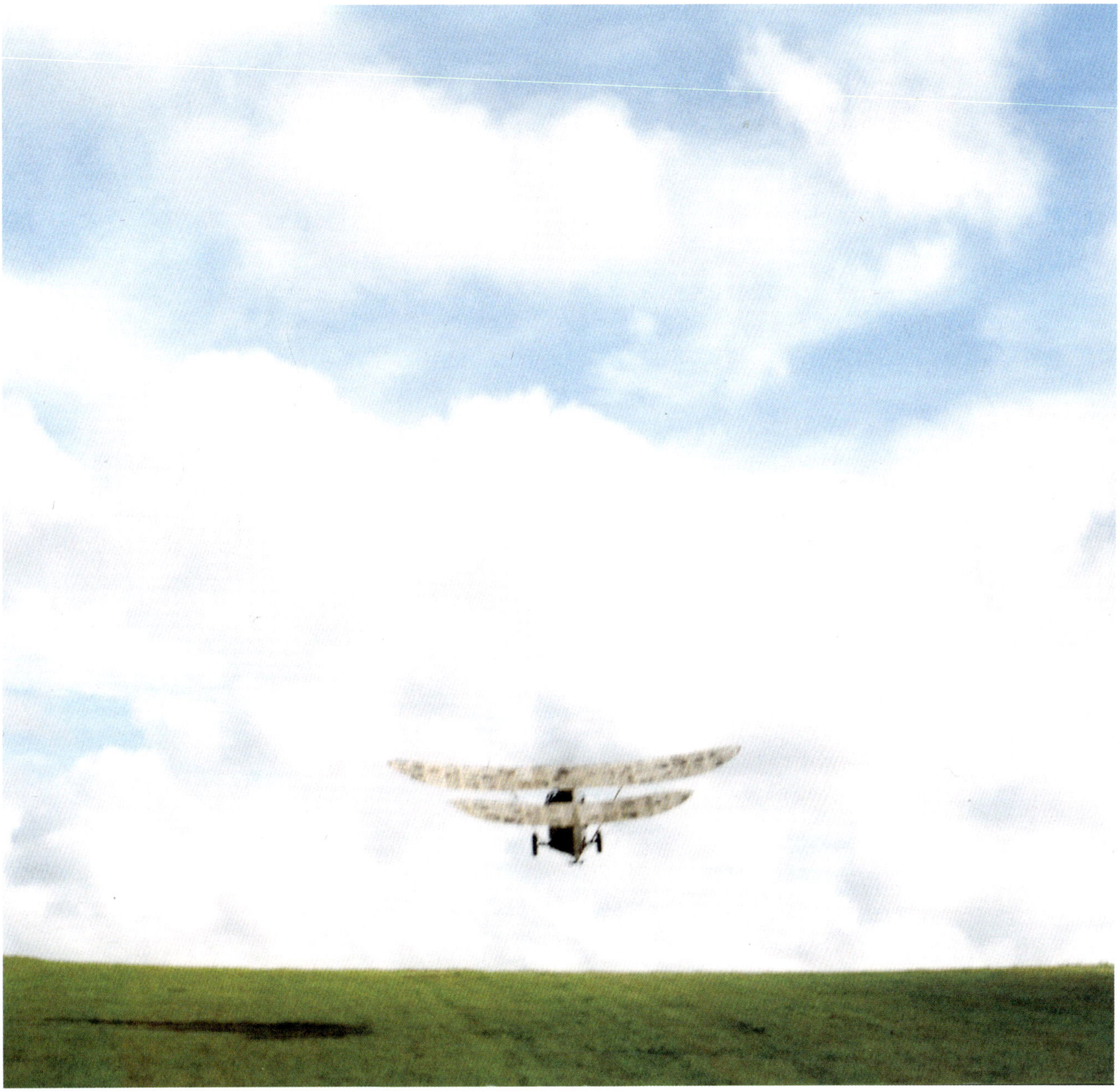

My highest flight – approximately 4 metres. I stalled and hit the ground a second later. [Jo Newman]

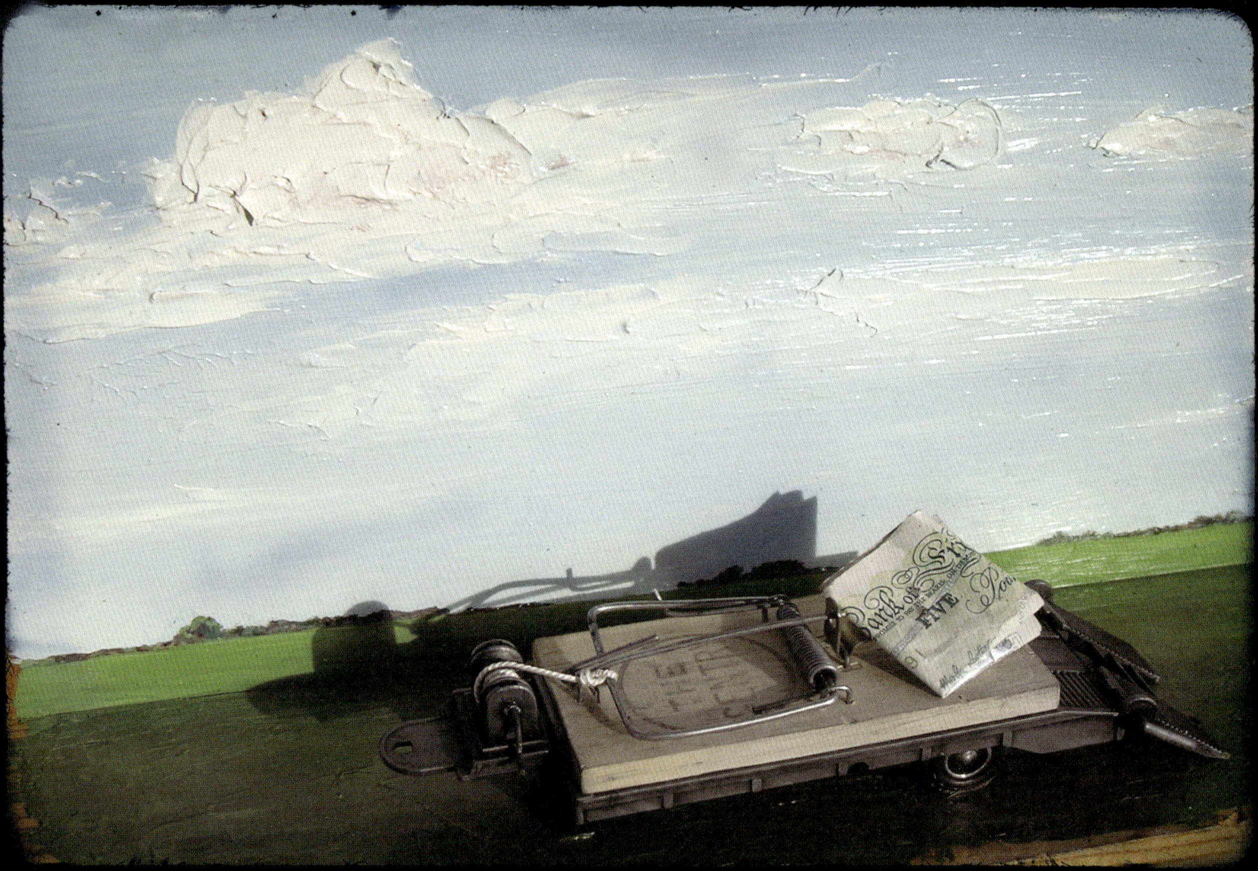
FIVE

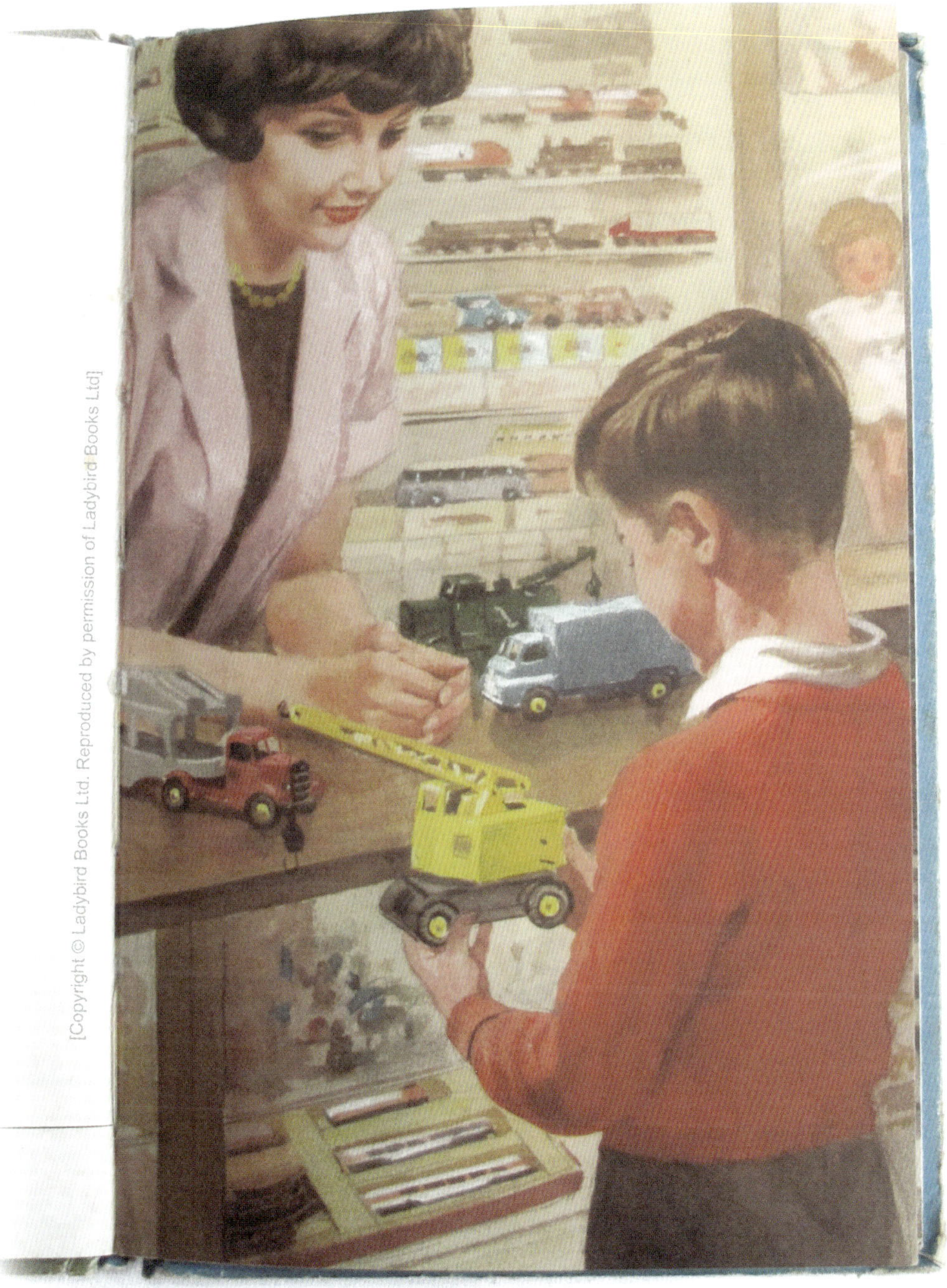

Transaction Transition

previous page: Offer Must End Soon. [Jo Newman]

None of the vehicles were ever sold but, in fairness, they were never made as a commodity. The other artist called Chris Dobrowolski has prices listed on his website. I don't know how successful he is at selling his work but I am rubbish. I spent a lot of my time trying to escape art college but, paradoxically, this in itself was a valuable learning experience. Escaping was born of the conceptual teaching I received there and it still informs my practice today. This academic influence is possibly why my work is still so painfully idealistic. In art college we learnt that contemporary art deals with loftier ideas and should therefore be raised above commerce. In practice, in the world outside college, it rarely is. A lot of well known contemporary artists nowadays are small companies with staff and overheads. Pressure is on them to manufacture and sell as much as possible to keep everyone in a job, pay their mortgages and feed their families.

Like so many financially unsuccessful contemporary artists I cling to the belief that it is my idealism that has trapped me in poverty. I scrutinise myself too much and constantly question my own motives. This has frequently led me into stupid, self-defeating situations that have perpetuated my love-hate relationship with the art world.

Not all collectors are super rich; some are just people with a small amount of disposable income. When someone like this wants to buy my work, I take it as a great compliment. I'm not a big name artist so I know it isn't an investment. This type of collector wants the work because they like it. A typical example of this sort of collector was Mrs Morrison. The Morrisons had seen a piece of mine commissioned by my local gallery in a nearby park. They asked someone from the gallery to approach me about doing something for their garden. I arranged a consultation. Already in their garden, impossible to miss, was a ten foot sculpture of an iguana made from welded steel.

'That's our other commission,' said Mrs Morrison proudly.

She carried on to the corner of the garden where there was a mature tree and a wire cage for her old vegetables and grass cuttings.

'This is where we want to commission you to make something. We've tried growing vegetables here but it's too shaded.'

I tried to find something positive to say and while I stood there looking around me I happened to rest a hand on the wire container. Mrs Morrison continued, 'Obviously, we'll tidy it up a bit'.

Then she noticed my hand on the cage and thought I was trying to make a point with it.

'No, the compost has to stay.'

In short, my brief was to make something that would compete visually with a ten foot long welded steel iguana, a bonfire and compost heap. There was also a clear understanding that from its very conception this commission was always second choice to potatoes. Instead of walking away like any sensible career-artist, I came away thinking:

'What a challenge.'

I spent the next couple of days at my desk with a sketch book pondering the different aspects of the garden. I was finding it hard to find an 'inner need'. What was my motivation? I wondered if I could address my fears about commercial artwork in Mrs Morrison's garden so that I could maintain my artistic integrity. Then I realised that I was spending so long contemplating these issues that the project probably wasn't going to be economically viable. I thought I had better call her and find out exactly how much I was getting paid: 'We were thinking £800.'

It wasn't a lot but I felt relieved. Then I had to be honest with myself and accept that the money mattered. It seemed disingenuous to pretend it didn't. Once I accepted this, it was easy to develop the work. I decided to make something that belonged in a garden already; something that wouldn't look out of place next to Mrs Morrison's compost heap. I decided to make a bird box. But no ordinary bird box. This one would address my issues with commercial art.

Mr Smith, my parents' next door neighbour, used to make bird boxes and I remember him once telling me that the ideal size for the entrance hole was the diameter of a two pence coin: big enough for bluetits to get in but too small for the common sparrow. Consequently, I made Mrs Morrison's bird box entirely from two pence coins. Since the coins were copper, the box was also weather-proof and ideal for the garden. I made two. As well as addressing the commercial context, they were also quite attractive objects and I felt that I had reached an interesting point in my artistic development. I took a photo and posted it to the lucky Mrs Morrison. A few days later she left a message on my answer machine:

'We don't like them.'

At the same time, I was invited as one of a group of artists to take part in an art trail in Hoek van Holland. Each artist was invited to find a setting they found inspiring and given ample time to go back to the studio and come up with an outdoor art piece. As well being given more artistic freedom, this project also had a lot more status attached to it. The organisers explained that, at the opening event, they were going to hire a special electric train to transport all of the visitors and artists from one art piece to the next. I had never heard of an art project with its own train before. The fee was £3,000.

£3,000 was a lot of money to me and I felt it warranted a lot of thinking time. Hoek van Holland is at the tip of mainland Europe. I once took the train from there all the way to Poland and it was possible to get a direct train all the way to Moscow. Since the Channel Tunnel however, this sea/rail terminal had become just a station for local trains and the huge international platforms were empty and silent. I planned to make an elaborate model train set in a railway carriage on the platform. I thought it could be an interesting psycho-geographic piece; a kind of homage to my father and his journey to Siberia by train sixty years before. I was very proud of my proposal and took a long time making a professional presentation of it. When I gave this to the organisers they asked me:

'Could you do it for three hundred? We couldn't get three thousand… Our funding fell through.'

I threw the £3,000 idea in the dustbin and sent them a picture of Mrs Morrison's bird boxes. I had found a children's petting zoo in Hoek and I told them I would put them there. Before I took them to Holland, I fitted the bird boxes with speakers and wired them up to a cassette tape player. I recorded myself saying the word 'cheap' over and over again. It was recorded onto an ordinary C60 cassette and the machine played both

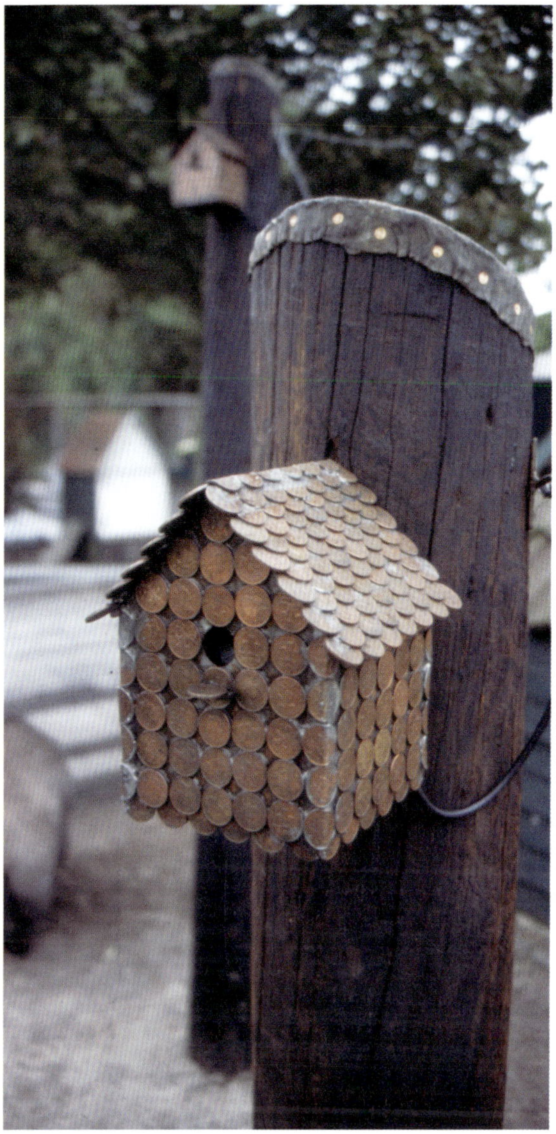

Bird box made from two pence coins soldered together.

C60 cassette of my voice saying 'Cheap'

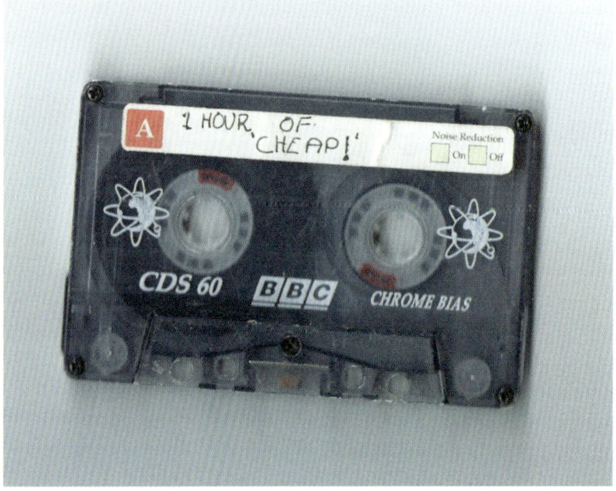

sides of it automatically and in stereo. The bird boxes were installed in an enclosure with a very old Vietnamese pot-bellied pig who was blind and deaf so wouldn't be disturbed by the cheaping.

The opening ceremony was held in an exhibition space on the edge of Hoek. Afterwards we were all invited to board the special train to view the artworks. I was particularly excited about the train – it was the only thing left that made it seem like a serious art event. I stepped outside the venue and was confronted by a giant blue plastic, seaside 'Noddy' train complete with funnel and bell.

At the children's petting zoo, the mayor and other dignitaries gathered around the pig enclosure for the curator to explain the artwork. I didn't realise that the Dutch don't say 'cheap' when they want to represent the sound of a bird, they 'chirrup' instead. The curator started to explain that 'cheap' was a similar sound to 'sheep' and this was a reference to its location on a children's farm. She eventually looked across at me for confirmation and asked 'Is that correct Chris?'

To which I replied 'No, it says cheap because you didn't give us the money you promised!'

As it turned out, the cheaping bird boxes became my most commercially successful piece of art. Before I sent the work to Holland, I had arranged for Mrs Morrison to come to my studio to see if we could find another way to fulfil her commission. Before she arrived, I installed the talking bird boxes outside the studio. On our way past, I nonchalantly explained that they were the finished piece she had rejected destined, instead, for an international exhibition in Holland. On hearing this, Mrs Morrison suddenly changed her mind and we agreed that, after the sculpture trail in Holland, I would bring them back for her garden. As far as know, they are still there, cheaping to Mrs Morrison's compost.

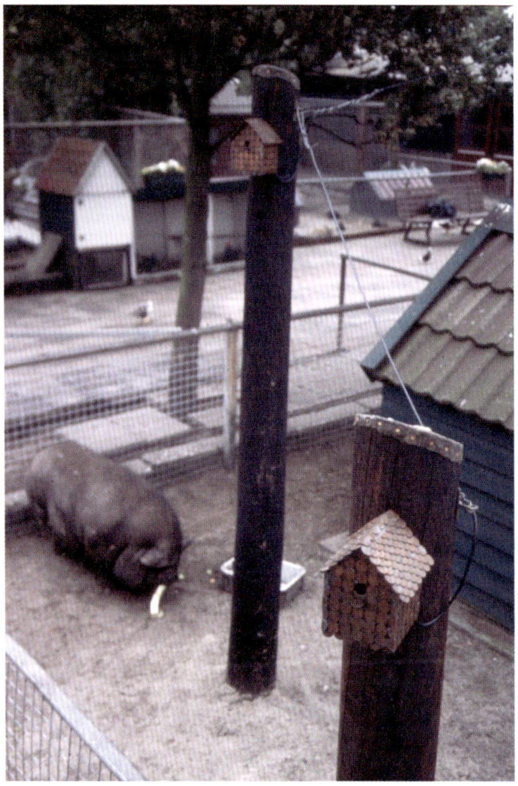

'Cheap' installed in the pig pen at the children's petting zoo. The deaf and blind Vietnamese pot bellied pig is in the background. He moved by sense of smell.

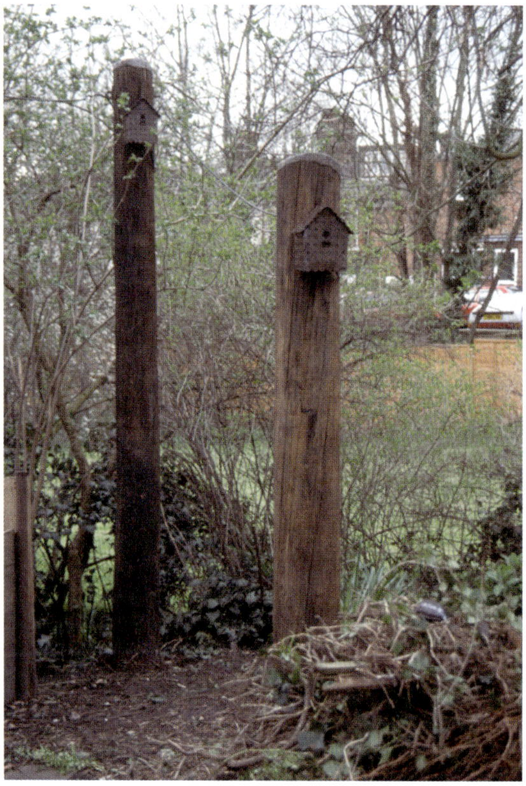

'Cheap' and Mrs Morrisson's and bonfire. The edge of her compost container is just visible on the left.

Landscape Escape No. 2 (the tank) was in a group show in London and a few days before the closing, one of the organisers told me that Charles Saatchi had been along and seemed interested in my work. Unfortunately, the warehouse containing his art collection burnt down the very next day. According to her, if it hadn't been for this distraction, he would have come back with his cheque book.

It probably wouldn't have happened but it made me think about what my reaction would have been. At the time Charles Saatchi's name was linked with many successful artists and he was key to making their careers. Arguably, he was the Establishment and, in the words of the girlfriend I was with at the time, I would have 'sold out to the man'. I consoled myself with the fact that I at least didn't have to deal with that moral dilemma.

By coincidence, an old friend of mine was in a similar position. In my friend's case, however, Saatchi had been to the exhibition and, cheque book in hand, did want to buy his work. My friend rang me up to ask my advice on what to do. I told him all about my near miss with 'the man' and how I didn't envy his decision but I would give the matter some thought. I ended up giving it a lot of thought and we made lots of phone calls over the course of the day looking at the situation from all possible perspectives. Finally, I came to the conclusion that he wasn't going to change the world by not selling his work. Satisfied that this was the right decision, I said goodnight and put the phone down.

My friend had a very interesting day job – he was technician to a very successful contemporary artist – and, as well as seeking moral guidance from me, he also asked his boss what to do.

'If you start picking and choosing who you will and won't sell your work to,' he said, 'pretty soon you will find yourself staring at the walls of your studio not selling your work to anyone.'

As my friend shared this information with me I realised it quite accurately described about ten years of my life.

Like most artists, I have done a lot of different jobs to make ends meet. One of them was as a modeller for a company that made toy cars and animal ornaments. It wasn't a factory; it was the place where the original models were designed. Once the model had been approved by the client, the original was shipped to China for mass production and then shipped back to be sold in the shops. In the hierarchy of the organisation, I was at the very bottom. One of my first jobs was a model of a duck followed by its ducklings crossing a hump back bridge. I wasn't trusted to make the duck; or allowed to do the ducklings. My job was to make the humpback bridge. On other occasions I was given the job of finishing off and modifying pieces that someone else had made. This often happened when the client wasn't happy with certain details. The following is a typical briefing from my boss for a model of two West Highland terrier puppies sitting in an old-fashioned school satchel:

Hi Chris, the client has been to see the new sculpture from the cute puppy series and we'd like a few alterations. Firstly, we don't like this puppy's face so if you could hacksaw its head off and replace it with this puppy's head that would be great. It's very important that the new head is looking upwards at an angle of 45 degrees to meet the customer's eye. Oh – and one last thing – We're not sure about both the puppies having both paws hanging over the side of the bag. Maybe just the one puppy with the one paw like so.'

He proceeds to snap the puppy's paws off:

'… After all, Chris, we don't want it to look kitsch.'

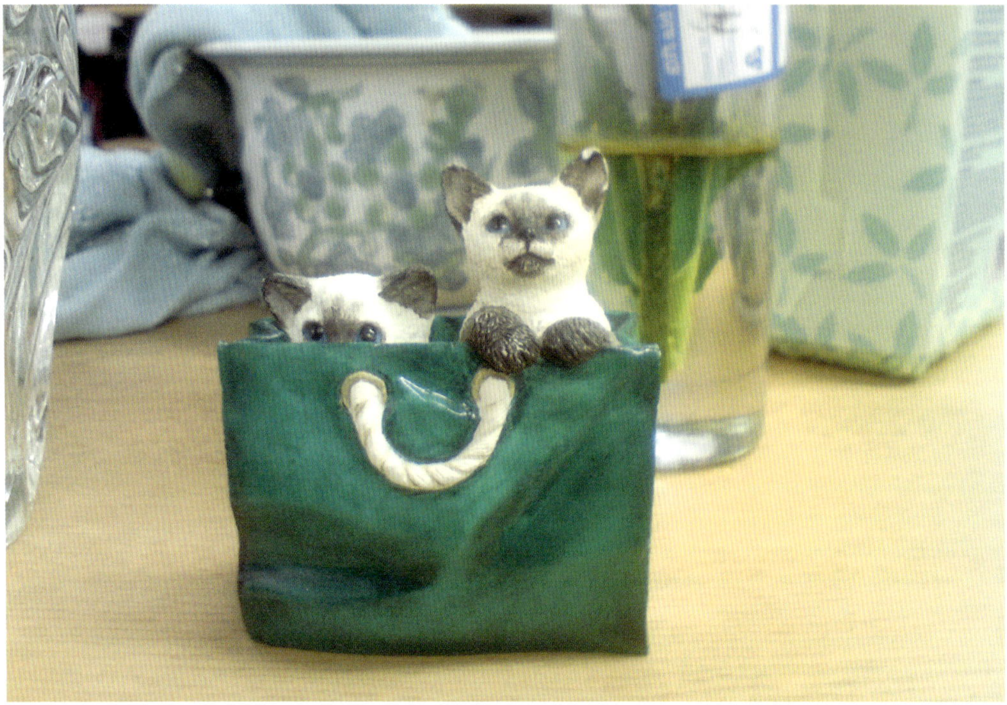

A typical example of kitcsh / not kitsch ornament I found in a charity shop.

Everyone who worked there was highly skilled and dedicated. They were also in complete agreement on which products they were proud of and which ones constituted bad model-making kitsch. I could not tell the difference. My years of art college training had absolutely no relevance here at all. Each model animal was referred to as a 'sculpture'. The original job was advertised as SCULPTOR WANTED. I could never bring myself to use the term in relation to these sentimental representations of animals but my conceited use of the term 'ornament' was met with laughter by the entire studio. There was limited room for self-expression; our main job was to make miniature replicas of things from the real world. We were not allowed to show any evidence of human contact with the object and were constantly smoothing out and hiding imperfections. After a mould had been taken from the original plasticine figure, a plastic version was cast. This would be sandpapered and worked with tiny files for hours and hours until every blemish had vanished. I can remember this part of the job being the most depressing, even the word used to describe this process annoyed me – it was called 'fettling'.

At the same time, my friend was working alongside a team of sixty or so other graduates making art for the successful contemporary artist. I told my friend about my world of 'fettling' and I was surprised to hear that they did exactly the same thing on some of their artworks too. Their current project was an installation in the form of a collection. There were thousands of small items mounted behind glass. Each was made from the same material and cast in the same way as my animal ornaments. Fettling however was not the only similarity. Even while it was in production this art piece was attracting a lot of interest. More than one gallery wanted it for their collection. As a result each component was reproduced several times so that the artist could sell it more than once.

The art pieces that my friend worked on represented the zenith of the contemporary art market but with this insight into the dispassionate production process, it didn't seem any more special than my plastic puppies. They were churning out stuff to sell just like we were.

I had very little affection for the model animals we produced but I quite liked the model cars. On one occasion I was allowed to make a bell for a fire engine. On another, I was told to make the dashboard for the model of an old truck. The person in charge of the model was very precious about it and I had to re-fettle the one and a half centimetre dashboard several times until he was satisfied. I don't think the final model even had opening doors; the only way to admire my work was through the tiny cab windows.

I think my fondness for the model cars came from having my own toy cars as a boy. I still had some of them from my childhood in the loft at my parent's house along with an old wooden garage that my dad had made for my older brother. It had been made from spare pieces of mahogany and oak that my dad had come across at work and he had made a nice job of it. The garage had a road leading to a rooftop car park and I thought the whole thing would make an interesting coffee table. I lifted it up on legs and installed lights so you could see inside. One of the rooms was a car showroom and it needed a few choice toy cars to go in it which gave me the perfect excuse to buy old toy cars from car boot sales.

After working for the model company I was indifferent to the pristine, highly detailed new toy cars and was drawn to ones that had been bashed about and scratched; what they call in the antique trade patina. The scratches, cracks and broken parts were evidence of their history. I started to place these impressionistic cars in landscapes painted in old wooden boxes and crates. I am quite a crude painter but it suited this context quite well. The paint looked like paint not a photograph; the boxes looked like boxes and not display cases and the toy cars looked like toy cars not slick models.

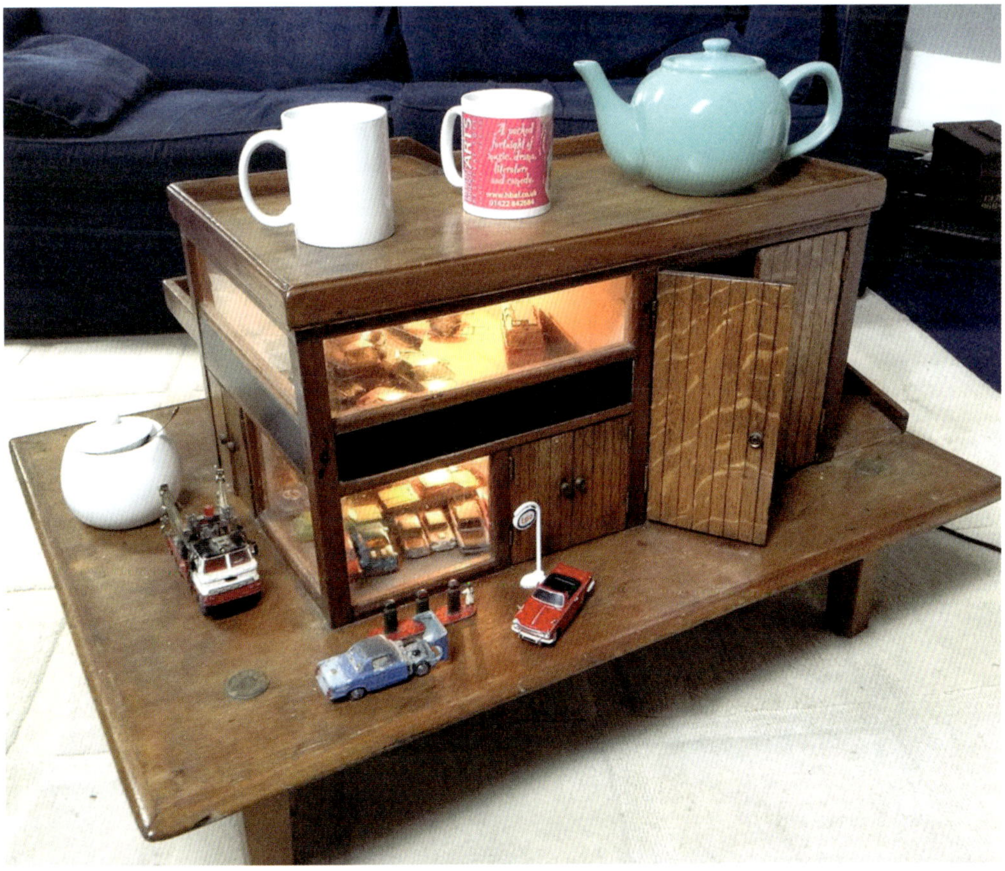

Wooden toy garage that my father built converted into a coffee table. [Priscila Buschinelli]

I was starting to make things that people might actually want to buy. Dangerous commercial territory. To begin with, I convinced myself that this body of work was not me 'selling out' but me growing up. As with Mrs Morrisson's commission, I decided to address the issue head on. I began to make the subject matter of each box 'selling out' and I set about making an entire show in which all of the pieces tried to sell themselves in a deliberately crass way.

I called the show Offer Must End Soon. The poster featured a toy trailer with a mousetrap fixed to it set in a painted box landscape. The bait on the mouse trap was a five pound note. A scalextric track followed the edge of the gallery wall. A large lorry drove around every time somebody came into the space. As it passed underneath the paintings on the wall a recording of my voice came out of a speaker as though through a loud-hailer:

'Buy my painting… Buy my painting… Buy my painting.'

Another piece was a representation of a car boot sale built on a cut down version of a decorating table. On it was an oil painting of a field. In this scene I placed a row of toy cars. In front of each was a miniature decorating table. Each one of these stalls was selling something that was in the painting. One had a few nails and screws and bits and pieces including a door bell switch. It was totally out of scale but it had a handwritten sign on it that said:

Giant switch 20p.

If the switch was pressed, it activated a cassette player connected to a 'giant speaker' on the next tiny car boot sale stall. This one said:

'C'mon make me an offer, don't make me take it all back home with me.'

This was quite a genuine plea because I really couldn't afford to take all this work back to my studio. Another piece was made from an old hearing aid mounted on the back of a toy lorry. It was made of Bakelite and had a lovely anachronistic logo that said, 'Ardent – for deaf ears.' It had a speaker attachment that amplified sound through what looked like a telephone receiver. I connected this to another tape recording of my voice. In this one, I imitated the way people talk to an elderly relative who is hard of hearing:

'BUYYY… MYYYYY… PAAAINTING! BUYYY… MYYYYY… PAAAINTING.'

The gallery of work was quite noisy but popular. A friend of mine asked the curator what the response had been like and he said:

'Very good! Everyone leaves with a smile on their face! Oh, apart from two people. Charles Saatchi and Nigella Lawson… they didn't find it amusing at all.'

Afterwards, my friend told me it was probably a waste of time trying to sell my work in the first place. As an unknown artist, there was a limit to the amount I could ask for my work. I spent too many hours making each piece and I would never be able to ask a price that would reflect this. For the amount of time I invested in the work, I needed to be selling to people with several thousands of pounds in spare cash:

'Chris, I see this type of person at work all the time. I don't know the exact reason, maybe it's the money that makes them that way, or they have to be that way to get the money but, in my experience, every single one of them has been a cunt. Even if you could start making a living from selling your work, you would have to deal with cunts on a regular basis and I know you wouldn't like it.'

Staring at the walls of my studio was lonely as well as financially unrewarding. It was clear that I needed to find another way of disseminating my work.

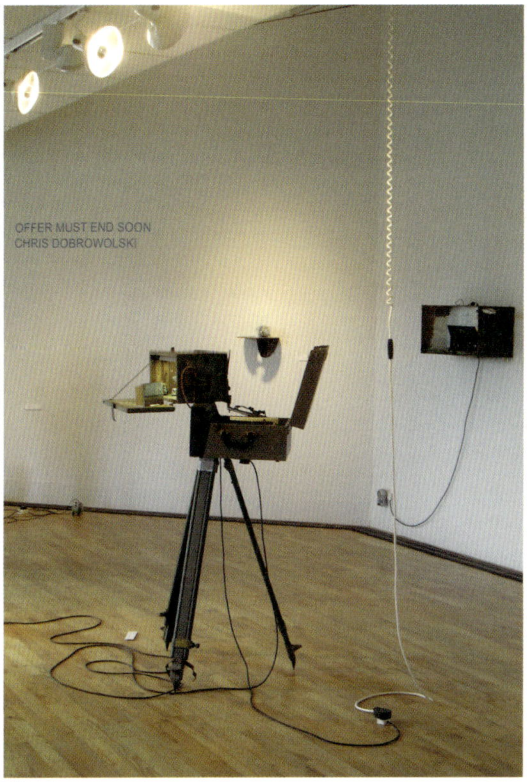

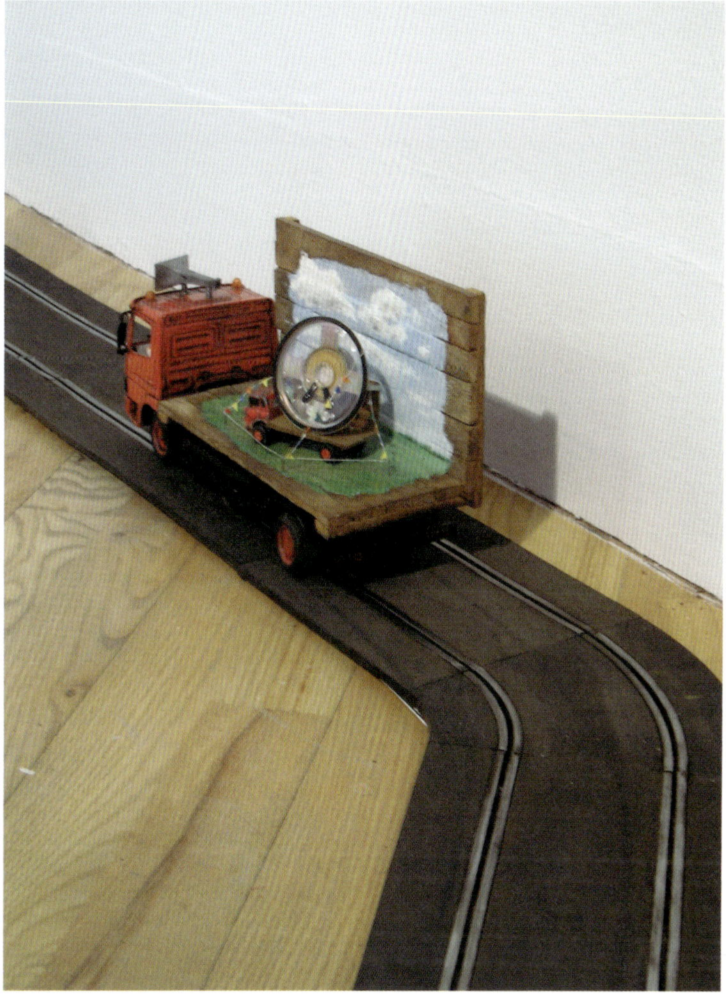

above: Overall shot of Offer Must End Soon – Essex University Gallery (Art Exchange). [Jo Newman]

right: 'Buy My Painting' [Jo Newman]

below: 'Dont make me take it all back home with me'. [Jo Newman]

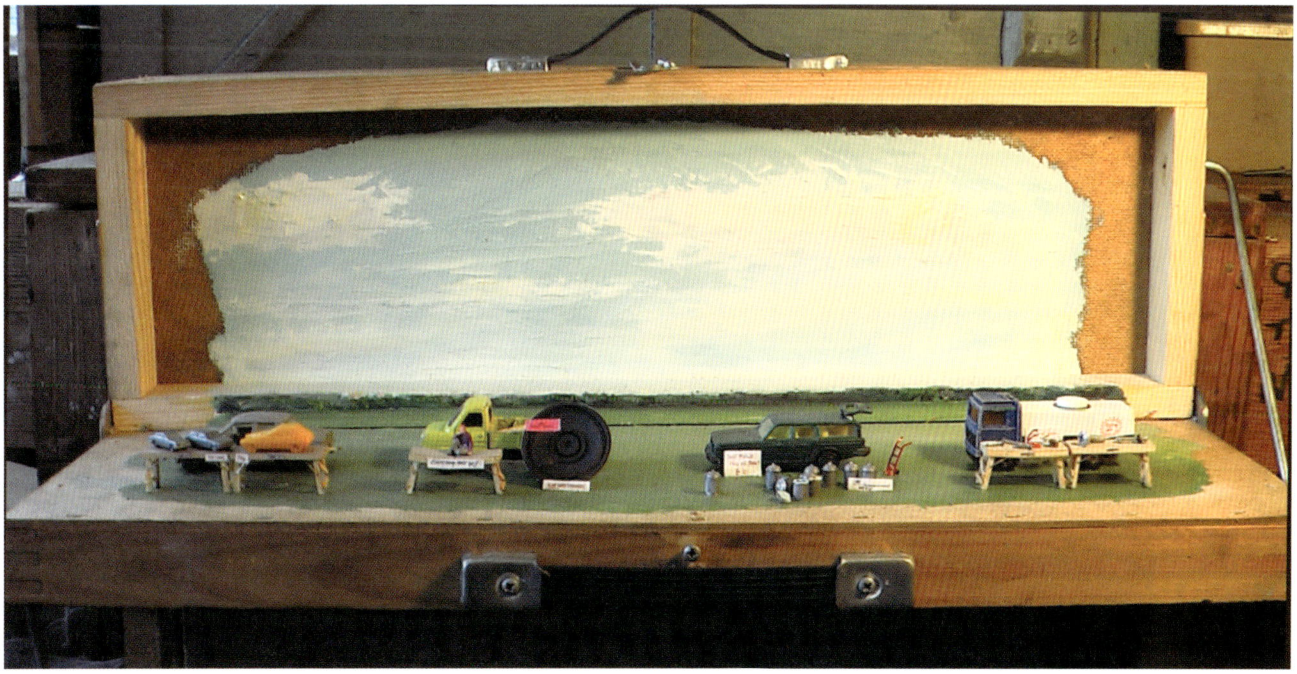

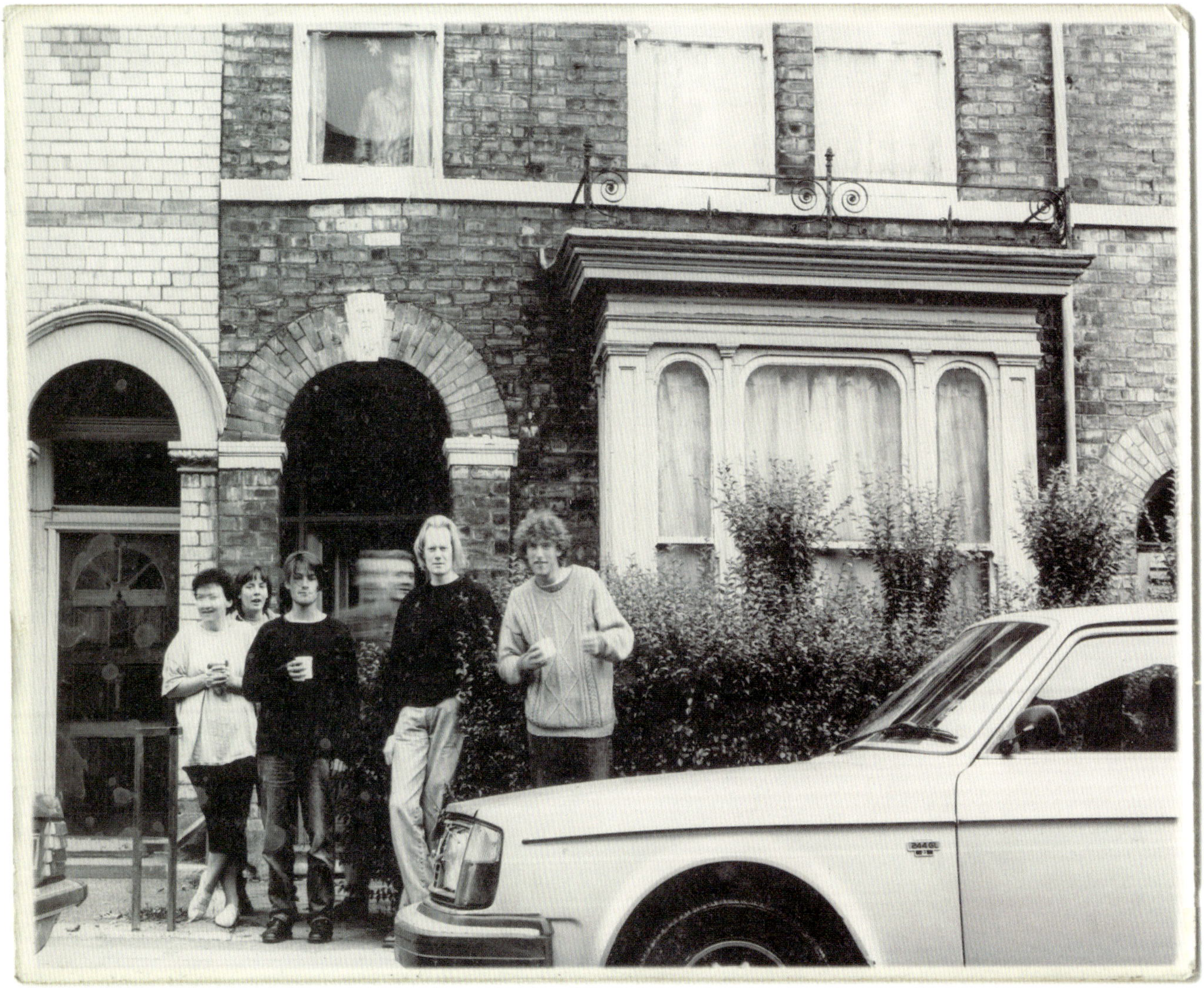

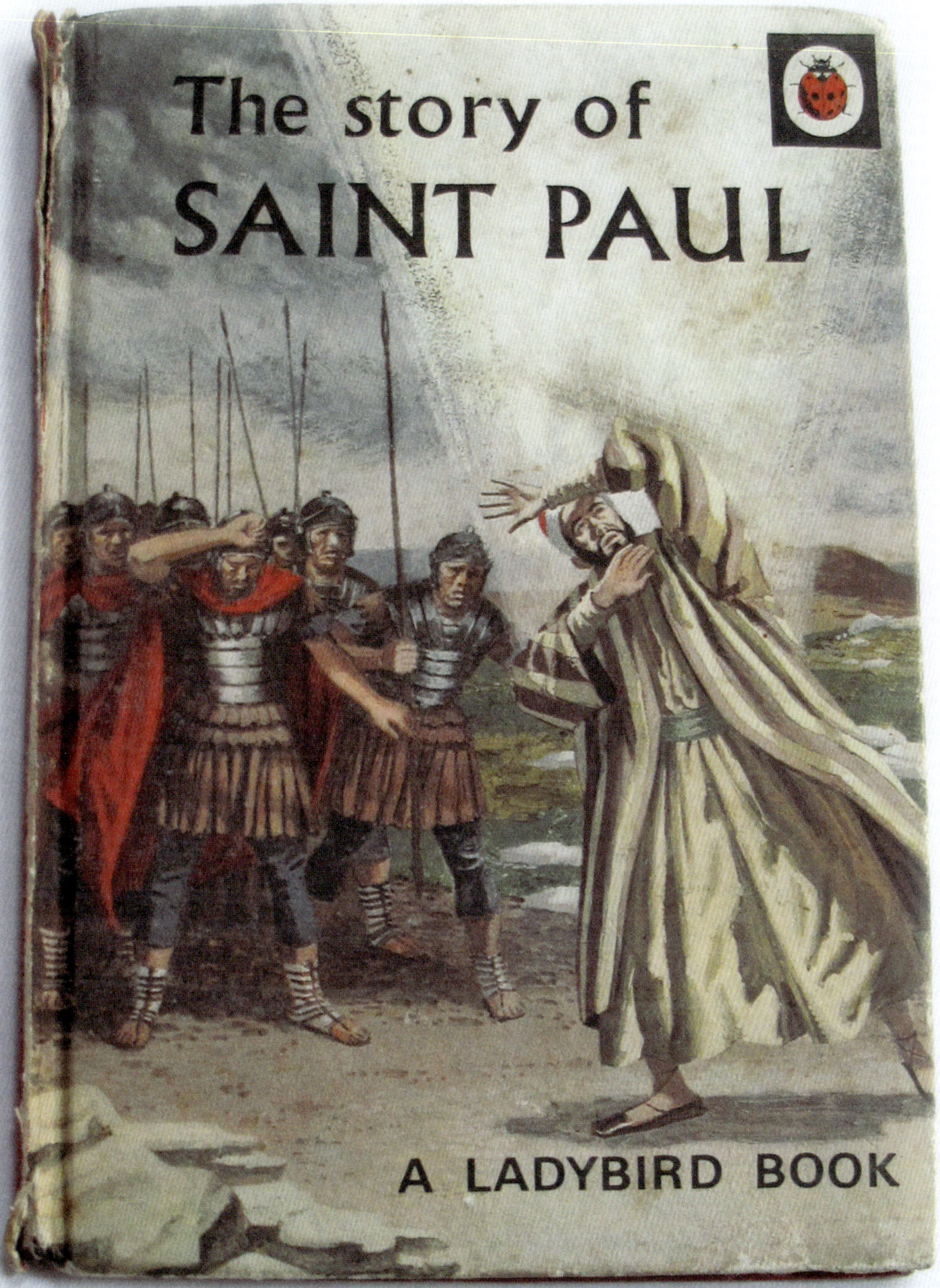

Lecture… Theatre

previous page: The occupants of 56 Park Grove. Including Eddie and Leo. [Leo Hazelrigg]

In my last two years in Hull, I shared a house at 56 Park Grove. It was a typical Victorian house divided into bedsits. My bedsit always reminded me of the poem Mr Bleaney by Phillip Larkin. The poem stuck in my mind because Larkin had lived and worked in the next street in Hull for a large part of his life. In Mr Bleaney, Larkin describes a miserable bedsit that used to belong to someone else. The landlady refers to it as Mr Bleaney's room and his presence still pervades the space. The new lodger is left with a morbid sense of inevitability as he stubs out his cigarette in the same miserable ash tray.

56 Park Grove had not been decorated since the days of Mr Bleaney. We were all art students and my flatmates included Eddie and Leo. We never locked the doors to our bedsits and turned it into a shared house which meant that there wasn't a communal sitting room. We would try to cram into the kitchen of the three person flat on the second floor but, eventually, we discovered that the best room for socialising was the bathroom at the top of the house. It was a ridiculously large bathroom and, as well as a bath and a toilet, the room had a coffee table, dressing table, armchair and, eventually, a three seat sofa. We would often congregate here after a night out at the Polar Bear pub and sometimes we would entertain guests by showing them my Super 8 films. They were silent films so we picked some accompanying music from our vinyl record collections. It was my job to explain what the films were about and why I had made the vehicles. They became spontaneous performance lectures.

Three years after graduation, some ex-students from Hull that included Leo organised an exhibition in South London and invited me to be in it. I was living in Essex at the time so London sounded unfeasibly glamorous. The venue, it transpired, was a squat with a vegetarian café and art gallery that had been used for raves. In exchange for using the gallery, my friends were asked to organise a 'Café Night' to raise funds for the squat. Leo told me to bring my Super 8 films along to entertain people with my stories. I refused. Leo explained that 'Café Night' wasn't such a big deal and that hardly anyone ever turned up. It was just an excuse for old friends to see the films again – like a family watching their home movies.

The night of my presentation, I went to London with an old film projector and a carrier bag of LPs and films. When I got to the venue, a new age traveller had set up camp on the forecourt in an ancient coach. One of its windows had been kicked in and replaced with a sheet of corrugated iron. It looked as though it had crashed into the building. The finishing touch was a crooked hillbilly chimney belching out smoke from a stove inside. As we surveyed the scene, a friend asked sarcastically if I was going to put the gig on my CV. Sadly, that's exactly what I had been hoping to do.

I went upstairs and began to set up my film projector. Slowly the room filled with about forty people I had never met in my life before. I spent about an hour showing the films and talking about my work. I had a lot of nervous energy and managed to give explanations whilst spooling on the next film. There was a synergy between my antiquated film projector, my temperamental vehicles and my nervous, stumbling presentation style. Everyone thought it was part of an act. A few years later in south London, I was approached by a slightly intimidating stranger who said:

'I know you!… You did that talk!… That was one of the best Café Nights we ever had.'

With new found confidence in my presentation skills, I became a frequent Visiting Lecturer giving lectures in art colleges about the vehicles I had built to escape from art college. Over several years, my lecture developed into a kind of show. I even had a finale – a musical instrument made from an old tool box with a car radiator fixed to the front. On the outside, it was covered in different car lights connected to car horns and wired up to a small keyboard and car battery. It could only play one song, Tequila by The Champs. Its limited capabilities were mainly down to the fact that it was impossible to tune the car horns.

To find the notes I went to the scrap yard with my friend Steve. I had no musical talent whatsoever and had no idea what notes we needed so Steve brought along an old school recorder and the notes written on a piece of paper. I climbed up the stacks of old cars with a car battery to set off the horns and Steve stayed on the ground to find each note on the recorder. Looking at his finger position and the scrap of paper he would then work out which note it was:

'No, semi-tone too high. Let's try the Cortina over there.'

Each note in my finale machine made a brake light or indicator flash. There was one note in Tequila that we could never find, it was just too high for any car horn. As a substitute, I connected the note on the keyboard to a car alarm siren which also triggered a windscreen washer and sprayed water into the audience.

One summer, the Director of my local arts centre, Anthony Roberts, organised a venue at the Edinburgh Fringe Festival. The venue was an old Routemaster bus that Anthony described as the 'Fringe of the Fringe'. Initially, I thought a bus didn't sound that appealing but there was an obvious link with my vehicles so I made an application to be part of 'Dr Roberts' Magic Bus' with my show 'Landscape, Seascape, Skyscape, Escape'. After rejecting my application, Anthony kindly gave me some feedback:

'You're not ready Chris. The Edinburgh Fringe can be a harsh, critical place. There may only be five people in your audience but two of them could be critics for the Guardian or the Scottish Herald. The Edinburgh Fringe is full of deluded people who convince themselves they are funny or interesting and they are going to get discovered. They spend a fortune and then come home demoralised. You have been doing your show in art colleges so you've only ever had a "soft" audience.'

As consolation and to give me some experience of a theatre audience, he offered me a gig at the arts centre the following week. Thursday night was experimental performance night with an average audience of about ten. I managed to get ninety people to turn up. I suddenly looked a lot more popular and little less deluded. A couple of days later I was summoned into Anthony's office:

'I've been giving the idea of you coming to Edinburgh some more thought. We want to challenge the formulaic conventions of the Edinburgh Fringe and your show fits the bill. To start with, it's too long and listening to you for two hours is certainly quite challenging. Ordinarily, it would be commercial suicide to send such a show to Edinburgh but our venue isn't ordinary so, Chris, you can be as deluded as you like – you're on the bus!'

In Edinburgh my audiences started very small but gradually improved so that, towards the end of the festival, I was filling the bus. I had more good reviews than bad ones and, in the context of

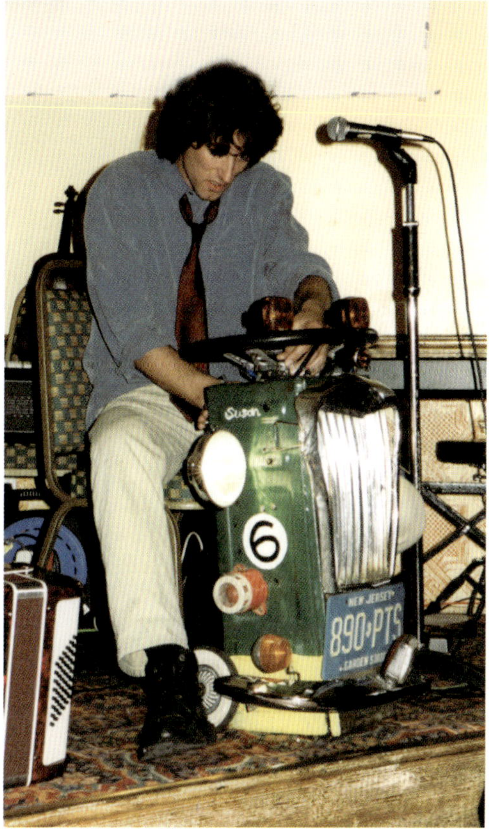

above: Playing the Tequila machine. [Clare Allen]

below: Dr Roberts' Magic Bus, the Meadows, Edinburgh Festival Fringe. Waiting to go on stage. [Natalie L'Herroux]

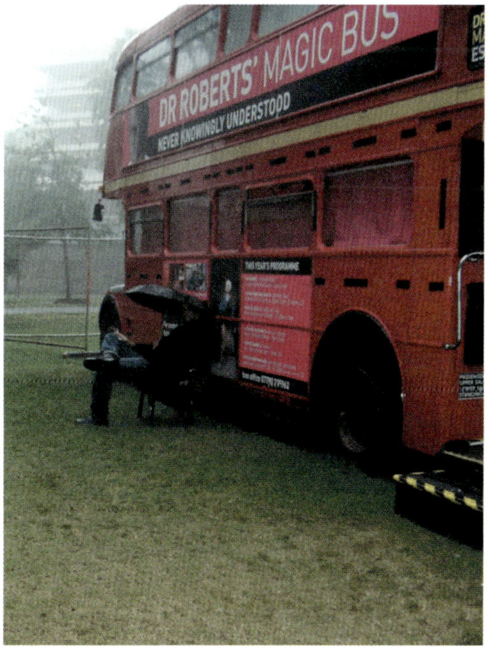

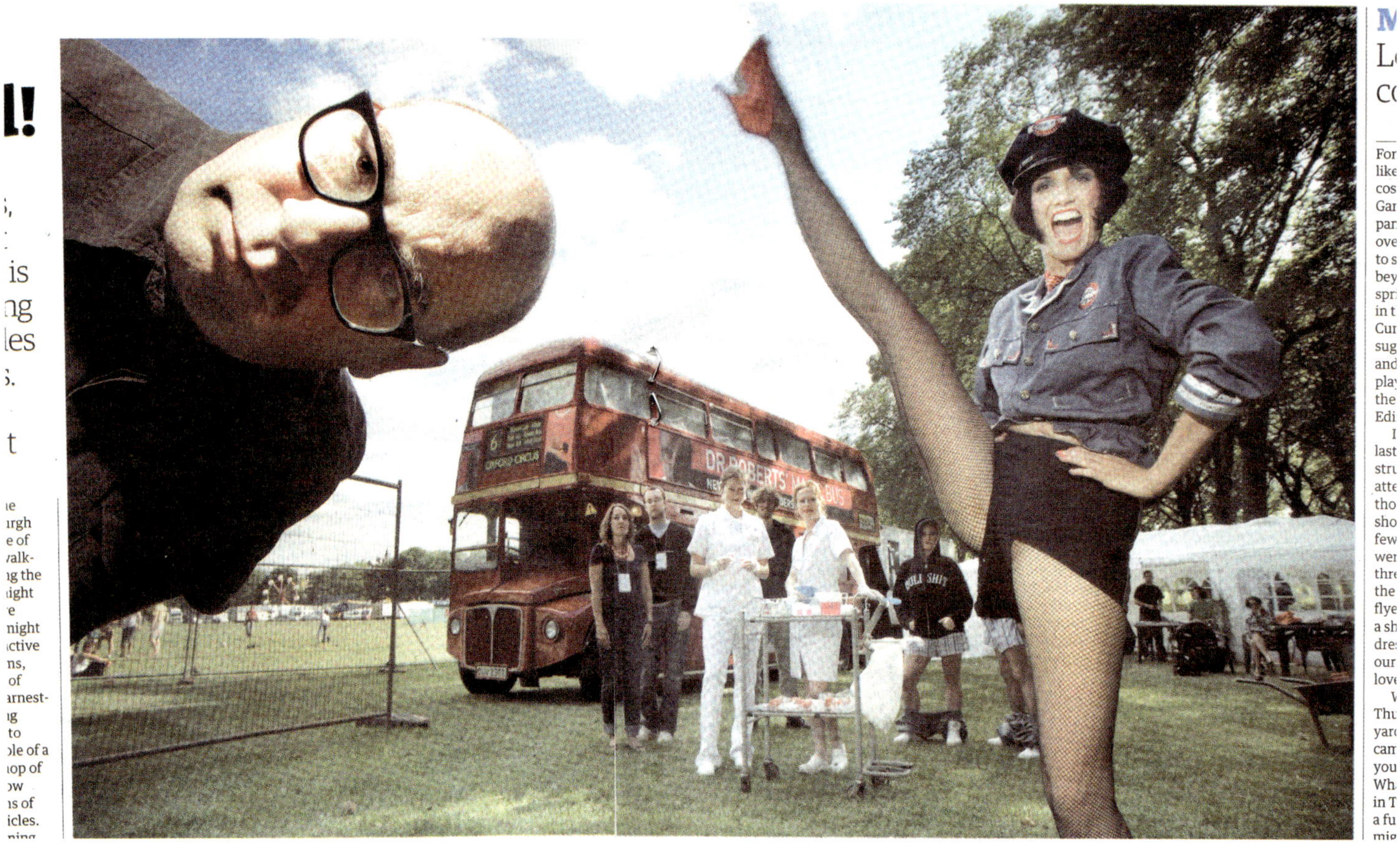

Anthony and some of the performers on Dr Roberts' Magic Bus, Edinburgh Festival 2006. I'm at the very very back between the dental hyginists underneath Miss High Leg Kick's leg. [Guardian newspaper 10.8.06 Murdo McLeod]

Edinburgh, this meant the show was a success. I couldn't exactly say I was discovered in Edinburgh but I handed out my phone number a few times and, when it was all over, I waited for the offers to come in. My first job came almost immediately. Anthony said: 'You like vehicles Chris, I bet you'd like to drive the bus back to Essex.'

Then a theatre company contacted me by phone: 'Hello, are you the guy who did the show about making things? Do you wanna earn some cash making some shelves for our office?'

Then I met a theatre producer called Paul Bourne. Paul didn't mind speaking his mind and was incredibly confident and self-assured. To my surprise, he wanted to discuss a possible collaboration:

'As you know I am a theatre producer and theatre is my passion but I only work in theatre for 90% of my time. For the other 10% I work with business but, let me tell you Chris, the money is reversed! I make 90% of my money from business and it's this side of my operations where you fit in.'

He took a quick look around my living space before he continued:

'If this plan works we might be able to improve on this for a start.'

I knew absolutely nothing about business. In my entire artistic career, I had never even made enough money to pay tax. I was certainly not someone you would approach for business advice. Maybe he had done an internet search and got me muddled up with the other Chris Dobrowolski. But no, it was definitely me he wanted:

'I do management training specialising in personnel development. I have several clients in this country; one is a bank, another one a brewery, but I also have other contacts all over the world. I teach them about creativity, communication and thinking differently about their business. I'm working on a workshop at the moment called 'Re-evaluating Success' and I think you would be perfect. My clients are professional people who are used to digesting sophisticated business presentations. All you have to do is give your vehicles presentation and, with your lack of sophistication or professional equipment, I can see you slipping in under the radar and getting them to drop their guard.'

I knew what he meant about the equipment. The rest of the world had moved onto laptops and Power Point whilst I was still using 35mm slides and Super 8 film projectors. Paul proceeded to describe his vision:

'I'll start things off with a few ice-breaking techniques I've learnt in the theatre – put them in a circle; get them to throw a bean bag to each other – say their name when they catch it – stuff like that – it's a great little warm up exercise that one. While I'm doing this you can start setting up the slide projector. After a few more games, we'll break for coffee, come back and I'll introduce you.'

I agreed to try it out. The morning went pretty much as described. After the ice-breaking, warm-up games and coffee, Paul introduced me:

'OK, welcome back. Now I would like to introduce you all to Chris. Chris is an artist and he's going to be giving us a talk about his work. I want you to pay close attention because Chris is going to be our case study for today since, as well as being an artist, Chris is also – more importantly, a failure. OK Chris, take it away.'

It was abusive, exploitative, belittling... and well paid. Some of my art college jobs often treated me far worse and paid me less money so I ended up doing quite a few management training days. It was certainly no worse than selling my work to an art collector. I didn't earn enough to move house but I did earn enough to pay my rent and it became my main source of income. I had become a professional failure.

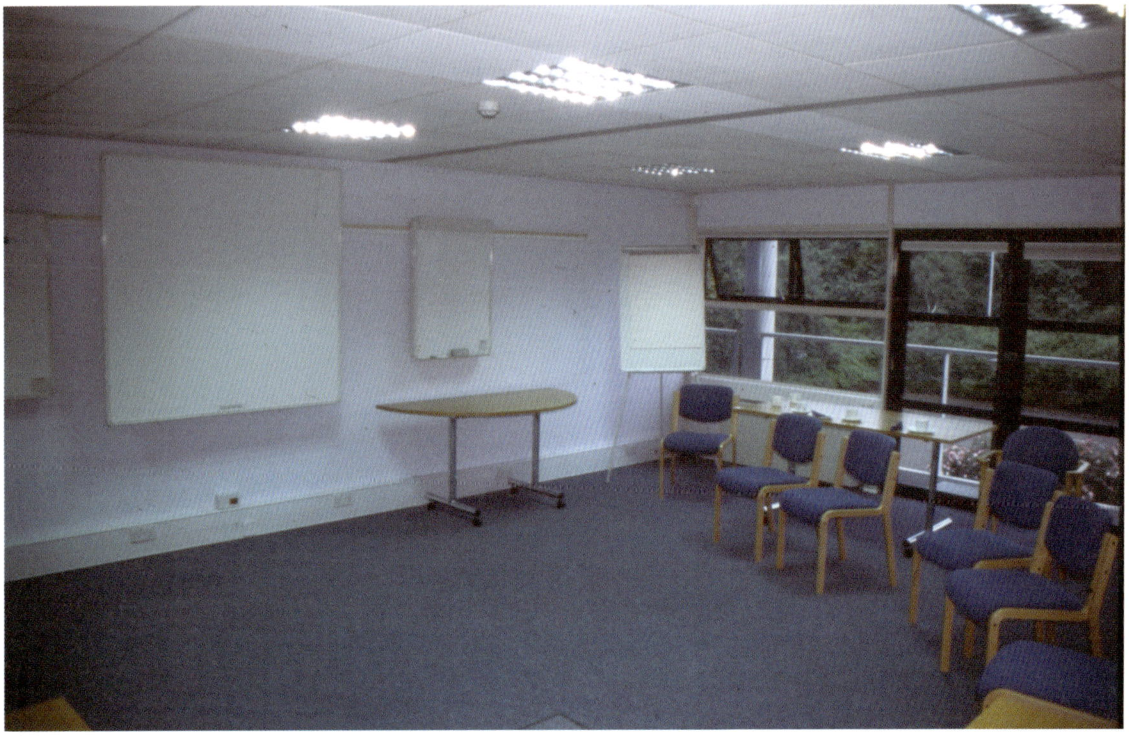

Nondescript conference room after one of my management training days with Paul.

One day Paul told me that our next job would be in Louisville, Kentucky. On the plane I asked, 'Who are we going to work for exactly?'

Without lifting his head from his newspaper, he said: 'The MWR – Morale, Welfare and Recreation.'

As I thought about it, the word 'Morale' stood out as a strange word to use in the name of a company. I rolled the word around in my head:

'We're not going to work for the US army are we? I'm not sure what I would think about that. The last time we did that talk for Zurich Bank my girlfriend said, 'you're not exactly sticking it to the man are you, Chris?' If I get home and she finds out I've been…'

Paul reassured me:

'Look Chris, I told you from the very beginning of this project that neither of us would do anything politically sensitive where we felt morally compromised in anyway. The MWR has loose connections to the US government but is not part of the US military.'

Our first workshop was attended by about fifty people. Paul arranged them in a circle and started the warm up exercises. As I put my slides into the carousel, from the corner of my eye I saw a bean bag fly across the room. A short haired man stepped forward to catch it and shouted his name smartly:

'Sergeant Major Vega –'

I had been conned.

My first impulse was to pack up my slides and leave but I had no idea where I was or how to get home. I decided to see it through and end the partnership when I was safely on the plane going back to England. I delivered the talk as usual but, when I got to the section about the tank and how my father was in the war, it took on a whole new resonance. My father was not a career soldier. He joined the army because it was a sure way of getting food in Stalin's Russia. He was just an ordinary man who ended up in the army. Over the next few days, I got to know some of the people I was talking to. Most of them had clear negative views on President Bush and the war in Iraq. I also found out that a large proportion of the US military is recruited from the poorest sections of society. They weren't that different to my own father. My friend had told me that 'you can't pick and choose who you will and won't sell your work to' and, in Kentucky, I realised that you can't pick and choose who your audience is either. Anyway, that's what I told my girlfriend when I got home.

The Post Production Meeting

I had no idea what a post production meeting was until I met Paul and it's a slightly overblown term in the context of my show which is essentially me telling stories while I play films and point at pictures. There wasn't really a production team so at my first post production meeting it was just me and Paul. He started proceedings by saying:

'Landscape, Seascape, Skyscape, Escape? What's landscape got to do with it?'

I started to explain how, though the landscape only features as a backdrop, it is still essential to the piece as a whole. Its true impact was on a subliminal level but essentially the landscape was where the true intellectual and spiritual content lay.

'What bollocks!' said Paul:

'We don't need any of that. We just need the failure! Let's change the title to Embracing Failure. It's the title of someone else's show but I know him and he won't mind if we borrow it. In fact, while we're on the subject, I want more failure in the show, better failure. Can you FAIL BIGGER?'

I left the post production meeting like a hurt child. I went home to my girlfriend who consoled me:

'The significance of the Landscape in your work? I know how to explain that, you've made me sit in the audience and watch it enough times. There is always one point during each film when the vehicle goes off into the distance. This gesture is a vital element that gives content to the whole talk. The audience watch you get into these incredibly temperamental, fragile vehicles and, as you disappear, you become smaller and smaller. You become overwhelmed by the landscape. You become insignificant.. ineffectual… pathetic. It's as if the landscape absorbs your failure and our collective disappointment in you.'

The Post Post Production Meeting

I was lying on the sofa in my bedsit one evening when my girlfriend came in from work with a copy of Artist's Newsletter. We couldn't afford to buy A-N so she photocopied it from the library. Artist's Newsletter is bought by artists mainly for its opportunities section; adverts for the latest open submission commissions and competitions. In truth, the main reason we photocopied Artist's Newsletter was to read out the ads and try to guess the underlying meaning. If we read:

'OPPORTUNITY. / Where – Preston, Lancashire. / What – Commission to make sculptural interactive piece for public space in the commercial quarter of the city. Sculpture should reflect the vitality of this new dynamic commercial hub. Proposals should have an interactive element that might include seating. Must comply with all health and safety requirements.'

We would translate it like this: 'We've been told that we have to have a sculpture in our new shopping centre. We don't want anything controversial. We were hoping you'd come up with an arty bench so that it doesn't look like art at all. PS, it mustn't have any sharp bits. We don't want to get sued by people who stumble into it drunk on a Friday night.'

The advert was placed by the British Antarctic Survey, there were no artistic restrictions and the concept of 'art' in an inhospitable hostile environment appealed to me. The first thing that sprung to mind was that I had the specialist training for this residency – I had been to art college in Hull. Then suddenly it struck me!

The predominant associations we have with this frozen land mass are Captain Scott and his agonising death after coming second in the race to the South Pole; Shackleton's stoic yet unsuccessful attempt to cross Antarctica and, more currently, impending environmental disaster. In the British psyche,

Antarctica is an entire continent synonymous with losers and failure, a place where landscape and regret meet and I thought, 'I'm your man!'

The first thing I did was visit the Scott Polar Research Institute in Cambridge. The museum holds artefacts related to Scott as well as equipment from other Polar expeditions. There are a few oil paintings of famous explorers and a chalk drawing of a penguin signed by Scott himself. There are also lots of old sledges. One of them, a 1930s Nansen, became the reference point for my proposal.

The design, named after Fridtjof Nansen, a Norwegian contemporary of Scott, was favoured by Antarctic explorers because of its light weight. Earlier sledges were solid constructions designed to smash their way through the sastrugi. The strength of the Nansen is its flexibility which allows it to travel over the sastrugi by twisting its shape. This means that the weight is always distributed evenly, giving less chance of a sudden jarring action that could snap the frame. It works in synthesis with the landscape and the design is so good that a modern version is still in use today. All the sledges in the museum are mounted high up on the wall. A member of staff lent me a stool so that I could reach up and take the dimensions. I also made a few rudimentary sketches so that I knew how it was fixed together. It seemed natural for me to try to make my own sledge but deciding on the material required a lot more thought.

In post-modern culture everyone can be an artist and anything can be art. In the Antarctic everyone has been employed for a clearly defined purpose. This makes the artist's role in the Antarctic a particularly self-conscious one. I was looking for a symbol, therefore, that accentuated and parodied the role of the artist in the blank canvas that is Antarctica. In my application, I proposed to make my Nansen sledge from gold picture frames.

The application form was more or less the same form that BAS used for scientists hoping to do research in Antarctica. It didn't call for the standard art application jargon and asked a lot of specific questions like: 'Where exactly do you want to go in the Antarctic?'

For scientists, this would make a big difference. I hadn't even considered that there was more than one place I could go. I needed to do more research. At the time, I didn't even have my own computer, let alone internet access, but, luckily, I still had my staff card from the college down the road. Each evening, I sneaked into the library to make use of the free internet access and, slowly, I built up a picture of the British Antarctic Survey and its resources.

The largest base is Rothera, just off the Antarctic Peninsula on Adelaide Island. This was where I proposed to make the sledge. I found out that BAS regularly move their own sledges around Antarctica by Twin Otter and Dash 7 aircraft and, in my proposal, I suggested that I hitch a ride on one of these flights. The most remote British base I could find on the map was called Sky Blu. Rothera is relatively far North at latitude 67°34'S and some of the snow around the base even melts in summer. By contrast, Sky Blu is 500 hundred miles further south and is properly on the Polar ice cap.

The reason for Sky Blu's existence is its blue ice runway; an area of compacted snow that has turned to ice hard and flat enough to use as a runway by aircraft landing on wheels instead of skis. This means that BAS can use its larger Dash 7 aircraft instead of the smaller Twin Otter and make a stockpile of fuel at this southerly outpost. The Twin Otter aircraft can refuel there en route to temporary field camps even further south. It is, in effect, an Antarctic petrol station.

Sky Blu is pretty basic. There is a radio mast, an underground garage, a couple of fibreglass huts and a handful of tents. It is reached and supplied by air. There is little of interest nearby so people don't travel very far from this spot over land. It is, quite literally, nowhere. BAS had gone to the trouble of making a map of the place; a blank piece of paper with the runway and fuel stores marked on it. There is an arrow coming from the word 'hut' pointing to a dot in the corner.

I reasoned that if I could get the sledge to this point and head off the base in any direction, I would be somewhere nobody had ever been before. This was my objective.

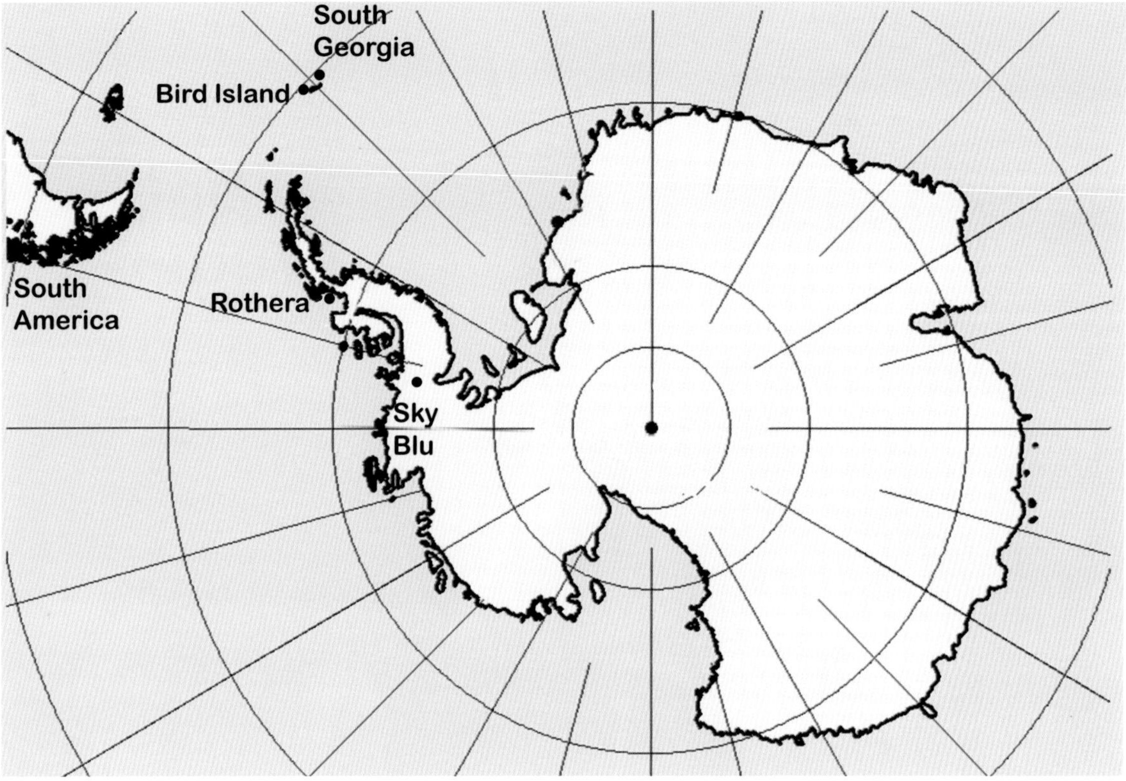

It seemed quite a grandiose plan. In fact, considering my circumstances, it was verging on the delusional. I was shuttling backwards and forwards on a bicycle to sneak into the library of the art college that used to employ me because of an advert in a magazine that I couldn't afford to buy. Yet, however inauspicious, my research process had the intensity of planning for an expedition.

I buried myself in the research and worked out things like how many picture frames I would need and how much equipment I could bring with me. It was like having a virtual trip to the Antarctic and, at this stage, I was potentially going. When it was time to hand in my application, I drove to BAS headquarters to deliver it by hand. I don't know why I did this but I think it was my way of holding onto that potential for as long as possible. I took a good look at the building from the outside and handed over my A4 envelope. Deep down I knew this was the closest I was ever going to get to the Antarctic.

One nice thing about my rejection letter when it arrived was the envelope. The British Antarctic Survey had their own franking machine so the envelope had been rubber stamped with a picture of a penguin. After my imaginary trip to the Antarctic this red faded outline of a penguin seemed like a perfect souvenir.

It was an unusual rejection letter and used certain phrases I was unfamiliar with. For example, it started with the phrase:

'I am pleased' – which I thought a bit harsh for a rejection letter. It also used other terms unfamiliar to me like:

'Congratulations.'

At this point, I stopped scan reading the rejection letter and realised it was, in fact, an acceptance letter. There was a horrible moment when I thought that they had confused me with the other Chris Dobrowolski. I had noticed on his website that he had started doing some paintings of whales in a Polar landscape with icebergs, but no, it was definitely me they wanted. I was going to Antarctica!

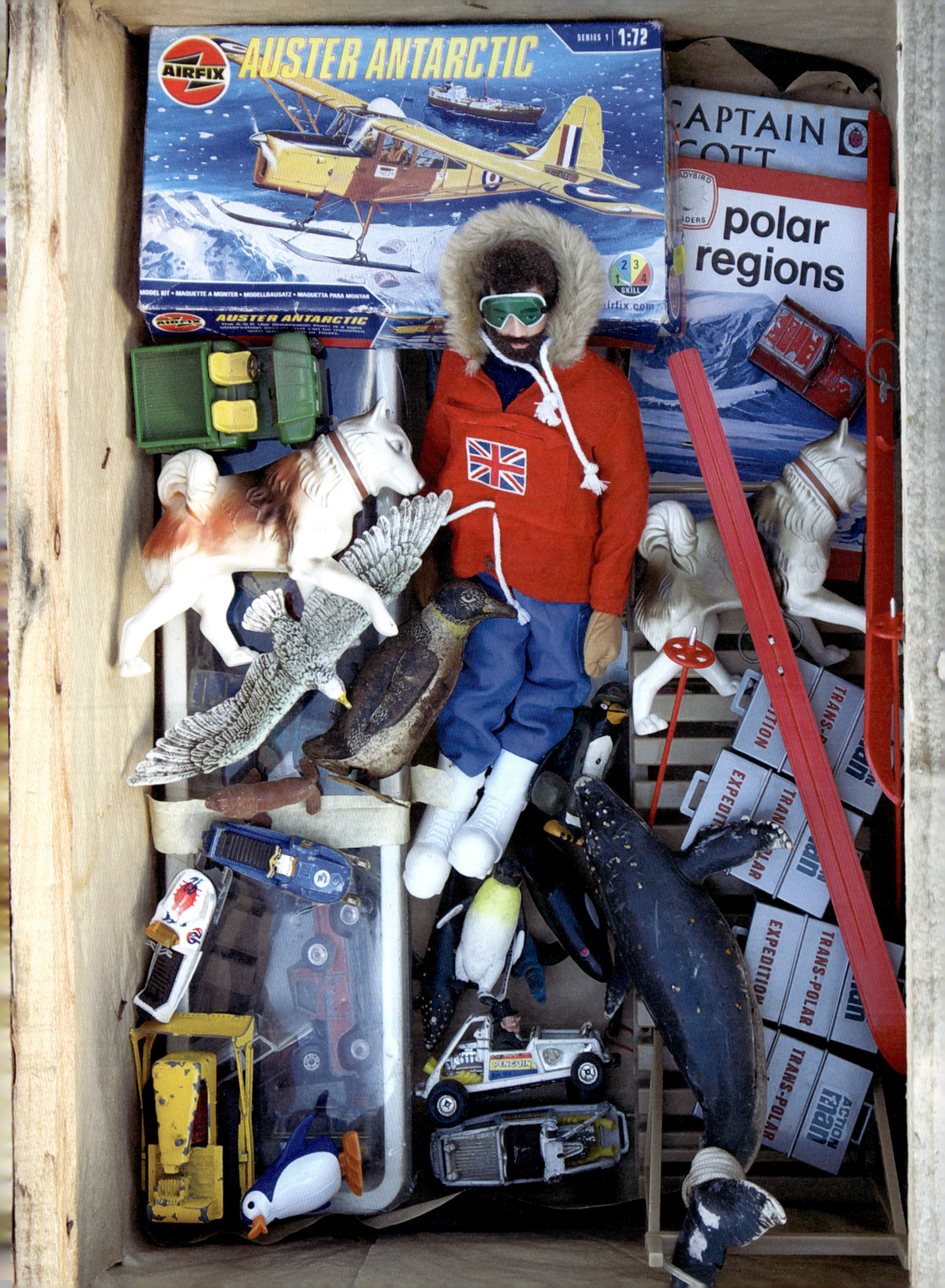
AIRFIX
AUSTER ANTARCTIC
SERIES 1
1:72
SKILL
MODEL KIT • MAQUETTE A MONTER • MODELLBAUSATZ • MAQUETTA PARA MONTAR
AUSTER ANTARCTIC
CAPTAIN
polar
regions
EXPEDITION
TRANS-POLAR
PENGUIN
Action
man

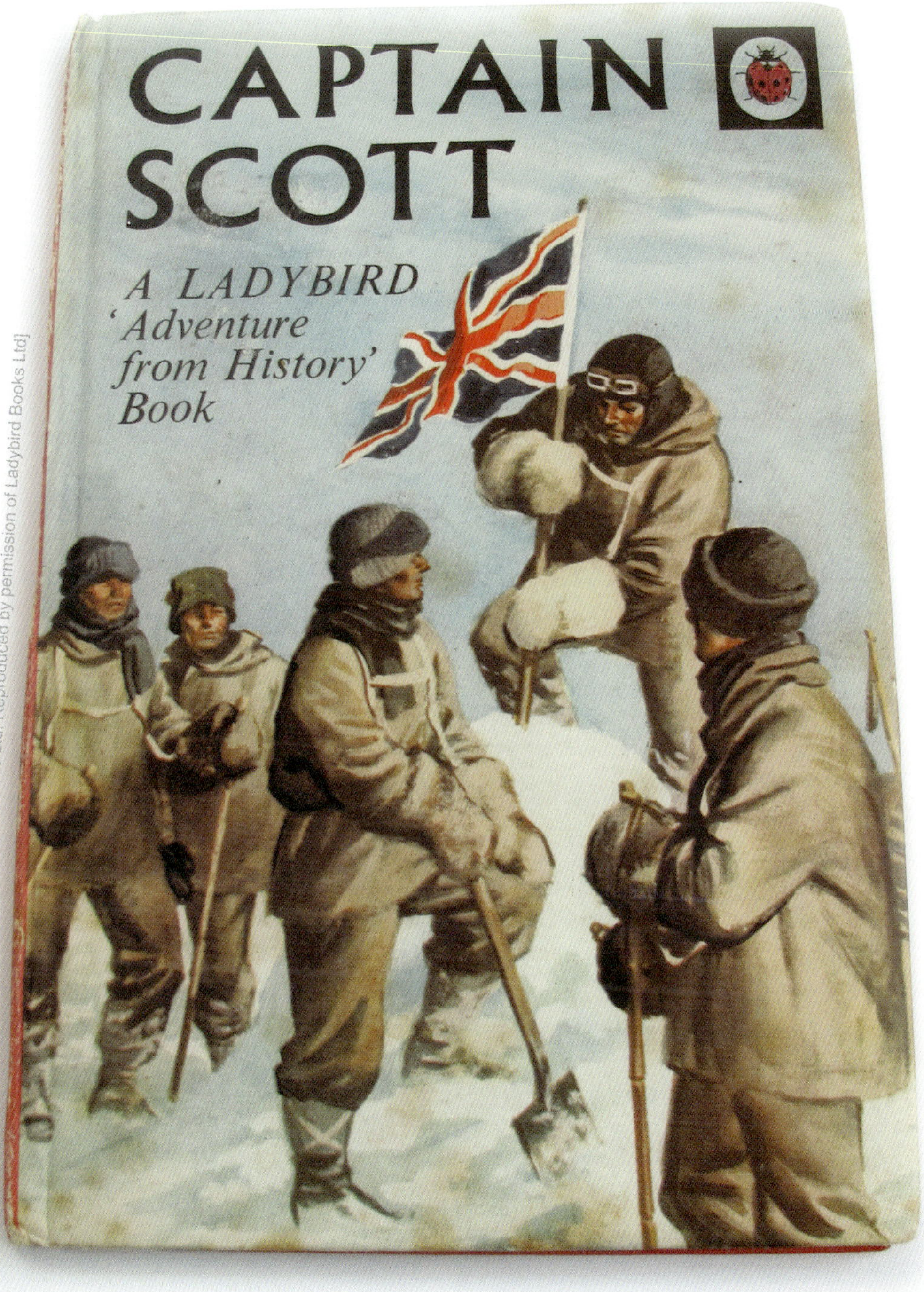

The Real Thing

previous page: Collection of Antarctic toys including Antarctic Action Man with sledge and dogs and an Auster Antarctic Airfix model aeroplane kit. LadybirdBook of Scott of the Antarctic, and a toy sledge by Herald Toys and Models.

Up until this point, the landscapes that I had travelled through on my own creations were relatively unremarkable and certainly not heroic. Despite this I still thought of these journeys as romantic adventures. Made in a similar vein to children's go-karts, often these projects felt like childhood games of pretend yearning to be real life. Antarctica, by contrast, was 'the real thing'.

Along with my gold picture frame sledge, my proposal had a second line of enquiry that reflected on these notions of real and unreal. The crates of gold picture frames were not the only strange cargo heading to the Antarctic. Packaged up in boxes and shipped ahead of my arrival was a large collection of toys that related in some way to Antarctica. This included the Ladybird Book of Captain Scott and the Antarctic Polar Explorer Action Man doll. When I was doing my research on the internet, I kept a record of every vehicle I saw there and tried to find a toy version of it on eBay. I also looked for Antarctic toys at car boot sales and managed to find various toy snowmobiles and lots of cheap model penguins, seals and killer whales. Some of the Antarctic links were quite tenuous; I bought a toy van purely because it had an advert for Penguin biscuits on the side.

At the Scott Polar Research Institute I had noticed some objects that, on the face of it, seemed quite arbitrary. In one display case there was a bottle, in another there was a basic telescope and a flag. There were ship's biscuits and lots of other things that were quite unremarkable but for the fact that they had been on a great journey. Antarctica has a way of endowing everyday objects with a mystique, an authenticity, that continues to this day. I was told that when BAS employees are issued with their clothing it includes thermal underwear that, unlike the rest of the kit, they are not expected to give back at the end of their season. These pants often end up on eBay as genuine Antarctic underwear.

My collection of Antarctic toys were, on the other hand, representations or pretend Antarctic things. My intention was to take these fakes with me to the real Antarctic, document them there then bring them back as the genuine article; real pretend Antarctic things. I planned to use this documentation as part of a series of new art pieces when I got back to the UK. Their tackiness might also make an interesting juxtaposition with the majesty and grandeur of the Antarctic.

When I tell people I was at sea for six weeks they automatically assume that I was on the ship all the way to Antarctica. I wasn't. My journey was a lot less intrepid and started on a bus hired by BAS to take their employees from the headquarters in Cambridge to RAF Brize Norton to catch a military flight south. The bus developed engine trouble two miles down the road and had to limp back to the depot. We got out, climbed onto another one and tried again.

When we finally reached RAF Brize Norton, the military flight wasn't quite what I had imagined either. It turned out to be a very ordinary civilian jet chartered by the military. The only things that signified it as military were the paper, RAF antimacassars and the fact that most of the other passengers were teenagers with short haircuts. Someone told me that the army likes to send the youngest recruits to the Falklands because it gives them a first taste of being a long way from home without the complications of getting killed. In their civilian clothes they looked like an inner city comprehensive school going on a field trip.

After a ten hour flight, the plane refuelled at Ascension Island in the middle of the Atlantic just south of the Equator. We all disembarked and, to pass the time, we queued to get an Ascension Island stamp in our passports. In exchange for this we had to make a £1 donation to the local wildlife charity. A short time later the plane took off again and, after another ten hours, we landed in the Falklands at the huge military air base called Mount Pleasant. Then we got on another bus to Port Stanley.

I joined my ship at Fipass Jetty. I thought Fipass was quite a nice name until I realised it was just the acronym for the temporary port facility where the ship was moored. We didn't leave immediately as the ship was waiting for an important spare part so we stayed at the 'Floating Interim Port and

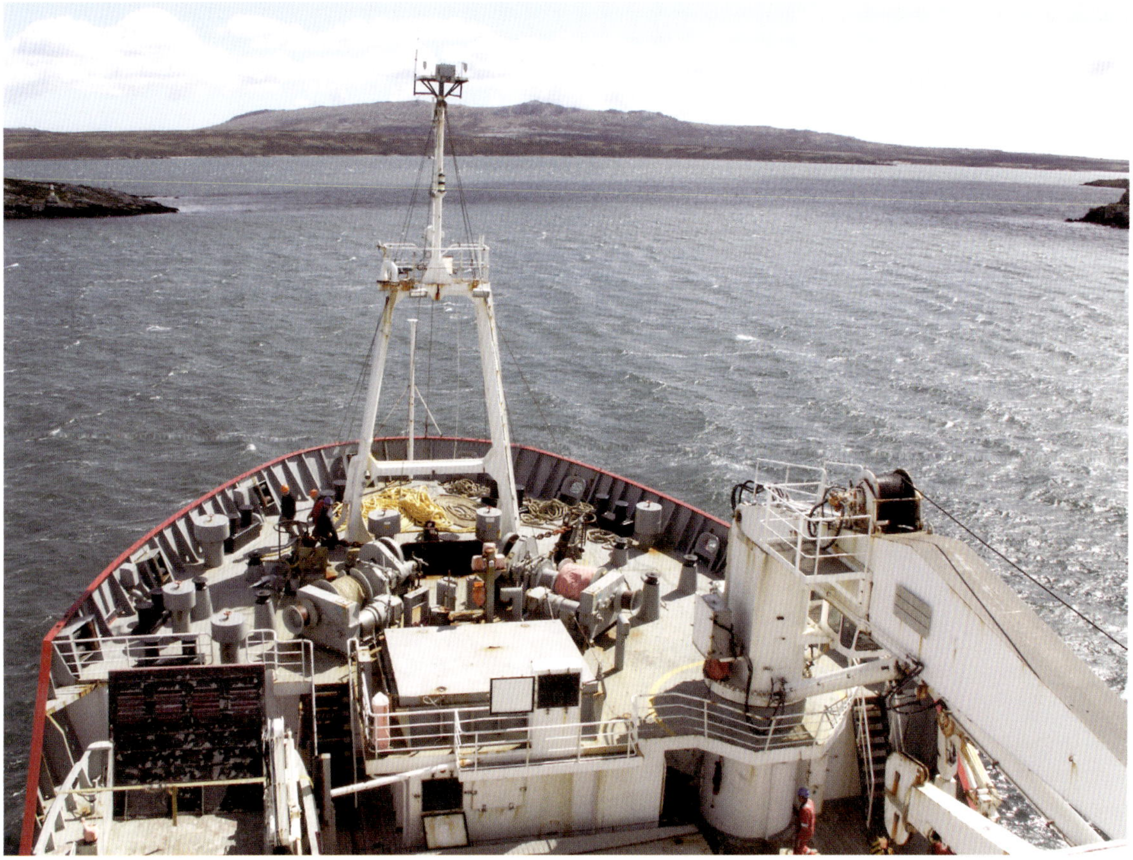

View across the bow of the James Clark Ross as it leaves Port Stanley.

Storage System' for the next couple of days. The ship was a BAS research vessel called the James Clark Ross. It was kitted out with laboratories and equipment for scientists to do all sorts of marine research. This usually meant studying the smaller creatures in the sea like phytoplankton or other suspended water matter that I had never considered before. The water itself was also the focus of much scrutiny. Samples were regularly sucked up into the laboratory and syringed into test tubes. Temperatures were noted and microscopic and chemical contents were meticulously analysed.

On the starboard side of the ship there was a special winch that lowered the sampling equipment to thousands of metres below the surface. The equipment consisted of a series of cylindrical containers or bottles arranged in a circle on a metal frame. Each one of these bottles had a door that revolved shut, a bit like the door on a bread bin. They were closed by remote control at the required depths and the samples were analysed later on board the ship. The water bottle carrier was built to work at tremendous pressure below the surface of the water and winching it up and down can take a few hours.

To while away the time, it is customary for the scientists to amuse themselves by drawing designs on polystyrene cups from the ships mess. When the water bottle carrier comes back to the surface everybody attaches their cup to it ready for the next descent. On the way down, the pressure crushes all the air out of the polystyrene leaving a shrunken, distorted cup with a highly detailed miniature drawing on it. The best way to attach the cups to the water bottle carrier is to put them in a small mesh net or a cloth bag. If there are a lot of people on board feeling creative, it is not unusual to see the water bottle carrier disappear beneath the waves with several people's socks tied to it. Each sock contains a cup carefully decorated in felt-tip pen and often dedicated to a loved one back home. Hours later, when the cups finally surface, they are transformed into unique, handcrafted, polystyrene souvenirs from the Southern Ocean.

When I first moved onto the ship there were only a couple of scientists left on board. Most of them had been studying the waters on the way down through the Atlantic and had left the day before I arrived. At this stage of its voyage the ship was fulfilling its more utilitarian function as a supply ship. As well as dropping people off at their various Antarctic and sub Antarctic bases, the James Clark Ross carried a large cargo of fuel, food and equipment. In amongst this cargo were my own supplies; the gold picture frames and the Antarctic toys. I had delivered them to BAS headquarters several months in advance so that they could be packaged up in carefully labelled crates and sent on ahead of me with the ship. Six months later, I had caught up with them. The boxes of toys had been designated 'wanted on voyage' and the gold picture frames were somewhere in the hold. The crates were more than just packaging for my materials, they were themselves going to be important elements in my artworks.

My visit to the Scott Polar Research Institute had shown me the power of the Antarctic to transform everyday objects into icons. The crates with their 'Bill of Lading' cargo labels were an ideal example of this type of artefact. The labels, or BOLs, were bureaucratic and concise. They described what was in the box, how much it weighed and, most importantly, where the crate was going and where it had been. It even said Northbound or Southbound in big letters.

The crates were not arbitrary containers either. In the yard at headquarters I had found several old sledge boxes. These were a standard BAS issue box made to hold equipment and supplies. They are roughly ten inches high and one foot by two foot wide which allows them to be stacked securely and neatly on a standard Nansen sledge. The ones I found were mainly the cheaper, disposable, wooden food boxes that are often reused to send things back to the UK. They had already been to the Antarctic and back again, now I was sending them there for a second time. Later I supplemented this supply of boxes with others I found on my journey.

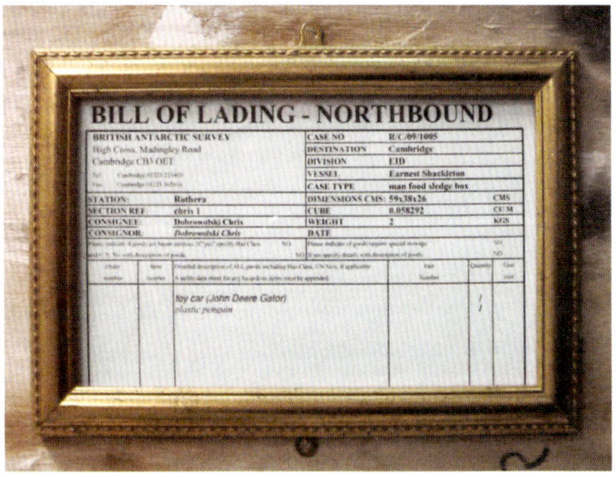

Gold-framed Bill of Lading.

right: Two of my crates 'wanted of voyage' in the laboratory / artist's studio on board.

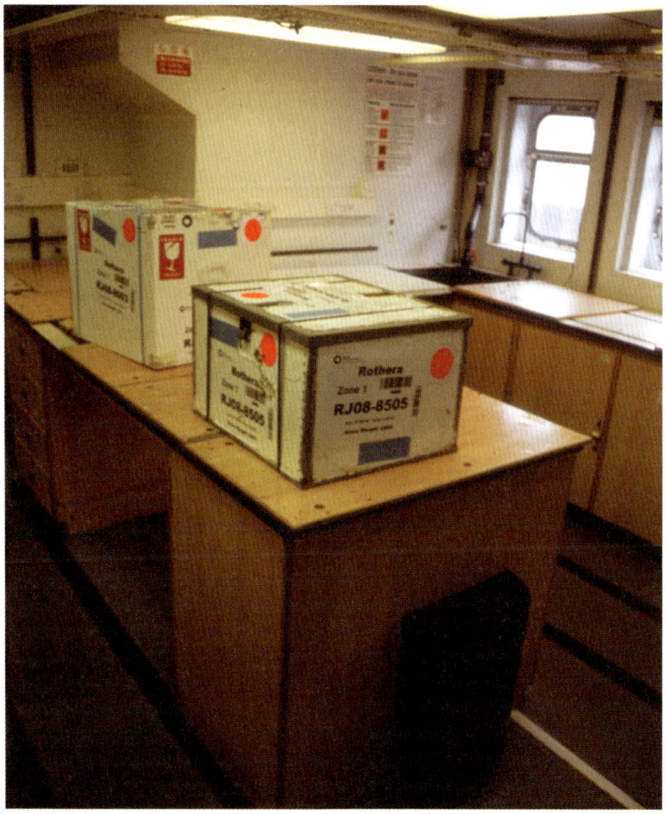

I wanted to use these boxes on my return to the UK. Back in my studio, the plan was to use images of the toys in the Antarctic, the toys themselves, sound recordings and film as my visual source material for a new series of paintings in wooden boxes – genuine Antarctic boxes complete with their authenticating Bill of Landing.

In contrast to the sledge, I'd left the toy part of my proposal deliberately flexible. I had such a variety of toys that I could respond to things I saw by chance and come up with ideas and images intuitively. This is how I saw the work coming together:

1. The toy, a plastic penguin for example, would be photographed in the Antarctic with a typical background including actual penguins.

2. The toy penguin would be shipped back to the UK in a wooden sledge box with BOL sticker declaring 'Plastic Penguin'.

3. I would paint a crude Antarctic landscape in the box and glue the photograph of the toy penguin in Antarctica to the inside of the lid.

4. I would then add the real plastic penguin to the painted landscape.

When I came to attempt number '4' in my studio, the way in which the toy penguin fitted into the painted landscape gave me the most concern. This was where real and unreal came together and was the conceptual point of the piece. I spent weeks contemplating the possibilities. I would stare at the penguin on and off for a few days whilst rubbing my chin. Then I would suddenly announce to myself, 'yes – that's it!' Two days later I would realise I hadn't made the breakthrough I thought I had and move it again. A plastic penguin placed in a painted landscape is naturally perceived by the viewer as a representation of a real penguin in a representation of a real landscape. This wasn't what

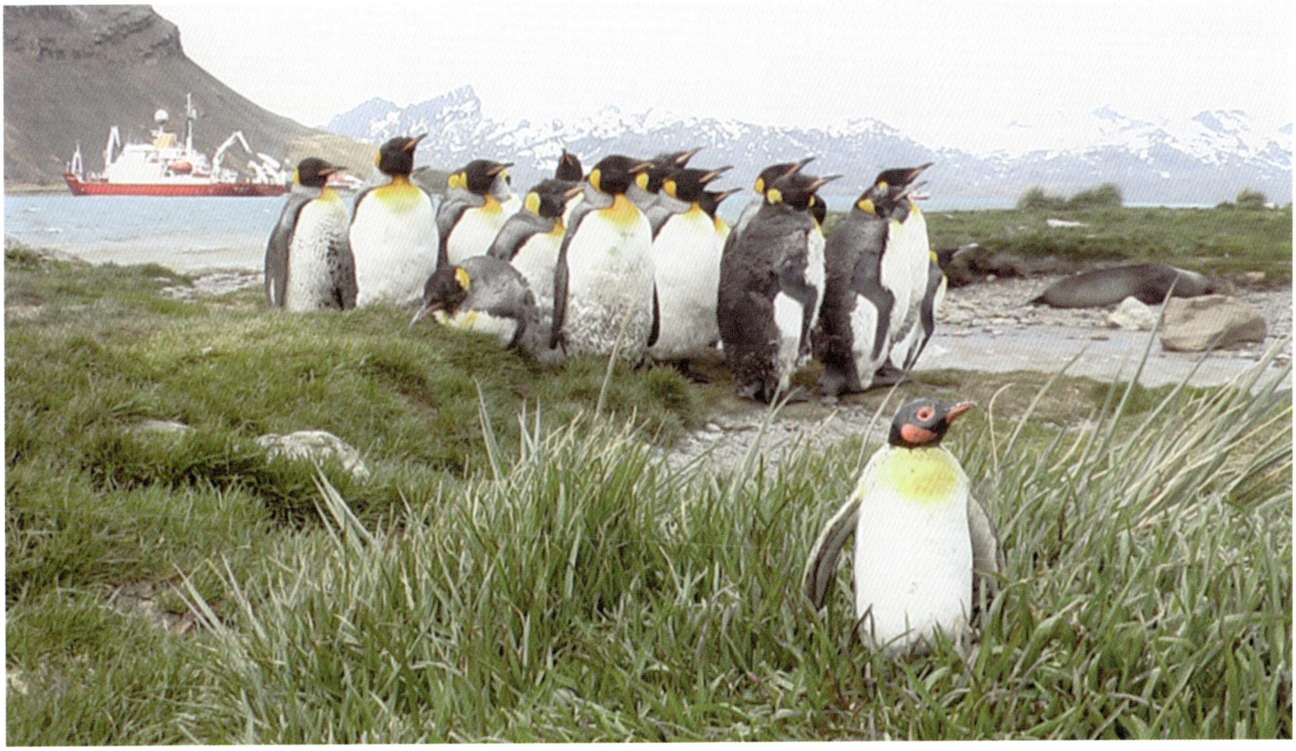

South Georgia. King penguins with the James Clark Ross in distance. The cheap plastic penguin from a car boot sale is standing in the foreground whilst one of the real ones has fallen over.

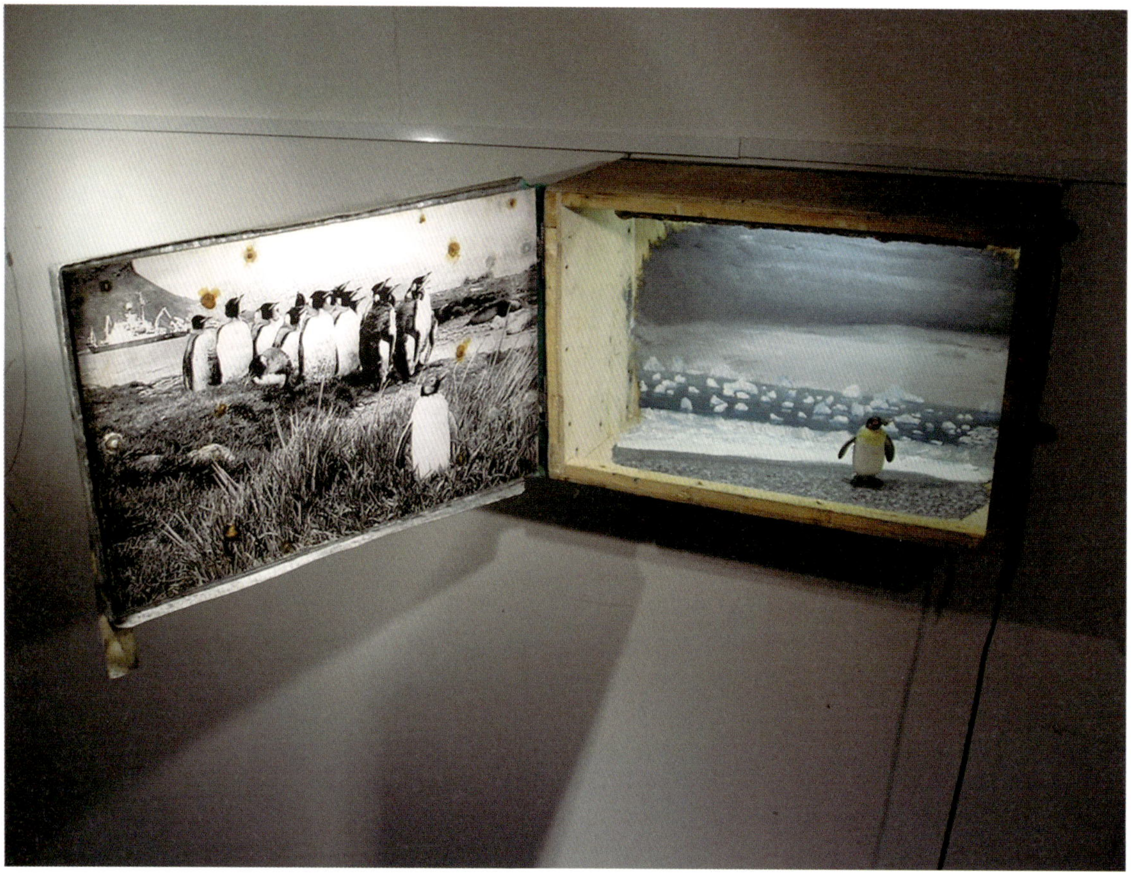

Gallery installation shot. Plastic penguin in painted landscape in sledge box.

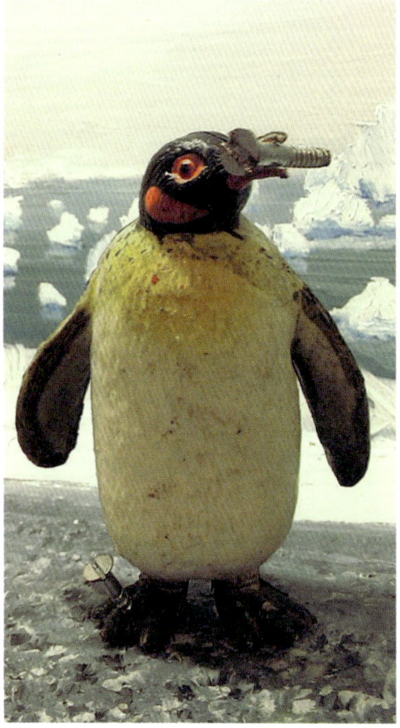

Detail with penguin holding one of the screws that secure it to the floor.

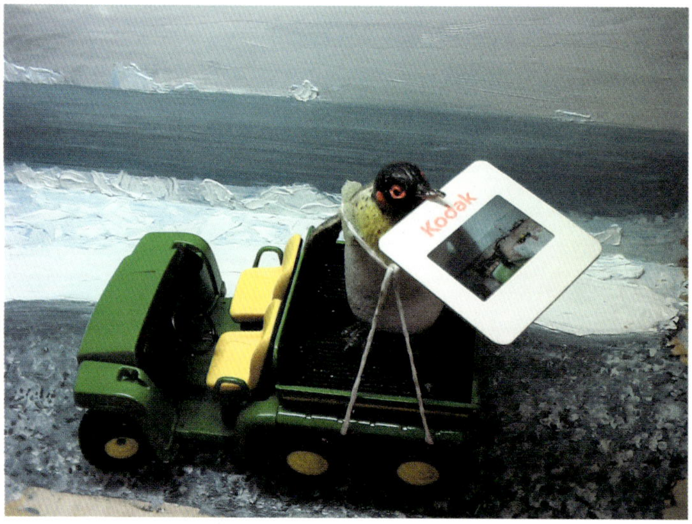

An earlier discarded composition showing the penguin tied in the back of a toy John Deere Gator holding a slide of itself.

I wanted at all; I wanted to show a cheap plastic penguin in a crude painting of the Antarctic. I tried all sorts of ways to break the natural interpretation. At one point, I roped the penguin to a toy car with a Kodak slide of itself in its beak. It was a ludicrous composition that couldn't possibly be misunderstood as a representation of real life. I was happy with this and about to start my second piece when a friend visited my studio. After studying my masterpiece for a minute or so she asked:

'So is that how you moved penguins in the Antarctic then?'

I dismantled it and started the process all over again.

Eventually, I decided to emphasise the falseness of the penguin by fixing it into the painting in a deliberately crude way. I screwed the penguin to the floor of the box through its feet, leaving the screw conspicuously half out of its foot. I put a second screw in its mouth. The process I went through to arrive at this was time-consuming and difficult to justify rationally to other people. The first piece was the most difficult but, over the period of a year, I slowly made an entire series of work in my studio in the garden shed at home.

I also had a studio on the ship. As there weren't many scientists on board I was given the main laboratory as my work space. Though this was a very generous offer, I spent very little time there. When I first opted to go on the ship it was only for two weeks so that I could experience some of the Sub-Antarctic bases and see what I could find on the beaches for my project. The waters between the Falklands and the Antarctic include an area called Drakes Passage known for some of the roughest seas on the planet. In the past, I have managed to be sick on a cross Channel ferry. My studio/laboratory was quite a few decks below my cabin and I seldom managed to get that far before needing to throw up. I was warned that schedules could often change and, sure enough, the ship was re-routed to do some survey work. From the vantage point of my cabin toilet bowl, I saw my two weeks on board stretch to six.

There's a point at which the body gets used to being at sea and you stop throwing up. For me that point comes after about three days. Unfortunately for the first month on board we were at sea for periods of about two and a half days so just as my body was about to come to terms with the motion of the ship, we would reach the next base and stop to unload. This pattern continued until I found myself back in Port Stanley. We had gone in a complete circle. We did not head in the direction of my own Antarctic destination until our third outing.

The ship's doctor, Nerys, was carrying out tests on sea sickness cures and wanted volunteers to participate in her survey. Consequently I wore a wrist band with a pea stitched into it. The pea was supposed to press against a specific point in my wrist as a reflexology cure. Each day I had to fill out a small questionnaire:

Retching or vomiting 0 1 2 3 4 5.

0 being fine and 5 being severe. I invariably circled 5.

I spent a lot of my time at sea laying on the bunk in my cabin. The mess was a couple of decks below; not as far as my studio but still too far to go without being sick so I didn't eat much. This had a negative effect on my health since having an empty stomach makes the nausea even worse. At one point, knowing I needed to eat, I called out and a Good Samaritan came back with two apples and a bread roll. I savoured the smell and taste of the fresh green apple right down to the last bite before running to the toilet to vomit it all back up again. That night I was woken by a particularly rough sea. I was still hungry. Not daring to move, I lay in the darkness listening to the bread roll and the uneaten apple roll backwards and forwards across the floor from one end of my cabin to the other.

The next day I was told by Dr Zubkov that eating an apple in my situation was a bad idea. Dr Zubkov was not a medical doctor, he was a very learned, serious, bearded Russian scientist who had remained on board to study the waters of the Southern Ocean. According to him, my sickness was caused by stomach acid. The apple had overloaded my digestive juices so he was not surprised I had vomited. Although he wasn't a medical doctor he sounded convincing and there seemed to be a synthesis between studying the contents of the water below the surface of the waves and hypothesising on the churning of my stomach.

According to Dr Zubkov, the best thing was to eat as much starch as possible. No meat, no greens just starch to convince my stomach that it was full. Eggs were also allowed because they gave my stomach something to use its acid on. That lunchtime, the ship was stationary to do some scientific work and I was able to make my way to the mess. Whenever I managed to get there, I was always greeted by a look of surprise and amusement from the stewards who at one point thought I had left the ship because they hadn't seen me for so long. On this occasion, I amused them further by requesting four helpings of mash potato and three eggs followed by bread. To my amazement, the sea sickness eased off to be replaced by acute indigestion.

I eventually discovered my own seasickness cure. Richard, the Ship's Purser, told me that the scientists and artists on board sometimes gave a presentation about their work to the crew and other passengers. These were quite informal gatherings in the officer's bar and he asked me if I wouldn't mind giving one too. Seasickness must be a psychological thing. I'm sure there's a link between the part of my brain that I use to throw up and the part I use to give my presentations. As I was preparing my slides, the adrenalin kicked in and I forgot about being sick. Just in case, Richard got the ice bucket from behind the bar. I gave three talks whilst on board. Just before the second one, I heard Richard prepping a newcomer:

'Normally these talks last about twenty minutes but the last time this guy did one he went on for about hour, then he put up a slide that said Intermission.'

I had managed to take the odd photograph while the ship was in dock or stationary for scientific work. As well as giving respite from sea sickness, the talk was therefore a useful tool for explaining to everyone why I was embarrassing myself photographing plastic toy animals. Not everyone came to the talks, however, and quite rightly wondered what the hell I was doing in their workplace playing with toys.

'Play' is how I would describe what I was doing too. 'Working intuitively' is the grander title we gave to this process at art college. 'Trying things out', 'not working to a brief' and 'just seeing what happens' were other phrases. This was the approach I adopted with the toys in the Antarctic. Not having the pressure of a fixed outcome is the key to the success of this process. It's important to accept that sometimes mistakes will be made and the outcome might be nothing. When this happens, it's difficult to see the activity as anything else but simply… play. This was how I worked in my studio at home but, in the Antarctic, I was a lot more conspicuous.

I had also brought along an old-fashioned record player because, on eBay, I had come across an LP of Vaughan Williams' Symphonia Antarctica. I had also packed a few sea shanties and other records with a nautical theme from my personal collection of old 78s. One day, the scientists were lowering some equipment over the side of the ship with the help of the deckhand George. I tried to use this marine activity as a backdrop whilst I filmed my record player. The scientists also let me tie a toy rubber whale to their apparatus as they lowered it into the water. I got what I thought were marginally interesting images from my activity but nothing special. I knew the images might be part of something more interesting later when I got back to the studio at home but, at this stage, it was impossible to say.

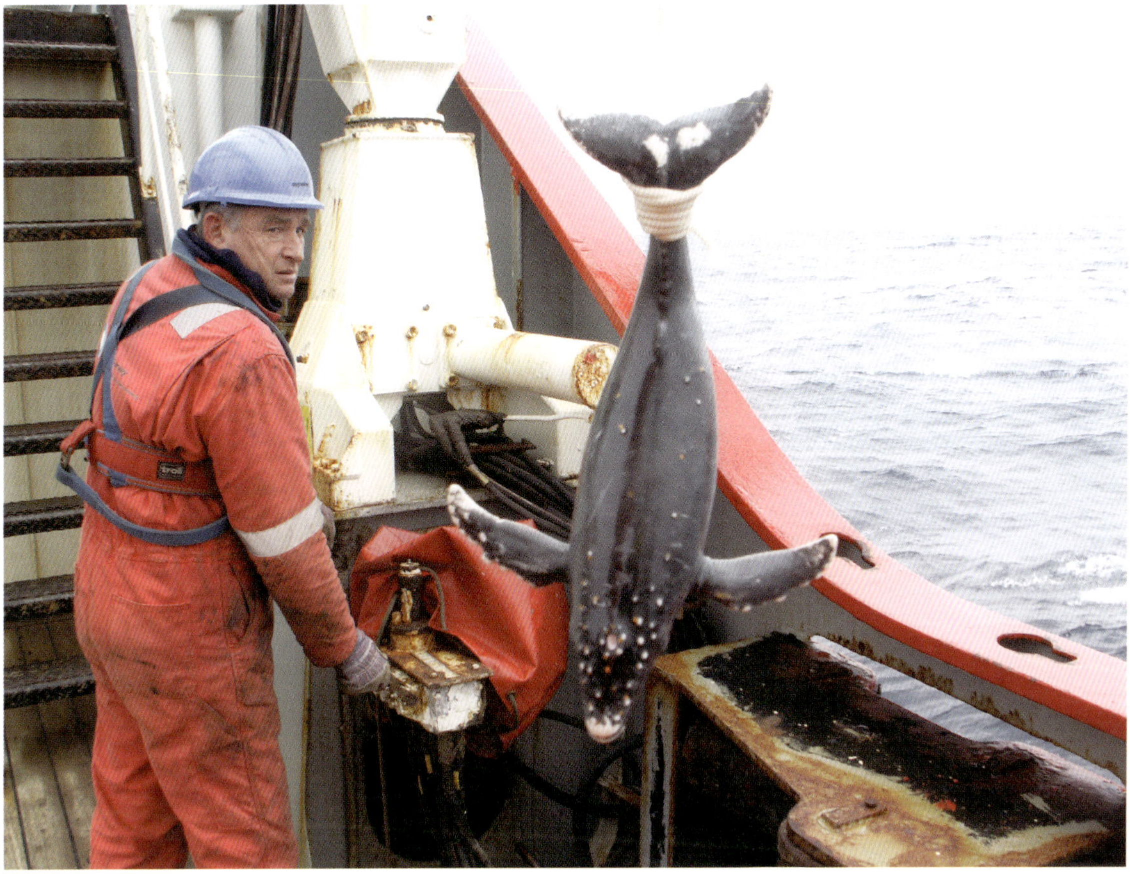

above: George and the rubber whale.

On one of our return visits to the Falklands, I was invited into the crew bar by a couple of the stewards for a drink. George walked in after an evening in Port Stanley. The crew bar was more George's territory than mine. Like the scientists, the artist was supposed to be upstairs in the officer's bar. Having had a drink and being on home turf, George was full of confidence. When I was an art student, it was always useful to have people around to give you their opinion or encouragement on your work. In that environment, it was also reassuring to know that others were having the same self doubts or that they noticed something in your work that you had overlooked. I do miss that kind of environment so I was pleased when George spontaneously started a one-to-one tutorial with me. In his broad Glaswegian accent he said:

'Plastic whale… shite!'

'Record player! Shite!'

He paused for a second or two while still maintaining his disgusted face and finally said.

'Yuh shite!'

I could see his point but I tried to explain it was early days yet.

below: Record player in the lab/studio.

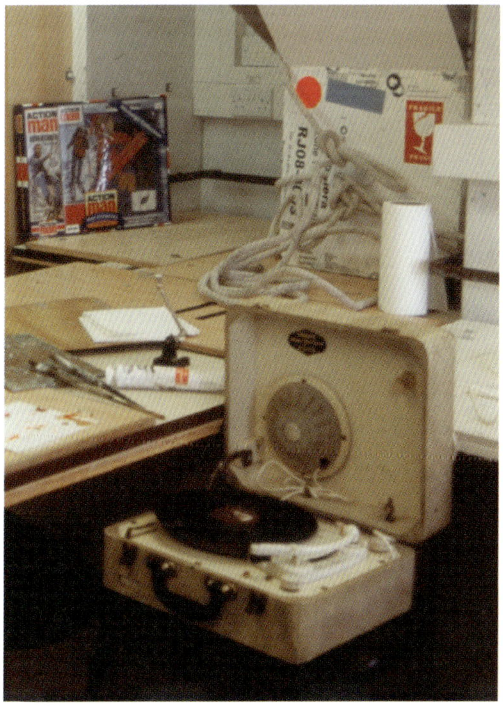

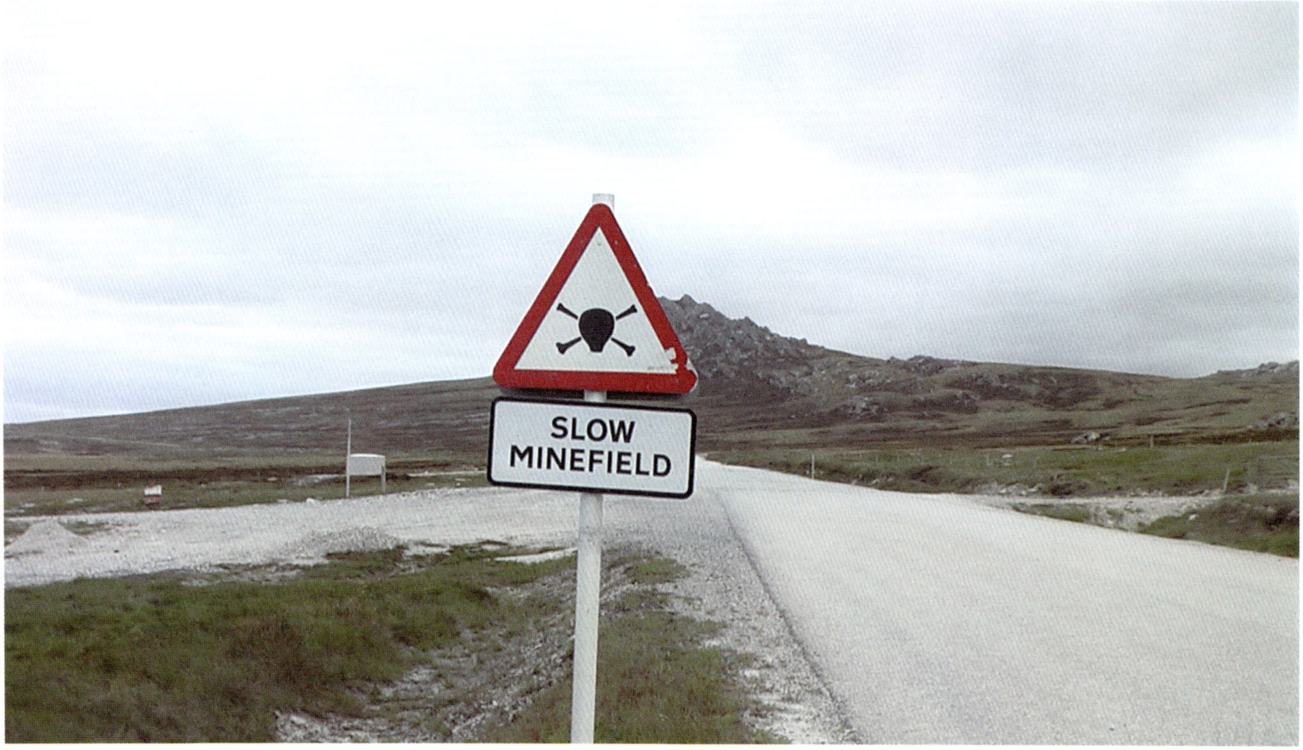

There is no shortage of land in the Falklands. As a result the inhabitants have not missed the fenced off areas that were turned into minefields by the Argentine forces during the invasion in 1982. Expensive and dangerous to clear, the government declared it would prefer to see the money spent in other countries around the world where minefields were more of a daily problem.

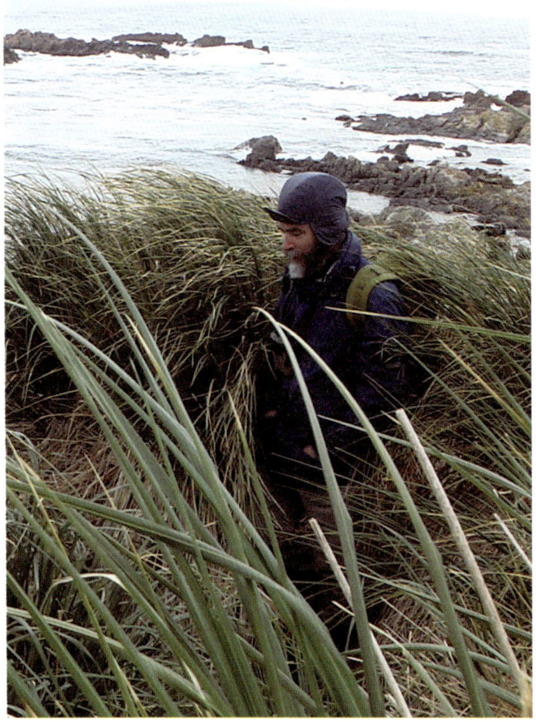

Dr Zubkov examines the giant tussock grass on the Falklands.

On another occasion, this time in the officer's bar, I had some more, indirect, feedback, this time from my friend Dr Zubkov. On one of our visits to the Falklands, we hired a Land Rover to explore the islands further. For two or three days, we visited battlegrounds and other sites of interest. I brought along my camera and filled my pockets with small toys. At the end of each day, we returned to the ship and finished off with a drink in the bar. On one of these occasions, I sat with Dr Zubkov. He was happy in silence savouring his drink but I always feel awkward in a communication vacuum and need the reassurance of trivial conversation. Dr Zubkov didn't really do small talk. To break the silence, I probed him with a few questions:

'Good day today Dr Zubkov?'

I could see him smile slightly behind his beard then very slowly nod his head in acknowledgement. I persisted:

'What was the most interesting part of your day Dr Zubkov?'

Dr Zubkov finally answered my questions with all the solemnity of a Chekhov character, slowly pacing his words to emphasis their gravity:

'As you know… I am… an oceanographer…… but my other great passion… is Geology!

'Do you remember the first day we arrived on these Islands? I pointed out to you that the land we could see at the side of the bay was actually… the beginning of a geological feature. It turned out to be part of the very sub structure for… the entire island. It was in fact… the beginning of a mountain rift running the entire length… of the Falkland Islands… Did you know… a rift is merely… nature's… crack?

'We drove… all day… in the Land Rover… but we ne-ver reached the end… of this crack.

'When we stopped to climb to the top of one of these mountains I had the opportunity to study… the strata in the rock.

'It was almost vertical.

'Imagine… the forces… of nature… over millennia… to force… these two tec-ton-ic plates… almost perpendicular!

'It is… experiences such as this… that make me realise… my insignificance… in time… and the universe!'

He paused for reflection before he finished:

'And this was the most interesting part of my day.'

I sat in silence hoping he wouldn't ask what the most interesting part of my day had been. The only thing in my head at the time was a collection of photographs that included a toy Land Rover, a plastic penguin and a rubber whale. I asked Dr Zubkov if he would mind participating in my project and he very graciously said:

'If your project will increase the accessibility of science to the general populace then of course.'

He kindly posed for me with my Action Man who, I noticed, had a similar jumper and beard.

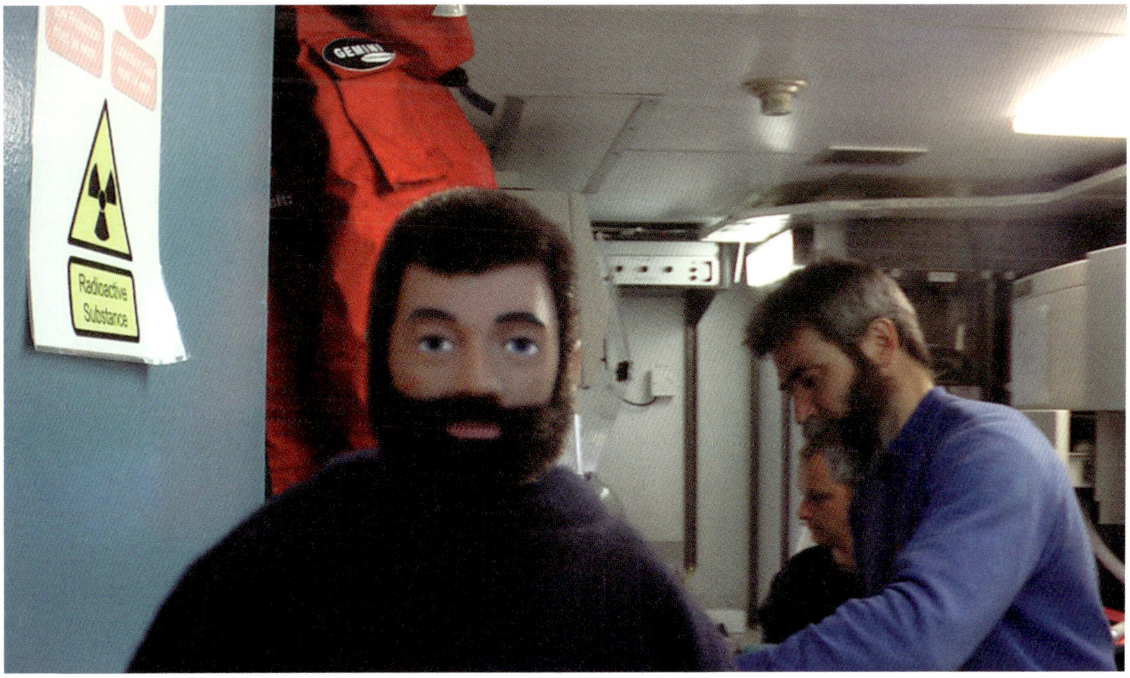

Action Man and Dr Zubkov in his laboratory on the JCR.

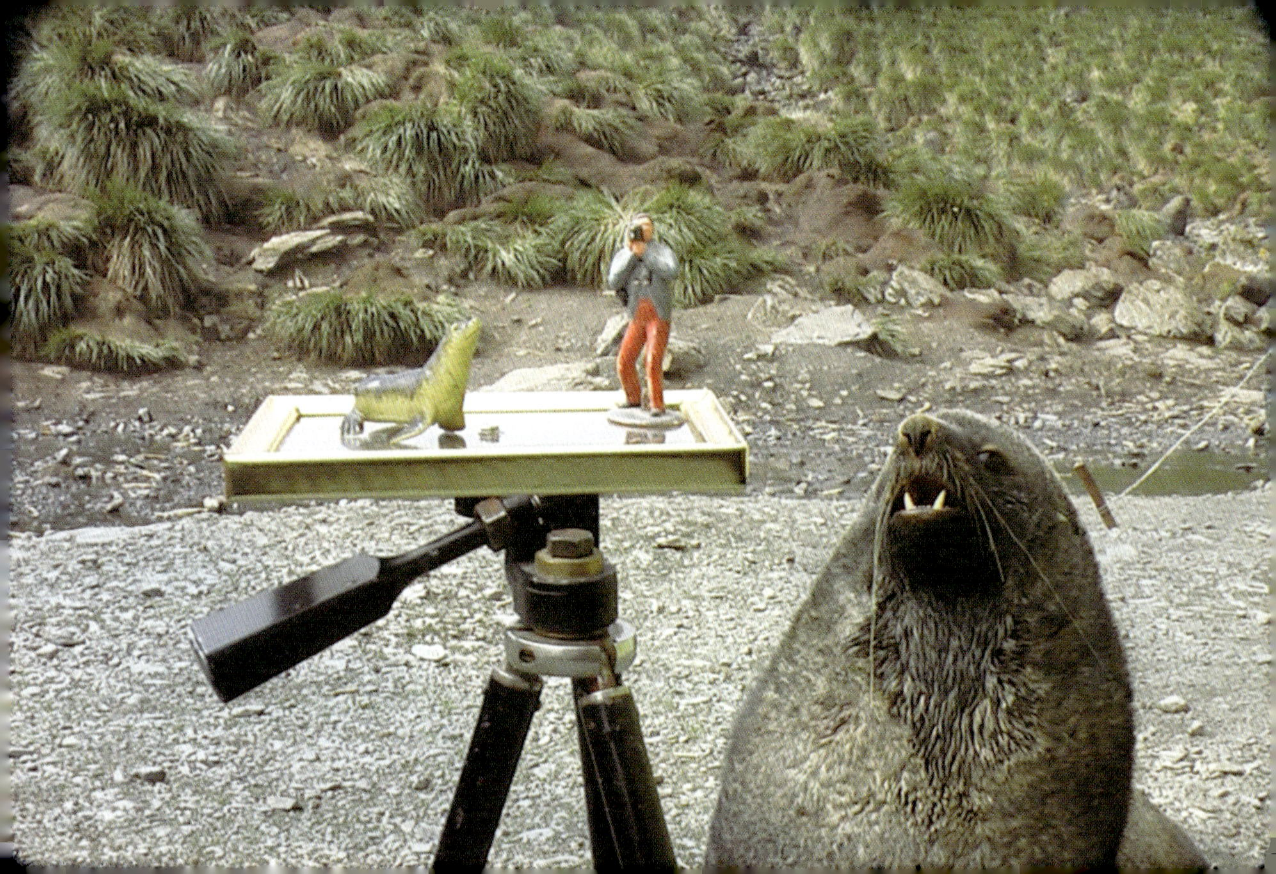

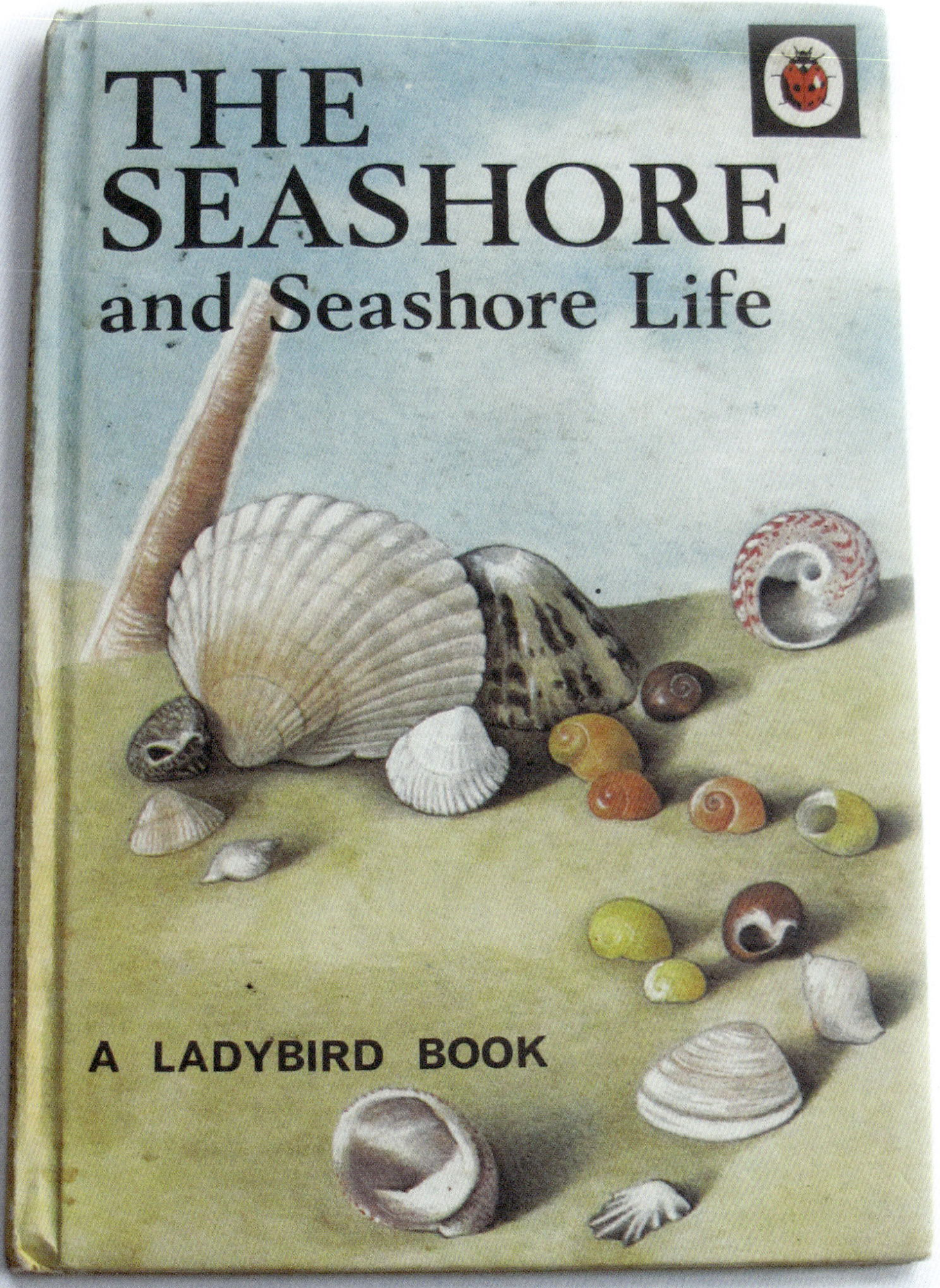

No Man's Land
No Man is an Island

previous page: Scalextrix model camera man spectator and plastic seal on a picture frame mounted on the top of a camera tripod. Fur seal.

In 1982 South Georgia was in the news as the initial flashpoint for the Falklands War. The news I saw on telly as a fourteen year old included footage of the dilapidated whaling station at Grytviken, abandoned since the early sixties. It made a lasting impression on me and I had wanted to go ever since. Moby Dick is also one of my favourite books so, when I arrived there, I had high expectations. My disappointment was probably inevitable. In the intervening years, the site had become a stop-off for cruise ships and the time capsule, built of sheets of corrugated steel that blew around in the strong South Atlantic gales, had been dismantled and turned into a museum. It's brilliant, as far as museums go, but it was a far cry from the news item I had seen as a boy.

Our next stop was a base at the end of South Georgia called Bird Island. Bird Island is separated from the mainland by a narrow stretch of water that is vital to the preservation of this nature reserve because it keeps the rats away. The base was very small and, to get the supplies ashore, they were transferred to a smaller cargo tender. The ship itself remained at anchor almost a mile offshore. It was obligatory to take part in the unloading of the cargo. In total, I couldn't have spent more than a few hours unloading on Bird Island but it made an indelible impression on me.

As the cargo tender approached the island, a flock of birds started to settle on the wooden crates and cardboard boxes. They were Sheathbills* – a little bigger than a dove and pure white in colour. They reminded me of white cockatiels and, perched so close to us, they felt almost tame. Their presence gave the boat a tranquil ambience. One of the birds stood out from the rest. It was exactly the same shape as the others but it had distinctly different markings. From its head all the way down its neck it had a vivid red plumage that made it look very exotic indeed. I studied this specimen through the viewfinder of my camera and slowly realised they were not red feathers at all. The bird was dripping in blood.

The boat chugged its way through a mist and the mood changed. As I looked down into the water, it seemed to churn with life. Giant Petrels and Skuas floated on the surface and black, slimy shapes kept emerging from beneath. Even on the ship, a mile off-shore, we had noticed a distinct odour. Now, as we got closer to the island, it became a more pungent mixture of musk, excrement and death. Through the mist, we could hear infant screams and cries drifting across the water from the shore. It was like a sequence from a cheap Hammer House of Horror movie and it stunned us into silence.

Bird Island has a simple eco-system; everything survives by waiting around for something else to die so that it can eat it. The birds on the beach casually peck at sleeping seals and, if they don't get a response, they assume the animal is dead and, by working a hole through the skin, they start to pull out lumps of meat. The bird on the cargo tender had obviously just joined us after its meal. The blood came from thrusting itself, neck deep, into the carcass of a dead Fur Seal.

We had arrived at the height of Fur Seal mating season and the beach was covered in seals staking out territory to attract a female. Less than a hundred years ago, these seals, along with whales, had been hunted to the point of extinction. Though the hunting of both animals has almost stopped, the whale, being larger, is recovering a lot slower. Meanwhile Fur Seal colonies have accelerated wildly because there are fewer whales to compete for the krill. There are probably more seals now than at any other point in history. The black shapes under the water were seals swimming around the island trying to find a space on the beach.

Each male seal guards its territory viciously. To a female, the most attractive male is the one that controls a nice dry patch of beach near the water's edge. The males fight frequently over territory and these clashes often end in a bloody wounding. Some seals die of these injuries but others just die of old age and illness. When they die, the body is always to be found in a water-logged patch of beach. As the animal gets weaker, it is driven into this undesirable territory by the healthier, more

*** commonly known by BAS employees as the 'shit chicken'.**

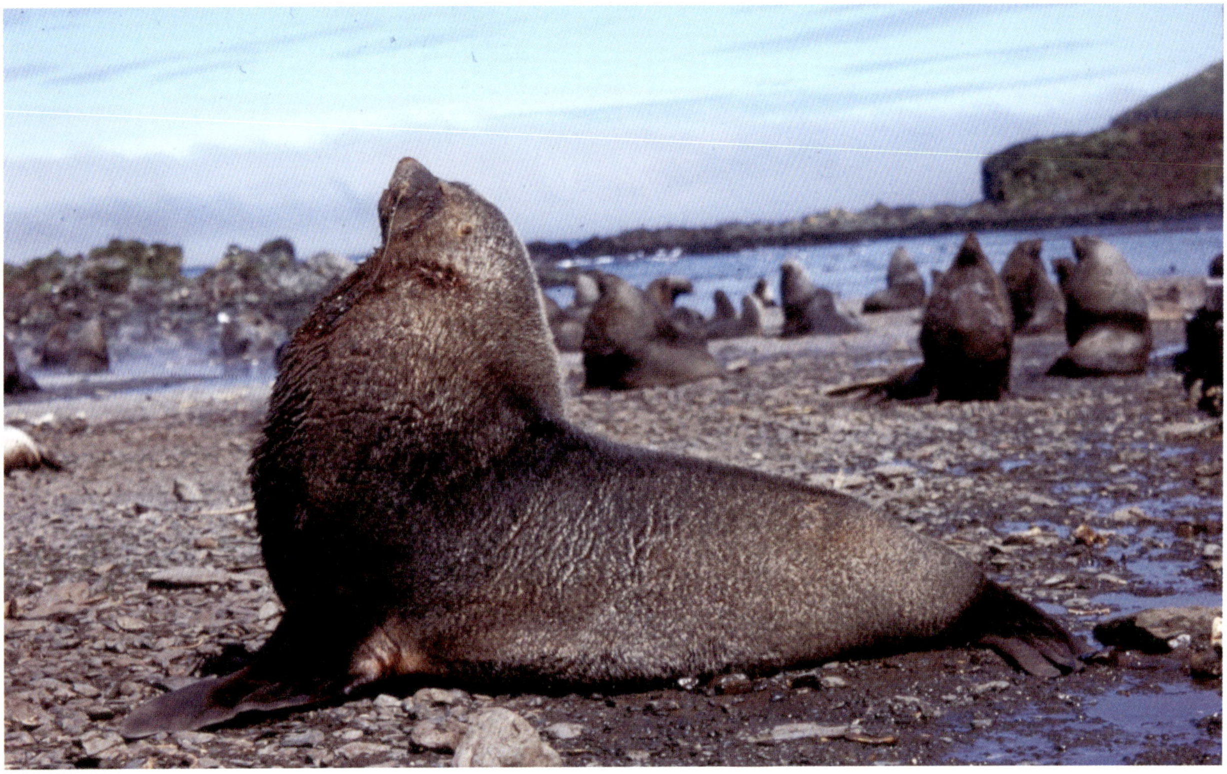

Male fur seal.

virile males. The noises we could hear were fights mixed with the cries of new born pups calling out for their mothers. The beach itself was made of mud, rocks and seal bones in various states of decay. I had never seen Dr Zubkov quite so happy:

'It is nature in the raw!'

He proclaimed. As the mist cleared, I could see nothing but seals disappearing into the distance. Their black forms were even distinguishable high up in the foothills of the mountain behind the base. These males were not likely to breed. Dr Zubkov pointed them out to me and said:

'You see? They are the losers!'

Wildlife in Antarctica has evolved without fear of human beings so penguins and other birds are completely indifferent to human presence. I once saw a Skua help itself nonchalantly to mashed potato while an intimidated crew member tried to eat his dinner from the other side of the plate.

Like the bird life, the seals also had no fear of human beings and, if they thought their territory was threatened, they defended it fiercely. We had received a briefing from the doctor Nerys before we left about the problems of being bitten. We were told that, although it would be painful, the bite itself wouldn't kill us. It would, however, go sceptic and we'd have to have an injection of antibiotics. The mouth of a Fur Seal is a particularly unpleasant place where microbes are forever mutating and there is a danger that doctors may, one day, run out of antibiotics to combat new infections. The doctor's advice, therefore, was 'Don't get bitten!'

Some more useful advice was that, if a Fur Seal decided to attack, it would probably raise itself up first. In this position, its mouth is roughly in line with the genital area and that is often the place it will strike. I was told to let my trousers hang as low as possible in an attempt to get my would-be attacker to bite cloth instead of genitals. The seal is, in fact, reluctant to attack. It is essentially a sea mammal, not designed to manoeuvre quickly on land. As you get closer, the seal starts to psych itself up like a tired old dog with rheumatism. With much huffing and whining it awkwardly raises its wallowing, blubbery bulk from the ground and points its

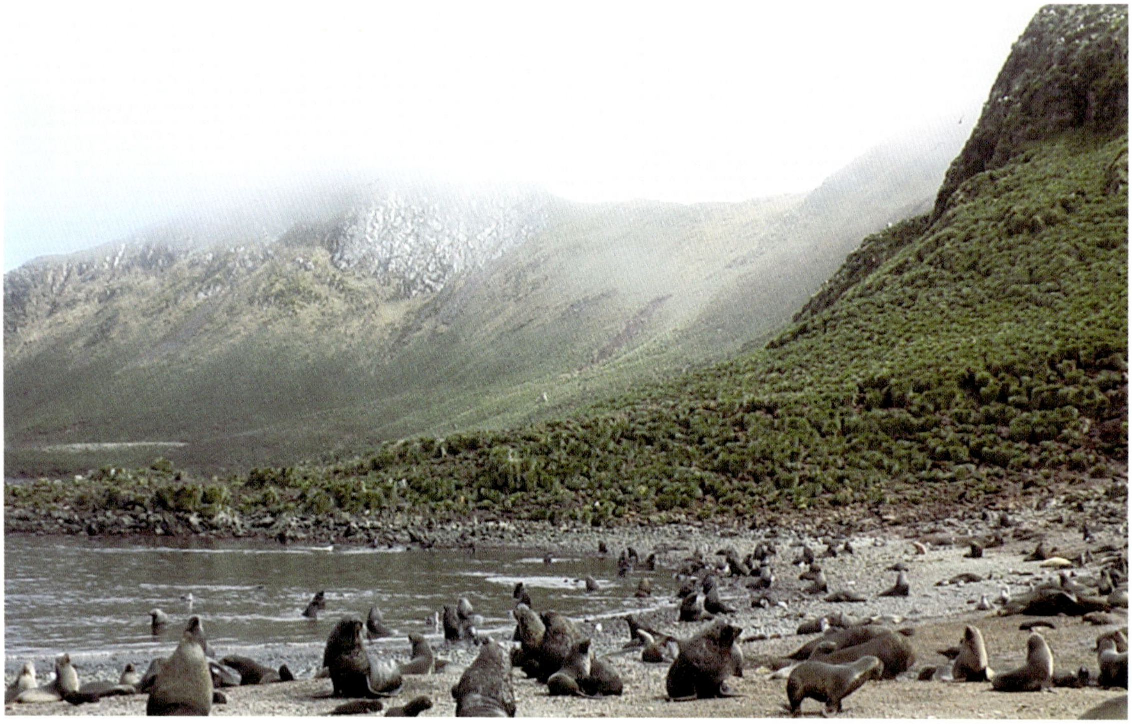
The beach in front of the BAS Bird island base.

nose in the air. At this stage, the effort has made it even more annoyed and it opens its mouth to bear its fangs, hiss and look pure evil at you. People aren't always bitten by the Fur Seal in front of them. Often, frightened by a hissing seal, they will impulsively jump back into another one and it is the startled neighbour that usually bites them.

One of the most desirable dry parts of the beach, close to the water's edge, was the jetty where we were trying to unload the cargo. The first seal to greet us, therefore, was the biggest, nastiest, alpha male of the lot. Faced with the hazard of an aggressive, rearing Fur Seal, I naturally assumed there would be a trained professional amongst us with the proper equipment to deal with the situation. They gave me a broomstick. Armed with this equipment, I was told the best thing to do was tickle its whiskers and it would back down. I did this and the seal tried to bite off the end of my stick. Somewhere in the cargo tender, under a year's worth of supplies, was an anonymous cardboard box with that year's supply of new broomsticks. Unable to find it, we armed ourselves with last year's broomsticks, some of which were bitten down to short stumps.

The jetty made its way from the deep water across the muddy, bony beach to the main building. It was about eight foot wide and along its length several more Fur Seals had decided to set-up camp. We had to roll sixty oil drums along this walkway. We later realised that the best thing to do was not antagonise the seals but, within half an hour of landing, inexperienced, frightened and flailing broomsticks, we had a jetty full of angry Fur Seals who objected to being an oil drum slalom course. Eventually we learnt to work around them and they settled down. There seemed to be logic to their behaviour and at one point I even felt a sense of pride that I had mastered their reactions. Just then, a particularly aggressive seal climbed up onto its flippers and made a dash as fast it could go down the length of the jetty heading straight for us. There was nobody even close to it and I couldn't understand why it had just decided to run amok. At the last minute it took a leap from the jetty into the water. I turned to Dr Zubkov and said: 'But why? It shouldn't have done that – it doesn't make sense!'

To which Dr Zubkov replied: 'Who can say – it just felt like it!'

The base had a scientist whose job was to study the Fur Seals and live on Bird Island for up to two and half years. In comparison to the ecosystem on Bird Island, the social structure that we had all come from now suddenly seemed very superficial. I began to think about the disparate group of volunteers I was in. Anyone studying the occupants of the cargo tender would have found us a very strange collection of specimens; an artist, Dr Zubkov the scientist, Dave a plumber, and a representative of the British Antarctic Survey's Human Resources Department.

Each year, someone from Human Resources goes to the Antarctic to hear any grievances and make sure that everyone on the ships and the bases is content. A banal role in an ordinary workplace but, in the Antarctic, it felt like a sketch from Monty Python's Flying Circus.

Although we all referred to Dave as a plumber, I found out later he was actually an engineer. He had applied to work for BAS after seeing an ad for the role of Technical Support Officer on Bird Island. This trip from the ship with the cargo was his introduction to his new home and we were going to leave him there. In the cargo tender, he suddenly went very quiet. Later that evening everybody, apart from Dave, came back to the ship. The ship was still at anchor so sea sickness hadn't kicked in yet and I felt well enough to go and have a drink. The man from Human Resources was holding court at the bar and talking about Dave:

'I could tell the plumber was getting shaky about staying on Bird Island. That place makes a terrible first impression on people. The animal lovers can't get enough of it but technical support staff? In the boat this morning, I could see the signs on his face – the look of mild shock, the jaw drops a little then they go all quiet. That's when I have to do my bit for Human Resources.'

As he said this, I recalled him making his way over to Dave in the boat to have a one to one. That day, a prominent piece of debris on the beach had been the rib cage of a dead seal. The white bones still had quite a bit of meat on them and the flippers and tail were still attached. A collection of Giant Petrels were helping themselves.

I always found the eyes of the giant petrel particularly unnerving. They stare grotesquely and are very pale in colour, like those of an alcoholic. By the back door of the base there was an assorted collection of birds fighting over a fresher corpse in a muddy puddle. A Giant Petrel was burying its head in the body whilst fending off competition from a smaller Skua. Ingeniously, the Skua had found the end of the seal's intestine and dragged it about ten feet away while the other end was still connected to the seal. It pecked at this extremity at a safe distance from the petrel. When the petrel next took its head out of its bloody hole, the Skua knew it had a ten foot head start.

These two were joined by a third species of bird; a rather ordinary and harmless-looking duck. This bird was a species peculiar to the Island being the only one in the world that is carnivorous. As Dave surveyed the bloody carnage, the man from Human Resources placed a reassuring hand on his shoulder and said:

'The Technical Support Officer at Bird Island is one of the most popular postings in BAS. You're a very lucky guy!'

As we stood at the bar, he recounted all the other things he had said to Dave to reassure him that he had made a good career choice: 'A fantastic group of people to spend the next year and half with. You can't leave so you will learn to be resourceful. Friends you make here will last a life time. The brilliant wildlife…' He admitted at this point he was pulling at straws. '…A good DVD collection and some great books in the library too.'

'Did you think Dave might be having second thoughts this morning Chris? I noticed you had words with him after I did.'

As I slowly realised that the chat Dave had been having with the man from Human Resources had been a counselling session, I started to reflect upon the comment I had made not long after:

'FUCKING HELL! Nice place to visit. Wouldn't wanna live 'ere… eh Dave?'

The ship weighed anchor and headed back to Port Stanley. I finished my drink and went back to my cabin to prepare for the next two days of throwing up.

A week later I was in the ship's bar again. We must have been at sea for at least three days because my body had grown used to the movement and I didn't feel ill. I was in a good mood. Somebody came in and casually told everyone that we were returning to Bird Island to unload some more supplies. My good mood subsided and an atmosphere of dread descended upon the whole bar.

This time we had a rough idea what to expect and, on coming ashore, we braced ourselves accordingly. It was a mild day and, to our surprise, even Bird Island can look better when the sun is out. I was relieved to see that Dave had fitted in and looked quite content. He had even given a name to one of the seals although 'Bitey' wasn't exactly endearing.

We all carried boxes of food, including frozen pork chops, along the jetty, past Bitey and handed them through the window of the food store. Gradually, we filled up the row of freezers and emptied the cargo tender. With our work done, we found ourselves with some spare time.

I had brought my camera and a few toys with me and the scientists stationed at the base offered to lead groups of us to the Macaroni Penguin colony, taking in the albatross nests on the way. One of the toys was a plastic model of a farmer pushing a broom. The head of the broom had come off and it looked like one of us wielding a broomstick at a Fur Seal. Although there are various plastic penguins on the market, I couldn't find many toys or models of the albatross. Eventually I found a company on the internet that made books for dolls houses including Coleridge's Rime of the Ancient Mariner. My only other albatross object was an image of one printed on a small card that had come as a free gift in a packet of tea. I had bought various other Antarctic related cards at car boot sales but this particular one had actually belonged to me as a small boy and I had found it by chance in my parent's loft just before I left for the Antarctic. I put my cards and toys in my pocket and set off to follow the guide.

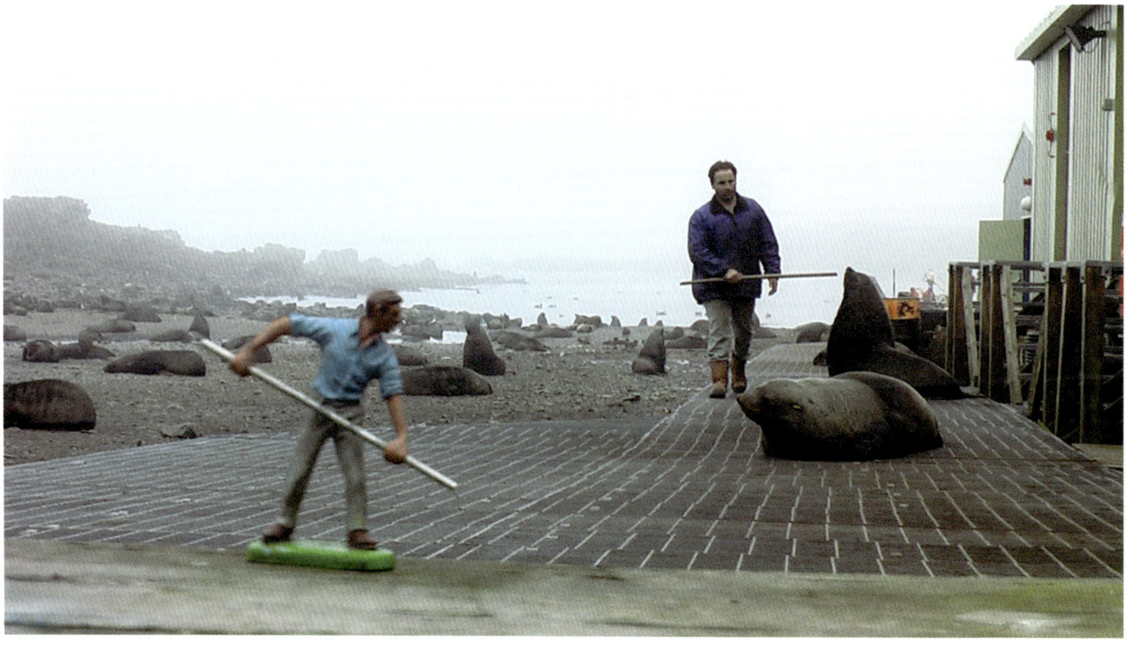

Bird Island base commander makes his way past Fur Seals and a Britain's toy farmer.

Where the beach ends and the foothills begin, the steep ground is covered in tussock grass. Some of these thick sprouting balls of vegetation can be waist-high and easy to trip over. Fur Seals slept between the tussocks and sometimes leapt out at us. We hiked higher and higher and still we kept finding seals. Even though we knew that these seals were the losers, they could still be quite aggressive. Then, suddenly, we reached a point beyond which the seals could not climb and there was a totally different mood. In this place, the Wandering Albatross sat on top of their nests. As with the other species, they were completely indifferent to human beings and were more interested in each other as I took out my tiny copy of the Rime of the Ancient Mariner and started to take photographs.

My English teacher once told me that because the albatross was found so far from land, sailors used to think that it gave birth in the air and never touched land. This myth would have persisted right up until 1775 when the first person stepped onto South Georgia and saw the albatross nests for the first time.

The others were anxious to move on to the penguin colony but I hadn't finished photographing. The scientist suggested I tag onto the next group so that I could have more time. I wasn't sure if this steep, grassy prominence constituted a small mountain or a big hill but it felt as though I was on the very pinnacle. I had a vast panoramic view of the horizon and, apart from a few icebergs in the distance and our ship, like a toy, clearly visible in the bay below, there was nothing. The only noise came from the birds themselves; clattering their beaks, calling to each other and swishing past me.

Apart from being sick in my cabin, climbing to the top deck of the ship and a few blustery walks around Port Stanley, this was the first time I had been alone for weeks. I took the Brook Bond tea card out of my pocket and pictured the loft at my parent's house. There were toys there from my childhood that I still didn't have the heart to throw away. This personal time capsule was now the other side of the equator and thousands and thousands of miles away over the horizon. I made a clip from a piece of coke can to hold the edge of the card and tied this to a rusty nail with string to act as a flag pole and took this photo.

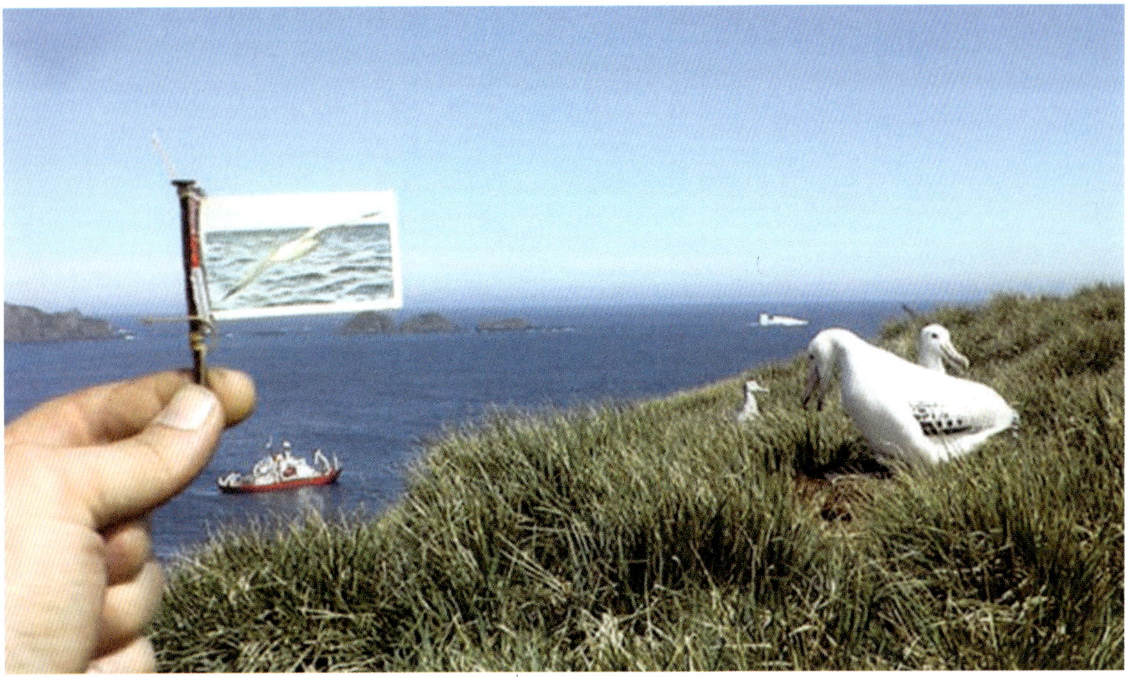

Brook Bond Tea collector's card of a Wandering Albatross in front of the real thing.

When the other group came along, I followed them to the penguin colony where 40,000 breeding pairs covered the steep slope down to the water. Dave was there waiting there for me:

'Wow Dave!' I said, 'it's just like one of those BBC wildlife documentaries!'

Dave pointed out that, in the long grass over to our left, there actually was a BBC wildlife cameraman. Luckily, I had brought a few model spectators from my racing car Scalextric set and one of these figures was carrying a film camera. I managed to photograph it with the real cameraman in the background. Guessing that this figure would come in useful, I had bought a couple more at a car boot sale and I modified one by extending the coat and adding a hood. I then painted it in the colours of the BAS cold weather gear so that it looked like a BAS employee. I referred to this model as my 'toy me'.

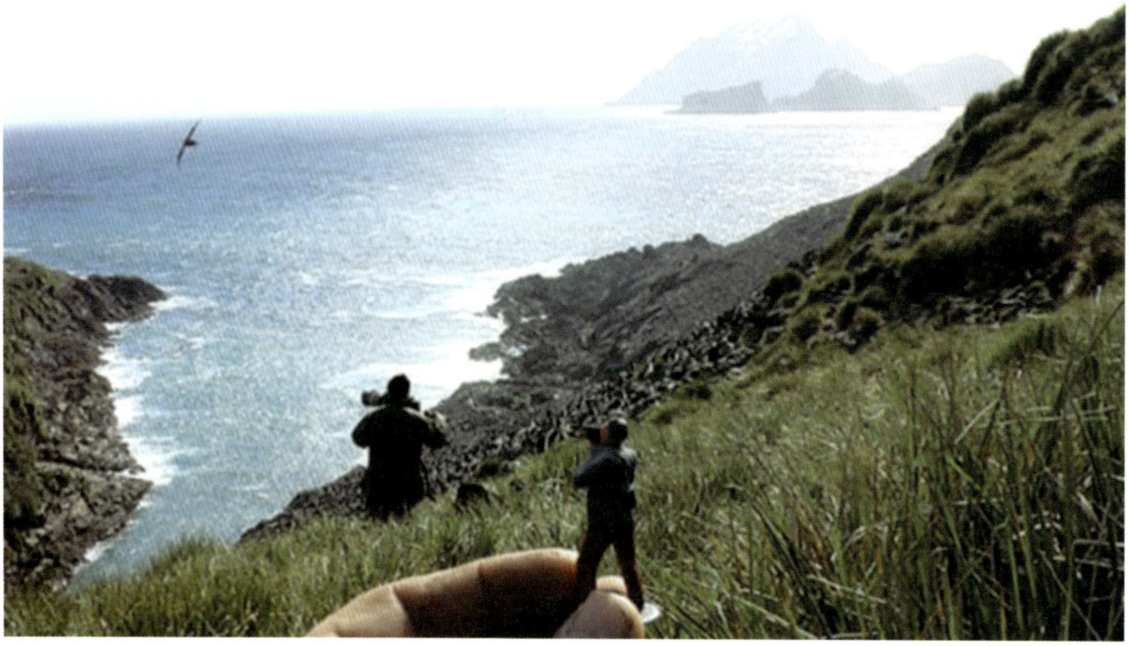

Scalextric's cameraman spectator model in front of a BBC wildlife documentary film-maker in front of the Macaroni Penguin colony in the distance.

The last two weeks on the ship were spent sailing from Port Stanley down the Antarctic Peninsula. On board was a new group of passengers on their way, like me, to Rothera. The straight two weeks at sea meant that my body became used to the motion and I stopped throwing up. The ship felt like my home and I felt like I belonged. I even had the cheek to give one or two of our new guests a tour. One evening in the bar the phone rang. With my new found self-importance I instinctively picked it up. It was the bridge and it was me they wanted:

'Is the artist there? We want him up here on the bridge. There's something we need to talk to him about.'

It sounded a bit ominous. On the bridge there were two officers looking at the charts. We were so far South by this point that, even at midnight, it was still quite light outside. The officers on watch called me over and pointed to a dot on their map:

'We estimate that in approximately half an hour we will be passing Dobrowolski Island. You should be able to see it on the starboard side.'

Like most people, I have put my name into Google to see what came up. This is how I found the other artist called Chris Dobrowolski but I had never heard of an island called Dobrowolski. I later

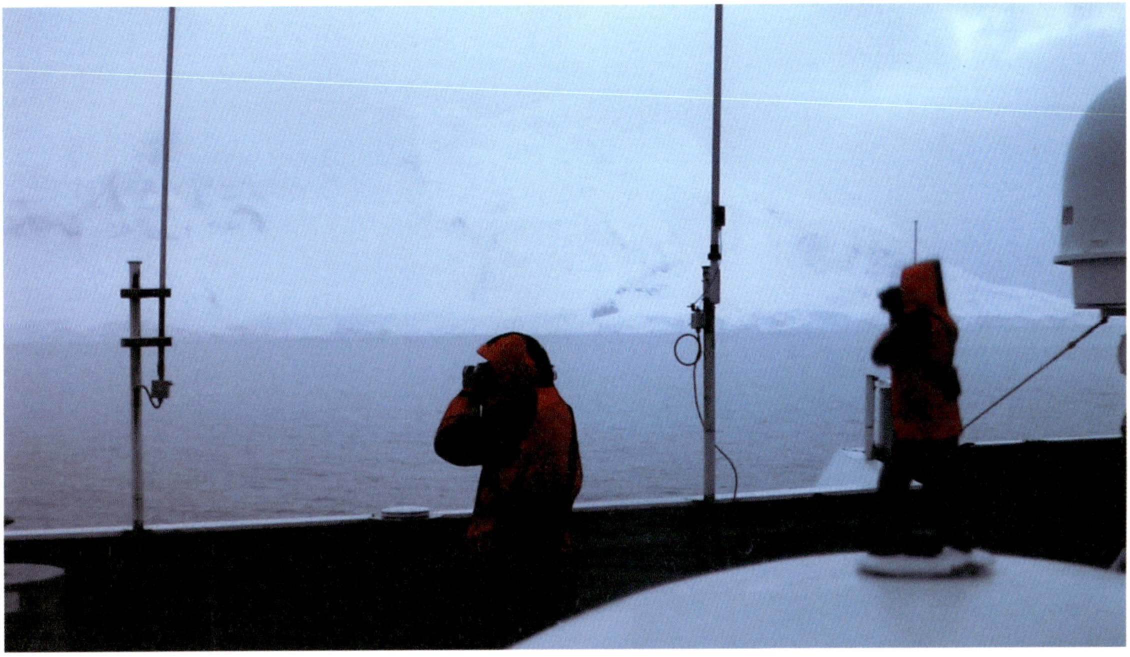

The Scalextric's cameraman adapted to be a BAS employee filming me filming Dobrowolski Island. [Terri Souster]

discovered that it had been named after a Polish Assistant Meteorologist on a Belgian expedition in 1898. It is very small and just off another island called Anvers Island at 64°36 S 62°55 W64.6°S 62.917°W. At half past midnight, I went to the top deck with my camera and I got someone to photograph my 'toy me' photographing the 'real me' photographing the real Dobrowolski Island.

The next day, the Chief Engineer offered us a tour of the engine room. It was a very noisy place and, as well as the loud, rhythmic engine noises, there was also the constant alarms of the watertight doors opening and shutting as we moved from one compartment to another. We went all the way to the back of the ship and saw the propeller shaft as it exited the hull to churn up the Southern Ocean. An hour later, we emerged and went back to the bar. In the hour I had been away, the Radio Officer had brought the schedule for our disembarkation from the Base Commander at Rothera. The ship was due to dock for several days and we were to disembark in order of importance or demand for our particular skill. I was to be one of the very last people to leave the ship.

Star Ship Rothera was how the crew referred to the base. A man-made environment surrounded by the vastness of space. At the height of the summer season Rothera could be inhabited by over 100 people and there were regular flights to the Falklands and Chile. It had a laboratory, various offices, mechanic's garage, store rooms and accommodation. There was a brand new building housing the dining hall, library, computers and common room. It did feel a bit like a space ship but with table tennis, pool table, gym, recreational skiing and snow-boarding. It was like a youth centre at the end of the world.

When I finally came to leave the ship, I borrowed a hard hat to stand alongside and say goodbye to all my friends on board. I waved to people on the higher decks and shook hands with George who was about to cast off. The ship pulled away from its berth then slowly became smaller and smaller until it disappeared. I turned back to Rothera, my new home, and realised I had to start all over again. There were nearly a hundred new people here, some of whom would doubtless think that the artist was pointless, draining resources from scientists working to save the planet.

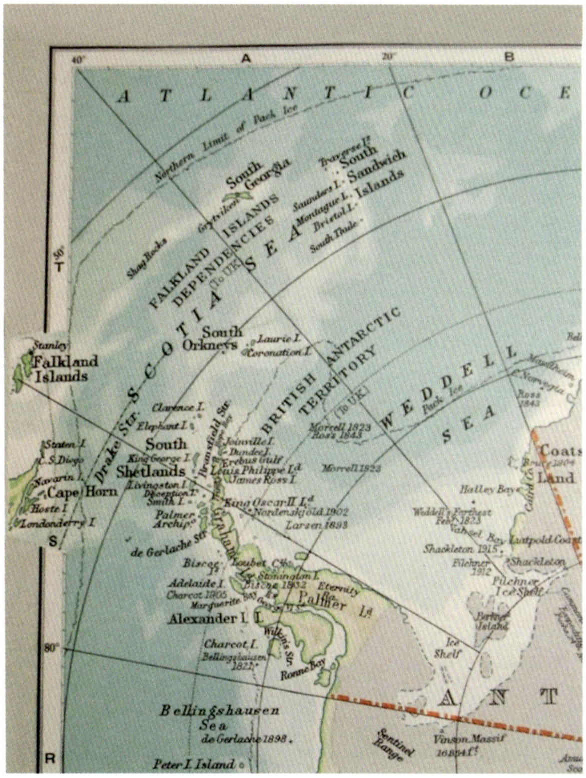

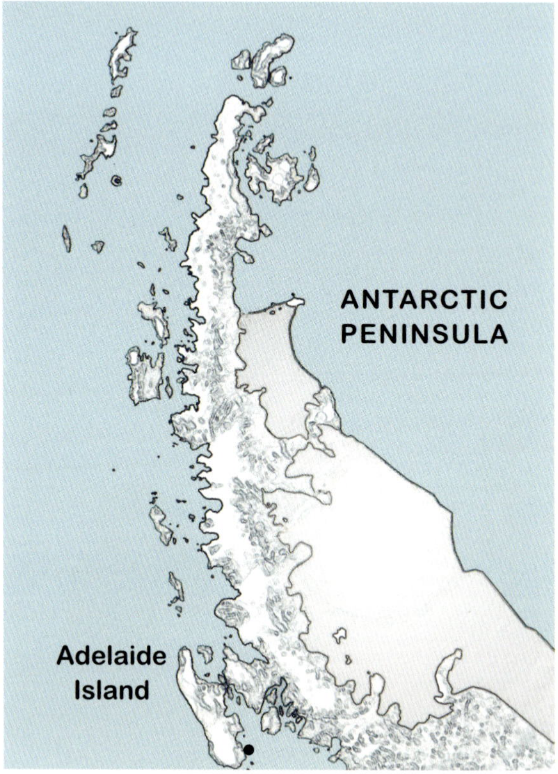

Rothera Point is on the tip of Adelaide Island which is 75 miles long by about 20 miles wide. It lies just off the West coast of the Antarctic Peninsula. The base itself is a few metres above sea level and surrounded by water on three sides which only freezes in winter. There is a steep snow ramp that leads up from the base to the mountain range and the ice cap which makes up the interior of the island. To the right of the ramp, the ice slowly descends to the water's edge as a glacier, ending abruptly in a sheer wall of ice. Every few days, a big lump several metres high will calve off and crash into the cove with the sound of a rumbling explosion that makes a dramatic spectacle from the window of the dining hall.

Despite the modern facilities we all had to learn how to camp in the snow to prepare for work off-base and to survive should something happen to the base. The first stage of integration into life at Rothera was a day learning how to melt snow for drinking water and how to put up the BAS issue Scott Polar tent. We also had to sleep in the tent. On my first evening, I therefore sat in the passenger seat of a Sno-Cat and rode up the ramp. Near the top of the slope we veered right and traversed the incline until the terrain levelled out. A bit further along, we came to a caboose – a hut on skis – at the base of the recreational skiing slope. The place was known to everyone as Vals and here we pitched our training camp.

That morning I had bumped into the previous training group just as they came down. They said it was a simple task and surprisingly warm in the tent. It was very peaceful and they had slept incredibly soundly. My cabin on the ship had been quite noisy so I was particularly looking forward to a good night's sleep. There were four of us in the last group to leave the ship – me, an electrician, a carpenter and the Business Development Officer who was clearly considered pretty low priority because he had to share a tent with the artist.

We were only about ten minutes drive from Rothera Point but up here, just out of earshot of the generators, I felt I was properly in the wilderness. Visibility was uncannily good and I could clearly see the mountains on the mainland miles away across the water. It was eerie to be able to see clearly for a long way knowing that there was nobody in the vast space between me and that horizon. I walked some distance away from our camp, there was no wind and it was totally still. Very quickly, the only thing I could hear was the crunch of snow beneath my boots and when I stopped it was as if the sound had been sucked from the atmosphere. I stood in the mute stillness and contemplated the abyss. Then, in the distance, I heard voices:

'F U U U C K I N G C U U U U U N T!!'

'A R R R R S E H O L E!!'

Having finished putting up their tent, my companions were having a competition to see if they could start an avalanche with swear words. They were trying to decide which swear words were the most effective. I spent the rest of the night trying to find ways to sleep in the twenty-four hour sunlight and the noise from my team as they built an igloo, had a snowball fight and pulled down their trousers to photograph each other's bottoms. I was in the quietest place on earth and I ended up stuffing things in my ears to shut out the din.

The artist's role in society is usually one of voyeur, someone who looks at the world from the outside and reflects back through their artistic medium. Surrounded by idealistic scientists who were trying to save the planet, I felt ashamed of my profession and found it difficult to think of my presence in the Antarctic as anything but exploitative. My one saving grace had always been that I was a failure. However, the fact that I had been selected to go to the Antarctic now made me look slightly more successful and my nagging self-doubts made it even more difficult to sleep that night. A few hours later, although the light outside the tent hadn't changed, it was morning. I was keen to be up but I lay in my sleeping bag listening for any sign that someone else was awake. I didn't have to wait long:

'M E R R Y F U U C K I N C H R I S T M A A A A S!'

It was Christmas day.

I had spent a month longer on the ship than anticipated but the date for my flight back to the UK was the same. I was scheduled to leave at the beginning of February and therefore had half as long to build the sledge as planned. I had been selected for the residency in May but I didn't actually leave for the Antarctic until November. In that six month period, people had asked me what I was going to do once I got there and I had proudly told them: 'I'm going to build a sledge!'

I would reach a whole new level of failure if I didn't fulfil this one basic objective. The strange contradiction about the Antarctic is that despite being surrounded by miles of empty space, there is nowhere to run away to. I was quite keen to lose myself in my work by getting into the carpenter's workshop to make the sledge.

The carpenter's workshop was the oldest building on the base. It had been erected in the mid-seventies when BAS moved their centre of operation from the other side of Adelaide Island. In the early days this modest prefab had been the base for the first team of four people. It reminded me of a school woodwork classroom. Behind it was another very basic hut which was even older since it had been dismantled and transported from the old base to Rothera. It served as an annexe to the main carpenter's shed and it had all the tools I needed. This was where I would spend the whole of the month to come. Admittedly, there was a fantastic view but, essentially, I had travelled several thousand miles to spend a month in a shed not dissimilar to the one in my garden at home.

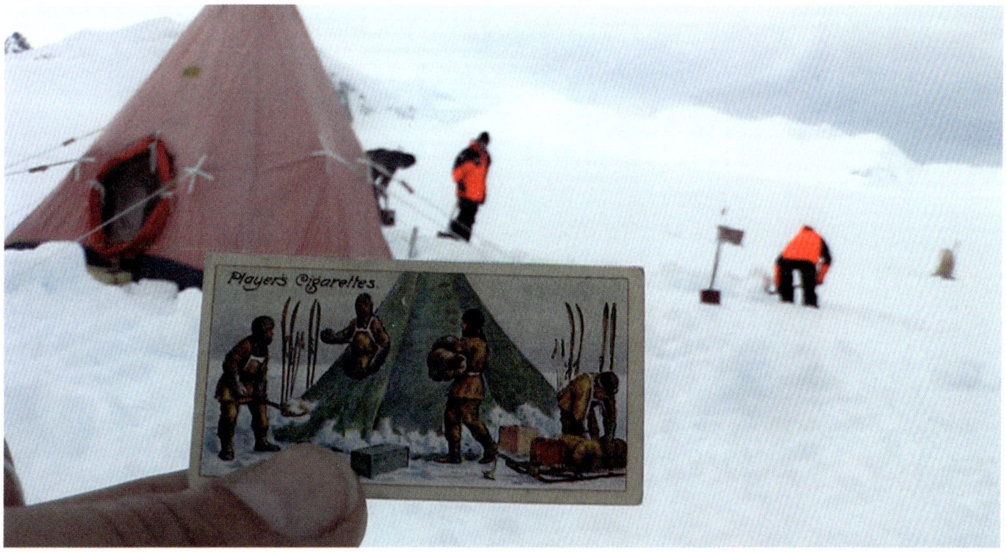

Player's cigarette collector's card of Captain Scott making camp whilst we learn the basics in the background.

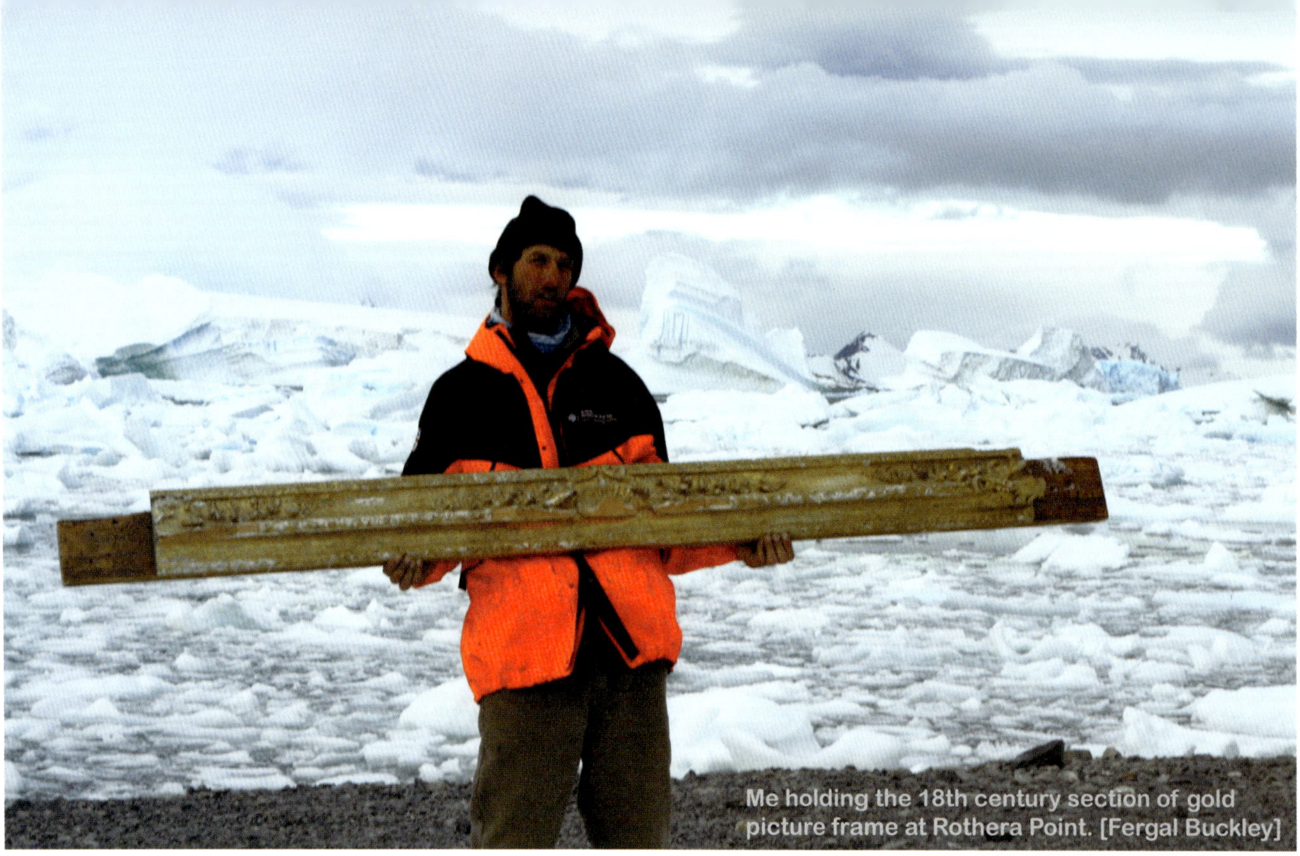

Me holding the 18th century section of gold picture frame at Rothera Point. [Fergal Buckley]

In Sheds

Before I went to the Antarctic, a friend put me in touch with a frame-maker who generously agreed to put some unwanted frames to one side for me. When I went to collect the frames, I realised that he wasn't just a frame-maker, he was also an antique frame restorer. One section of frame he gave me was 250 years old and covered in the remnants of real gold leaf. It was so old that it had been made before human beings had even seen the Antarctic. At eight foot long and eight inches thick, this section was too wide and heavy to use on the sledge but I took it to the Antarctic anyway and made a photograph of it there. The other frames were less remarkable and I'd bought them at my local car boot sale.

The wood used for a proper Nansen sledge is ash which is very solid, hard and durable. My picture frames were usually cheap pine or obeche often with plaster moulding stuck all over them. A Nansen sledge is about 12ft in length but most of my picture frames were a little over 2ft long. The longest sections are the two runners which go from the front to the very back. I managed to make them from my short sections by joining them side by side and doubling them up. I then staggered the joins alternately in each runner so that the potential weak spots would always be opposite a solid section of frame. I reinforced them by screwing the same mirror plate into the two separate pieces as they butted up to each other. Gradually, a long gold jigsaw puzzle came together which was surprisingly strong.

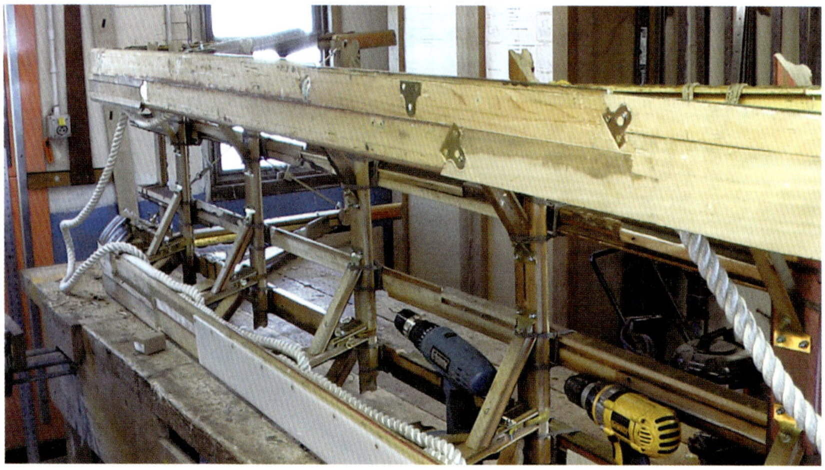

The underneath of the sledge showing mirror plates holding the sections of picture frame together.

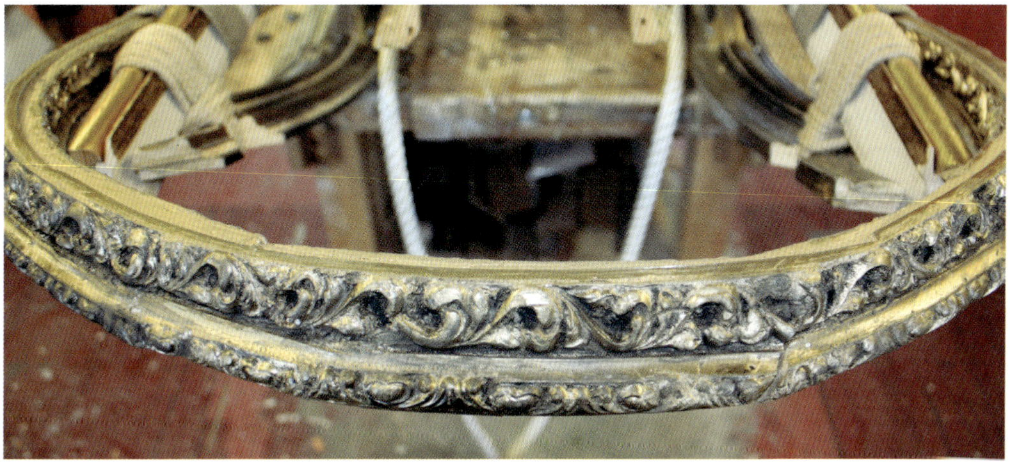

Close-up of the cow-catcher [Alister Doyle]

I began by cutting the wood on the circular saw in the carpenter's workshop. The blade was blunt so the wood got hot and started to smoulder slightly which set off the fire alarm and the entire base had to stop and go to the fire assembly point. At the assembly point, four people were donning asbestos suits ready for their fire rescue procedure and some people had wet hair because they had been in the shower. By following the burning smell, it was quickly established that the false alarm was the artist's fault. I returned to work sheepishly.

As well as length, the other difference between a sledge and a picture frame is the curvy bits. I seldom found curved frames at the car boot sale and when I did they were never the uniform curve required of sledge runners. For this reason I planned to make some kind of enclosed container to put pieces of frame into and fill it with steam. Under a bit of pressure, the steam gets into the wood grain and makes it more flexible so that it can be bent into shape. I had brought an electric hot plate with me to heat up the water. It was a large, very old piece of kit that Eddie had left behind in his studio. He used it for melting rabbit skin size to prime his painting canvases. The hot plate made me smile. On the side, my old friend had painted EDDIE in big letters. It was a reassuring presence. I plugged it in and all the electricity in the carpenter's shop fused. I thought it best to find another way to make steam.

In training on the mountain we had been shown how to use an Optimus primus stove which was part of the standard issue camping kit for the British Antarctic Survey. I decided to use one of these but needed a big receptacle to put the water in. In the Antarctic all milk comes powdered and packaged in large yellow tins with the trade name Nido. One of these empty tins was just the right size. The next thing I needed was something to collect the steam in.

To get around on base there were several little green cars called John Deere Gators. They had chunky wheels and I was given an old inner tube from one. I cut it open so that I had a floppy black rubber pipe open at both ends. I then fixed one end over the top of my Nido tin with a very large jubilee clip. The water in the tin boiled on the primus stove and the steam filled the tube. In this receptacle I placed a length of gold picture frame. After it had boiled for about half an hour, I quickly removed the frame, clamped it to the work bench and bent the front end up onto a temporary support that gave it the required angle. At this point my first runner snapped. I persevered and eventually used a technique that I had noticed on the other Nansen sledges at Rothera. I cut lengthways into the wood so that, instead of trying to bend one thick section, I was simultaneously bending three thin slivers. The saw cuts between these pieces were later filled and glued and this helped strengthen and hold the curve.

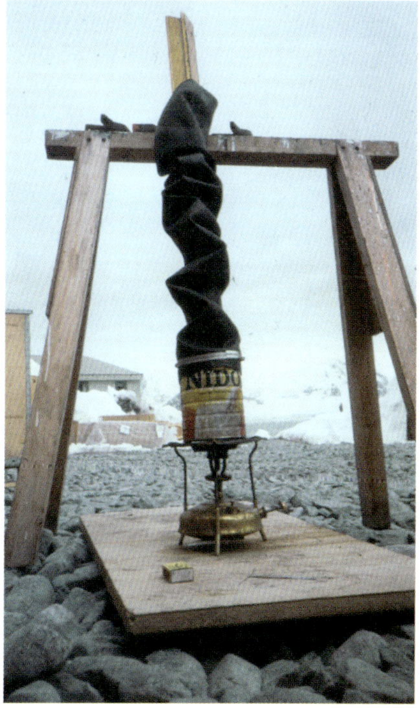

The steaming device

The next sections to be built were the supports that held the runners together in parallel. These sections also make the raised area of the sledge that takes the weight of the payload. There are five of these supports or chairs and, on a modern sledge, they are made from one section that comes up, over and down to the other runner in one curved piece of very strong laminated wood. It would be technically difficult to make the chairs in this way from frame wood but it was for aesthetic reasons that I didn't actually want to do it this way.

Having gone to the trouble of bringing picture frames to the Antarctic it would have been pointless if they didn't look like picture frames once they were turned into a sledge. One of the things I had to be careful of was not to plane and cut the wood in such a way that it lost its picture frame-ness. If the frames were overworked they would start to look like any other second hand wood. My aim was to find a way of working that struck a balance between making the sledge look like a sledge but one that was made of picture frames. Luckily, the sledge that I had seen in the museum used a more suitable method.

This old-fashioned sledge design made each chair from three sections plus two smaller pieces that triangulated the corners to brace the joins. I fixed these braced corners together with a combination of sledge building and picture hanging techniques. The small bracing section was held with large, bent picture-hanging mirror plates, whilst the corner itself was joined in the traditional way with a leather thong. I heated the thongs in an electric kettle of water to make them more pliable for squeezing through the joining holes. When they cooled down they shrank and tightened. I used this thong method again to join each finished chair to the runners.

The base of each chair is usually pretty wide and solid. This gives rigidity and stops backwards and forwards movement caused by the forces of inertia whilst in motion. It was difficult to find such a wide section in a typical piece of picture frame wood so I braced each chair with a corner of picture frame. If seen from the side, it appears that there are a series of five gold triangles along the edge of the sledge. This method also accentuated the fact that the sledge was made from picture frames.

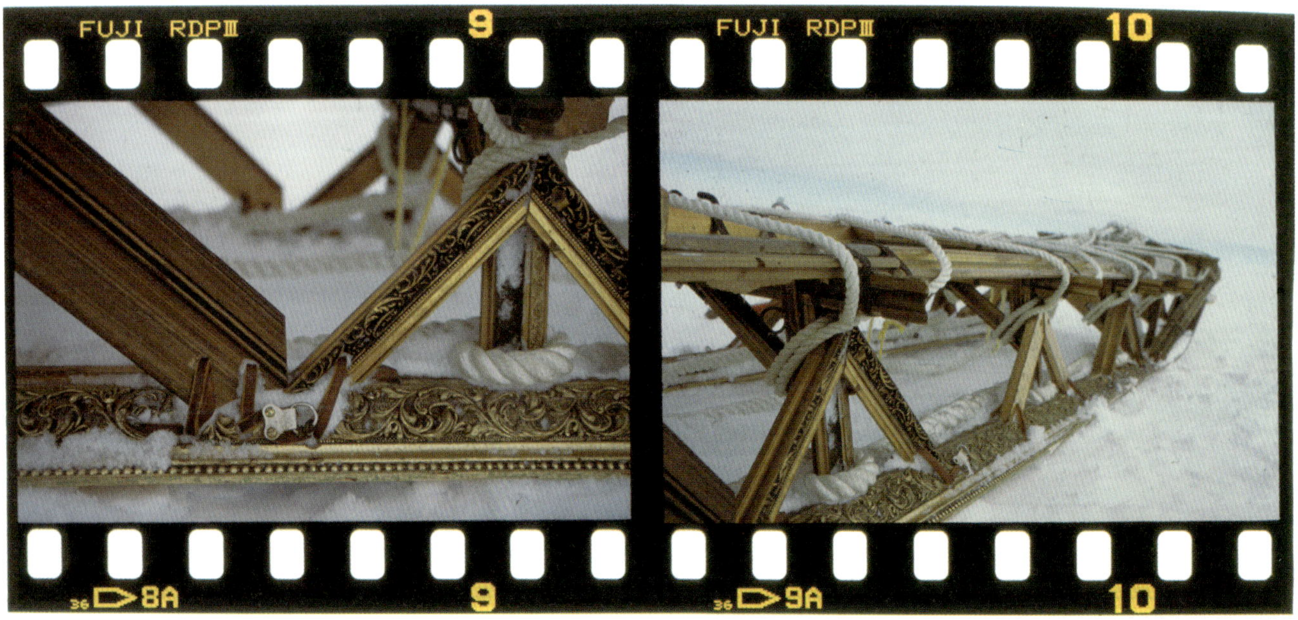

Gold picture frame corners along the side of the sledge.

The next stage involved connecting the tops of the five chairs to each other. The four long, thin connecting pieces were called longies and, again, I made them from connecting short pieces of frame together. The two outside longies were especially long because, as well as joining the chairs, they joined with the curved tips of the runners. As these sections crossed the chairs at right angles, they made a grid which would become the load carrying surface. At the points where the longies intersected the chairs they were fixed together with string. The strong string was wound round many times at these points and, after it had been tied off, it was painted with dope that shrank and tightened it. This string-fixing method, called whipping, like the leather thongs, made a strong joint that also gave the design its flexibility even in extreme cold temperatures.

Each longie is fixed to each chair, making a total of twenty joins that have to be whipped together. The two outside longies are fixed to the curved runners at each corner in a similar way. There were several other joins for the remaining components. This was a long, laborious job that had to be mastered before I could do it in a reliable, efficient way. At this point I realised that I would not finish in time for my scheduled departure in early February.

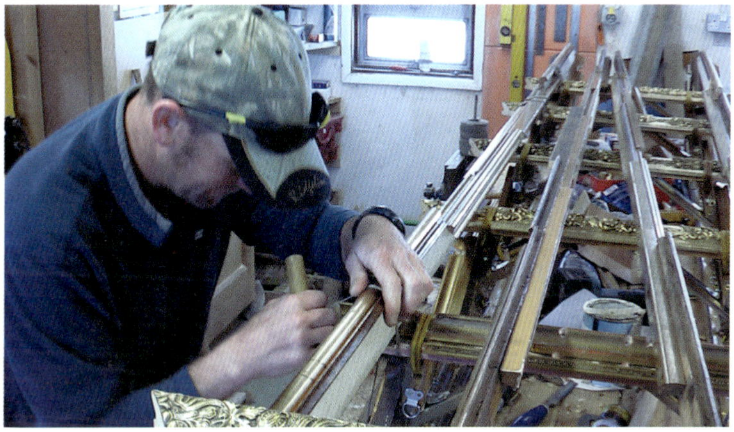

The four longies about to be connected to the chairs by whipping.

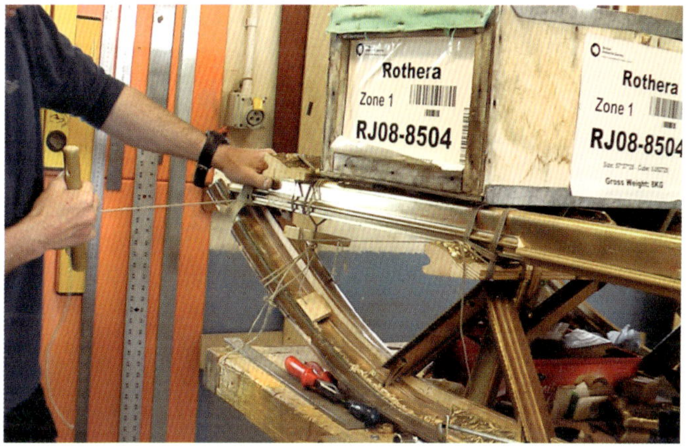

Attaching the curved end of one of the runners to a longie.

One of the few commitments I had during my stay was to give a presentation about my work one evening to everyone on base. I had brought along the machine that played Tequila on car horns and films of the other vehicles going all the way back to the driftwood boat. By now the films were quite fragile and, over the years, the footage had become tattered. Although I had copied them digitally, a part of me was always slightly disappointed with the results – not visually or technically, but conceptually.

Super 8 film is like 35mm slide. There is no negative, the original film is a transparency and this becomes the film that goes through the projector. This strip of film was physically there on the day and I was always worried that if I copied the film it would lose its authenticity. Eventually, I came up with a compromise and copied the 8mm film onto 16mm. It was a costly way to reproduce the film and only a bit more durable. Being a copy, it wasn't really any more authentic either but somehow it felt at least one layer closer to the real thing.

When I was a student, I used Super 8 film because video equipment was expensive and hard to get hold of. In those days it was easy to buy a Super 8 camera at a car boot sale because it was out of date. Nowadays, it is difficult to get hold of the old equipment because it has become a painfully fashionable way for artists to make work and the projectors are ridiculously expensive. Luckily, I have a contact who can still get the equipment for me at a sensible price.

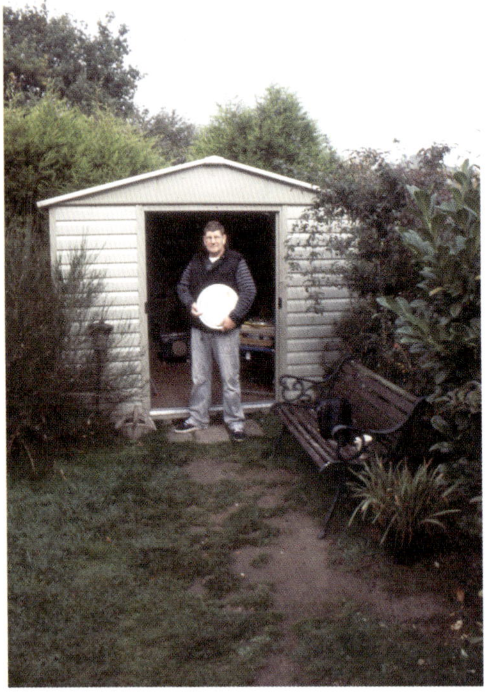
Brian outside his shed.

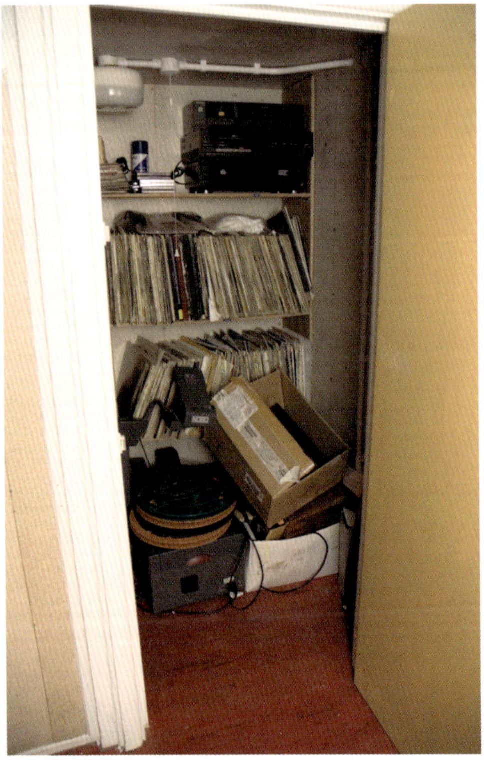
The obsolete media cupboard under the stairs at Old Bransfield.

I first met Brian at a car boot sale. He gave me his phone number and invited me to his house to look at his projectors with a view to selling me one. Brian is a projector enthusiast, he loves the process of getting them working and will spend ages rebuilding each one. He will often sell them on for little more than he paid for them in order to make room in his shed for the next one. Brian also collects 16mm films. When I visited we sat in his 8ft shed with cups of tea and watched his latest purchase – a public information film from the 1940s.

Before I went to the Antarctic I had been told that there was an old film projector at Rothera left over from the days before video entertainment. I was given an email address for someone on the base who took it out of storage and kindly emailed me some photographs. I took the pictures to Brian who recognised the model immediately. He also knew exactly what all the weaknesses were and sent me to the Antarctic with replacements for the things that were likely to break. Before I could service the projector, however, I had to find it.

Storage was in the next oldest building on the base called Old Bransfield. It had two floors and had been altered many times. Old Bransfield had once been the main part of the base but was gradually being decommissioned. Architecturally, Old Bransfield was unremarkable and sometime in the last twenty years it had been made even blander by covering it in green corrugated metal cladding. The interior was also functional but, unlike the outside, it retained its original 1970s condition. One feature that stood out for me was the deep red linoleum floor because it was strangely familiar. When we were growing up, my brother and I had a play-shed in the garden made by our father. Inside there was a table that hinged down from the wall and inlaid was a sheet of linoleum exactly like that in Old Bransfield.

Under a seldom-used back staircase of this half-abandoned building there was a cupboard and I was told that the film projector was last seen in there. When I looked inside I found historical layers of obsolete media equipment. There were CD players that had been replaced by I-players and cassette tape players that had been superseded by the CD players. There was a large row of vinyl LPs, video recorders and slide projectors. Underneath were rolls of old newsreel and, finally, the 16mm projector. It was in good condition and the Base Commander even knew where the stand was, in one of the many empty rooms. After replacing one suspect rubber drive belt I tested my films and took the projector to the presentation room. The slot for my talk was on an evening normally designated for a half hour educational presentation by one of the scientists. I spent the day before testing equipment, remembering my lines and preparing the room.

It could get quite soporific in the presentation room so, despite the fact that we were in the Antarctic, I opened the windows and turned the heating off to keep people awake. I went to a lot more trouble than most people did and, in retrospect, it was probably worth it. After my presentation, I'm sure I detected a difference in the way people related to me. It was a mixture of understanding and pity and it got me some badly needed help with my project. The next day the Head Field Assistant, Fergal Buckley, paid me a visit.

A Field Assistant knows a lot about Antarctic survival and safety. They are outdoor types and keen mountaineers. Their role is to support the scientific expeditions. They also rebuild sledges. Ferg's latest expedition had been cancelled at the last minute so he had some time on his hands. After a quick assessment of the sledge he offered to help. Ferg had been at Rothera a relatively long time and knew everyone and where everything was. He had access to all the materials we required such as a full set of ropes and the P-Tex nylon covering for the runners. He was liked and respected by everyone on base. My influence was zero but, with Ferg on board, people were far more likely to take me seriously.

Ferg rapidly set to the task of professionally whipping each join as I finished making the last components. One of these components was a curved bumper at the front of the sledge called a cow catcher. This was normally made from bamboo which curves easily. After snapping quite a few frames, I managed to get the correct curve by steaming and then bending the pieces around the rim of an oil drum. It was a very messy process which used every G-clamp in the workshop and totally covered my hands in glue that didn't come off for days. The only parts I had left to make after the cow catcher were the handles but I was in two minds whether to make them or not.

Traditionally, Nansen sledges have handles at the back to hold onto when running or skiing alongside whilst trying to keep up with the dog team. Standing on the back is not really encouraged because the weight of a person on that specific point tends to loosen all the joins. On a modern BAS sledge these handles are redundant as there are no dogs in the Antarctic anymore. Instead of being at the back, the driver sits in front on the dog's replacement – the skidoo.

The last dogs left the Antarctic in 1994 as a condition of the International Antarctic Treaty which banned non-indigenous species from the continent. There was a fear that dog distemper might mutate and infect seal populations, seals being genetically quite a close relation to dogs. These sledge dogs were all descended from a stock that had been brought to Antarctica in the late 1940s. In the intervening fifty years this genetic strain of dog had developed a weak immune system, probably because of the lack of diseases they were exposed to in the Polar environment. When the dogs were retired to Canada many of them died quite quickly.

The most prominent memento of the dog era at Rothera were the framed commemorative photographs still hanging on the wall in Old Bransfield. There was also a framed dog family tree that charted the lineage of every dog that had been on base to prevent in-breeding. In the carpenter's workshop there was also a particularly poignant reminder of their presence. In the earlier days of the base, the dogs had been housed in this building. There are two walk-in cupboards at the back of the workshop and one day the carpenter took me into one of them and shut the door behind us. On the back of the door were deep claw marks from dogs scratching to get out. When I saw these marks, I decided that I would, after all, make handles for the sledge.

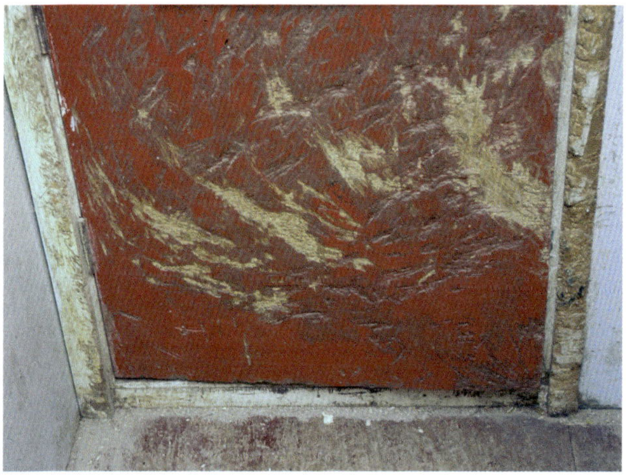

Dog claw marks on the back of the cupboard door in the carpenter's workshop.

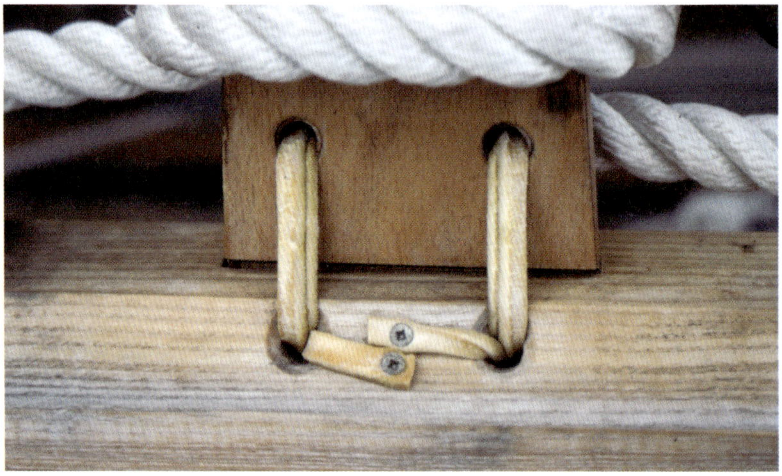

Holes in the runners of a sledge used to pass the leather thongs through.

After a month Ferg fixed the last rope onto the sledge and declared it finished. We had just under a week to try it out so the next day he planned to put me through a crash course in crevasse rescue training which was obligatory for operating a sledge off-base. It was as if the sledge made a transformation in that moment. Up until this point it had felt like a pretend sledge but, as the focus changed from preparing it to preparing me, the thing turned into something more real.

That evening as I tided and swept the workshop for the last time, I came across something underneath the work bench that had been puzzling me the whole month. Mixed up with my collection of spare sections of gold picture frame, I kept coming across someone else's mitred pieces of wood that looked suspiciously like they had come from a picture frame. Drilled through this wood were some quite crude holes about ten millimetres in diameter. The size and pattern of the holes were familiar.

One of the functions of the carpenter's workshop is recreational activity for the team through the months of total darkness and harsher weather. There are long periods of inactivity and often the winter team occupy themselves with a choice of different handicrafts. A popular activity is to make things from the wood of redundant sledges. The holes in the pieces of wood under the bench were holes for the leather thongs to pass through to join the separate components of a sledge together. I had come across a half-finished craft project; a picture frame made from the wood of an old sledge.

I had taken picture frames to the Antarctic to make a sledge from them not realising that in the Antarctic they cut up old sledges to make pictures frames.

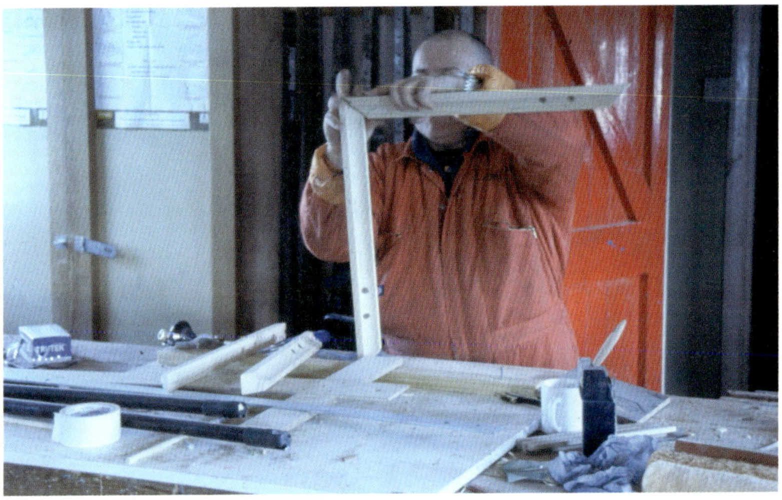

Making a picture frame from the wood of an old sledge.

Sledge on the snow for the first time at Rothera.

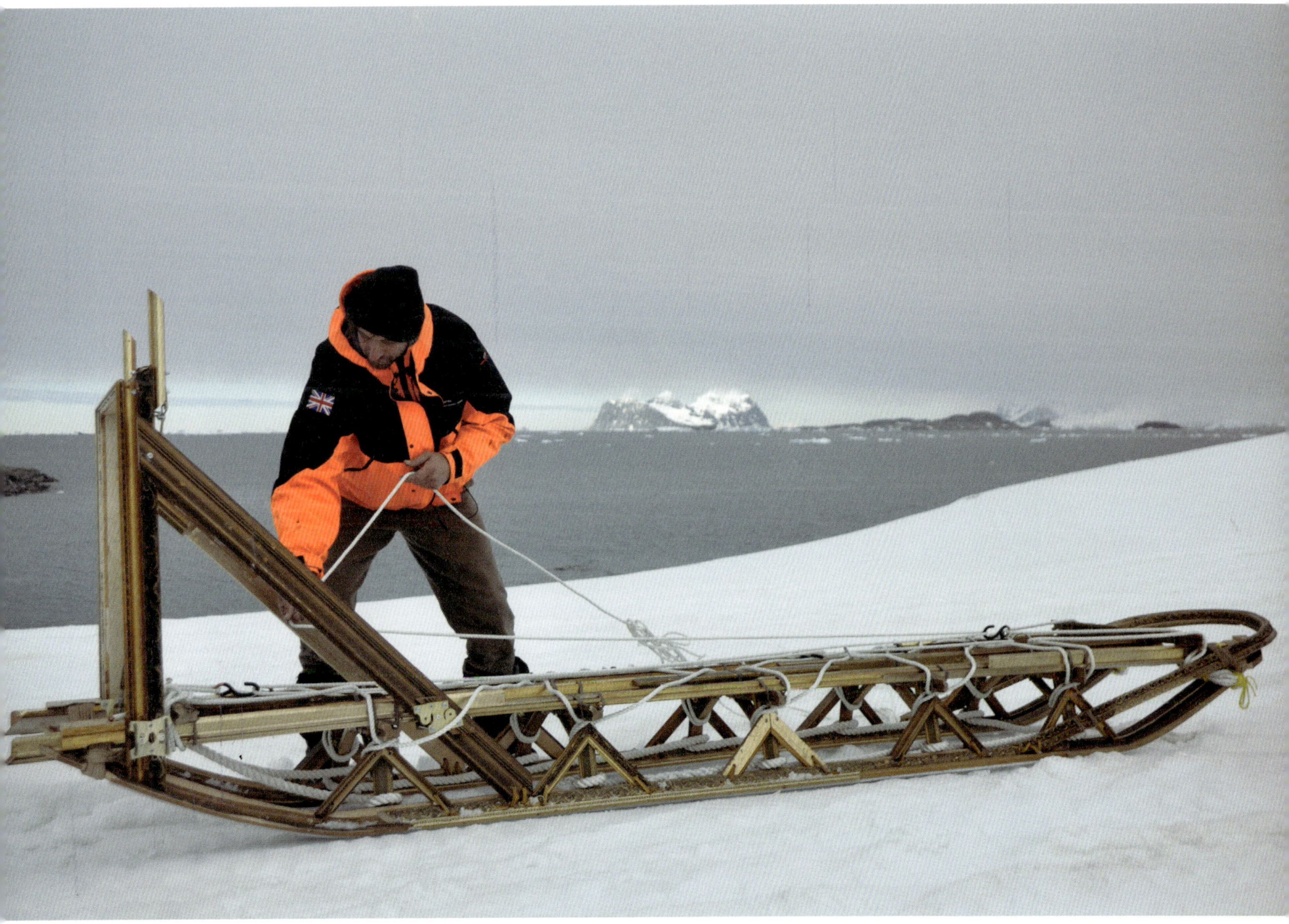

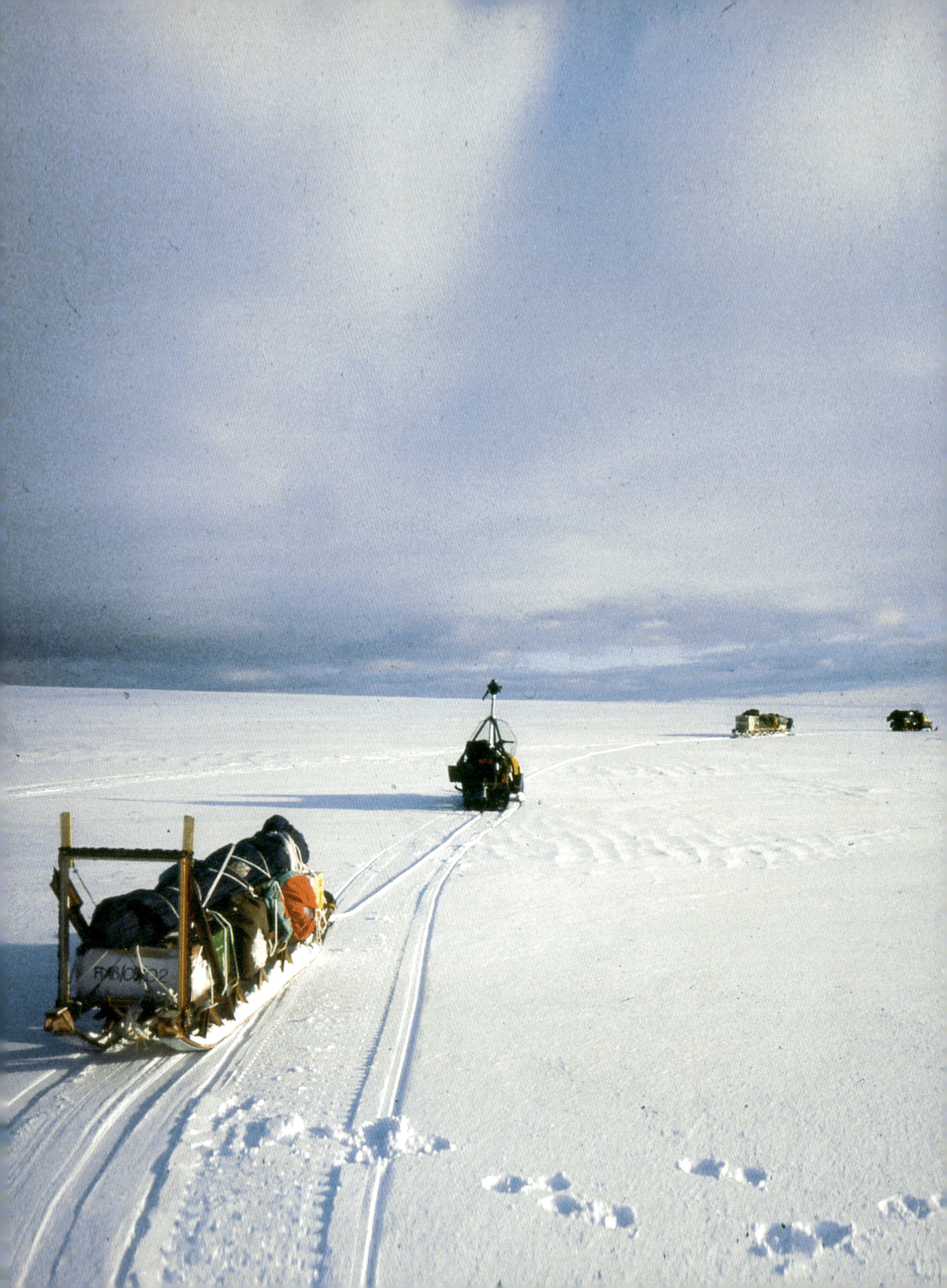

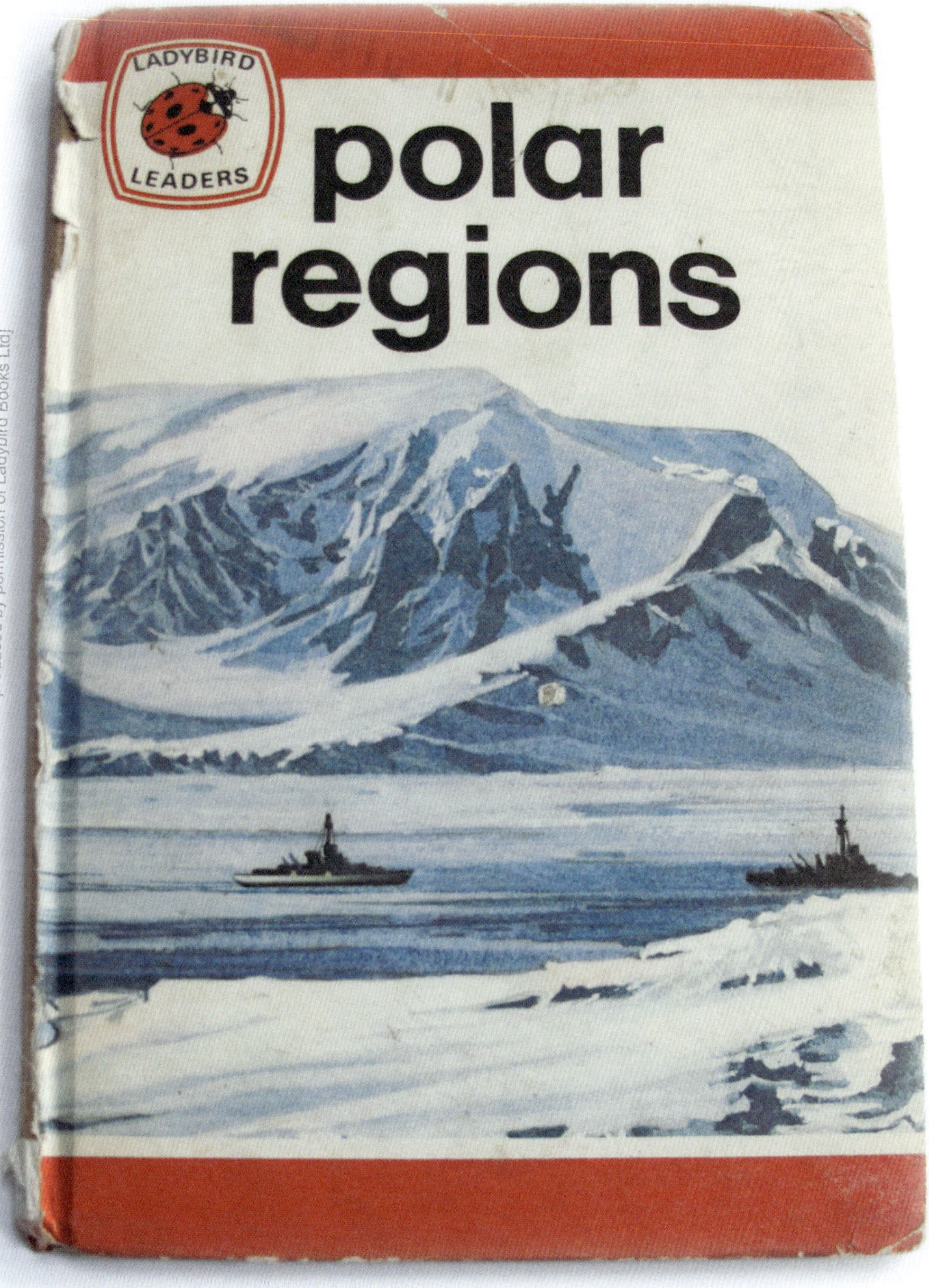

On the Blank Canvas

British Antarctic Nansen sledges always travel in pairs, tied together, one behind the other. The first sledge is tied behind the first skidoo on a ten metre rope. A rope then passes underneath the sledge that joins it to another thirty metre length which is tied to the following skidoo. This in turn pulls a second sledge on another ten metre line. This was to be the position of my sledge.

All the equipment is doubled up where possible and divided between the two sledges. In this way it is possible to lose one sledge without losing everything essential to survival. My sledge would have to take the weight of nearly half a metric tonne of equipment.

At all times drivers wear a climbing harness with a rope that ties them to the skidoo. The reason being; should the convoy accidentally cross an unstable snow bridge, the heavy skidoo and its driver are the first things to fall through into the crevasse beneath. The point where the tow rope meets the sledge is the point at which the system is designed to stop the descent. As the sledge is a rigid section along the sequence of sledges, ropes and snow mobiles, it can't bend over the lip of the hole. The driver is left hanging beneath his skidoo which is also hanging in mid air ten feet below the sledge.

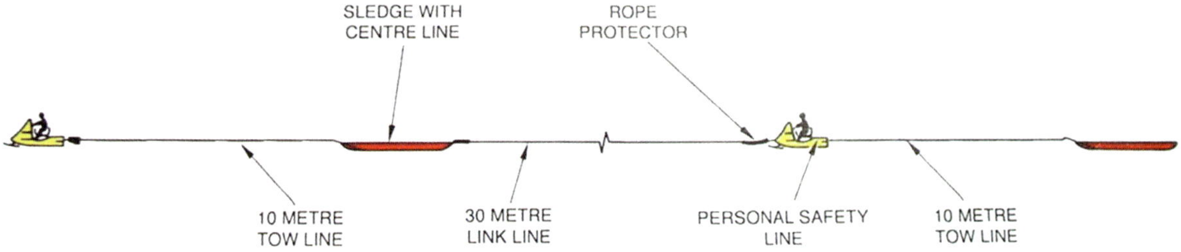

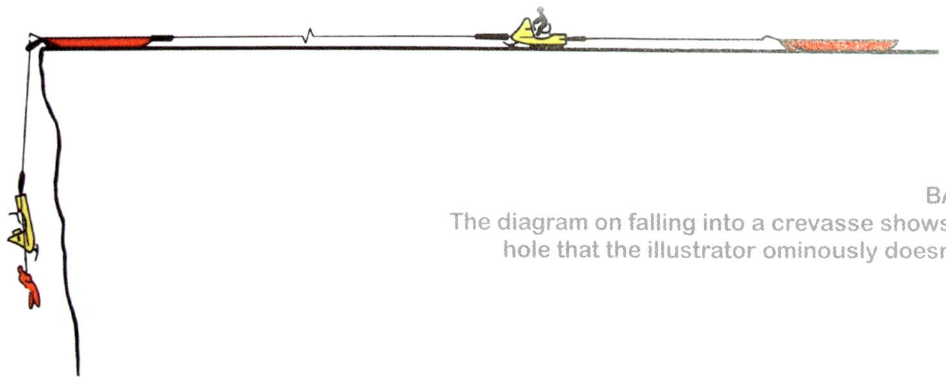

BAS Field Operations Manual
The diagram on falling into a crevasse shows the driver hanging down a hole that the illustrator ominously doesn't even draw the bottom of.

A crevasse is caused by movement in the ice and, as 98% of Antarctica is glacial, most of it is constantly moving and crevasses are common. The real danger occurs when snow builds up and completely covers fissures with a thin layer of snow. At certain times of the year these snow bridges are strong enough to support weight but, if not, they can give way to a crevasse up to 40 metres deep. This would be the equivalent of falling from the top of a fifteen storey building.

In areas that are susceptible to crevasses, the Field Assistant looks at the terrain ahead for tell-tale slumps in the snow that suggest a snow bridge is about to give way. Travelling in front, it is therefore the experienced Field Assistant who falls into the crevasse. It is the job of the driver on the second skidoo to put on the brakes and abseil down to perform a crevasse rescue. This second driver is often someone who is probably not, in any way, an outdoor person. They are normally a scientist or maybe the base cook on his recreational winter trip. It could of course, also be the artist. I was assured that it happens very rarely but it was strange to know that the landscape had the potential to swallow you up.

Crevasse rescue training consisted of a preliminary descent from the upstairs balcony in the equipment building. I had to abseil down into the room below and climb back up again by making footholds with an attachment called a dumar. Ferg then rounded up a small group of novices and we went up to the snow scoop – a big hole formed by the wind as it hit the base of the nearest mountain. We all took it turns to leap off the edge whilst our partner lay flat on their back ready to take the strain as we ran out of rope. The person being rescued then dangled off the end of the line while the rescuer worked out how to get them back up again. All the equipment had to be carried on the climbing harness whilst riding the skidoo just in case.

Although my final destination was Sky Blu, Ferg was conscious that the weather could change at any moment causing my flight there to be postponed. He therefore suggested that we made another trip to explore the peninsular of Adelaide Island whilst we had a day in hand. He also had an aesthetic reason for this extra journey since in his opinion Adelaide Island would make for much better images. Sky Blu, totally flat and virtually featureless, would make quite an unimpressive backdrop for the sledge and the toys. Ferg was a keen photographer and he said that photographs taken at Sky Blu often made people look as if they were standing in front of a large piece of white paper. They could be anywhere. He knew places nearby on Adelaide Island that offered much better composition opportunities.

It turned out that not only did my field assistant know the best way to pull a casualty out of a forty metre deep fissure he also knew how to take better photos than me.

The route from the base to the interior of Adelaide Island involved going up the mountain and then traversing across to the caboose where I had camped on Christmas Eve. Ferg was concerned about the route; it was so churned up by people going up to Vals to snow-board that deep ruts had formed and he thought there was a possibility of my sledge turning over and the handles snapping off. For this reason he loaded it onto a large steel trailer sledge that was about the size of a car. By hitching this to the Sno-Cat we could safely tow it up the slope and across the traverse.

When we got to the caboose there were some other sledges there already that had come back from various trips. Some had been left there in readiness for the next excursion, others were temporarily parked ready to be unloaded. Each one had a black flag on a bamboo stick. Ferg told me that earlier in the season the wind had dislodged a flag and a fully loaded sledge had been lost in a heavy snow fall. We had brought all the supply boxes separately in the back of the Sno-Cat so we still didn't know if my sledge would take the weight. Ferg had tried to keep it to a minimum but there was still quite a lot of kit including an extra box containing my toys.

Our sleeping bags came in a protective cover with a polythene liner that tended to hold a lot of air. Ferg tried to stuff the bags onto the sledge between some boxes and in an attempt to expel the air, he belly-flopped onto them so the sledge took his full body weight. I winced, expecting the sledge to give way. It didn't – this was the first test.

The next test was to pull it fully loaded so we tied it to the back of the trailer and towed it along very slowly with the Sno-Cat. I stood on the flat bed of the trailer with my tripod and camera. It was a tense time as we gradually got faster. The rope was the standard ten metres long so the sledge trailed behind, a little bit removed from us. As Ferg started a gradual turn in the Sno-Cat, the sledge kept a steady pace but veered off to the right. Bit by bit it came back in line with the Sno-Cat and trailer. It was a strange sensation slowly passing through the landscape and watching my creation momentarily wander off on its own.

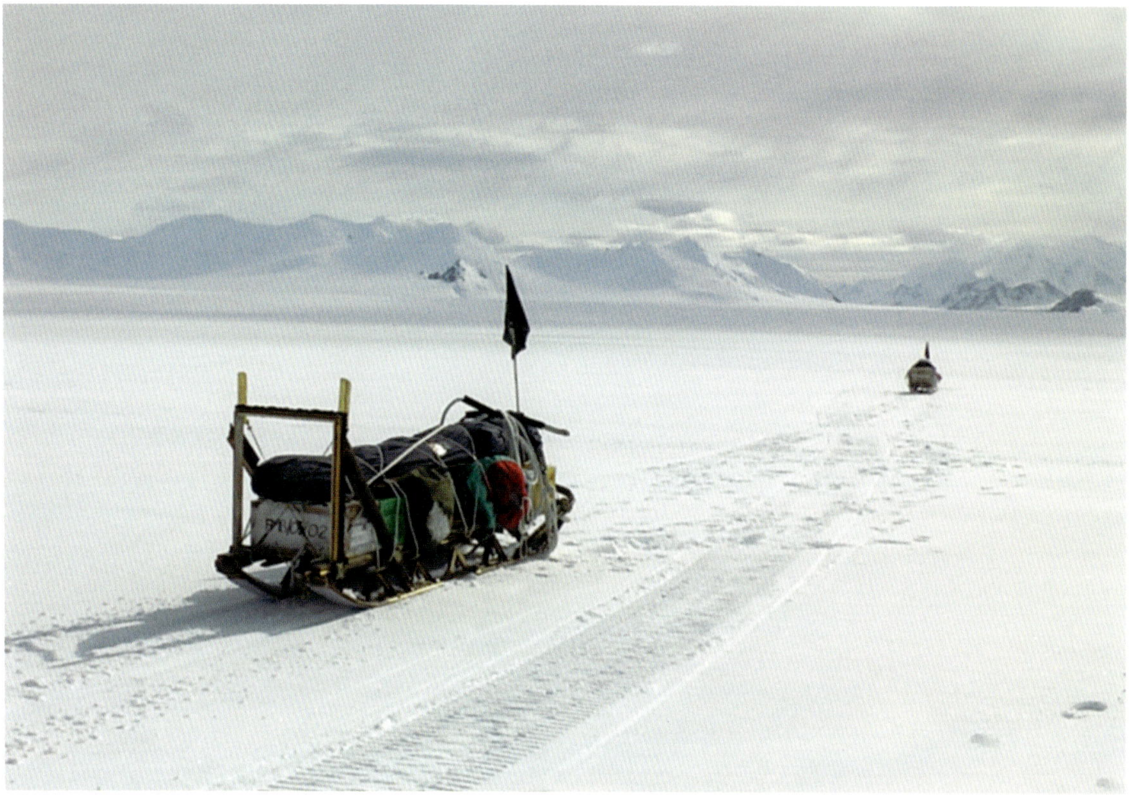

The two sledges parked at Vals near the caboose in readiness for its trip the next day. The gold picture frame sledge in the foreground.

I panned the camera through 180 degrees, pointing it at the sledge then pointing it at Ferg as he looked over his shoulder and gave me a thumbs up. It was working! I turned off the camera and we headed back towards the caboose, admiring my work as we went. As we turned, the sledge again veered off in another direction. This time, however, it found a deep hollow in the snow, disappeared and then rose up sharply so that I could see underneath as the runners briefly pointed skywards. It lurched up and out of the hole violently. I was expecting a snapping noise but, to our amazement, the sledge was perfectly fine. We had accidently given it a thorough test.

We were in self-congratulatory mood as we unhitched the sledge and left it with its own marker flag, planning to return the next day for our first trip. Ferg asked me if I would like to drive the Sno-Cat back to the base. Only certain people were allowed to do this so it felt like a great honour. More importantly, it also represented an opportunity to experience a little bit of history.

When I had visited the Scott Polar Research Museum there had been a special exhibition commemorating the 50th anniversary of the 'Commonwealth Trans-Antarctic crossing' in 1958. It was promoted by the museum as the 'last Heroic age' expedition.

The Heroic Age is a historical reference to a particular period in Antarctic exploration. The name celebrates the romantic motivation behind such expeditions and contrasts with current, primarily scientific, ambitions. The period starts in the earliest days of Antarctic exploration and includes Scott's doomed journey to the South Pole. It officially ends with Shackelton's 'Imperial Trans-Antarctic expedition' in 1917. However, some consider the 'Commonwealth' Trans-Antarctic crossing in the fifties as a 'last gasp of empire' and therefore, arguably, the last 'Heroic age' expedition. Typically it served limited scientific purpose but had immense inspirational value. I have met people in their sixties who refer to it as 'our generation's moon landing'. The exhibition included letters to Vivian

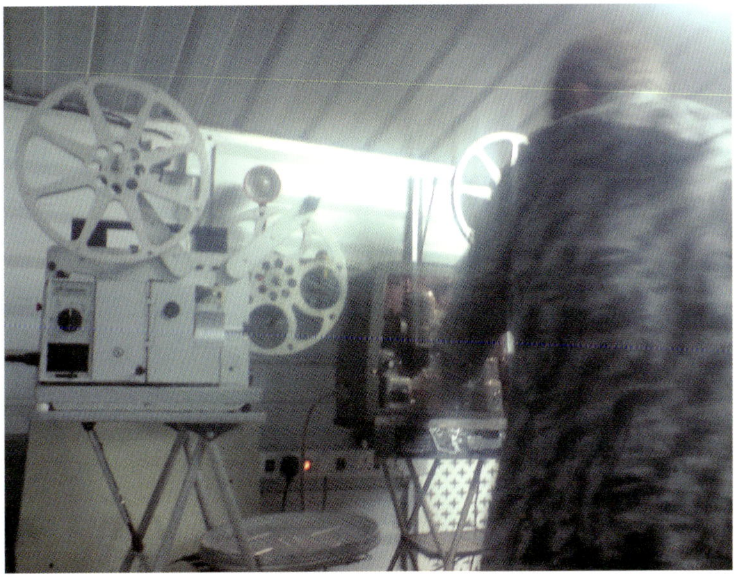

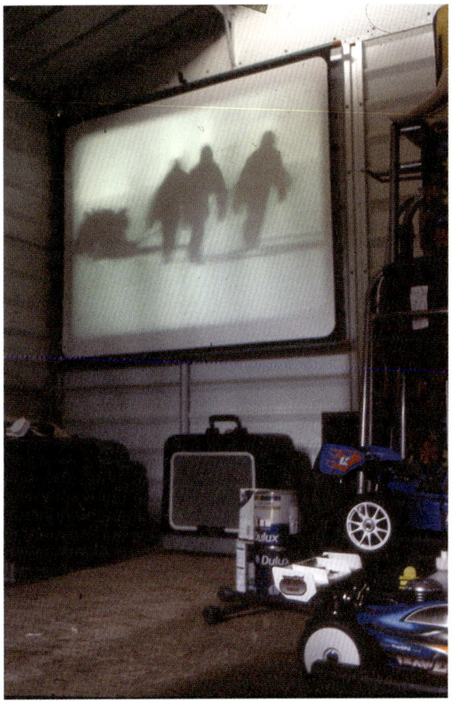

above: Brian rewinding a film.

right: Watching a 16 millimetre film of the Trans-Antarctic expedition in Brian's shed.

Fuchs, leader of the expedition, written by school children. The main transport for the expedition was the Tucker Sno-Cat and the children included drawings of the Sno-Cat in their letters.

In the gallery, there had been a looped projection of a film made at the time; a 16mm film that captured the expedition in full colour. On my first visit to BAS Headquarters, I was introduced to the archive department. The lady there told me that their archives included many rare documentary films including the 16mm original of the Trans-Antarctic Crossing. I was very excited by the possibility of watching the film in its original format instead of a DVD copy. For me, it was one step closer to the original, more authentic and closer to the real experience.

When I asked the lady from the archive department if I could borrow the film she gave me an emphatic NO. Every time a reel of film is put through a projector it wears slightly. Static electricity builds up and dust accumulates. This can scratch the film and there is always a possibility that the film will break. To splice it back together again, the film is overlapped and a frame is lost. The lady from the archive was happy to lend me a DVD but on no account would anyone ever be allowed to put the films through a projector ever again. I shared this information with my projector enthusiast friend Brian. I was trying to get advice from him on the best way to prevent damage but Brain seemed more interested in the actual content of the film:

'Was it about crossing the… Arctic… no… no hang, the Antarctic?'

'Was it made in the 1950s?'

'Was it that bloke, Vivian Foooch or sumint who was in charge?'

'Did it have them big orange snow cats in it?'

'Yes' I said, whilst trying to think of a way to steer the conversation back to my original enquiry. 'Why do you ask?'

'Cos I think I've got it in my shed! If you want to see it on the original 16mm you can come round here. I'll put the kettle on.'

In Brian's shed we sat in deckchairs and watched the rare film.

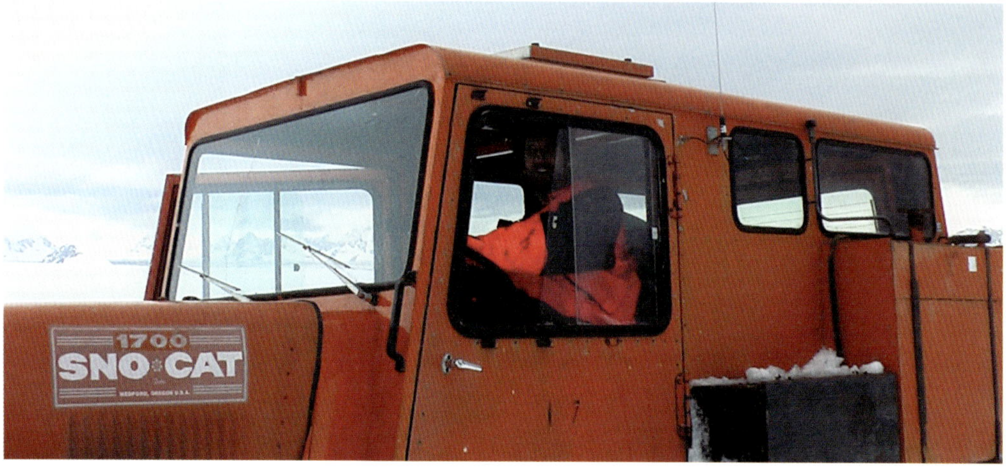

Me driving the
Tucker Sno-Cat.
[Fergal Buckley]

When Ferg offered me the chance to drive an actual Sno-Cat in the real Antarctic it felt like my little project had a proper link to the Golden Age of Exploration, the Trans-Antarctic crossing, and even Scott. When I clasped the steering wheel, I held history in my hands. As we set off, I remembered my disastrous Christmas Eve at the caboose only a few weeks before. On that occasion I had felt like a complete loser, now I was on the brink of triumph. The Sno-Cat thundered along the traverse. I was still contemplating the day's accomplishments when I suddenly felt the Sno-Cat sink as if it was falling into a hole.

It was not a crevasse about to swallow us up; it was something far more inglorious. A wheel had fallen off and taken one of the tracks with it. The forward momentum had forced the remaining trackless wheels onto one side, down into the snow. As we looked through the windscreen at a lopsided horizon, it took us a while to work out what had happened. Just before the Sno-Cat dug itself to a standstill, Ferg saw something go past the window. This turned out to be the black rubber track. When we got out we noticed that not only had the track come off but we had run over it with the trailer. When the mechanic came he laughed at the mess. He then gave me the wheel as a souvenir and took us back to base.

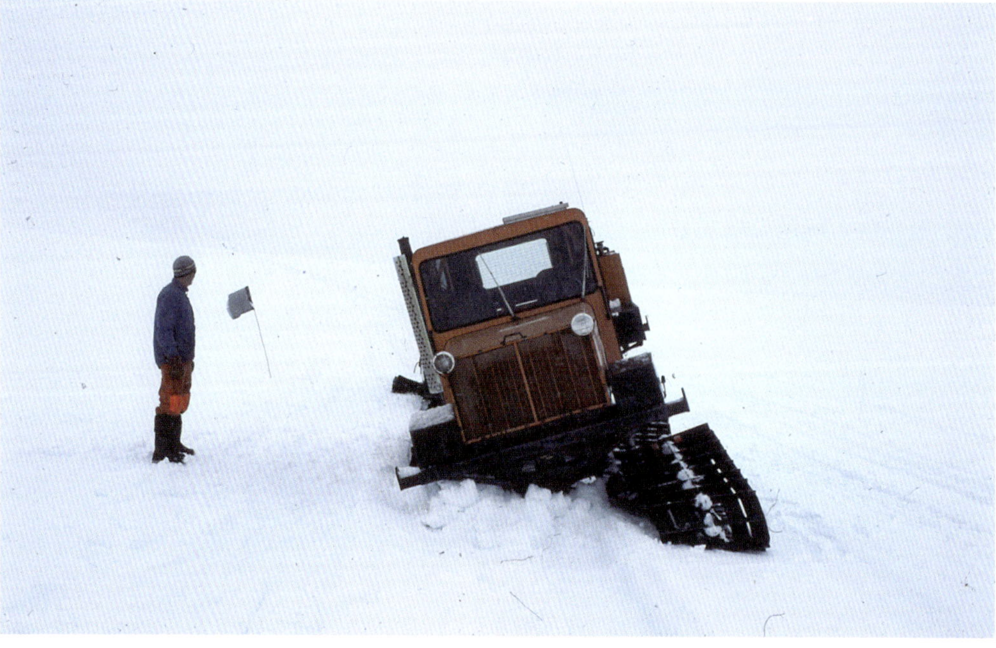

Sno-Cat half buried
in the snow after the
track came off.

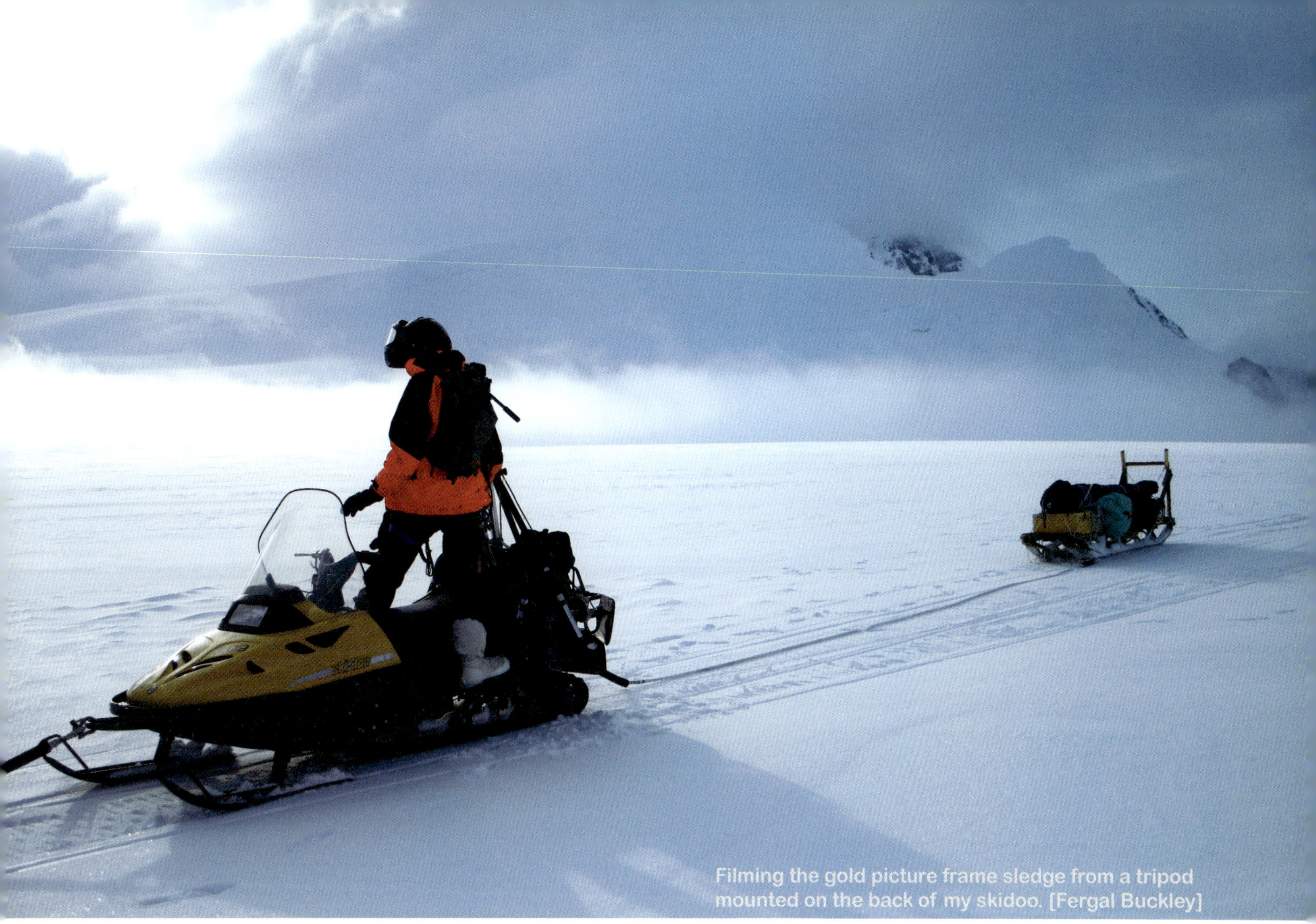

Filming the gold picture frame sledge from a tripod mounted on the back of my skidoo. [Fergal Buckley]

The next day we drove two very powerful skidoos back up the mountain to the sledge ready for our trip. Skidoos and sledges were all joined together by the 30 metre rope and we set off across the flag line. Little red and black flags on bamboo sticks are everywhere around the base. The black ones usually mark a path or road. The red ones are for danger and usually mean there is imminent threat of a crevasse. Whilst camping they are also used to mark the spot where everyone is expected to urinate so there is less danger of digging up toilet snow to melt for drinking water. They serve as a constant reminder that you are within an area that has been tested, checked and sanitised. The flag line is the point on the mountain where the flags end and untrained people like me are not usually allowed to cross.

Vivid blue patches of sky contrasted sharply with brooding clouds but it was the way these clouds interacted with the mountains that made the landscape spectacular that day. Sometimes they hid the peaks but, at other times, the peaks were exposed as the clouds appeared to tumble down the mountainside and along the valley floor towards us. The dry Antarctic conditions had frozen the moisture in the air and altered my perception of distance. Snow covered peaks were hit by the sun which made them stick out – they felt within touching distance. Through gaps between the mountains we could see down to the sea, speckled with small blocks of ice. Beyond was the Antarctic mainland in the dreamlike distance. Occasionally I gave a sharp tug on my brake to signal Ferg to stop so that I could take it all in. I marked these occasions by photographing a toy against the dramatic background.

When travelling tied together, it is advisable to keep looking back at the load to make sure it hasn't fallen over. The second driver also has to keep looking forward to make sure the rope joining the two units has not gone slack and been run over by the skidoo. I adopted a twisted position in my seat and looked forwards then backwards whenever we were moving. I met one Field Assistant who even sat on his skidoo side saddle. The skidoo, like my hovercraft, has a two stroke engine. The noise was not as loud but it did have a similar high revving, rattling type of din. We passed through the most majestic landscape sounding like a couple of teenagers on mopeds.

We couldn't go any further than McCallum Pass, the gateway from the mountains into the interior of the island. All of the snow bridges were slumped over the crevasses indicating they were unsound so we looked for a place to camp. Ferg found a picture postcard spot, unofficially called Sunnyside Glacier. It overlooked Stonehouse Bay and was in a gap between the Stokes Peaks. It was only about ten miles from the base but it was the real Antarctic. In the night the wind got up but when we awoke it was a bright sunny day.

The ground where we stood was totally flat but sloped down gradually to the sea in the distance. Either side of us was a steep wall of compressed snow that covered the mountains and created our own private valley. Although it looked narrow, the map said it was almost half a mile wide. At one point I heard the now familiar explosive sound as a huge lump of snow and ice fell from the wall. We were the only people for miles. I spent the morning photographing as many toys as I could; Action Man, a toy skidoo and the Ladybird Book of Captain Scott. I had also brought the record player and played Symphonia Antarctica to the miles of nothingness. We spent a long time photographing three plastic dogs that came with the Action Man sledge. We positioned the picture frame sledge a little way away and Ferg lined them up so they looked like they were the same scale.

Each mountain peak on the map had a strange name like Mouse, Arthur or Morgan. We are used to geographic features in the Antarctic being named after their discoverers but these names were especially odd because they were written on the map in blue biro. Ferg told me that each peak was unofficially named in memory of the last sled dogs from Rothera.

On the return journey we saw the beginning of a sun set. It was late January and the 24 hour sun was beginning to dip in the sky. My time at Rothera was coming to an end. We unhitched the sledges by the caboose and drove our skidoos back to base past the broken Sno-Cat.

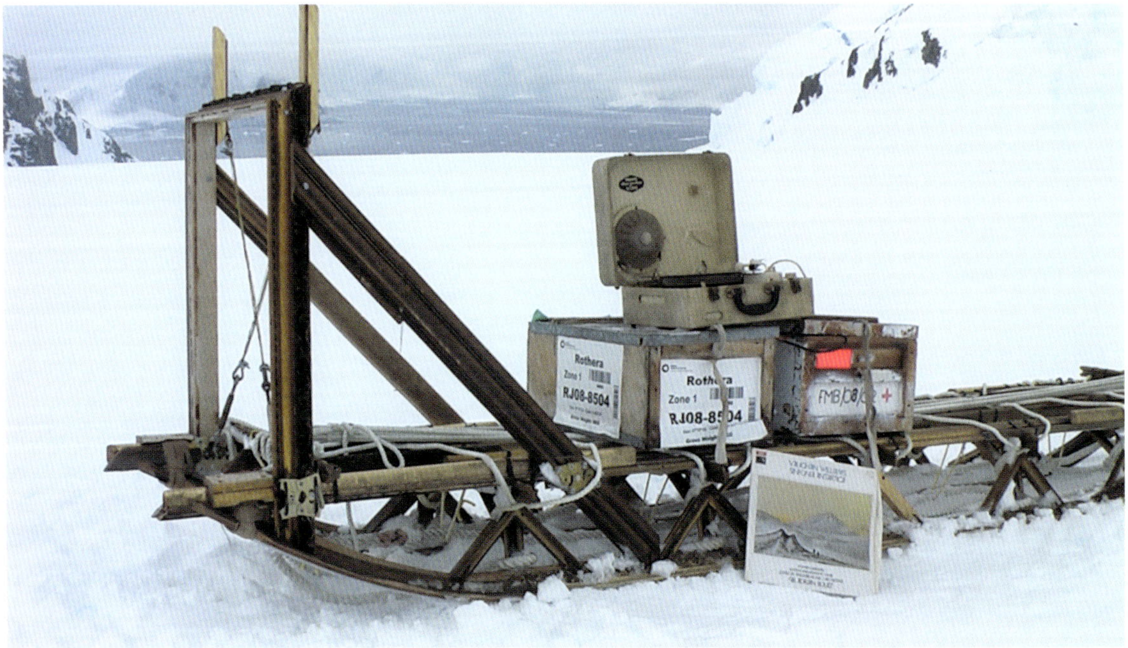

Playing Vaughan Williams' Symphonia Antarctica in Antarctica.

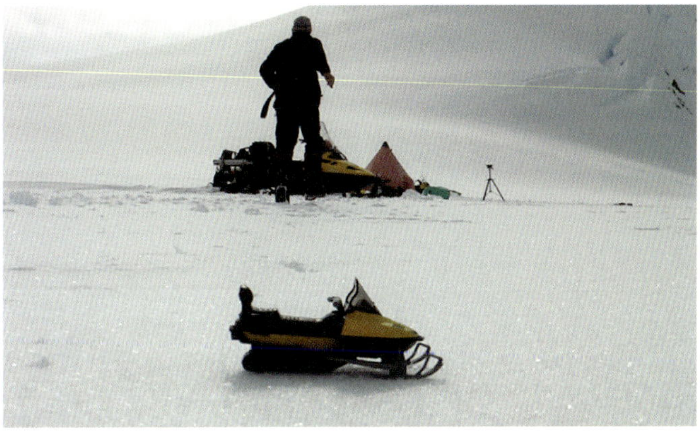

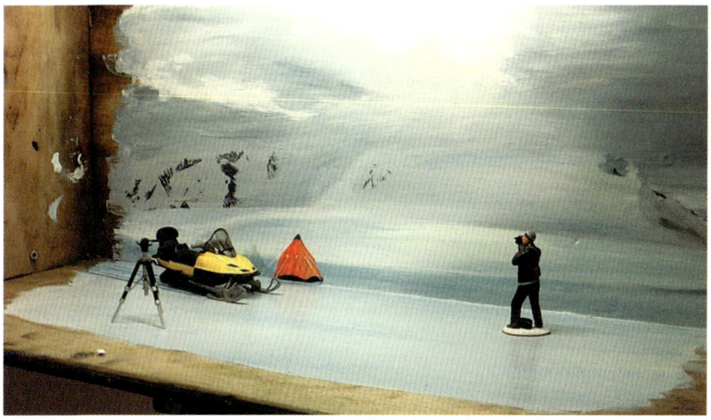

Model skidoo in the foreground. Our camp in the distance including Ferg, the camera tripod and the real skidoo.

Gallery shot: The same model skidoo, a model of the tripod and a toy Ferg. This sledge box was eventually mounted on top of the real tripod.

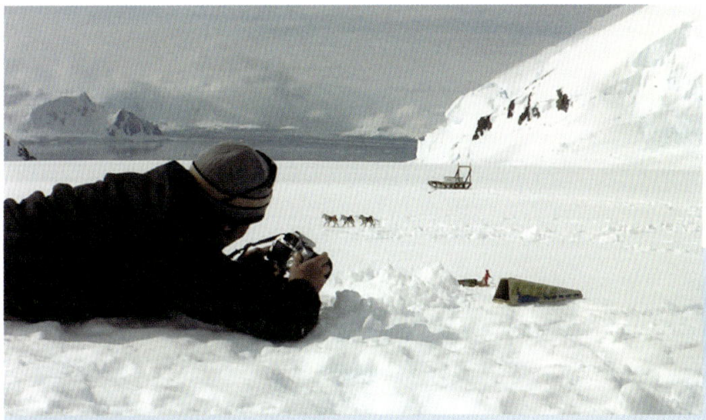

left: Ferg photographing toys on the Sunnyside glacier.

below:
Foreground: Action man, toy dogs.
Background: Me on gold picture frame sledge. [Fergal Buckley]

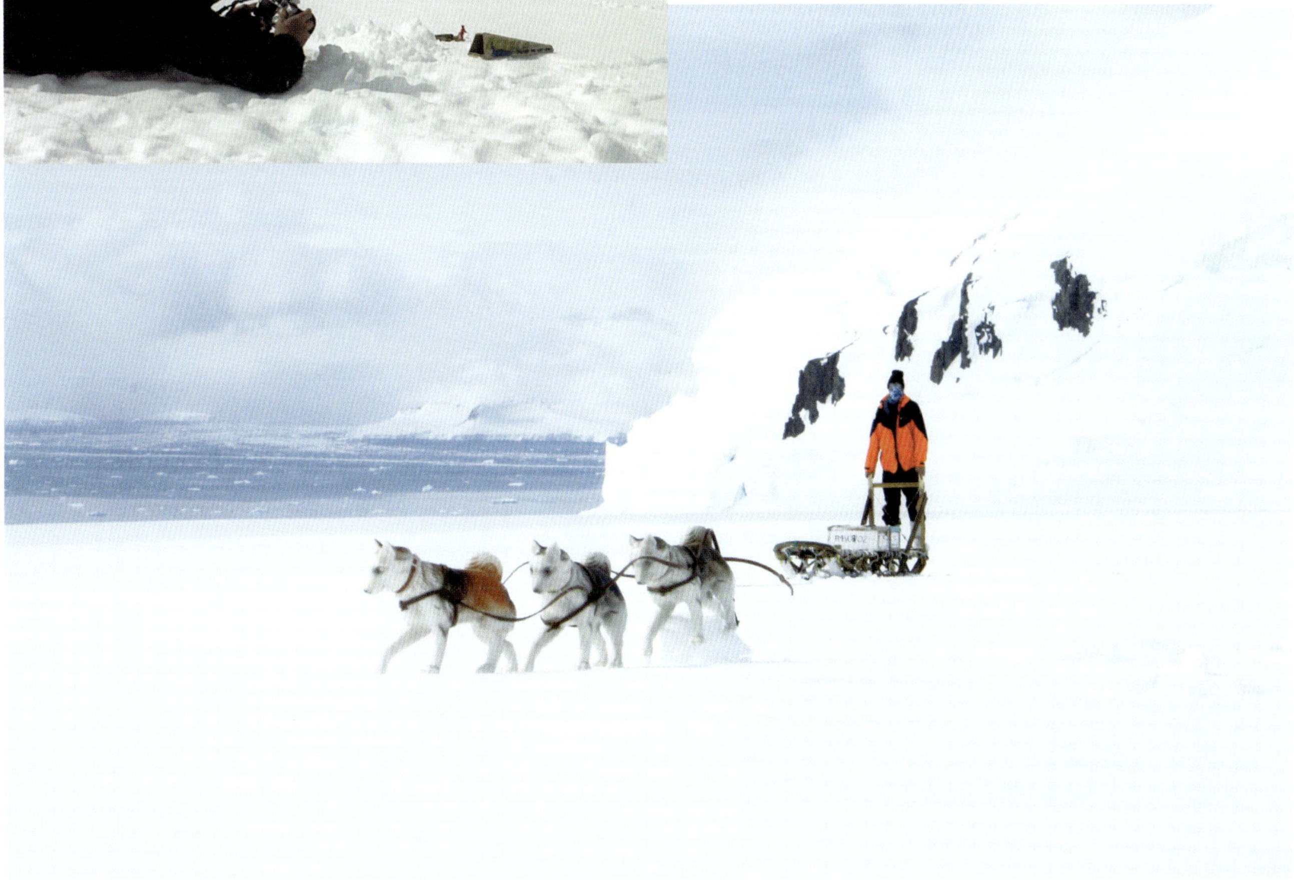

Not going to Sky Blu

As a child I made a lot of Airfix models. When I had finished gluing, painting and applying the transfers I proudly positioned them all around my bedroom. Some hung from the ceiling on lengths of fine thread, others were on shelves or the windowsill. Like a lot of busy mothers, my mum was more concerned with the dust the models attracted than with the skill they displayed. Her dusting technique could be quite heavy-handed and it was always worrying when she decided to clean my room. She made her assault with stealth, gradually vacuuming her way up the stairs to my room. On entering she would take the rugs from the floor and stuff them through the window to land in the garden below. Tiny details on Airfix models snagged on nylon pile as the synthetic rugs cut a destructive path through my fragile exhibition.

Sometimes I would come home and find the signs that my mother was halfway through operations; the rugs on the lawn, the vacuum cleaner at the top of the stairs, its flex stretching all the way down to the kitchen. All my carefully arranged and extremely fragile models would be 'stored' in a few plastic bags, crushed against one another, the tiny broken details mixed in the bottom with hair and dust. I learnt to hide the models away in cupboards and that's where they stayed.

About fifteen years later, when doing my post-graduate course in Sculpture, my tutors were becoming concerned about the time it was taking me to make my aeroplane. All I had to show were a few aircraft components and they encouraged me to make something a bit more achievable in the time I had at college. I went home and retrieved my model aeroplanes from the cupboard. At the time, I dismissively called these pieces 'gallery fodder'. Since then, I have realised they were, in a sense, sketches or experiments that enabled me to play around with visual ideas and I learnt a lot from them. For my first year show I tied a model aeroplane by thread to a vacuum cleaner on top of a record player. When switched on blow, the air made the model aeroplane fly to a musical accompaniment. Over the years I have made several record player pieces and this probably influenced my decision to take a record player to the Antarctic.

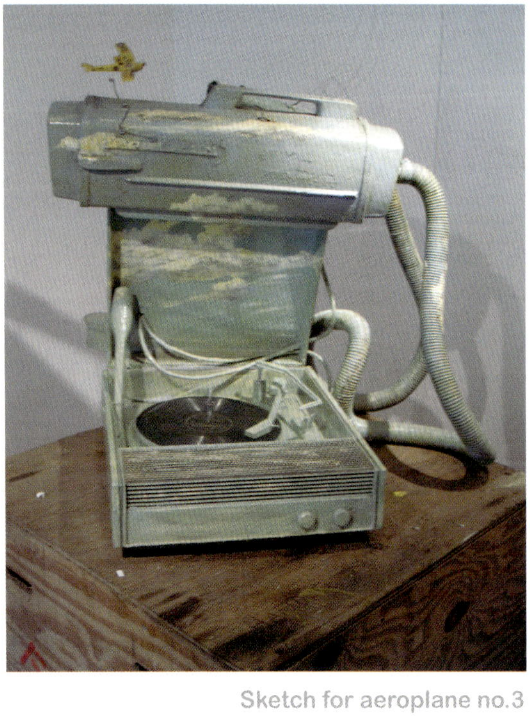

Sketch for aeroplane no.3
[Jo Newman]

In amongst my luggage I also had a1950s vacuum cleaner with runners to help it slide across the carpet. I had an idea that the runners might be good on snow. Airfix produced a model of the Auster Antarctic, a plane used in the 1958 Trans-Antarctic crossing, so I brought that along too.

There were only a few days before my flight back home and it was looking increasingly unlikely that I was going to Sky Blu. Ferg and I brought the sledge down from the mountain and left it by the aircraft hangar hoping we could load it onto to the next plane making a fuel trip to Sky Blu. The weather in the Antarctic can change very rapidly in a short space of time and sadly and almost predictably my luck ran out. The fuel flight was cancelled and therefore so was my trip to Sky Blu, my destination but also ultimately the goal of the project. My flight back to the UK had been scheduled months in advance and the plane never went back with an empty seat.

To make the end of my adventure even less heroic, I was on gash. Gash is naval slang, meaning surplus to requirement or rubbish. Being 'on' gash involved chores such as emptying the dustbins, recycling, cleaning the toilets and washing up. It was a great social leveller and everyone on base was expected to take their turn. On the wall next to the dinner queue was a 'gash duty' list. Each day we would see our name slowly edge its way to the top. My name was now at the top of that list and since I was not going to Sky Blu anymore – I was on gash.

The Saints were the employees hired each year to do the domestic work. They were from St Helena, a remote island in the South Atlantic. Whoever was on gash supplemented the Saints. I was to take my orders from Saint Justin who had lined up a list of chores for me starting with hoovering the back staircase.

The St Helena accent is a mix of old English, South African and Caribbean. I had spoken to Justin before but while he had my attention he decided to give me his personal take on my position within our Antarctic community:

'I've been coming here quite a few years now and I've met a lot of the artists. They is kinda important! They come here and they talk a lot of stuff that I don't always understand but I know they is important. Intellectual! It was kinda interesting meeting you for the first time, Chris, because I could tell from the very first time you opened your mouth. I thought this guy is, like, really… common!'

I plugged in the cleaner at the bottom of the stairs and gradually worked my way up to the landing, pretty much how my mother did. I made a thorough job of it too and lost myself in the work. The noise of the vacuum motor filled the space and I didn't notice that at the bottom of the stairs the 'head of operations' had walked into the hallway.

His job was to organise all of the flights in and out of Rothera and organise the supply of field depots. He was normally found in his office at the bottom of the control tower or on the runway supervising the loading of planes. It was unusual to find him here on this rarely used back staircase. He was looking for me. There was a window in the weather, another change of plan… I was going!

I started to wind up the cable of the vacuum cleaner but Justin took it from me and sent me on my way.

Half an hour later I was taking my own 1950s vacuum cleaner out of the hangar with the sledge and loading it onto an aeroplane.

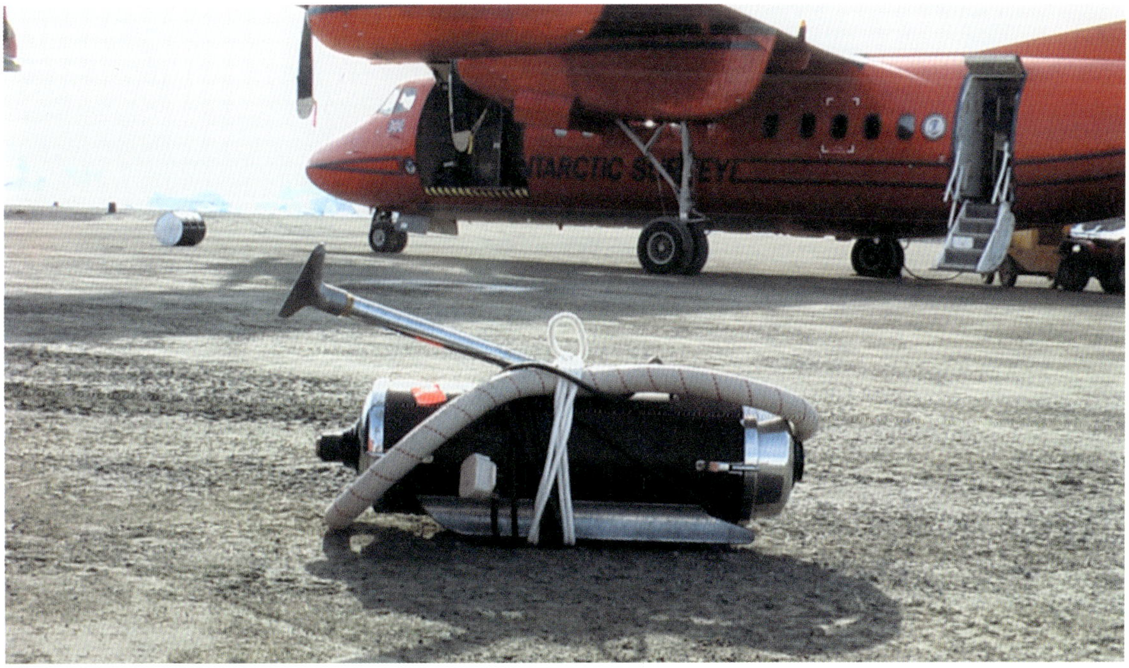

My 1950s vacuum cleaner, ready to be loaded onto the plane for Sky Blu.

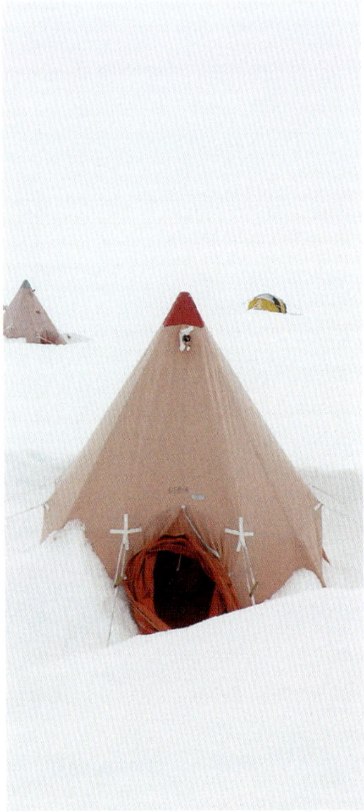

Toilet tent

I had just enough time to get to Sky Blu, come back, gather my things and get my flight home. I had to make arrangements for my sledge to be shipped home along with all the old sledge boxes. Inside these I had to delicately pack all the fragile toys and models. During the flight I sat between the two pilots in the cockpit. We spoke about the weather and they explained that it was quite possible that I would get stranded at Sky Blu. I didn't mind this because, if I was stranded long enough, I would miss my flight home and have plenty of time to do all my packing while I waited for next one. My worst case scenario was to get back late from Sky Blu and have no time to pack or make any of my arrangements.

We came into land at Sky Blu and it was exactly as I had expected. The runway was a barely visible pale blue smudge in the distance in front of a mountain peak protruding out of the ice cap. It is the wind vortex from this that blows the loose snow away to leave the blue ice runway. Close by were a few tents and a couple of bright red balloon shaped buildings called melon huts.

As Ferg had predicted the landscape was like a giant sheet of plain paper; the horizon barely discernible. At Sky Blu there were days of very low contrast when the light was so diffuse that it didn't give any indication of shade. Everything white had absolutely no definition. With sunglasses on or off tracks in the snow were difficult to see. Not long after I got off the plane I even fell three times on my way to the toilet tent. As my eyes focused on the bright orange tent triangle in the distance it was impossible to see the lumps and holes in the snow directly in front of me.

One of the problems of meeting new people in the Antarctic is that everyone wears the regulation sunglasses so you can never see their eyes. This makes it hard to read facial expressions and judge the reaction you are getting. When I met the Field Assistant assigned to me at Sky Blu he appeared particularly enigmatic behind his mirror shades. Dave Routledge was an extremely experienced Field Assistant who had been awarded the Polar Medal. I was slightly intimidated by him and knew he spent a lot of his time assisting with important scientific field work. Consequently my introduction turned into a bit of an apology. To stop me, Dave said:

'Don't worry, a lot of the scientists are fucking useless as well.'

I was reassured. Dave didn't want to waste time while the weather was good so he planned to leave within an hour of my arrival. I explained my plan; to head off the base in any direction so that we were somewhere that nobody had ever been before. Dave asked me what way I would like to go. I pointed purposefully. He turned, pointed in the opposite direction and said.

'We're going this way!'

There was no point to me disagreeing. Every direction was nowhere.

We set off roped together on our skidoos and sledges at a speed I wasn't used to. I could see the sledge twisting and bouncing as it adjusted itself to the contours of the ground. The square frame of the handles accentuated the twisting as it changed from a square to a rhomboid and back again. It was designed to do this but it was alarming to see it happen so violently. I just carried on behind Dave and hoped for the best.

The snow surface was different to that of Adelaide Island because it was about 20 degrees colder. The snow was frozen and powdery rather than clumped and stodgy. We soon made camp. It wasn't far from Sky Blu but it didn't need to be. At one point the Dash 7 aircraft flew low over us and it reminded me of the target I had set for myself when I made my own aeroplane. On that occasion I had realised there was a space not high above the garden that nobody had ever been in. Here, the air above had been colonised more than the ground we stood on.

In the morning I planned to photograph objects and toys then film the sledge with a special movie camera I had brought with me. Instead of my old Super 8 camera I decided to bring a 16mm camera so that the original film would be a little less fragile. More importantly, I would be documenting the sledge on the same format as the 1950s film I had watched in Brian's shed. I had, in fact, bought the camera from Brian not long before leaving for the Antarctic. Initially, he had been reluctant to help:

'I don't do cameras Chris, I'm only really interested in the projectors.'

But, after a while, he changed tack slightly:

'I've got a mate who's got one! I think it's from the 1950s.'

I thought this would be an interesting object from the era of the Trans-Antarctic Crossing and told Brian to buy it on my behalf but, instead of buying the camera from the 1950s, Brian came back with something from the 1920s. Instead of a camera from the time of the Trans-Antarctic crossing, I now owned a camera historically closer to the era of Captain Scott. It was clockwork and had a handle that wound up a spring to pull through the film. It was made before the invention of colour film and didn't have the required filter inside. I couldn't shut the aperture enough to stop the film overexposing. Where I was going, there was twenty-four hour daylight and it was really bright because of the snow. There was, of course, no light meter or focus indictor.

I managed to buy a colour film filter and a polarising filter to make it slightly darker. Both were too big for the lens so I invented an attachment made from a Marmite jar lid with springs to hold it on. I also had to buy a focusing device and a light metre. Loading the film was a complicated procedure that involved threading it through a series of catches and pulleys that were, awkwardly, in a compartment within the camera behind a second door. It was fiddly at the best of times but this had to be done in total darkness. The expensive film did not come in a cartridge and one false move would expose and ruin it. I had to keep a black changing bag with me at all times. It was not a practical camera!

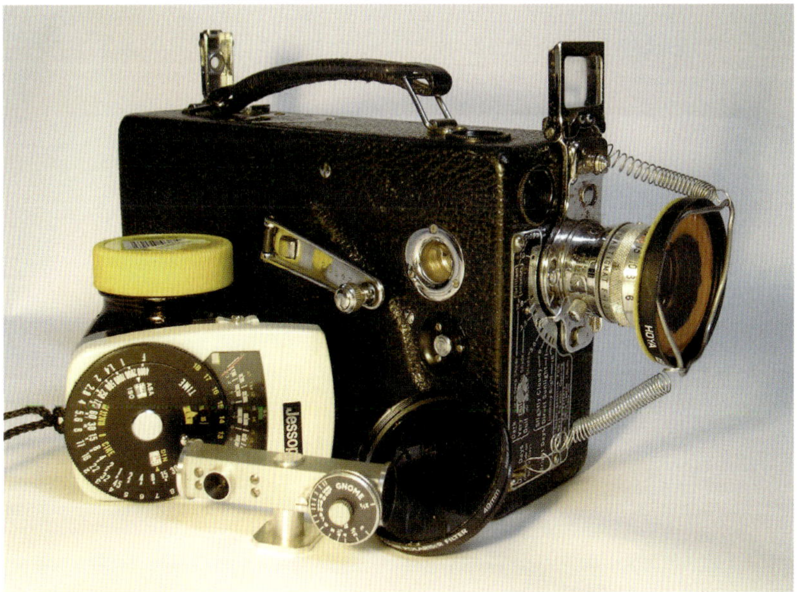
The 16mm camera and accessories. Light meter, rangefinder, polarising filter, colour film filter and adaptor made from a Marmite jar lid.

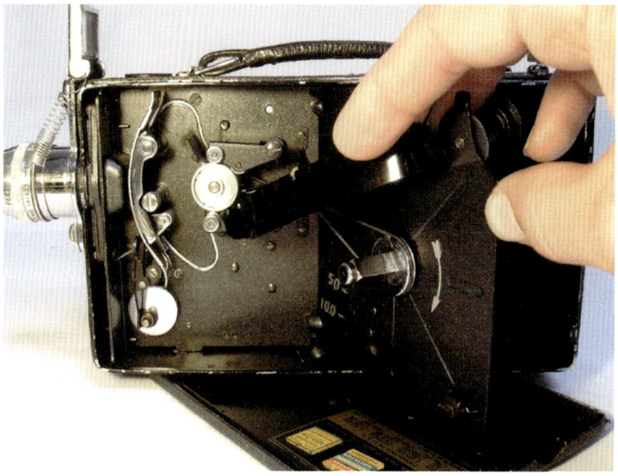
Opening the camera to load the film.

That night in the tent with Dave we passed the time by talking about my project and the problematic camera. This led onto the other difficulty of filming the flat featureless environment. I showed Dave some of the toys I had brought with me. One of the things that always seemed to work as a social ice breaker was a children's booklet that came with the Action Man Polar Explorer. It had lots of handy tips inside on how to make a penguin from a cardboard toilet roll tube and black and white paper; a design for a Sno-Cat made from a cereal packet and a shoebox, plus an illustration of how to make an Antarctic base from a cardboard box. As we laughed at the book I relaxed with Dave and felt free to express creative ideas. I thought more about the problems of filming the next day and then, suddenly, I had a eureka moment.

There was going to be nothing in the background to make for an interesting composition but I started to think about the documentation in terms of time rather than image. I remembered what my girlfriend had said about my disappearing into the distance and realised that the sentiment of this gesture would be heightened by the significance of the environment.

As I told Dave about my girlfriend and expressed my vision to him I probably started to become more animated and excitable. As the plan unfolded in my head I became full on 'arty'. I'm sure I sounded like a delusional Hollywood film director.

Dave hid his embarrassment with my pretentious outburst very well.

'I've got it Dave. It doesn't matter that there is nothing to film out there. I will just keep the camera rolling on the nothingness. OK! Picture it Dave. You drive off into the distance and I will just film you and film you until you become a dot; a speck and then disappear. It will be a lot of film but... It's the Antarctic Dave, it will be worth it. Then… after I've filmed you going into the nothing I can film you coming out of the nothing as well… Think Omar Shariff's entrance in the film Lawrence of Arabia.'

Dave was confident that the ground for miles and miles was safe to travel without me being tied to him. I set up the old camera and gave him some final instructions:

'It's important that you keep going until you disappear out of sight. When you have disappeared I want you to come back to me from another direction so that you approach the camera across virgin snow.'

When I think back on it now, I am amazed that the stupidity of the next instruction was lost on us both:

'You keep going Dave and when you get to the point where I can't see you anymore, I'll give you this signal.'

As I said this, I waved both my arms high in the air so they crossed above my head.

Dave dutifully set off into the big white emptiness. It looked fantastic. Then the film ran out.

After I gave up waving my arms about, I watched him become a dot in the distance then disappear. When he came back an hour later, in exactly the right spot and right on cue, I had to explain to him that the spare films were on the sledge he was pulling:

'Is that the sort of fucking useless thing that the scientists do Dave?'

I was hoping for a conciliatory answer but, instead, Dave said:

'Yes.'

The weather began to change again and the light contrast lowered. We packed up the tent and headed back to Sky Blu while Dave could still follow our skidoo tracks from the day before.

When the film was processed the grainy image did give a sense of other-worldliness and I often show the footage whilst playing Symphonia Antarctica on the record player I took to

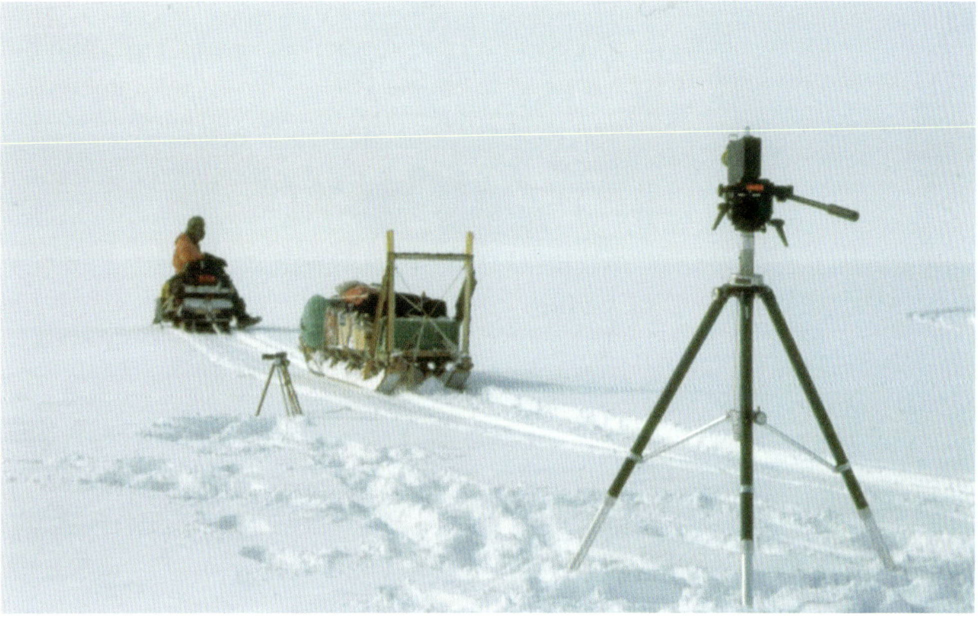

Dave getting ready to set off into nothingness.

right: Dave going.

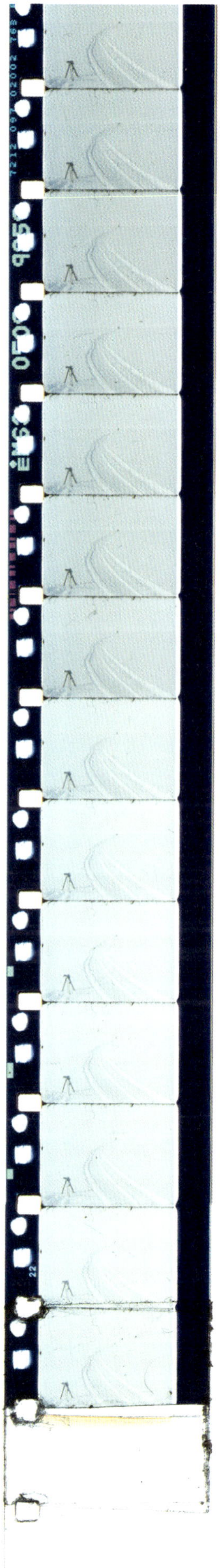

the Antarctic. One of the consequences of the old camera was that, as the spring wound down, it took the film past the aperture too slowly and these parts of the film become progressively over exposed. Played through a projector at the correct speed these sections also speed up as they fade away. Before I ran out of film the spring in the camera had run down. The sledge travels into the distance but, instead of disappearing into the whiteness of the Antarctic, it bleaches away and disappears into the whiteness of the world created by the camera.

Dave gone.

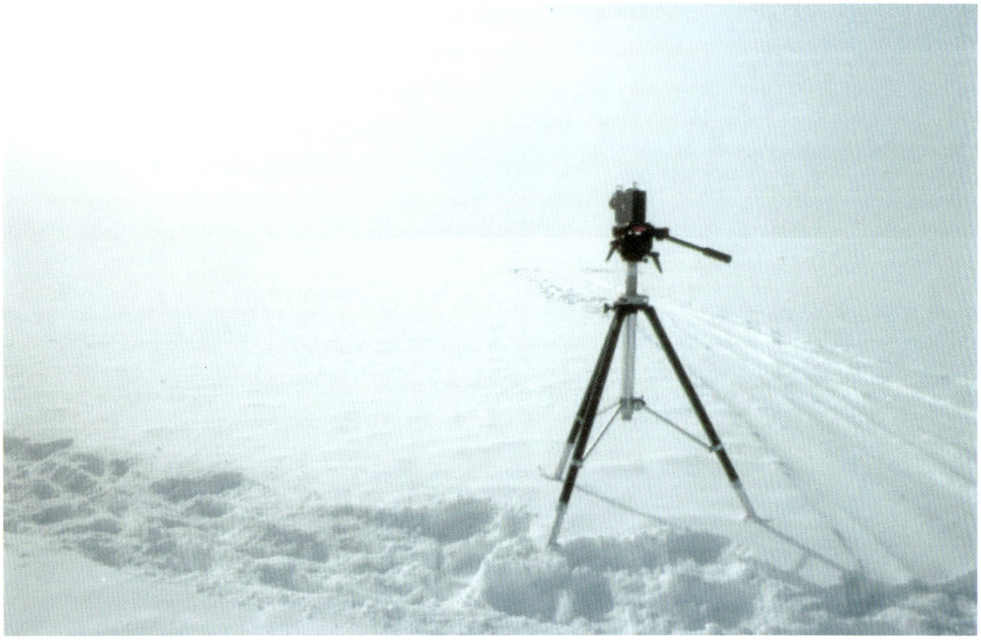

When we got back to Sky Blu the weather had changed for the worse at Rothera and all the flights had been suspended. Nobody could be sure for how long but, for the time being, I was stranded and it looked like I would miss my flight back home after all. Sky Blu was still operational however and Twin Otter aircraft continued to land for refuelling and unloading. At this point in the season they were returning equipment from field parties hundreds of miles to the south. I busied myself by helping to unload. There were six of us there and once a fully serviced plane had taken off we waited for the next one in the relative comfort of a Melon Hut.

The hut was about fifteen foot long, bright red and a bit like a giant melon. It had round windows and, from the outside, looked very modern. On the inside however, there was a crude bench seat and a table made from rough wood which curved round one side. The radio was by the door and, on the remaining side, were shelves of food and a stove for heating. Cooking utensils hung down from the ceiling and there was a camping stove so we could fry bacon for sandwiches. Occasionally someone would get up, put on a pair of rubber gloves and go outside. They would come back with a couple of blocks of snow, melt them in a saucepan and make tea. The gloves had the word 'water' written on them which was reassuring as I had noticed an identical pair in the toilet tent with the word 'shit' written on them.

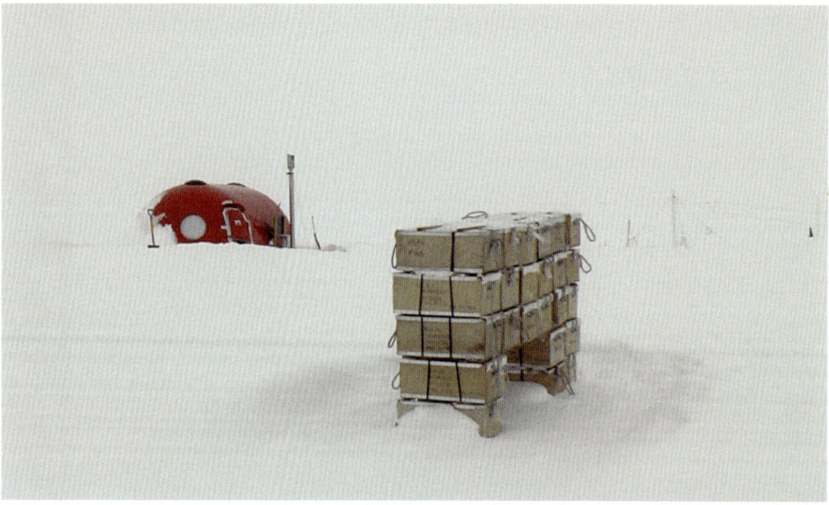

A stockpile of 'Man food boxes'. The term 'man food box' is a throwback to the days when dogs were still used in the Antarctic. The term differentiated them from 'dog food' boxes. Food supply dumps like this can sometimes stay in frozen limbo for years. In the background is one of the Melon huts at Sky Blu.

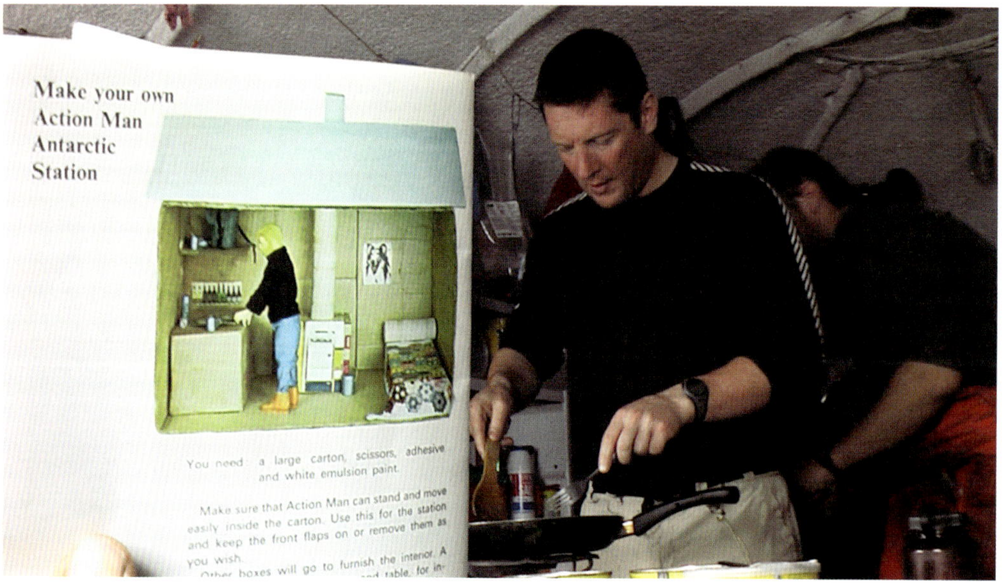

Inside the melon hut. On a break between flights Doug fries bacon whilst I hold up a page from the Antarctic Action man explorer booklet.

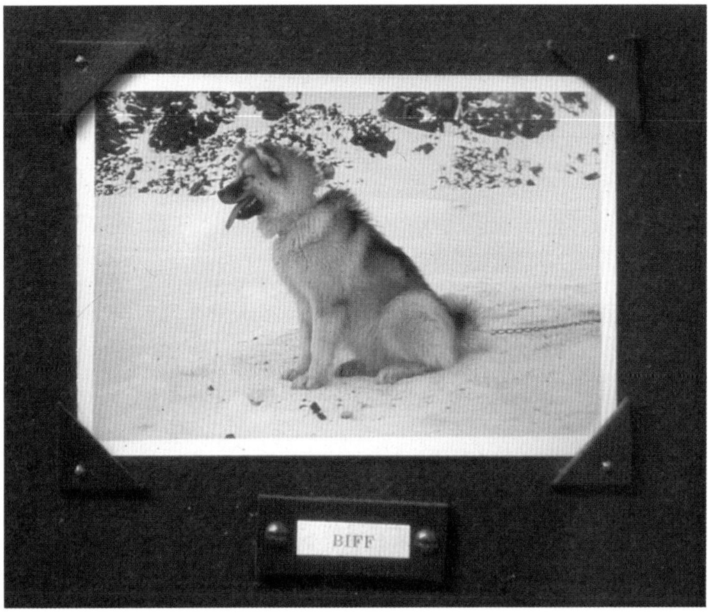

Biff, the shit-eating winner. Photograph on the wall at Old Bransfield. Photographer unknown.

Dave had been coming to the Antarctic for so long that he had worked with dogs. As we sat around in the hut, he gave us a history lesson about dog culture that I couldn't have imagined reading in a history book. According to Dave, controlling a team of dogs is done solely through the lead dog and relies on reinforcing this dog's superiority over the others by giving it special treatment. Dave described an effective method that was used to instil loyalty and strengthen the chain of command. Apparently, Antarctic dogs loved to eat human excrement so, rather than burying it in the snow, it was far more useful to let the lead dog eat it. Whilst they ate the special treat it was important to let the other dogs see this favouritism. On no account however, were they allowed to share the special fecal treat. A lovely example of success and reward.

I had achieved my objective by taking the sledge and camping on the ice cap at a spot where possibly no-one had ever been before. Also, just being selected to go to the Antarctic was an achievement in itself and certainly looks good on my CV. I guess on these terms I was a winner, but what constitutes success can often be forever illusory and mercurial.

Like success, the parameters of what constitutes 'good' art are also constantly shifting. There is a school of thought that says all good art comes from an environment where there is permission to fail. Failure is almost a prerequisite to authenticity and learning new things. In short, it can be 'good' to fail. As I write these words, a friend has posted me a book they have found in one of the bastions of British contemporary art literature: the Whitechapel Art Gallery bookshop. When I opened the package, an inch thick paperback fell out that looked like a typical piece of intellectual marketing for some very successful contemporary artists. It is entitled 'Failure – Documents of Contemporary Art'.

On a yellow post-it note stuck on the cover, my well meaning friend has written in blue biro, 'Saw this and thought of you, Chris!'

It appears that not only is it good to fail, it is positively all the rage.

Soon after my return to the UK I was invited onto a public discussion panel to share my experience of the Antarctic residency. On the panel with me was another artist who had made a conceptual application to the British Antarctic survey residency to NOT go to the Antarctic. His work of 'not going' highlighted the obvious delusions of self-importance that any artist must have to ultimately send themselves on such privileged journey. Going to such an environmentally sensitive area could be tasteless if ultimately the only purpose it serves is one of self-promotion.

Suddenly, my big achievement of going to the Antarctic, wasn't a good thing after all.

This other artist had even been short listed to do the residency before making it clear that he REALLY didn't want to go. His work parodied the notion of an artist going to the Antarctic and he made pieces that were set in a pretend Antarctic with plastic animals and figures. Coincidently he used some of the same plastic Antarctic animals in his work as me. Mine were in the real Antarctic; his were in blocks of ice floating in his kitchen sink.

The title of the discussion was 'Antarctic – To Go or Not to Go?' As he delivered his presentation it became clear he was winning over the audience with his humble, self-deprecating style. We were fighting over the same intellectual territory with me cast as the 'successful' villain of the piece. For the next hour of panel discussion, we vied for the position of underdog. It became a perverse parody of the Darwinian struggle for survival I had seen on Bird Island. We politely played down our achievements and competed fiercely with each other to be the biggest loser.

Failure is relative. Captain Scott only knew he was a failure once he saw evidence near the South Pole that he had not been there first. Up until that point he must have considered himself a winner. I realise now that there was a very short period of time when I was truly a success. It started in the melon hut at Sky Blu, after the point I had achieved the goal of taking the sledge to 'somewhere no-one had ever been before'. It probably ended at the point I came back to the UK and became part of the art world's twisted reality again.

Since I couldn't go back to Rothera, Doug, a pilot I had met on his break, took me with him on his next flight south. Every flight in the Antarctic has to have a co-pilot or second person on board. At Rothera everyone took it turns to co-pilot in order to get off base for a while. At Sky Blu the limited amount of people meant the selection process was more casual. The flight took a few hours so I thought I would carry on swapping stories over the plane's intercom with Doug. I had just started when Doug interrupted: 'Is this going to take long?'

I thought it might be time for me to shut up but Doug showed me a switch on the dashboard to lock the intercom so that I could talk without holding my thumb on the control. There is no in-flight entertainment on the Twin Otter so Doug didn't mind listening to me telling stories because it was better than the noise of the engine. It's not saying much but halfway through our flight to a field station called Rabid, near the Ellsworth Mountains, I was the most entertaining thing for thousands of miles. He explained that sometimes the sky became the same featureless white as the ground and if there were no mountains to break up the monotony, the sky and the ground became one. After several hours it could be disorientating and felt like flying around inside a giant ping pong ball. I had a use!

We went south to Rabid to help the Scientist and Field Assistant there pack up camp and close down the supply dump for winter. Packing up camp took longer than anticipated and we had to stay the night. In the morning I walked across the ski-way we had landed on. The Ellsworth Mountains were a little way off to the south. I took out a toy sledge, placed it on the ground and made a photograph. It was a pretty special sledge, bought on eBay, with a set of plastic dogs, a figure and a detachable load of equipment and supplies.

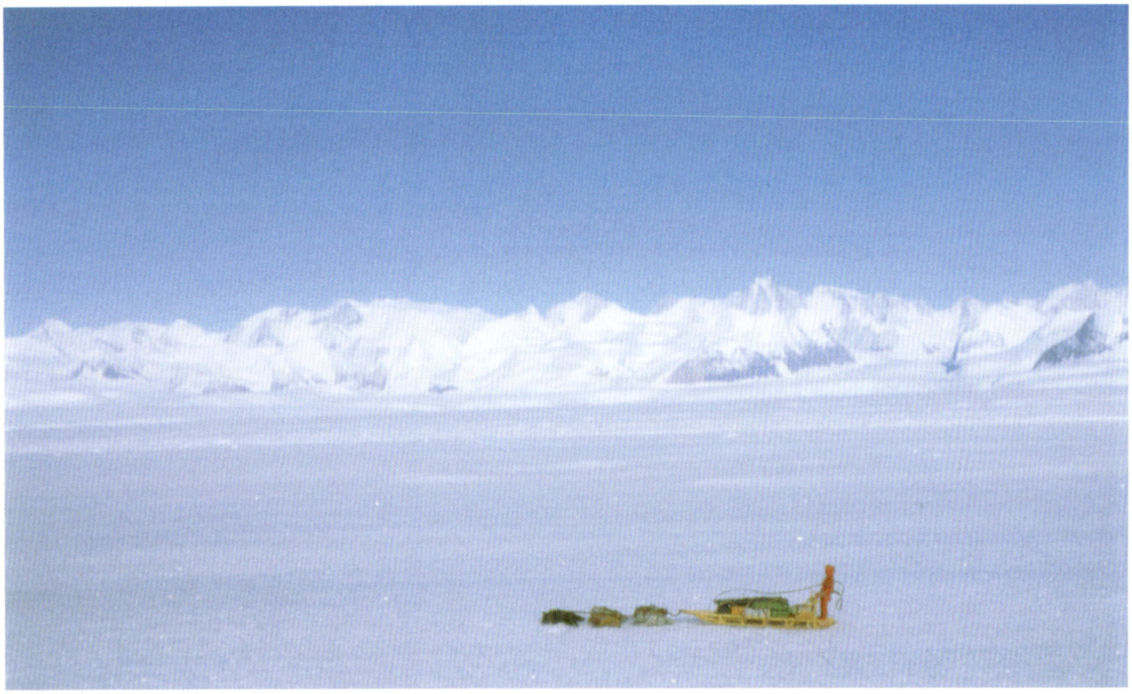

'Herald toys' Antarctic dog sledge. This plastic toy was produced in the late 1950s after the successful Commonwealth Trans-Antarctic expedition. The Ellsworth Mountains are in the distance.

These plastic boxes were pretend versions of the ones I had stacked the day before when we had packed up the camp. I laid the toys out in front of me and knew this was the furthest south I would ever go. Doug had just received a radio message saying there had been a change in the weather at Rothera and he had to get me back as quickly as possible. It appeared that I was going to catch my flight after all.

I was going to have to make a series of flights to Rothera. Once there, I would have a very short space of time to pack my things and get on another plane heading for the Falklands and eventually home. My worst case scenario was about to happen.

During the flight back to Rothera I took random pictures of the landscape beneath me for no special reason other than it was my last chance to see it. I visually took in as much as I could; finding it difficult to equate what I was looking at with the reality of going home. Doug had swapped with another pilot at Sky Blu and as we flew along he kept receiving radio messages from Rothera asking about our progress. He kept looking back over his shoulder to give me the latest news. With his face full of sympathy, he told me that he was going as fast as he could but I was only going to have twenty minutes maximum once we landed at Rothera for me to pack my bags. As I wondered how I was going to organise the packing of the more fragile things, Ian had another radio message. He turned around, shook his head and looking pityingly at me said:

'Someonc has been into your room at Rothera and thrown some of your possessions into a bag. They will chuck it to you as you get off of this plane and onto the Dash 7 to fly on to the Falklands.'

I had boxes of toys that I needed to bring back with me. I had the photos but I needed the genuine objects otherwise they would be meaningless. My things needed delicate handling and sorting. I was having a flash back to my childhood. As I pictured someone even more heavy handed than my mother stuffing my carefully arranged models and toys into a plastic carrier bag, I realised I had another pressing problem. There are very few facilities at Sky Blu; there is no shower for example. When people came back into the warmer environment they start to smell. In my rush to leave

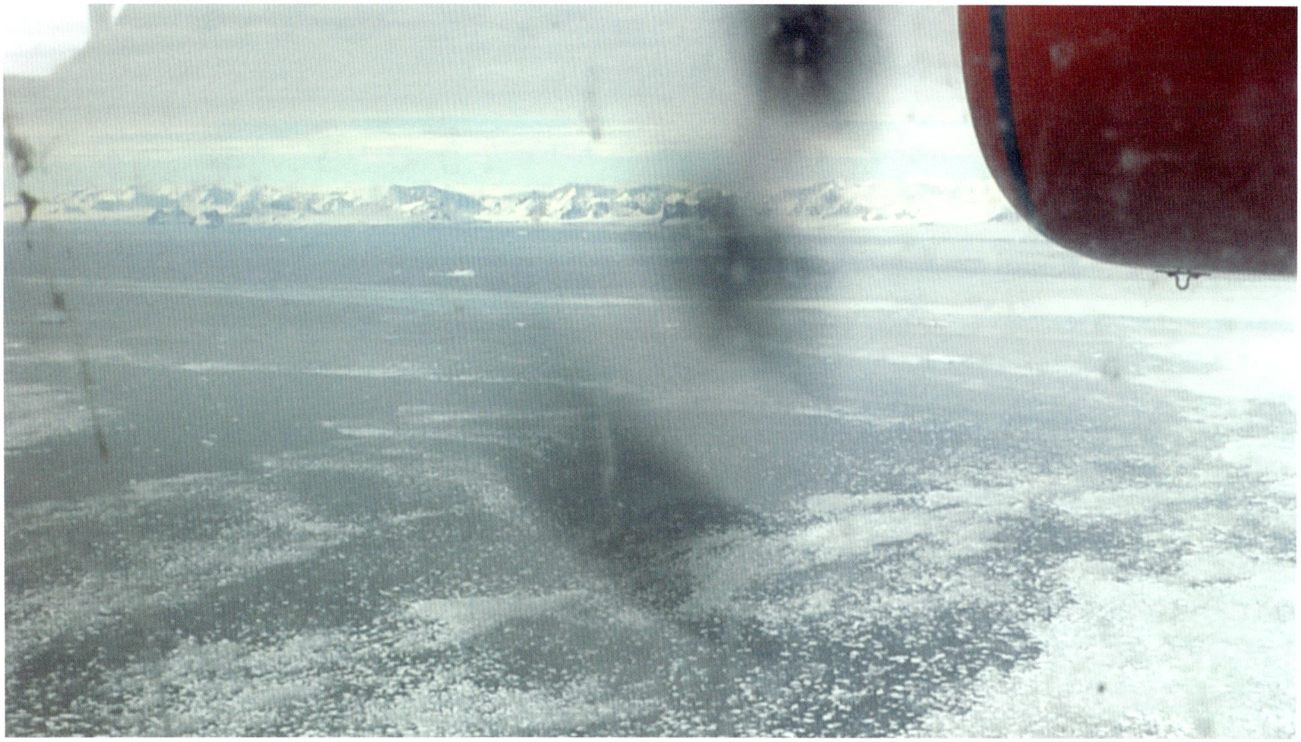

Heading back towards Rothera from the trip to Sky Blu.

Sky Blu I hadn't even been to the toilet tent. I thought I might be able to negotiate a trip the toilet before getting on the plane at a stretch, maybe a shower but definitely not both. As the plane came into land at Rothera and the propellers stopped turning I climbed out and ran over to the Head of Operations standing on the runway:

'Andy! PLEASE can I have ten minutes to go to the toilet?'

To which he smiled and replied, 'Chris… Take as long as you like… you aren't going home for another two weeks! We rescheduled your flight yesterday. We were having a laugh with you!'

I had made the mistake of telling the flight crew on my way down to Sky Blu that this would be my worst possible scenario and so, for a joke, everyone had pretended that this was what was going to happen. The only person who didn't know was the pilot who was deliberately left out so that the others could use his sincere face to make the fictitious radio messages appear more genuine.

I had taken unreal objects or Antarctic toys from home to photograph them in this real dreamlike environment. During this flight however, something else had happened as I anxiously looked at the fantastical landscape beneath from the window of the plane. I was contemplating going home, back to the real world – but in that instance, home itself had become fiction, a mirage.

Someone asked me once if I was annoyed at having to stay for another two weeks, but of course I wasn't. The two extra weeks in the Antarctic were given to me as a gift and that's how I received them. Unlike the scientists and other important professions, the artists only get one chance to go there and rarely have a reason to be invited back. There was no sense in hurrying home I had the rest of my life to never go there again.

THE END

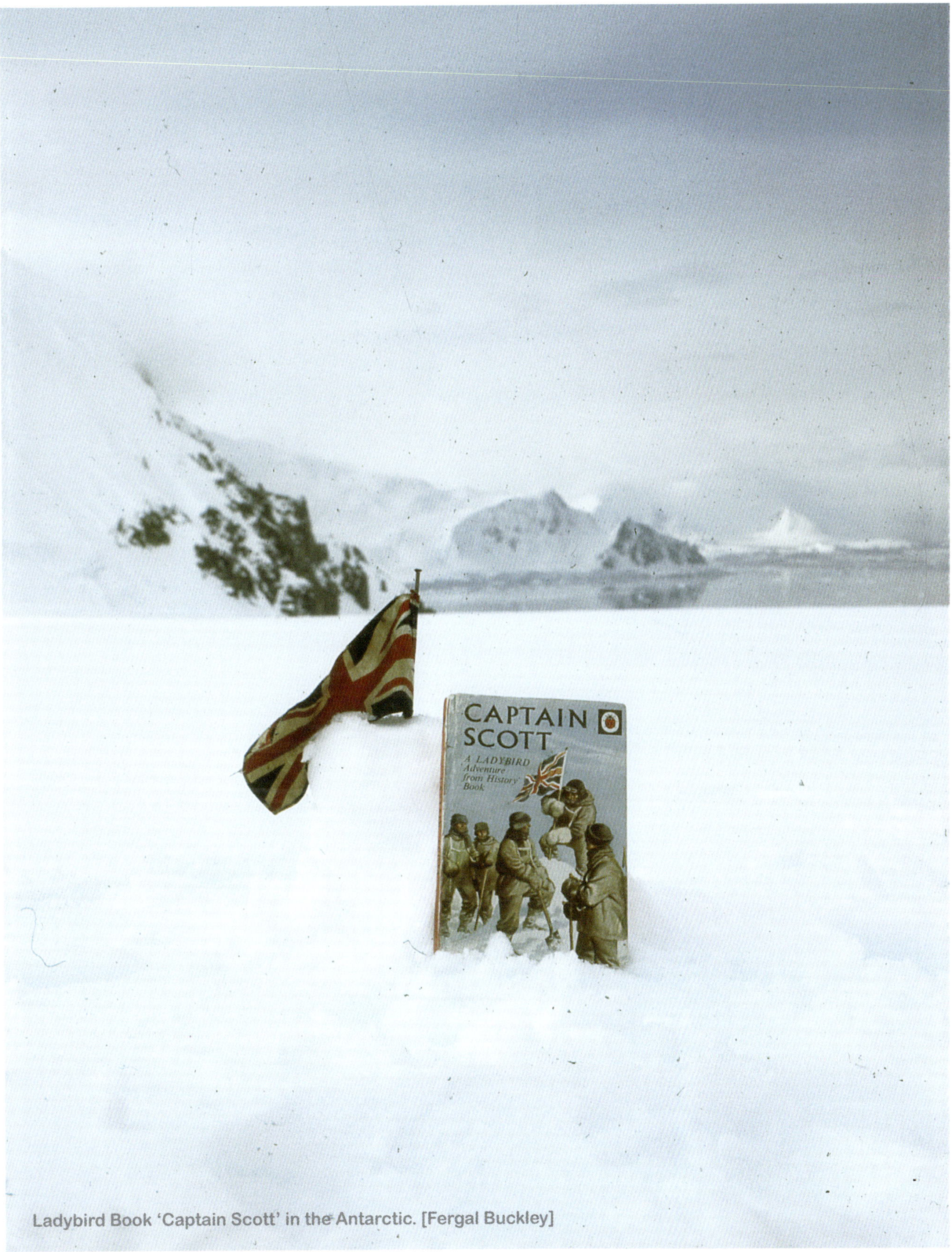

Ladybird Book 'Captain Scott' in the Antarctic. [Fergal Buckley]

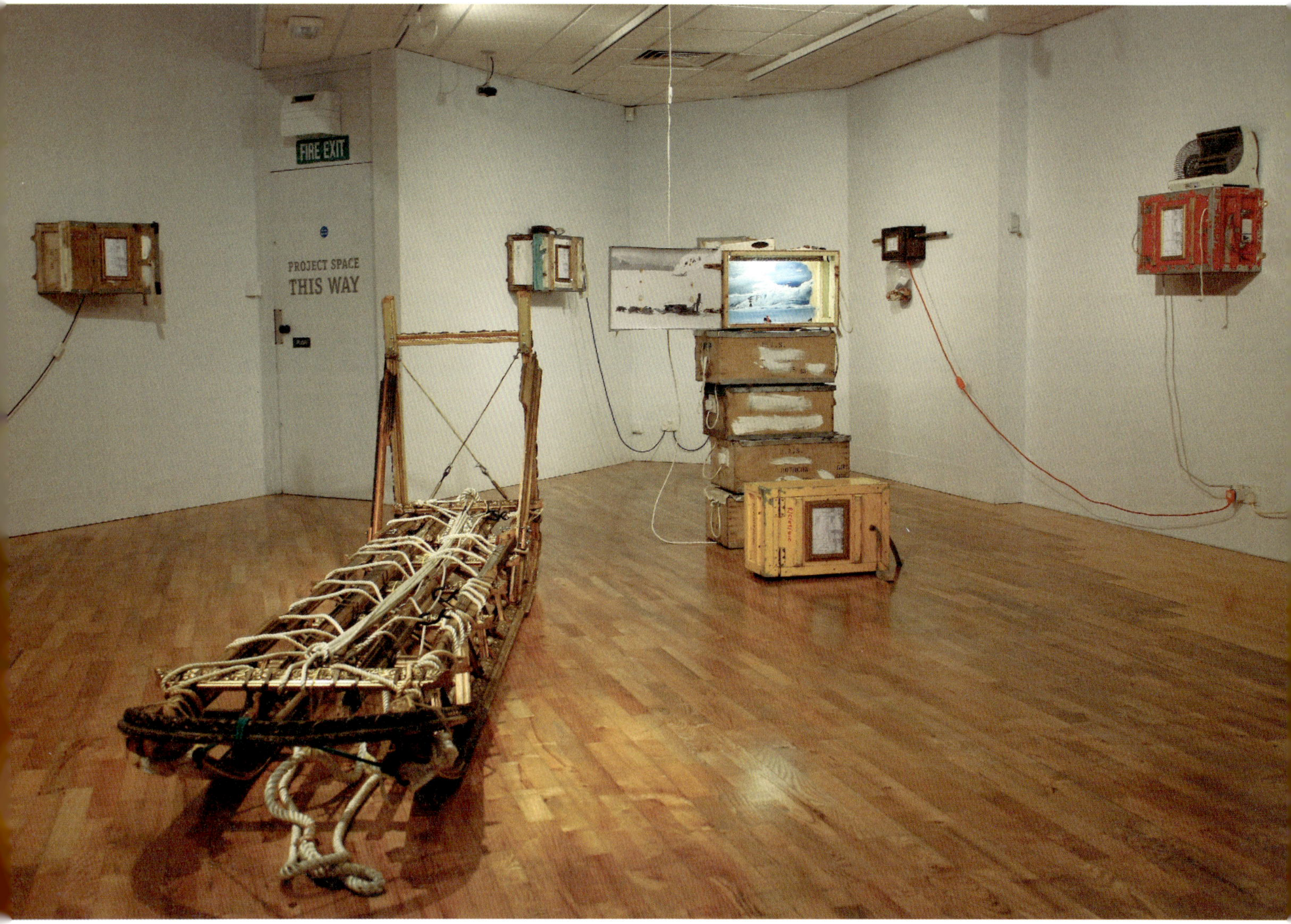

Gallery installation shot of the sledge and painted sledge boxes. Essex University gallery (Art Exchange) [Matt Bowman]

Time Line

1986–1988	**Art Foundation, Braintree Essex** The Roses were posted – February 1987
1988–1991	**Hull College, school of Art, Architecture and Design.** Toy boats sailed sent down the river Humber – March 1989 Driftwood boat launched and destroyed – August 1989 First trip in pedal car – May 1990 Found toy boat while collecting plastic bottles for hovercraft – November 1990 Hovercraft trip – May 1991 Trip to London in the pedal car – June 1991
1991–1992	**Living back in Braintree, Essex.** Repairing the Triumph Herald
1992–1994	**Moved to Colchester Essex.** Tank built – 1993 First live Art lecture, Cool tan Arts, Brixton – Spring 1994
1994–1996	**Royal College of Art.** First aeroplane components made – 1994 Aeroplane only half complete shown on top of a shed for MA show – May 1996
1996–1998	**Residency at Ardleigh Park, near Colchester.** Aeroplane wings completed – February 1998 'All at Sea'. An exhibition in Hull of the Ferrens gallery's maritime art collection. On the strength of building a boat from driftwood to escape from art college in; I was considered a contemporary 'maritime' artist. Consequently I was invited to make a piece for the collection. Title 'Siren' – March 1998
1998–1999	**Moved back to Colchester.** Working at the model factory – Summer to Autumn 1998 Aeroplane engine started for the first time – Summer 1998 Tank is on the front cover of Colin Painter's book – 'The Uses of an Artist'. The book has a disappointing review in Frieze magazine – October 1998 Commission from Christchurch Mansion/Wolsey art Gallery, Ipswich – 'Aerial' (wind powered sculpture in the park). Had to give a slide talk about my work. It was about this time the title 'Landscape, Seascape, Skyscape, Escape' started to be used – Summer 1999

2000–2003 **P.T. Art Lecturer at Colchester Institute.**
Invited to give 'Landscape, Seascape, Skyscape, Escape' talk at Musoshino Art University, Tokyo Japan – Spring 2001
'Constable Country'. A three minute short film of the tank by Dan Saul was shown on 'The Slot', a fill in programme after the Channel 4 news – 2001
Retrospective including all of the vehicles at the Ferrens gallery Hull – 2002
Fired from Colchester institute – June 2003
Plane flies for the first time – August 2003

2003–2008 **Visiting lecturer at Leeds Metropolitan University, Ruskin (Oxford University). Reinstated at Colchester Institute.**
'Model Village' pop up gallery in Northdown Street, Kings Cross, London. Where Charles Saatchi did NOT buy the tank – Spring 2004
Aeroplane flew again and crashed – August 2004
Aeroplane repaired and flew for the last time – August 2005
Fired from Colchester Institute again – June 2005
First Arts Council Grant -– 2006
'Offer must End Soon' – 'Art Exchange' University of Essex Gallery. January-February and 'Studio One Point One' February-March 2006, where Charles Saatchi did NOT buy my painting.
Review in Modern Painters – May 2006
First show at Edinburgh festival Fringe (Landscape, Seascape, Skyscape, Escape. Dr Roberts Magic Bus) – August 2006
First management training session with Paul – 2007
Performed 'Landscape, Seascape, Skyscape, Escape' at Lakeside theatre, Essex University. Met Jardine Press.

2008 **Selected for the British Antarctic Surveys 'Artists and Writers' Programme'**
RRS James Clark Ross – November-December 2008
Rothera research station – December 2008-February 2009
Sledge at Sky Blu – Beginning of February 2009
Second Arts Council Grant – March 2009
First Antarctic talk, Junction theatre, Cambridge – Summer 2009
'Antarctica' 'Art Exchange' University of Essex Gallery – March 2010